*Seeking Social Justice*

*Through Globalization*

# *Seeking Social Justice Through Globalization*

## Escaping a Nationalist Perspective

### GAVIN KITCHING

The Pennsylvania State University Press
University Park, Pennsylvania

Library of Congress Cataloging-in-Publication Data

Kitching G. N.
   Seeking social justice through globalization : escaping a
nationalist perspective / Gavin Kitching.
      p.   cm.
   Includes index.
   ISBN 0-271-02162-4
      1. Social justice.  2. Globalization.  I. Title

HM671 .K57  2001
303.3′72—dc21

                                        2001021563

It is the policy of The Pennsylvania State University Press to use acid-free paper for
the first printing of all clothbound books. Publications on uncoated stock satisfy the
minimum requirements of American National Standard for Information Sciences—
Permanence of Paper for Printed Library Materials, ANSI Z39.48–1992.

*for M.P.C.*

*Mankind* always sets itself only such problems as it can solve, since on reflection it will be seen, that the problem itself only arises when the material conditions for its solution already exist or are at least in the process of formation.

—Marx, *Preface to a Contribution to the Critique of Political Economy,* 1859

# Contents

# Preface

In 1982 I published a critical essay on what were then dominant and popular themes in development theory under the title *Development and Underdevelopment in Historical Perspective: Populism, Nationalism and Industrialisation.* In the eighteen years that have elapsed since the book's publication much has changed in the world; and since the original text was moderately successful, its publishers approached me several times to update it in the light of new trends and events. However, in the 1980s the focus of my empirical research moved away from Third World or development issues altogether, and this made me feel less and less confident that I had anything substantively new to say, or possessed the academic expertise to say it.

I continued to teach the politics of development, however, and to read widely in the secondary literature for teaching purposes. In 1998 I decided that a major revision and restructuring was required of the upper-level undergraduate course I was presenting under that title at the University of New South Wales. In undertaking that revision I found myself deeply immersed in the rapidly expanding literature on globalization. That reading, plus the experience of teaching the revised course for the first time, led me to reengage with some of the same issues in the economics and politics of development that had led me to write *Development and Underdevelopment* in the first place. Gradually I realized that, in preparing the new course, I had gathered together research materials and thoughts from which I could also provide a commentary on the globalization literature and its debates, reflections on changes in the real world of development since the early 1980s, and reflections upon, and a partial self-criticism of some of the views I had presented in my original book. So what had begun as a series of lecture outlines gradually transmogrified into this more or less coherent text.

However, while it contains some implicit and explicit criticisms of my earlier textbook on development, this text also has some important traits in common with the earlier book. Like *Development and Underdevelopment* this book too aims to be a sustained commentary on, and argument about, the current literature on globalization, rather than a comprehensive textbook in the traditional style. Thus its readers will find a maximum of contentious and sustained argument in its pages and a minimum of statistical data or detailed empirical description. The literature already abounds in books containing lists of the one hundred or five hundred largest transnational corporations, graphs or bar charts of foreign direct investment flows and their changes over time, detailed institutional descriptions of the workings of the IMF or the World Bank. Should the reader wish to refer to them, abundant references to such texts can be found in this one. The aim of this book, however, is not to present such well-known data again, or to be another introductory textbook. Rather, its aim is to provide a sustained argumentative thesis about the process of globalization that I hope that readers will find stimulating and convincing enough to persuade them to read further. I also hope that it will help them to approach the more conventional textbook literature in a more questioning and insightful way. This "argumentative essay" approach appeared to work well in the case of *Development and Underdevelopment*. Certainly many teachers of courses on Third World development have told me that that text was generally successful in stimulating interest and debate among new students of the subject. I hope that *Seeking Social Justice Through Globalization* will be similarly successful as a first "shock" or "stimulus" text, convincing newcomers to the field that further exploration of the issues it raises would be rewarding and illuminating.

In addition, and also like *Development and Underdevelopment,* this book is based on the central methodological premise that the significance of contemporary events is more profoundly grasped if they are set in an historical perspective—if they are set, that is to say, against a deep historical backdrop through which both the continuities and discontinuities of the present with the past can be discerned. In fact it is my view that, just like the dependency theory which was the prime focus of concern and critique in the earlier book, the contemporary globalization literature too is often weakened, both as description and as explanation, by its lack of historical depth. Most of the authors on globalization are either economists or human geographers, and neither of these disciplines is noteworthy for its strong historical sense. Indeed, I think one of the most disturbing traits of social science and humanities scholarship generally at the beginning of this century is its increasing lack of interest in the serious study of history. Like many other scholars, I think this trait may be both an effect and a reinforcing cause of the cult of the present and of the immediacy of "experience" which is such a hallmark of the postmodern world in which we live. However, like Terry Eagleton[1] and some other traditionalist scholars, and unlike so many postmodernists, I see this loss of a sense of "the present as history" or of "the present in history" in postmodern culture as, precisely, a loss to be mourned and lamented, not a liberation to be celebrated.

It is not only the world and the academic literature on development, however, which has changed markedly in the last eighteen years. My own views and beliefs, not only on questions of development but on social science generally have also altered significantly in the same period, and those changes have affected not only what I choose to write about but how I choose to write about it. I have, in particular, been profoundly influenced by the philosophical ideas of Ludwig Wittgenstein in ways that have affected the whole basic infrastructure of my thinking—on the nature of knowledge and of language, on the possibility of a science of society, on the relationship between political views and activities and personal life. Readers of this book will not, I think, require any knowledge of Wittgenstein or Wittgensteinian philosophy in order to appreciate it (or condemn it!). But those who are familiar with his ideas will undoubtedly see traces of them on many of its pages, and especially of course on those which are concerned with language and with the relationship between social change and changes in language use. Any reader who is stimulated by this book to find out more about the Wittgensteinian perspective, and in particular about the relationship of that perspective to Marxism, is referred to my two books on the subject which appeared in 1988 and 1994.[2]

1. T. Eagleton, "Where Will It All End?" *The Sunday Times,* November 13, 1994, pp. 7–8.
2. G. Kitching, *Karl Marx and the Philosophy of Praxis* (London: Routledge, 1988) and *Marxism and Science: Analysis of an Obsession* (University Park: Pennsylvania State University Press, 1994).

It is usual in prefaces such as this to refer to a long list of people who have influenced the author of a book during its writing and to whom she or he feels indebted. However, over the last decade in particular my major occupation, aside from university teacher, has been that of partner and parent. As a result the intensity of my involvement in academic life has slackened, certainly in comparison with my time as a young scholar in the 1970s and 1980s. To that extent, and fittingly, the major personal and intellectual influence on the making of this book, aside from my own, has been that of my partner, Dr. Pamela Cawthorne, with whom every one of the major ideas in this text has been discussed innumerable times. I have also made use of her own empirical research on globalization and economic restructuring in several parts of the text, and she was certainly the major influence in persuading me that what began as a set of lectures might make a worthwhile book. I therefore owe her profound debt for the book's existence but for many other things as well—things far more important to me than this or any other book.

Aside from Pamela, I should make mention of Dr. Richard Bryan of the Department of Economics of the University of Sydney, whose books on the political economy of globalization have certainly influenced this text, as have a number of conversations on those themes which I have had with him on and off the golf course. I would also like to thank Dr. Nigel Pleasants of the University of Exeter. Nigel has not only supported and endorsed my inexpert delvings into Wittgenstein and Wittgensteinian social theory over the last ten or so years, he has also influenced my thinking in a whole variety of ways—ways that find indirect expression in this book and which will find much more direct outlet in my forthcoming *Wittgenstein and Society*, which I hope will follow this book in short order. In addition, the final draft of this book has benefited considerably from the comments made on an earlier draft by two readers commissioned by Penn State Press. I would like to thank both of them for their careful reading of that draft and for their always constructive and helpful criticisms. One of them—Professor Herman Schwartz of the University of Virginia—was happy to make personal contact with me, and I have gained further both from several long e-mail exchanges with him and from reading his own excellent book on globalization, *States Versus Markets*.[3]

Perhaps the most direct acknowledgments for the making of this book,

3. Herman M. Schwartz, *States Versus Markets: The Emergence of a Global Economy*, 2d ed. (Basingstoke: Macmillan, 2000).

however, are due to the undergraduates who attended my Politics of Development course at UNSW, and in particular the cohort of the academic year 1999. This latter group had to cope with the often bewildering transmutations of lectures which were turning into a single argumentative text in the mind of their lecturer even as they were being presented as discrete entities. I would like in particular to thank Tom Dawkins, Miriam Lyons, Rebecca Hewett, Deborah Muir, Geoff Connell, and Mabel Wong, who did me the great favor of responding to these changes with excitement rather than dismay, and who, through the questions they asked, the objections they raised, and (indeed) the essays they wrote in response to my course, have contributed in no small way to the construction of this text.

This book was written in Australia, and that—the whole experience of living in Australia, with its proximity to Southeast Asia, its own particular political traditions and concerns, and its rather charming but odd conceptions of itself and its position in the world—has influenced the writing of it. This Australian influence is often reflected in the choice of examples or empirical illustrations in my text, but does not, I hope and believe, detract from the general applicability or relevance of its ideas. Where I think that the Australian case is in some way discrepant with other "rich world" experience—in Europe or the United States—I have usually signaled that by a qualification in a footnote. Otherwise the reader may take it that those generalizations which I offer about Australia and globalization, I also believe to hold for other societies like it.

Mention of qualifications found in footnotes brings me to the topic of footnotes in general. The notes in this book are genuinely *foot*notes—they are found at the bottom of each page. Some are very long and consist indeed of qualifications to, or elaborations of, an argument found in the text. Some are full of statistics. Others are full of references to and comments on, books and articles. Very often they also contain thoughts or beliefs of my own which have been formed in reaction to those books or articles. In other words, taken together these footnotes constitute a kind of parallel text to that in the main body of the book. I hope that this parallel text is both of interest in itself, and serves to strengthen the often bald and polemical case argued for in that main body. In contrast to the ahistoricity of much contemporary scholarship mentioned above, many of this book's footnotes are deeply historical in tone. That is to say, they contain references to a large number of the history books and articles I have read over my working life and to the influence they have had on my thinking. In particular the deep debt that this book owes to the wonderful historical scholarship of Eric Hobsbawm will be obvious at almost every turn of its footnotes. In other words, I think any reader of this book will get more out of it if they read the footnotes—or at any rate many of them—as well as the main body of the text. I have, accordingly, tried to write those notes in a way which will make them enjoyable and interesting to read.

Finally, I am aware that the argument of this book will be found controversial. Most especially, some at least of its readers who think of themselves as on the political left may find its major argument profoundly antithetical as well as controversial. The reason for this is simply that this book aims to present a strong case for the merits of globalization, but from a left perspective. The literature on globalization to date is, with but a few exceptions, polarized into right-wing "free market" or "neoliberal" celebrations of globalization and left-wing polemical denunciations of it—often with a strong nationalist tinge. Therefore, a text that holds that globalization can be of enormous benefit to the poorest and most oppressed people of the world, *but only if the process is carried much further than it has been to date,* is bound to seem both anomalous, contrary, and (or certainly I hope) enormously provocative. I make no apology for this. My private life over the last decade or so has been very happy. But my public life, or the public/political dimension of my life, has been very sad. For I have seen a large number of my most cherished hopes disappointed and an equally large number of my most fundamental beliefs problematized or undermined by events in the world. This has led me to rethink many of my views in fundamental ways, and this book is one of the products of that rethinking. It is in many respects a product of pain, but it is, or aims to be, an honest product of an honest facing of that pain. I ask only that it be read and criticized in the same spirit—a spirit of honesty and not of avoidance or of retreat into arguments that leave one with a clear and easy conscience at the cost of a soft head.

Gavin Kitching
Sydney, Australia.

# An Additional Note

In February 2000, as this book was being completed, I received news of the death of Michael Cowen, professor and director of the Institute of Development Studies at the University of Helsinki, Finland. In the 1970s and early 1980s I was just one of several students of African Studies in general, and of the political economy of Kenya in particular, who was profoundly influenced by Mike's path-breaking rural research. I met Mike, briefly, while in Kenya in 1972–73, and also enjoyed his company as a colleague in the Centre for Development Studies, University of Wales, in the late 1970s. He was a man of deep intellectual honesty and originality and with an abiding personal warmth and loyalty lying just below his trademark grumpiness. He taught me a lot, most especially a profound skepticism of nationalism in all its many and varied ideological forms. And since that skepticism is at the heart of this text, I dedicate it to him. He would not, I am sure, have agreed with everything in it, but that is just the point. I and many other people are much the poorer for no longer having Mike's disagreement from which to learn.

PART ONE

❦

# Globalization,
# Some Conceptual Issues

# CHAPTER ONE

ॐ

# Globalization: Buzzword or New Phenomenon?

As well as teaching the upper-level undergraduate course in the Politics of Development which gave rise to this book, I also teach a first-year introduction to political sociology under the title "State and Society." One of the prime aims of that course is to break down, or at any rate challenge, a very commonplace and commonsense way of thinking about politics and society. That commonsense understanding says that there are certain things happening "out there" in the real world, and that when those things change or are changing, the language that we use to describe and explain those things itself changes to reflect those real-world changes. Thus, to take the central topic of this book, if a global economy or a global society is emerging out there, then we will find new words ("globalization") or new phrases ("global economy," "global society") appearing in our language in order to describe that new reality. However, as I will stress repeatedly, this commonsense idea is misleading because it underestimates the extent to which the appearance of the new word or words is itself a part of the *creation* of the new things out there that they describe.

It is important not to misunderstand what the above assertion means. It does not mean that if I (as an individual) start using the word "globalization" or the phrase "global economy" regularly, that will, in itself, create a global economy. Nor do I mean that if a restricted human group, such as students in my courses or readers of this book, start using such words, that will, in itself, have the same creative effect. Rather I mean that when new ways of speaking—new words or phrases, or new uses of words or phrases—appear in our language and are taken up not by hundreds or thousands of people, but by millions or even hundreds of millions of people, this is nearly always both a sign that something is going on and *a part of* that "going on" in itself. In other words, very widespread talk and writing employing the word "globalization" in a whole variety of different contexts is itself part of the real process of globalization.

But (and this is equally important) it is only part of that process. That is, the whole world simply talking and writing about a global economy would not create a global economy. Rather, it is hundreds of millions of people talking and writing about globalization and a global economy *in conjunction* with their doing a host of other things (investing in stock markets around the world, migrating for thousands of miles in search of a better life, doing business by internet and e-mail, ordering clothing to be produced in India from designs made up in Australia, but for sale in Australia, Europe and the United States) that creates, or may create, a global economy.

In short then, when some part of language changes and that language change is taken up in a very short space of time, this is, in itself, a fairly sure sign that something important is going on in, as we say, "the real world." But it is not, in itself, a clear or infallible guide to what that something is, or to exactly how important it is. That is, it is still open to people to say (as for example Paul Hirst and Grahame Thompson say in their recent book *Globalization in Question*)[1] that the real significance or importance of globalization has been exaggerated, and that the real process has not gone nearly as far as (in their words) the "most enthusiastic proponents" of globalization have suggested in their writings and speeches. And that it is possible to be questioning in this way is both fortunate in itself and shows the profound misunderstanding of language embodied in the commonsense idea that I mentioned above. Because if the word "globalization" were simply a label for something already existing in the real world, then Hirst and Thompson (and other skeptics about globalization) could themselves not exist. That is, if the word "globalization" only appeared in our language when globalization as a real process had occurred, or if the phrase "global economy" only appeared when there was

---

1. P. Q. Hirst and G. Thompson, *Globalization in Question: The International Political Economy and the Possibilities of Governance* (Cambridge: Polity, 1996), chap. 1.

a global economy, then the question, but is there really a global economy? or the question, has the real extent of globalization been exaggerated? could not be asked. But such questions can be asked (and are indeed being asked all the time) so clearly the word "globalization" or the phrase "global economy" are not labels in this simple sense.

So what are they then? That is, if such words are not used simply as labels[2] which we "stick" on something or some things that already exist in the real world, how do we use them? Well, as we shall see, we use these words and phrases in a whole variety of ways. We use them to describe what is going on, to explain what is going on, to recommend what is going on, to deplore what is going on, and to suggest that what is going on is not what others think is going on—and probably to do a lot of other things as well.

In the case of "globalization" in particular, the third point above is paticularly important. For as Hirst and Thompson also stress, the word "globalization" was originally put into linguistic circulation by people who were not just describing and explaining something that they thought was going on, but who wished to praise or commend what was going on and indeed to encourage more of it to go on. That is, and again in the words of Hirst and Thompson, "globalization" was a word originally coined by neoliberals. That is, it was coined by contemporary thinkers and theorists (often referred to in Australia as "economic rationalists") who are enthusiasts for so-called free markets in general and for the new global free market in particular. They were people who, quite openly and explicitly, wished to see ever more free market globalization going on unhindered by what they would describe as "irrational" or "misguided" state or other regulations or by other forms of, what they would call, political interference with market forces.

However, although the first users of the word "globalization" were, overwhelmingly, those who wished to commend and encourage the process (and to do so, in part, simply by talking and writing about it), the word has now been taken up and used by many other people. That is, it is now used by those hostile to globalization, by those sympathetic to it (but on different grounds from the free market economic rationalists), as well as by those simply curious or puzzled about the phenomenon, and by those

---

2. On "labeling" conceptions of language and the confusions to which they can lead, see, for example, Hanna Fenichel Pitkin, *Wittgenstein and Justice: On the Significance of Ludwig Wittgenstein for Social and Political Thought* (Berkeley and Los Angeles: University of California Press, 1972), chap. 2.

(like Peter Dicken,[3] for example) who think it may have both positive and negative features.

Or, in other words, while the word "globalization," and its derivative phrases, may originally have had a fairly clear ideological use (and perhaps still have that use predominantly), the linguistic water has now been much muddied by a whole variety of other people taking up the word and using it in quite different ways for quite different and varied purposes. So now there is, as they say in standard academic euphemism, "a widespread debate" about globalization, which means that there is now a whole cacophony of voices, using the idea in a whole variety of different ways, and often focusing on quite different dimensions of, as it is said, "this multi-dimensional process."[4] But always, it is to be noted, the ultimate point of all these varied analyses and descriptions of globalization is to come up with some *judgment* about it—to commend and celebrate it, to decry and denounce it, to declare that the whole thing is overblown or not original at all (which is usually a sotto voce way of denouncing it), or to provide a Solomonic inventory of both its merits and its demerits in the manner of Peter Dicken.

And this book will be no different. It too is not simply about what globalization *is* in some factual sense. Rather, I too wish to encourage the effort at judgment. That is to say, I too wish readers of this book to decide for themselves both how real they think globalization actually is, and whether, on balance, they think it is a good or a bad thing. But to properly accomplish this task, I must first of all emphasize how difficult these judgments are—both the judgment of fact ("How real is globalization?") and the judgment of merit ("Is it on balance a good or a bad thing?"). In particular, it is vital to clarify the issue with which I have begun this book—the issue of the relationship between the language of globalization and the reality of globalization. For this relationship has a vital implication for the judgment of fact—an implication that works dialectically or double-sidedly—through the effect of language on action and the reciprocal effect of action, and the results of action, on language.[5]

---

3. P. Dicken, *Global Shift: Transforming the World Economy,* 3d ed. (London: Chapman, 1998), see especially 429–40.

4. For a very useful brief but comprehensive overview of the varied literature on globalization, see L. Sklair, "Globalisation," in *Sociology: Issues and Debates,* ed. Steve Taylor (London: Macmillan, 1999), 321–45.

5. J. Israel, *The Language of Dialectics and the Dialectics of Language* (Brighton: Harvester, 1979), has this point as its unifying theme.

So let me try to make that relationship clear by referring once again to Hirst and Thompson's *Globalization in Question*. As the authors of that book rather indignantly point out (and with much quotation to back up their indignation), it is a hallmark of the more enthusiastic neoliberal writing on globalization to stress, not merely the desirability of free market globalization, but also its *inevitability*.[6] That is, in the worldview to which Hirst and Thompson take objection, capitalism or the free market economic system has now simply outgrown the limits of the nation-state (and in particular, the European and North American nation-state) that gave it birth. The volume of physical commodities requiring consumption, the volume of financial capital requiring investment, the range of modern communications media (and of the messages they carry), have now simply grown too big—or so it is argued—to be contained within any nation-state (even the United States). Moreover, new electronic means of moving capital, new "space and time collapsing" technologies of production and distribution, new satellite-based communications media, now make all attempts at nation-state regulation (let alone control) of these phenomena effectively impossible. Hence, on this account, it is not a question of whether we want a global economy or not, it is simply a question of our adjusting ourselves to the global economy, which, as it were, we "have to have."

Now, as Hirst and Thompson point out, any statement of the form "X *is* (present tense) inevitable"[7] used of any present-day economic, social, or political phenomenon, carries a risk of becoming a self-fulfilling prophecy. That is, if enough people come to believe (and if, in particular enough crucial nation-state politicians and policymakers come to believe) that globalization is inevitable, then they will take actions that will ensure that globalization *becomes* inevitable. In other words and more tersely, getting enough people, or enough powerful people, to believe that the linguistic proposition "globalization is inevitable" is true is itself part of making globalization inevitable, and, therefore, of making the linguistic proposition

---

6. Hirst and Thompson, *Globalization in Question*, 1–7.

7. I stress the present tense use here because that is the interesting or nontrivial use. There is also a past-tense use, of course—"X was inevitable"—often found in history books or in writings about history. But so far as I can see this is a rather trivial use, being simply a synonym for "X happened" (although not always recognized as such). In other words the logic of the present- and past-tense uses of the word "inevitable" and its derivatives are significantly different. The former involves important and substantive claims about the future (important because uncertain and, therefore, disputable). The latter, however, usually amounts to nothing more than a portentous and overblown way of stressing the facticity or indubitability of a past event or events.

come true! Hirst and Thompson (and a number of other authors on globalization, such as Hans-Peter Martin and Harold Schumann)[8] make a lot
of this point. They stress repeatedly how a variety of governments have
enacted deregulation legislation unleashing globalizing economic forces—
and most especially vast global movements of speculative capital—and
then justify what they have created on the grounds that they have not *created* anything but are just "bowing to the inevitable."

So we can put it this way. When we read a supposedly factual account
of globalization which leaves us (and which is intended to leave us) with
the strong impression that we are dealing with some massive, steam-
rollering "purely economic" or "purely technological" process that cannot
be reversed and which must just be adjusted to in a variety of ways, we
have to be aware that what we are dealing with here is an attempt to *persuade*—not, or not simply, an attempt to describe something. And we have
to take that into account in trying to come to a judgment of fact about
how real globalization is. But how do we "take that into account"? We
do so by reading other factual accounts of the same processes which are
trying to persuade us of the truth of some other judgment (accounts that,
for example, are trying to persuade us that globalization is not inevitable,
or that it partly is and partly is not, or that it is not a single process with
a single cause at all).

## Conclusions

Globalization is just one example of a very common phenomenon in history and especially in modern history (understood here as history since the
first capitalist industrial revolution in Britain). This is the phenomenon of
human societies changing when people act differently from how they have
previously acted. Part of that acting differently consists in their talking
and writing differently about both their own actions and those of others.[9]
But though the matter is essentially simple, its implications are very

8. H.-P. Martin and H. Schumann, *The Global Trap: Globalization and the Assault on
Prosperity and Democracy* (Leichhardt: Pluto Press Australia, 1997), especially chap. 8. A
similar, though much less stridently expressed version of the same thesis is in Hirst and
Thompson, *Globalization in Question,* chap. 8.

9. For a fine analysis of language change in the period of the industrial revolution, see
N. W. Thompson, *The People's Science; The Popular Political Economy of Exploitation and
Crisis, 1816–34* (Cambridge: Cambridge University Press, 1984).

complex and apt to lead to a lot of confusion. One very common confusion arises from the question, are they acting differently because they are talking differently, or are they talking differently because they are acting differently?

This question confuses us because both the "becauses" in it are misplaced. That is, it is not a question of our acting differently because we are talking differently or *vice versa*. It is rather that our talking differently *is part of* our acting differently. That is, our talking differently and acting differently are not two separate "things" and because they are not two separate things they are definitely not two separate things that can have a causal relationship. Rather, they are just two aspects of one thing—one single process—which we usually call something like "structural social change." But even this formulation does not capture the full complexity of what happens in periods of rapid economic and social change. It does not do so because formulated this way it leaves the false impression that during such periods of rapid change, everybody acts differently *in the same way*, and therefore talks differently *in the same way*. But that is not, typically, what happens at all during such upheavals. And it is certainly not what is happening now with respect to globalization. Rather, periods of rapid social and economic change are nearly always periods of enhanced political conflict and that for quite obvious reasons. Some people like and approve of those changes and others do not. Some people benefit from those changes and others do not. So they *quarrel* (in language) over such changes as they are making them and as part of the very process of making those changes. And sometimes those quarrels go beyond language into forms of conflict that we call social, political, or even military.

This conclusion enhances our first suspicions about globalization—that something historically important is going on here—not just because people are talking and writing about globalization a lot, but because they are *quarreling* about it in that talking and writing.[10] And when people are quarreling (think of family quarrels) and when part of that quarrel is about the facts (that is, about some event or events present or immediately past), it can be very difficult for an outsider or arbitrator in the quarrel—even a fellow family member—to get a clear unbiased account of the facts over which people are quarreling.

---

10. A useful survey of some of those quarrels, with abundant quotation of sources, is to be found in Dicken, *Global Shift*, 4.

"You agreed to pay me back at the beginning of last week!"
"No, I didn't."
"Yes, you did!"
"No, I didn't. I just said I'd try to."
"You're such a liar!"
"No, I'm not!" And so forth.

In this book I am going to both review and take sides in the quarrel over globalization. This means that I will have to describe what's going on with regard to globalization as fairly and as comprehensively as I can. But it also requires me to review the quarrelers as well as what they are quarreling about. I will have to find out who they are, what they want to see happen in the world and why, and what interests they have at stake in the quarrel.

All these issues are important because they will tend to lead quarrelers not, or not usually, to lie, but to *select* the facts they present to us in quite different ways—to emphasize some facts and to deemphasize (or even omit mention of) some others. Perhaps most difficult of all, however—especially for readers trying to make judgments of fact about globalization—the identities, values, and interests of the quarrelers over globalization will tend to lead them to run together descriptions of what is the case with prescriptions of what they want to be the case. (The use of the proposition "globalization is inevitable" being a classic example of doing just this.) Moreover, it will often lead them to do this in subtle ways that can make it difficult for unsuspecting readers to tell one from the other, or even to tell that this elision is occurring.

༙

# CHAPTER TWO

# Defining the Term:
# A Useful Way to Start?

In one well-known work reviewing the debate (or rather debates) around globalization, James H. Mittelman offers the following useful (and oft-quoted) sentence providing a thumbnail sketch of the main features of globalization. He writes: "The manifestations of globalization ... include the spatial reorganization of production, the interpenetration of industries across borders, the spread of financial markets, the diffusion of identical consumer goods to distant countries, massive transfers of population within the South, as well as from the East to the West, resultant conflicts between immigrant and established communities ... and an emerging world-wide preference for democracy." And he goes on to add: "A rubric for varied phenomena, the concept of globalization interrelates multiple levels of analysis: economics, politics, culture and ideology."[1]

Well, everybody likes definitions. They give us a feeling of having "pinned down" something, especially if that something is rather complex and multidimensional (like globalization). Moreover, definitions can be memorized, which makes them useful for tests and examinations. But of course definitions are at best a starting point. This is partly because they often have to be rather vague simply in order to be comprehensive (for example, what precisely does "the spatial reorganization of production"

---

1. J. H. Mittelman, ed., *Globalization: Critical Reflections* (Boulder, Colo.: Lynne Rienner, 1996), 2.

mean?). But in addition, definitions of any complex object or process will vary from author to author. For example, Mittelman's definition of globalization contains no mention of the new global electronic communications media—such as the internet—which figure prominently in other peoples' accounts. And finally, like many similar definitions of complex phenomena, Mittelman's sentence is really only a *list* in continuous prose. In fact it can be written out as a list, as follows:

1. Spatial reorganization of production
2. Interpenetration of industries across borders
3. Spread of financial markets
4. Diffusion of identical consumer goods to distant countries
5. Massive transfers of population within the South and from the South and East to the West
6. Conflicts between immigrant and established communities
7. Emerging worldwide preference for democracy

But, in the end, a list is just a list. It does not tell us, for example, which items in the list are the most important or most significant characteristics of globalization, nor does it tell us how, if at all, the items on the list are connected. Are some of the items, for example, "causes" of other items, these other items being "mere effects"? If so, then we might want to rank the causal items as more important or significant than the effect items.

Most importantly, if we begin our analysis with a definition of globalization, we may risk begging the most important question. Because, as noted in the first chapter above, the most fundamental of the current debates about globalization is over whether it exists at all. So if we begin by defining "it" (in the way Mittelman does), then we seem to have already committed ourselves to saying that globalization does exist, since one can hardly define something that does not exist!

So perhaps the best way to begin is not with a definition. But if we do not begin with a definition, how do we begin? Well, perhaps with the word itself—"globalization." Perhaps the most significant part of the word is its suffix—"ization." For in English we use that suffix when what we want to describe *a process,* not a thing—hence "democratization," "socialization," "liberalization," etc. So, if we say that we are interested in globalization, we are saying that we are interested in studying a process, and processes occur over time. But what process? Well, obviously, the process of creating something "global." But *what* something global? Interestingly, as we will see, this itself is an important source of disagreement. Most authors on the subject would say that globalization is about the process of creating a global *economy,* but a few think that this may also mean the creation of a global *society.*

But leaving that disagreement aside for a moment (we will come back to it), we will concentrate first on this "process" business. If globalization *is* a process, not a thing, this means of course that it is a process that is still "going on." It is a process that is incomplete. So we do not yet live in a global economy or a global society, but we may come to do so if current processes continue—this is the implication we commit ourselves to in using the word "globalization" at all. For if the process were complete, then presumably we would be speaking, not of "globalization," but of the workings of a fully fledged "global economy" or a "global society" or whatever.

Very well. But even this approach raises a formidable problem. If I choose to describe anything that is currently going on in "ization" terms, I am implicitly making the claim, not only that I know what is going on, but that I know "where," as it were, what is going on is leading us. In other words, to describe any process in English in "ization" terms is to make a claim not only about the present but also about the future. It is to make a claim that you can see the direction of change, the "way the wind is blowing." It is to make a claim that you can see not only a movement but a tendency, a movement in a particular direction, or even toward a particular destination. To put it another way, "ization" words, in English, always have predictive as well as descriptive uses.

And to return to the subject of Chapter 1, this dual "predictive/descriptive" use of "ization" words can itself be a source of controversy. Someone can always say that in describing something as "globalization" one is not merely describing a historical process, one is engaged in trying to bring about a particular result.[2] They can claim, that is to say, that someone is engaged in predicting that something will happen because they approve of that something—that end state—and want it to happen. To put it in a really mind-boggling way, one can think one is just describing a process, but can be accused by others, not just of predicting an outcome, but of actually prescribing an outcome in the disguised form of a prediction!

---

2. Or, as my editor, Andrew B. Lewis, pointed out to me, to prevent a particular result. Some particularly nasty "-izations" have been coined to serve that purpose: "bastardization," "balkanization," "mongrelization."

Now all that may lead readers to think that perhaps "ization" words are more trouble than they are worth. Perhaps we should perhaps dump them altogether, and try to find more neutral, less loaded ways of describing what is going on. But unfortunately this is not really an option open to us. If you think about it, just to describe something—anything—as a process, is to describe it as a kind of movement, a movement, however, through time rather than through space. But, for human beings, movement, whether through time or through space, is always movement *in a particular direction,* and so is inextricable from ideas like "destination" or "goal."[3] After all, a person cannot move at all without going somewhere, and if they keep moving in one direction they will presumably end up in one specific somewhere, which we can properly call their destination. So in other words, we cannot avoid the predictive, even teleological implications of the process words in our language. All we can really do, is to keep in mind two things: First, that if we perceive economic or sociological movements in society, then, just like the movement of physical objects in space, we can only say that there is movement in a certain direction "up to now," as it were—up to the time of observation. We cannot—and certainly should not—preclude changes in the direction of movement, if certain crucial forces change. In short, we must keep our minds open to the possibility that the movement toward globalization, even if it currently exists, may be halted or reversed if, as we say, "things change." But this also means that we have to understand precisely what is propelling the movement toward globalization. Of course if we understand this—the cause or causes of the globalization process—then we understand not only what is, as we say, "driving it forward," but also what precise things would have to change for the process to be halted or reversed.

So then, in analyzing globalization we must keep constantly in mind the conditionality of what we are doing. That is, we are engaged in an intellectual exercise which has the logical form "if things continue as they are, then so-and-so may happen." But of course things might *not* "continue as they are," and we must always keep that possibility in mind, and we must also clearly understand what these "things" are—what political, institutional, and other conditions must remain stable, must not change— if the process is to continue. Indeed understanding what logicians call the

---

3. For a more detailed discussion of the analogical use of "movement" vocabulary in socioeconomic description and the conceptual confusions to which it can lead, see my *Karl Marx,* 200–209.

ceteris paribus conditions of the globalization process is an especially important part of understanding the phenomenon as a whole.

## Concepts and Methodology

With all those provisos we can continue. Globalization then is a process, a movement of the world, in a particular direction. In what direction? Well obviously toward the creation of something global. And it is probably best, for the moment, if we take that "something" to be the something favored by most of the authors on the subject—a global *economy*. Now economics is about the production, distribution, and consumption of goods and services. So applying that idea globally, we might say that a truly global economy would be one in which (1) everything that is produced is produced globally, (2) everything that is produced is distributed globally, and (3) everything that is consumed is consumed globally. Note, however, that there is a crucial ambiguity in phrases like "produced globally," "distributed globally," and "consumed globally." In all cases those phrases can be understood to mean produced/distributed/consumed *in different parts of the globe,* or they can be understood to mean produced/distributed/consumed equally *in all parts of the globe.*

This distinction turns out to be important, because in fact most authors who are impressed by how far the process of economic globalization has "processed" understand "globally" in the first sense. They are impressed by the fact that the process of market and industrial production, distribution, and exchange of goods and services has now spread to a much larger *geographical area* of the globe than was the case one hundred years ago, fifty years ago, or even thirty years ago. Those, however, who are much less impressed by the extent of genuine economic globalization, are apt to point out that this spread is both geographically and socially highly uneven. Thus, for example, while certain areas of Latin America and East and Southeast Asia have increased both their production and consumption of goods and services in the last thirty or so years, the increase in South Asia, and in particular in the whole continent of Africa has been markedly less. Indeed in large parts of Africa real per capita production and consumption of goods and services has actually fallen absolutely in the last twenty-five years. Such people—the skeptics about globalization we might call them—are also apt to point out that, even within Latin America or Southeast Asia, increases in production and consumption have been markedly unequal and uneven across different social or class groups

within the population. So, for example, within even a supposedly successful economy like Malaysia or South Korea many poor people are to be
found who are marginalized in both production and consumption. And
this is even more true in Latin American countries such as Mexico, Brazil,
or Argentina.

However, while the unevenness or inequality of the globalization process can be a cause of concern, it would be nonsense to make an absolutely
equal spread of production, distribution, or consumption across the globe
a defining criterion of economic globalization. After all, some forms of
production are still tied to the presence of certain natural resources which
are, of necessity, unequally distributed across the globe. You cannot mine
iron ore where there is no iron ore, or set up wheat-processing mills where
it is too cold to grow wheat. A pineapple cannery set up in northern
Canada would struggle to obtain raw material at a competitive price.
Also, there are some forms of consumption that are of necessity globally
unequal. Again you do not require combine harvesters where you cannot
grow grain, and you do not require air conditioners in climates where the
temperature never arises above 10 degrees Celsius. Clearly furs—whether
real or synthetic—will not sell well in Indonesia or Thailand. Finally, and
probably most importantly, highly unequal distributions of income (and
thus of market consumption power) have been, and remain, a feature, not
only of the new parts of the global economy—like Southeast Asia or Latin
America—but also of the "old" parts of the global capitalist economy—
like Europe or North America. Thus, if you refuse to count Brazil, for
example, as part of the new global economy on the grounds of its internal
inequality, then you would logically have to refuse to count the United
States either. This procedure would soon lead one to the (presumably
ridiculous) conclusion that not only was there not a global economy everywhere, but that there was not a global economy anywhere! So while social
inequalities, particularly where they are very extreme, should lead us to
ask—quite proper—questions about the distribution of the economic
*benefits* of globalization, I do not think that either geographical or social
unevenness of the process can be a ground for denying its *reality*. We
should also remember in this context that any process of economic development must, of necessity, be spatially and temporally uneven, and to that
extent it must also be socially uneven and unequal. That is, if an office or
an industrial plant is placed in location X and employs Y group of people,
it cannot simultaneously be placed in location A and employ B group of
people. Of course, at a later time a company that has set up operations in

location X can expand its operations and also set up in location A. But until it has done so there is a necessary inequality between location X and location A. Moreover, even when there has been expansion to location A, locations B ... n (and all the people who live there) can still be regarded as "left out in the cold" (unless and until they get included at some later stage or stages in the process). In fact to an extent the phrase "uneven development" must be regarded as a classical case of linguistic redundancy. That is, s/he who says "development" says "uneven process"—as an adjective of "development" "uneven" is otiose.

However, the discussion to date has provided a useful example of one methodological approach to the study of globalization. In this approach (perfectly exemplified in *Globalization in Question* by Paul Hirst and Grahame Thompson) an ideal type of a perfectly globalized economy is set up and the current imperfect reality is compared with it in order to demonstrate how far short of "true globalization" the world actually is.[4] There is nothing wrong with this method, provided that the model of "perfect" or "complete" globalization is at least moderately realistic and sensible. But when reading such texts it is always important to examine the postulated end state carefully to see that it indeed is both realistic (realizable in the real world) and sensible.

The other approach to globalization as a process, however, begins "from the other end," as it were. That is, instead of measuring current levels of globalization against the standard of a perfect, "complete" economic globalization, the procedure is reversed and the current reality is compared with some historical "pre-globalization" starting point, usually in order to show "how far we have come" down the road of globalization. So classical propositions generated by this method might be:

1. National and even regional economies are much more deeply interdependent than they were thirty years ago.
2. The global movement of capital is much more extensive and has much greater effects than it had thirty years ago.
3. The global movement of labor is much more extensive than it was thirty years ago.
4. Multinational or transnational companies dominate world production and trade much more than they did thirty years ago.

---

4. Hirst and Thompson, *Globalization in Question,* chaps. 2–4.

5. Communication links—and particularly electronic links—between different parts of the globe are much more developed than they were thirty years ago, and

6. Because of (1) above individual states have much less control and influence over crucial economic variables than they had thirty years ago.[5]

But again such formulations are not immune to problems of vagueness and (thus) from complexities of measurement. For example, a lot turns on what the phrase "much more extensive" means in propositions (2) and (3). People (authors/analysts) who want to impress you with the advance of globalization over the last thirty years will provide figures on the absolute amounts of money that are now invested by companies in assets held abroad or outside their own country (estimated to total U.S.$2.5 trillion dollars in 1995). Those who want to downplay this will say that this amount, although absolutely huge, is smaller, *as a proportion of world output,* than the amount of capital that was invested abroad in the late nineteenth century. Or again, those who want to impress you with the rapid globalization of world labor markets will point out that in the year 1992 alone about 100 million people moved their country of residence, the vast majority of them voluntarily, in search of better employment in some other part of the globe. Those who wish to minimize the phenomenon will point out that 100 million people equaled about 1.7 percent of the world's population in 1992, and that *as a proportion of the world's population* labor migration was actually greater in the nineteenth century—the century of the great mass migrations from Europe to the United States, of the Russian colonization of Siberia, and of considerable labor movements in the British, French, German, and other European colonial empires.[6]

Equally obviously, "much more deeply interdependent" is a rather vague phrase and raises questions about how we measure the level or degree of interdependence among economies at any one time and changes through time. There are many ways of doing this. They include measuring an economy's level of dependence on exports to other countries, on imports from other countries, on investment from overseas, and on technology from overseas. Moreover, when you apply these different measures to a single

---

5. Lester C. Thurow, *The Future of Capitalism: How Today's Economic Forces Shape Tomorrow's World* (St. Leonards, New South Wales: Allen and Unwin, 1997), esp. chap. 8.

6. For the growth of FDI over the last forty years, its countries of origin and destination, see Dicken, *Global Shift,* 42–48. For the arguments and statistics on global labor migration, see Hirst and Thompson, *Globalization in Question,* 22–26.

economy you sometimes get broadly consistent results and sometimes inconsistent results. For example, Japan's economy shows a very high level of export dependence but a rather low level of import dependence. The British economy shows a very high level of export and import dependence, and that of the United States shows a relatively low, but rapidly growing, dependence on both exports and imports.[7] Or again, some economies are highly dependent on foreign capital and technology for their economic development (most of the Southeast Asian economies fall in this category), while others—like the German economy—are much less dependent on other economies by both these measures than most other industrial economies in the world.[8]

So just as with the "ideal type future" method, there are lots of technical and statistical difficulties with the application of the "how far we have come" method, and you must always be aware of these complexities and difficulties when reading this, or any other, text about globalization. And indeed, as readers become aware of these complexities, they may begin to wonder how real the whole phenomenon of globalization is. More subtly still, they may begin to wonder how one might even answer that question.

7. For the United States and Japan, see Thurow, *Future of Capitalism,* 147–51, chap. 8. Over the period 1960 to 1995 the value of exports from the U.S. economy averaged 7.7 percent of its GDP and the value of imports 8.3 percent, but these averages disguise the fact that the export figure grew from 5.2 percent to 11.3 percent over those thirty-five years and the import figure from 4.5 percent to 12.8 percent. By contrast exports averaged nearly 25 percent and imports 24.4 percent of Britain's GDP over the same period. (The figures for Australia were 15.8 percent and 16.6 percent.) Rather surprisingly, Japan's (annual) exports averaged only 11.3 percent of the value of its (annual) GDP over this period (imports 10.1 percent). However, the former figure is highly misleading in that sales of Japanese-owned multinational corporations from subsidiary companies *based abroad* are not counted as "Japanese" exports in national accounts statistics, although a part of the profits from such sales are typically remitted to Japan. Thus, this figure for Japanese exports of goods and services does not include *any* of the revenue earned by *any* factory in the United States, Europe, or elsewhere in Asia that is owned by Sony, Mitsubishi, Canon, etc. What's more, the figures for U.S. exports does not include *any* of the revenue earned by *any* factory *in* Europe, Latin America, Asia, or wherever that is owned by Ford, General Motors, IBM, etc. This is just one of the ways in which national accounts data now provide a very partial and misleading picture of the workings of the global economy. For further remarks on this, see note 13 of Chapter 15. Figures quoted are from OECD Statistics Directorate, *Historical Statistics, 1960–95* (Paris: OECD, 1997), tables 6.12 and 6.13, pp. 75 and 76.

8. For the Asian "Tiger" economies and foreign investment, see Dicken, *Global Shift,* table 2.10, p. 48. This same table shows that whereas in 1994 foreign investment in the British economy was equal to 20.9 percent of its GNP, the figure for Germany was only 6.8 percent and for Japan only 0.4 percent!

### *A Suggested Criterion for "Determining" the Reality of Globalization*

Resolving these difficulties, or at least some of them, is a task for later chapters. But for now, let me at least offer my "bottom line" measure or a "bottom line" criterion for assessing the extent and importance of globalization. It is this. In this book globalization will be treated as an important and significant economic and social process insofar as it can be shown that the material welfare of the majority of people in the majority of countries of the world is now far more dependent on decisions and activities taken by people far removed (geographically speaking) from those people and countries, than was the case thirty years ago. And here "far removed" is to be understood as "*at least* resident outside the boundaries of the country in question." It will, I hope, be clear that this is just a variant of the "how far we have come" measure of globalization mentioned above. But there is also an "ideal type" variant of the same idea. In this variant globalization is an important and significant process, insofar as the degree of disruption of the material standard of living of the majority of people in the majority of countries of the world that would be suffered as a result of the breakdown of international economic relations is much greater or more profound than it would have been even thirty years ago.

These are "bottom line" measures of globalization, in my view, because it is only if globalization is coming to affect the basic economic welfare of ever more ordinary people in the world (rather than minorities or elites alone), that it is likely to have profound social and political implications, as well as economic ones. And as you might have guessed, I think that this is the case—that globalization *is* touching the lives of more and more ordinary people in more and more profound ways.

PART TWO

*Globalization
as a Contemporary
Phenomenon*

# CHAPTER THREE

ᕽ

# The End of the
# Postwar Long Boom

Toward the end of Chapter 2 I offered a list of six propositions that someone might put forward to show how far globalization had advanced, as a
process, over the last thirty or so years. The first of these propositions was
that "national and even regional economies are much more deeply interdependent than they were thirty years ago." I then went on to list, briefly,
the measures of economic interdependence (export dependence, import
dependence, and so forth) that economists frequently use in this context. In this chapter I want to return to this proposition, because in some
ways it is perhaps both the most general, and the most important proposition in that list of six. In fact the other five propositions[1] that followed it
may all be seen simply as different expressions and/or effects of the "much
deeper economic interdependence" of national and regional economies
referred to in that first, very broad or general, proposition.

In this chapter, therefore, I want to consider in more detail the deepening interdependence among economies brought about through the process
of globalization. I also trace the origins of this economic globalizing process to a major crisis that confronted virtually all the advanced industrial

---

1. Just as a reminder, these were increased global movements of capital and labor,
increasing importance of multinational corporations (MNCs) in global trade and investment, rapid improvement of global means of communication through advances in
telecommunications, and the declining influence of individual states over crucial economic
variables that affect the welfare of their populations.

economies of the world in the early to mid 1970s. That crisis is often referred to as *the end of the postwar long boom* in the world economy. This boom began in the late 1940s or early 1950s. It saw the longest, most rapid, and most sustained growth in world output and world trade since the origins of industrial capitalism as an economic system in the late eighteenth and early nineteenth centuries. During the long boom, not only did output and income grow more rapidly on a world scale than ever before, but the real incomes and standard of living of a minority of people on this planet (basically the populations of North America, Western Europe, and Japan) rose more rapidly and more consistently than at any other period in human history.[2]

However, that boom came to an end with the oil shocks of 1973 and 1979 and the onset of the "stagflation" of the early 1980s. In that latter period inflation rose to levels unprecedented in the postwar period (never less than 10 percent and sometimes over 20 percent in all the OECD countries save Japan in the early 1980s), and unemployment began to increase rapidly. In addition, the rate of growth of output and incomes slowed markedly, and (most significantly of all perhaps) profit rates dropped sharply across all the major industrialized economies. By 1981 for example, profit rates as a whole were typically half or less of what they had been in the United States, Europe, and Japan in the peak boom years of the 1960s, and in manufacturing industry in particular they were typically less than a third of what they had been at their postwar peak.[3]

In fact, in retrospect, the early years of the 1970s can be seen as a kind of fault line in the economic history of the postwar world economy: in the peak years of the long boom, the GDP per capita in all the advanced industrial economies of the world had grown at an average rate of nearly 4 percent per year; but in the thirty-five or so years from 1973 to the present that figure never exceeded 2 percent. Eric Hobsbawm, in his history of the twentieth century, has suggested that both the postwar long boom itself, and the long recession that followed it, fit very closely the thirty-year "long-wave" cycle of expansion and stagnation that the Russian economic historian N. D. Kondratiev suggested, in the early years of this century,

2. For a good account of the long boom, its origins, and consequences, see P. Armstrong, A. Glyn, and J. Harrison, *Capitalism Since World War II* (London: Fontana, 1984), especially chap. 8. See also E. J. Hobsbawm, *Age of Extremes: A History of the World, 1914–1991* (London: Jonathan Cape, 1996), chaps. 9 and 10.

3. Armstrong, Glyn, and Harrison, *Capitalism Since World War II*, chap. 14 and data appendix, tables A1–A4, pp. 464–67.

has punctuated the entire history of industrial capitalism since its inception in the late eighteenth century. On this basis Hobsbawm suggested that a new long wave of expansion might begin either at the end of the 1990s or sometime in the first decade of the twenty-first century.[4]

But whether this is so or not (and the whole existence of Kondratiev long waves is a subject of considerable controversy in the professional literature), it is clear that, in the period since the mid 1970s, virtually all business firms everywhere in the world have faced much stiffer competitive conditions than they did in the thirty or so years from the end of the war to the mid 1970s. That is, they have all been operating in a situation in which both output and income has been growing much more slowly than it was in those economic "golden days" and in which, therefore, they have had to fight much harder just to keep their existing shares of a (much slower growing) demand cake, let alone to increase that share.

And this is not their only problem. For not only has the economic cake been growing only about half as fast as it was in the postwar decades, but *there are now many more firms competing for the business that is available,*[5] at least if the matter is considered on a global scale. That is to say, in the middle of the 1970s the only serious players in the world market economy were firms based in the United States, Western Europe, and Japan. By the end of the 1990s, however, firms based in those economies were facing ever stiffer competition from firms based in Southeast Asia and China and (to a lesser extent) from firms based in India and Latin America as well. In other words then, the number of players competing in the world

4. Hobsbawm, *Age of Extremes,* chap. 14, and more especially 87, 403–5, and 570–71. And indeed, as the year 2000 progressed, there seemed to be some signs that the world economy might be set to return to growth levels of 4 percent and above. (See for example, *The Economist,* April 15, 2000, pp. 13 and 78–80, commenting on upbeat IMF growth forecasts.) Given the notorious unreliability of such forecasts, this should not be taken as anything like definitive proof of the Kondratiev hypothesis. But it is interesting that recent developments in computers and telecommunications constitute a perfect example of the sort of "batch" or "clutch" of technological developments whose commercial exploitation both initiates and fuels "long waves" of growth in his theory.

5. This way of formulating the matter, although broadly correct, also has its problems. For competition in the capitalist market can occur, not only among firms as a whole, but among *sections* or *parts* of firms as well. This is particularly the case where large firms are loose "conglomerate" structures made up of what were independent firms operating in widely diverse markets. The composite parts of such conglomerates may then continue to compete in widely different product or service markets even when they are formally part of one economic entity.

capitalist market has increased markedly in the very same period in which the rate of growth of the market has slowed down.

But what does all this have to do with globalization? A great deal, as may already be obvious. For faced with much stiffer competition and sharply declining profit rates in the late 1970s and early 1980s firms across the world have reacted in the economically classical manner. That is, they have all tried to increase profits *by cutting costs.* They have had to do that because the ever increasing intensity of competition in the world market has meant that it has been very difficult even for the very largest firms (including the multinational corporations or MNCs, which I shall consider in detail in Chapter 4) to raise profits by raising prices. On the contrary they have tended to find, not only that raising prices in overseas markets risks losing market share to another competitor or competitors in those markets, but that even raising prices in their home markets risks a loss of market share to foreign competitors.[6]

How do firms cut costs in order to raise profits? Well, in most firms in most lines of business there are basically three categories of cost—energy and raw materials costs (in manufacturing), "overhead" costs (such as rent of premises), and labor costs. Now in the early 1980s (when the profits squeeze was at its worst) it was hard to cut energy and raw materials costs precisely because the sharp oil price rises of the 1970s increased energy costs directly and also impacted on the cost of all raw materials and components made using petroleum or petroleum derivatives. Moreover, overhead costs were usually not a very large component of costs for most firms. So most firms across the world at that time chose to cut costs by laying off workers and reducing the real wages of the workers they retained. Laying off workers, of course, increased the rate of unemployment. Reducing or holding down real wages, while it may have helped to restore profitability for individual firms, also meant a slower growth of demand in the system as a whole and hence a further intensifying of competitive conditions.

Hence, while the initial assault on labor costs by firms across the world was first provoked, in the early 1980s, by the attempt to reverse the profits squeeze that came with the end of the long boom, this assault did not end once the oil shocks had been absorbed and inflation had been brought under control (roughly by the mid 1980s). On the contrary, the continued

6. For a most interesting analysis of the problems of MNCs in Britain in the early 1980s focused on just this issue, see A. Glyn and J. Harrison, *The British Economic Disaster* (London: Pluto Press, 1980), especially 5–13 and 34–36.

intensification of competition brought about both by the declining growth of the system as a whole and the entry of new competitor firms (on a world scale) all led to further cost-cutting efforts, and in the later 1980s and 1990s in particular these efforts took two main forms:

1. The use of new computer and information technologies to cut workforces and (simultaneously) to increase the productivity of the remaining workers. This occurred first in manufacturing processes themselves, but by the late 1990s had also affected a whole variety of administrative, managerial, and service occupations and business.
2. The relocation of certain production, distribution, and service activities to lower-wage areas of the globe, relocations that could involve movements of activities to lower-wage areas or regions within a national economy as well as international movements across borders.[7]

It must be emphasized here that this strategy of cutting costs by cutting wages in order to meet the demands of a much more intensely competitive global market has had profound implications for ordinary people (worker-consumers) in the advanced industrial economies as well as for the ordinary people (worker-consumers) in the so-called developing economies. That is, the recruitment of millions of people in South and Southeast Asia (including China) or in Latin America into relatively low paid employment provided by relocating MNCs and other firms has been frequently commented upon in the globalization literature. But a rather less frequently remarked upon consequence of this same labor-cost saving strategy in the OECD economies has been a slow but continuous reduction in real wages and standards of living for the majority of the labor force in both North America and Europe since the mid 1970s. Thus, in a fascinating text, *The Future of Capitalism*, Lester Thurow cites data for the United States showing that for the poorest 60 percent of full-time male workers real wages fell by nearly 20 percent between 1973 and 1992, while real household incomes for the same bottom 60 percent have fallen 2 percent in real terms over the same period. According to Thurow: "From 1973 to 1994 America's per capita GDP rose 33% yet hourly wages fell 14% and real weekly wages 19% for nonsupervisory workers. By the end of 1994 real wages were back where they had been in the late 1950s. With current

---

7. For good empirical discussions of both these trends, see Thurow, *Future of Capitalism*, 26–29 and chap. 4, and Martin and Schumann, *Global Trap*, 96–108.

trends, by the turn of the century real wages will be below where they were in 1950."[8]

Thurow also suggests that the same pattern of falling real wages has marked the British economy through the 1980s and 1990s. In Western Europe real wages have not fallen as sharply for the employed as they have in the United States or the United Kingdom, but this has been done only at the cost of a much higher overall level of unemployment and a severe fall in the standard of living of the unemployed, since the real value of unemployment benefits has been eroded.[9]

There are many further complexities in this process of cost reducing and economic restructuring both of the advanced industrial economies of the world and of the global economy as a whole. But at the moment readers may be wondering what the connection is between all this and the "deeper interdependence" of national economies that has emerged globally over the last thirty years.

### Cost Cutting and Global Economic Integration

The connection between these two phenomena is as follows. If a firm is looking to increase its competitiveness and profits by reducing costs, it is in fact extremely rare (despite some media impressions to the contrary) for it to do this simply by closing its business in high-wage location A and moving lock, stock, and barrel to low-wage location B. Rather a much more typical approach is that the managers of the business break down its activities into a number of component parts and try to reduce costs systematically in each part. Thus, for example, an American company manufacturing personal computers may stop manufacturing whole PCs, and instead subcontract the manufacture of different parts of the product (chips, motherboards, casings, monitors) to a variety of independent supplying companies around the globe (perhaps simply keeping the final assembly process in its own hands and moving that to a lower-wage location). At the same time it is doing all this, however, it may also be reducing the number of its middle-level administrative staff at home by computerizing much of its routine record keeping, *and* subcontracting its product research and design activities to a number of small independent

8. Thurow, *Future of Capitalism*, 24. Real wages in the United States rallied somewhat in the later 1990s, but again, the distribution of this growth was very unequal among groups of workers, and in any case, that rally may now (2001) have exhausted itself.

9. Ibid., 172–75.

consultancy companies (perhaps made up of former direct employees). This kind of subcontracting also reduces the restructuring firm's labor costs because, when it hires these now "independent" consultants, it is not responsible for a whole range of payroll costs that it used to have when it employed the same people directly.[10]

The net result of this kind of systematic cost cutting through a combination of various strategies for various activities (relocation, automation, subcontracting, and outsourcing), when it is being carried out simultaneously by hundreds of thousands of firms in thousands of sectors of economic activity across the world, is not only to vastly increase labor productivity (to allow a greatly increased output to be produced by a smaller and cheaper workforce), it is also—in geographical terms—to make production of a good or service increasingly dependent on interrelated activities carried out in a whole number of different places. Thus, to take the same example, Singapore and Malaysia are today (in the late 1990s) described in official statistics as the leading locations in the world for the manufacture of personal computers. More personal computers are produced there than anywhere else in the world. But the word "manufacture" here has to be put in quotation marks. For all that happens in factories in Singapore and northern Malaysia is the final assembly of PCs from components supplied from as far away as the United States, Europe, and Japan, based on research and programming done in locations as far away as the United States, Japan, Russia, and India.[11] And similar remarks could be made in regard to car "manufacture," to the "manufacture" of clothing, or toys, or sports equipment, or audiovisual technology, around the world.

10. For good discussions of these kind of cost-cutting strategies, see Thurow, *Future of Capitalism,* chap. 4, and Dicken, *Global Shift,* chap. 11. More recently, the world has had some rather dramatic evidence of both the economic efficacy and the social and political costs of this kind of labor market restructuring using outsourcing and subcontracting as important tools. For the year 2000 saw the first really substantial rise in oil prices since the 1970s but this did *not* lead, *contra* the 1970s, to sharp rises in inflation, although it *did* lead to mass demonstrations by truckers, farmers, and others against such rises. These latter two phenomena are connected. Because far more firms worldwide now subcontract their haulage to truckers operating as "independent" businesses on fixed-price contracts, rises in fuel costs for transport are generally not passed on (as rising prices) to final consumers, but "absorbed" by the hauliers as lower (or negative) profits on their haulage contracts. Thus, there was very little oil-induced inflation in the system but there were thousands of irate truckers demonstrating and blockading (and with much public support).

11. Dicken, *Global Shift,* chap. 11.

We can now look at this same process from a national point of view rather than from the point of view of the firm. Looked at in this way it implies, not just that (say) the British, U.S., or Australian economies are a lot more import and export dependent than they were thirty years ago, but also that now, as opposed to thirty years ago, a lot more of the goods which they both export and import are not final or finished commodities that can be consumed by any real final consumers—British or American or Australian citizens—at all. They are rather bits or components of products that can only be turned into useful final products by being circulated around the world in a complex chain of importing and exporting. This chain may link together several independent firms in the same sector of economic activity, or it may link many, widely dispersed subsidiary operations of a single, vertically integrated firm (in "intra-firm trade").

Now let us return to my preferred criterion of the significance or importance of globalization—its implications for ordinary people. The implications are that the material standard of living of many ordinary consumers around the world is made up of commodities that, if they were not being produced and distributed in this globalized fashion, would not be produced at all. That is, if the global design, manufacture, and distribution of cars ceased tomorrow, Australian car buyers could not simply substitute Australian cars for the missing global cars, *because there are no Australian cars any more* (in the sense of cars assembled in Australia from components made entirely in Australia). And what is true of cars is true of audiovisual equipment, a large range of electrical goods, all computer equipment, a lot of clothing and footwear, much sports equipment, and so forth. And what is true of Australia is equally true of the United Kingdom, most of Western Europe, and (even, to an important degree) the United States and Japan.

In the short to medium term then, a breakdown of this globalized production structure would have catastrophic implications for the real standard of living of hundreds of millions of ordinary consumers around the world. They would, overnight, lose access to goods (and actually quite a few services) they now take for granted as part of their normal standard of living. Of course, given time it might be possible, by processes of invention and investment, to substitute locally produced products for these globalized products. But even if that happened, it could only happen through a large rise in the price of these locally produced substitutes (compared with the globalized products they were replacing). And a sharp rise in the price of a large number of items which people routinely consume amounts to the same thing as a sharp decline in their real standard of living, if their money incomes do not increase proportionately.

## Conclusions

The strategies that hundreds of thousands of capitalist firms (not just the 39,000 or so so-called multinationals) have used to lower their costs and to remain competitive in an ever more "cutthroat" global economy have had, and continue to have, enormous implications for the lives of hundreds of millions of people around the world. Moreover, these strategies have had important implications for such people both as workers or employees and as consumers. In general terms those people have benefited, as consumers, from the cheaper goods and services to which globalized production and distribution has given them access. But as workers and employees, they have often had to pay a high price, either through falling real wages and dramatically reduced job security in the so-called advanced capitalist countries, or as newly employed but low-paid workers in the new industrializing countries and parts of the globe.

As we shall see, drawing up a balance sheet of the (economic, social, political, even moral) benefits and costs of this highly complex process is by no means an easy task. Moreover, at this point in my argument I am not going even to attempt to draw up such a balance sheet. For the moment I only wish to emphasize that this process of globalizing the production of many goods and services—a process carried out, quite unwittingly, by thousands of business managers worldwide for quite commonplace, short-term cost-cutting reasons—has drawn hundreds of millions of people across the world into a complex web of deep economic interdependency. Through this web, the most fundamental determinants of the material welfare of hundreds of millions of people worldwide are effectively in the hands of other people enormously distant from them culturally, socially, and geographically. These people they will never see or know, but they too (again usually quite unwittingly) can damage or enhance the welfare of millions of human beings enormously distant from them by actions which, they too, could not readily conceive as having such consequences. All this has come about, not only because of the globalized structure of *production*, whose origins and development I have traced in this chapter, but also because of a number of other economic processes (particularly the globalized circulation of money and capital) which I shall be discussing in Chapter 5. However, insofar as these other processes are all dependent in one way or another on the global integration of production processes, I have chosen to give that first priority in my analysis of the economics of globalization.

CHAPTER FOUR

ॐ

# The Role of the
# Transnational Corporation

*Multinationals or Transnationals?*

According to the latest statistics from the United Nations Conference
on Trade and Development (UNCTAD), there are now approximately
39,000 so-called multi- or transnational companies in the world, with over
265,000 subsidiaries or affiliates.[1] In a lot of the globalization literature, as
we shall see, the terms "multinational" and "transnational" are used inter-
changeably. However, some authors think there is a difference of substance
in the terminology. Hirst and Thompson, for example, argue that, at the
moment, the vast majority of these global companies are better referred
to as multinationals (MNCs), rather than transnationals (TNCs), since,
according to them, despite the fact that such companies typically operate
in a variety of countries, they are not—or not yet—genuinely transnational. They are not genuinely *trans*national, it is said, because they still
have a national "home" or base to which they relate differently than they
do to other geopolitical sites in which they may operate.

In fact, in their chapter "Multinational Corporations and the Globalization Thesis" Hirst and Thompson go to some length to demonstrate that

1. In UNCTAD (United Nations Commission on Trade, Aid and Development) reports
a transnational corporation (TNC) or a multinational corporation (MNC) is defined as
any company having at least one subsidiary or affiliate company registered outside the
country in which the company has its corporate headquarters.

both manufacturing and service multinational companies have the bulk of their assets held in their national home economy, have the bulk of their affiliate or subsidiary companies in that economy (and/or in economies geographically adjacent to the home economy), make the bulk of their sales there, and even (contrary to what is often claimed) declare the bulk of their profits there. Thus, for example, in 1992–93, German manufacturing multinationals made 75 percent of their sales into the German market, and the figure for Japanese manufacturing multinationals was 75 percent, for British companies 65 percent, and for U.S. multinationals 67 percent. Moreover, in 1987 U.S. multinationals declared 69 percent of their gross profits in the United States, while British multinationals declared 67 percent of their gross profits in the United Kingdom.[2]

However, while Hirst and Thompson make a great deal of the terminological distinction between MNCs and TNCs (arguing in effect that the difference is more than terminological), many other authors, as I have already noted, treat the two terms as synonyms, and that is the procedure I am going to follow in this chapter. That is partly because, for philosophical reasons, I think that a fluidity in terminology has, in general, much less damaging effects on the quality of social science description and analysis than many social scientists continue to suppose. But also, in this particular case, I happen to think that the Hirst-Thompson argument that these companies are multi- rather than transnational is weaker than it looks.

## Multinationals and Globalization

However, we shall come to that issue shortly. For the moment I just want to emphasize that MNCs or TNCs figure so early in this book because they figure so predominantly in the globalization literature generally. Indeed, in quite a lot of the literature economic globalization and the activities of MNCs are treated as more or less synonymous. That is, globalization is often seen as having begun with the first period of significant development and spread of Western MNC activity (from the United States and United Kingdom in the 1920s), and the degree of globalization is often more or less equated with the degree and extent of MNC activity. This is often

---

2. Hirst and Thompson, *Globalization in Question,* 77–98. Sales and profits data are from pages 90–91 and 89. Dicken makes a very similar argument to Hirst and Thompson and on rather similar grounds. Dicken, *Global Shift,* 193–99.

expressed statistically in the claim that the larger the share of MNC activity in global GDP and global trade and investment, then the greater the level of economic globalization. And this view is common both to enthusiastic advocates of globalization, such as Kenichi Ohmae,[3] and to the many skeptics or critics of globalization, for whom MNCs are a frequent *bête noire.*

For this reason I want to stress here, at this early point in the analysis, that I believe this view to be subtly but profoundly mistaken. That is to say, I think it is clear that the capitalist firms and enterprises engaged in global or globalizing economic activity run into the hundreds of thousands, even though it is true that the 39,000 or so formally multi- or transnational companies in the world account for a large proportion of global foreign direct investment (FDI) and a large proportion (about two-thirds) of global trade.[4] These hundreds of thousands of other global economic players are not counted as MNCs or TNCs because they do not possess any subsidiary companies outside their country of origin. But this fact does not prevent such companies from placing orders overseas for the manufacture of a commodity or commodities, investing in overseas businesses or assets, or selling commodities or services overseas.

Thus for example, the Australian surfwear manufacturing company, Rip Curl, owns no affiliates or subsidiary companies outside Australia, but the vast majority of the clothing and clothing accessories that bear its well-known brand name is manufactured by Chinese and Indian clothing companies. To reiterate, these companies are independently owned by Indian and Chinese capitalists. They are not Rip Curl subsidiaries in any sense. But they produce clothing to designs and specifications supplied by Rip Curl Australia, and in quantities and at prices laid down in contracts drawn up between these firms and Rip Curl. And in the case of some of the Indian companies for example, the production of Rip Curl products can account, at any one time, for 90 percent or more of their output.

In addition to this, however, Rip Curl also sells franchise rights to market its products to a large number of clothing wholesalers and retailers worldwide (everywhere from Europe to North and South America) and earns considerable revenues and profits from these global franchising arrangements. These generalizations, applying to Rip Curl, also apply to

---

3. See, in particular, K. Ohmae, *The Borderless World: Power and Strategy in the Interlinked Economy* (New York: Free Press, 1990).

4. See Dicken, *Global Shift*, 42.

its major Australian competitors in the surfwear trade—Quiksilver and Billabong—which also operate globally in these same kinds of ways, although they too, like Rip Curl, would not figure in any formal list of MNCs.[5]

Of course, most of these hundreds and thousands of smaller capitalist companies (the ones that make up the submerged part of the globalization iceberg, rather than its more visible and better-known transnational tip) are, generally, much smaller than the MNCs or TNCs by almost any measure. That is, these companies typically employ far fewer people directly than a statistically typical multinational, have a far smaller asset base, make a much smaller absolute amount of profit individually, and account collectively, for only a third or so of global trade and for a much smaller proportion of FDI than the MNCs. But these facts should not blind us to the aggregate importance of this mass of much smaller, non-multinational companies and firms in the globalization process generally. For example, a frequently quoted statistic suggests that, at the moment, the 39,000 or so parent MNCs in the world, with their 265,000 foreign affiliate companies, account for about two-thirds of world trade. However, about one third of this is so-called intra-firm trade—the trading of goods or services among MNCs and their affiliate or subsidiary companies—a form of trade whose size can only be estimated because it is not taken into account in formal trade statistics. Now assuming these estimates to be approximately correct, they imply that one-third of all world trade is conducted by non-MNC companies, and that indeed half of "official" or "visible" trade (the trade covered in national and global trade statistics) is carried out by such companies.

So to repeat, the fact that globalization as a process is dominated by, and perhaps even led by, MNCs/TNCs, should not confuse us into believing that if MNCs disappeared tomorrow, globalization would cease. For there are many other smaller but (in aggregate) important players in the globalization process, and some of these smaller players and companies will themselves grow to the point where they become MNCs/TNCs by the UN's formal definition. (In fact the number of MNCs is growing all the time by just this means.)

5. Pamela Cawthorne, "The Limited Usefulness of National Economic Identity in the Case of an Australian Networking Firm," Department of Economics, University of Sydney, Working Paper 98-10, September 1997, and "International Sub-contracting and the Australian and Indian Clothing Industries," Department of Economics, University of Sydney, Seminar Series Paper, November 1997.

I make this point for two reasons. First, as already stated, I want to challenge the commonplace understanding of globalization which equates it *entirely* with the activities of the giant companies whose names dominate the billboards and advertising waves of the world—Coca Cola, Macdonalds, Ford, IBM, Samsung, Mitsubishi, Canon, etc.—and who, just for that reason, constitute the far more socially visible symbols of the globalization process than the Rip Curls of this world. But second, and more importantly, if globalization is simply equated with the activities of MNCs/TNCs, it is very easy to slip into a comfortable nationalist myth which divides the world of business into nasty, unreliable footloose multi-nationals on the one hand, and good, local, even patriotic, national firms on the other. In this myth the latter's activities are deemed, somehow, to be inherently more desirable than those of the awful MNCs/TNCs.

But, aside from the frequently verified fact that MNCs are nearly always better employers—by a variety of measures—than local companies in a whole swathe of countries in the world,[6] this nationalist division often conveniently overlooks the fact that so-called national firms are often locked as firmly into global activities as any TNC. They are just locked in in different, less obvious or visible ways.

In a sense the attempt by Hirst and Thompson to show that transnational companies are not really transnational at all, but multinational, because they are still far more integrated into their home states than into other global locations is just a variant of this kind of nationalist logic at play. It appears, from their approach, that if, for example, Ford still depends more on U.S. sales than on global sales for its corporate revenue and profits, or Cadbury-Schweppes still gets greater revenue and profits from its British sales than from sales in any other single market, then we can, as it were, claim or reclaim that firm as nationally American or British after all (and therefore as "our" "good-guy" firm, rather than as "their" or, still worse, *nobody's* "bad-guy" firm).

But in any case it seems to me that the attempt to deny the genuine globality of MNCs by showing that the bulk of their assets or sales or profits are geographically concentrated rather than spread across the globe is itself a highly questionable procedure for a number of reasons. First, it involves assigning a nationality to a firm entirely by reference to where its

6. The most comprehensive account justifying this generalization and citing a mass of specific case studies and comparative data in its support, is the UNCTAD *World Invest-ment Report 1994: Transnational Corporations, Employment and the Workplace* (New York: United Nations, 1994). See also Dicken, *Global Shift,* 259.

global or corporate headquarters happens to be.[7] Surely this is rather odd. To call an insurance company (like AMP) Australian because it historically originated in Australia and has its headquarters there does not make a great deal of sense, since the bulk of its shares are not held by Australians at all, but by a number of large American and European institutional investors. Classifying the Ford Motor Company as "American" or the Cadbury-Schweppes corporation as "British" would be just as odd, for the same reasons.[8]

Second, the data on sales and profits presented by Hirst and Thompson is too aggregated and crude to do the "nationalizing" job they wish it to do. Thus, in the case of sales, the geographical location of the volume of total sales of a company does not tell us much unless we know the relative *contribution* of sales in different locations to a company's total profits, and the relative *rate of growth* of sales in different locations. The latter measure is especially important where a company is expanding its operations, since sales in new markets may be growing faster and be more profitable than sales in traditional markets, even if, for historical reasons its sales to traditional markets still dominate its aggregate sales statistics.[9] In the case of

7. An empirically useful and important text that, nonetheless, attaches "national" labels to multinationals in this same question-begging fashion is Michael E. Porter, *The Competitive Advantage of Nations* (London: Macmillan, 1990). This is not to deny the truth of the central contention in Porter's important book—that the national historical setting of an MNC/TNC may have been important in its growth and may continue to be important in its global competitiveness in the sector or product market in which it operates. But it does not follow from the fact that a given national location may be significant in these senses, that an entity called "the British nation" or "the American nation" or "the German nation" *benefits from* the success of globalizing companies that have originated and grown in these national geopolitical spaces. Interestingly, this is one issue which receives no attention at all in Porter's wide-ranging book.

8. It must, however, be said that the ownership structure of American and British multinationals is more diverse than that of German and (in particular) Japanese multinationals, the latter having their controlling stock "cross-owned" by other Japanese companies and by Japanese banks in a way that makes takeover by non-Japanese capital more difficult than it is in the United States or elsewhere. This, of course, does not prevent non-Japanese individuals and economic institutions from holding nonvoting shares or small blocks of voting shares in Japanese multinationals, and many such individuals and companies do. Nor does it entirely prevent foreign takeovers or mergers, as the recent Daimler-Chrysler/Mitsubishi merger shows. For differences in the ownership structure of American, German, and Japanese multinationals, see Dicken, *Global Shift*, table 6.4, p. 198.

9. Data on the growth rates of different markets and their contributions to the profits of individual MNCs are almost impossible to obtain. However, Dicken, *Global Shift*,

profits the situation is even less satisfactory, since the Hirst and Thompson data on gross profits only show where those profits were declared for tax purposes, not where they were earned.

And finally, all the Hirst and Thompson data is aggregated for whole national groups of multinational firms ("British multinationals," "U.S. multinationals," "Japanese multinationals," "European multinationals"), and I suspect that these huge categories serve to obscure enormous differences in the degree and type of globalization among different kinds of firms in different sectors.

But again, none of these technical problems with the Hirst and Thompson data is as important as the observation that claiming that any company or any group of companies is not genuinely transnational because it does not (at any given point in time) hold its assets in equal proportions all across the globe, or does not sell equally into all markets, or does not make profits equally in every location across the globe is not very sensible precisely because it ignores the fact that globalization is of necessity a spatially and socially uneven *process,* not an end state. It is an approach that measures the degree of globalization by reference to some postulated "fully global" end state (from which, of course, the present real level of globalization necessarily falls short) rather than by reference to the distance moved from the world of predominantly national firms and economies of seventy-five or so years ago.

But Hirst and Thompson adopt this particular ideal-type measure of globalization for a reason. They do so because they wish strenuously to deny what they think of as the overblown claims of certain advocates of free market globalization. These latter they accuse of claiming, not only that the globalization is far more advanced as a process than it actually is, but (and more seriously) that it is now a process beyond any form of political control or regulation—indeed, that it is a process which should not, if its dynamic is not to be impeded, be politically controlled or regulated at all. But Hirst and Thompson strenuously deny, in their later chapters, that this is the case. They point out that the process is already being regulated in a variety of informal ways, and indeed they advocate a marked extension of this regulation, both to keep the globalization process economically

---

324–25 and 360, suggests that "market saturation" in developed-country markets for both cars and television sets, and the slowing of turnover velocity that such saturation brings, has been a factor in MNCs in both sectors expanding sales in "new" "developing" markets (especially in Asia) since the 1970s.

stable and to rectify, or at least modify, what they see as its more pernicious social effects.[10]

So what we glean from this is the obvious point that Hirst and Thompson are, at bottom, very worried about globalization, which is why indeed
they have chosen to write about it and analyze it. And in this they are
highly typical. Most people who write about globalization are worried
about it, and indeed the majority of such writers are hostile to it to various degrees. In particular, as I noted earlier, they tend to be particularly
hostile to or worried about TNCs/MNCs.

### Hostility to Multinational Companies

But why? For this is perhaps the most remarkable—and least remarked
about—phenomenon of all. Here are these huge companies generating a
large part of the world's material wealth, satisfying a very large part of its
consumption requirements, and contributing directly and indirectly[11] to a
considerable amount of its wage employment, *yet nobody likes them or
trusts them.* And when I say "nobody" I mean "nobody." UNCTAD trusts
them so little that it has set up a special body of its own to monitor their
activities and to try and get them to abide by a code of conduct which it
lays down. They are disliked and distrusted by many, if not all, politically
involved people across the entire South or the Third World as agents of
Western economic and cultural imperialism.[12] But what is perhaps most
remarkable of all, these same companies tend to be no more popular in

10. Hirst and Thompson, *Globalization in Question,* chaps. 6–8.

11. Possibly more indirectly than directly. Dicken, *Global Shift,* 257, quotes an UNC-
TAD report to the effect that, in the early 1990s, MNCs employed about 73 million people directly worldwide, of whom about 12 million were in developing countries. Sanjaya
Lall, *The Indirect Employment Effect of Multinational Enterprises in Developing Countries*
(Geneva: International Labour Office, 1979), insists that reliable quantifications of the
indirect employment effects of MNC/TNC presence are hard to obtain, but cites a Korean
study to the effect that the indirect employment generated by MNC activity is about equal
to its direct employment effect. However, a great deal turns, as Lall insists, on the length
of time a country has been in receipt of MNC investment (generally speaking, the longer
the time the greater the indirect employment benefits) and the kind of enterprises involved.
As one might expect, agricultural or primary product processing industries on the one
hand, and capital goods industries on the other, tend to generate more indirect employment opportunities for a local population than "light" manufacturing industry.

12. It might seem that if the Chinese government, or any other Third World government, sets up export-processing zones (say) in which MNCs are offered multiple tax
and other incentives to locate there, this may stand as some kind of evidence against this

their home societies and economies in the West than they are in the non-Western world. Suspicions that such companies are exporting American, or German, or French, or British jobs; that they are bribing or bullying democratically elected politicians; that they are dodging taxes, polluting and destroying the world's ecosystem and atmosphere; and that they are reducing the entire world to a uniform acculturated mass of burger chains, violent videos, and a crass "materialist" "consumptionist" ethic are just as common among politicians and intellectuals in New York, Paris, and London as they are among similar groups in Bombay, São Paulo, and Jakarta.

*Nobody likes TNCs.* And though they spend billions of dollars on advertising themselves and their products, and hundreds of millions more on public relations ("Coca Cola—proud supporter of the Australian Olympic Team!"), this widespread—one might properly say "global"—unpopularity and suspicion just will not go away.

But again, why? Well, it might seem that I have already rehearsed some of the reasons for this unpopularity above. To repeat, TNCs are regularly accused of the following:

1. Moving investments (and thus jobs) around the globe, in search of the cheapest labor, the lowest tax rates, and the slackest environmental or labor regulations, without regard to the societies or communities (whether in the Western or non-Western world) which they disrupt and destroy by these activities.

2. Using their enormous wealth to bribe or influence politicians, state bureaucrats, and other power holders around the world, often in ways that are in direct disregard of the wishes or interests of ordinary people in the states affected.

3. Being effectively unaccountable to anyone—to any state or group of states, to their consumers, to their workers—for the decisions that they make, despite the fact that those decisions often have considerable economic, social, and environmental consequences of the greatest significance.[13]

4. Bullying or browbeating the governments, particularly of small or poor

---

generalization. But it really is no such thing. Third World states may feel economically constrained to deal with MNCs as sources of investment, technology, and (hopefully) employment. But this dealing, though perhaps celebrated in a thin rhetoric on certain formal occasions, is almost always underlaid by a strong distrust and—indeed—dislike.

13. Martin and Schumann, *Global Trap,* chap. 3.

states, which threaten, or seem to threaten, their interests in any way, often doing this in conjunction with the Western imperialist states which support their activities.

5. Spreading a uniform (and generally Western) individualist, materialist, consumptionist culture around the world, a culture which relentlessly undermines all alternatives to it across the globe, and thus results in the cultural oppression of a large part of non-Western humanity by these quintessential vehicles of Western cultural imperialism. (Western media and telecommunications TNCs are often singled out for particular criticism in this regard.)

Now I do not want to say that all such allegations are false. They clearly are not, and there are famous—or infamous—cases or case studies (ITT's role in the overthrow of the Allende regime in Chile; the Nestle corporation's marketing of baby milk powder in countries without safe drinking water; the dangerous and polluting activities of the Union Carbide company and of and other chemical multinationals, in Bombay, in the notorious Maquiladores border zone of northern Mexico, and in the hinterland of São Paulo and elsewhere; and the numerous reported and unreported oil spillages across the world), which can be, and constantly are, brought forward to justify the world's hostility to and suspicion of TNCs in general. But despite all this, I think a defense of MNCs/TNCs, and of their role in the world, can be mounted, and at the risk of incurring some unpopularity myself, I now wish to offer that defense.

### A Qualified Defense of Multinationals

I want to begin by claiming two things:

1. First, that the evidence justifying hostility to and suspicion of MNCs/TNCs is in general far more specific and more limited than the hostility and suspicion itself is. That is, there are 39,000 multinationals, but examples involving a few tens or hundreds of them at most (and often the same examples) are used to taint the other 38,000 or so by association, as it were.

2. Second, the unpopularity of MNCs owes far more to what we might call structural factors about the world over which MNCs, either individually or as a group, have no more control than their numerous critics have.

To take these points in order. In the first place, there is, as I have already said, a great deal of evidence to suggest that MNCs are generally better employers right across the world than are the national companies operating in the same geophysical spaces.[14] This means, to be more concrete, that multinational companies operating in (say) Thailand, generally pay better wages than Thai companies, provide better working conditions, and obey local labor and environmental legislation more conscientiously than local companies do. And there are good reasons for this to be so. In the first place, companies that have relocated globally in order to secure a cheaper labor supply can often save massively on labor costs (relative to the costs they would have to incur in their home economies) even as they are paying relatively high wages locally. That is to say, globalization allows them to "have it both ways" in many local arenas. They can make enhanced profits *and* be model employers in a cheap-labor market without any contradiction.

But the second reason why TNCs or MNCs are often better behaved than local firms in a variety of ways is that *they lack local political legitimacy* (in comparison with locally owned and operated firms and businesses) and are usually keenly aware of this lack. It is precisely because of this that they want to appear to be model employers. But it is also because of this that multinationals typically try to acquire a degree of nationalist "cover" or "protection" as quickly as they can. This is the reason why they typically, and quickly, move to sponsor local sports teams or cultural events, why they make deals (open and covert) with powerful local politicians and presidents, why they move, equally quickly, to recruit local people at least into the most socially visible managerial and functional roles in the local branches of their organization, and so on.

This is not to deny of course that predatory, polluting, and oppressive

14. See above, note 6. An important point here. UNCTAD's *World Investment Report* for 1994, which is the best source for these comparisons shows clearly that *directly owned MNC subsidiary companies* are in general better employers, by a variety of criteria, than local companies in a whole swathe of countries in the world. The matter may become more complex, however, when attention turns to locally owned companies who are acting as subcontractees for a multinational company or companies. Thus, for example, the poor wages and conditions in so-called Nike factories in Indonesia and elsewhere, are not in fact wages and conditions in factories *owned by Nike* at all, but wages and conditions in locally owned shoe and clothing factories making products under contract for Nike. The issue then becomes one of determining how far low wages (for example) in these factories are in fact "forced" by the terms of the supply contract between Nike and the local producer and how far they reflect profit desires and expectations of local capitalists.

multinational company behavior cannot be found. But it is to say that, where it is found, it is often because it has been overtly politically encouraged, either by the MNC's "home state" government (for example, the U.S. government's use of ITT to destabilize the Allende government) or by local political elites. Thus, in Mexico under the PRI government, for example, the national government showed itself willing to sacrifice the welfare of the people for whom it should have been responsible (the workers and families of the Maquiladores border zone) for what they saw as a broader economic or political payoff.

In this context it is also important to note that the oft-quoted willingness and ability of multinationals to shift their investments and the locations of their operations if they are threatened—or even seem to be threatened—with any local political interference with their operations is, again, a rather exaggerated phenomenon. In general terms it is, as one might expect, much more a feature of financial multinational companies (banks, insurance companies, investment funds, and brokerage houses), who are exclusively involved in moving money (or more exactly, transmitting information about money electronically) around the world, than it is of either manufacturing multinationals or service multinationals (like McDonald's or Pizza Hut), who have significant physical presences in particular economies or societies. Generally speaking, the greater the financial investment a company has in fixed plant and equipment in a particular location, and the more important that location is in its total (global) sales, the more reluctant it will be just to "up and move" when something goes wrong in the local political or social scene. Thus Volkswagen Brazil, for example, which now provides a larger share of Volkswagen global sales than the German mother company, is not an asset that Volkswagen will lightly abandon (and the Brazilian government has used that fact more than once in negotiations with Volkswagen Brazil).[15] On the other hand, of course, a small rented clothing factory with a couple of hundred easily transported sewing machines can be more readily closed and moved than a massive car plant.

So the picture is complex. But in general it is not one found in some more impressionistic radical accounts of MNCs/TNCs, in which all states around the world cower at the first threat of relocation by a company or

15. On this, see, for example, "Former GM Executive Puts Dream Factory in Brazil" (a *New York Times* story concerning the further expansion of Volkswagen's activities in Brazil in late 1999), viewable at www.nytimes.com.

companies and in which all multinational companies brandish the threat of relocation at the first whiff of political interference with their affairs by any and all governments everywhere. The real situation varies enormously, both by state and by company, with, as one might expect, the poorest and smallest states (with the most limited internal markets) having the weakest bargaining positions, and with financial and light manufacturing and service multinationals having the most mobility with which to threaten political authorities.

But, as I have said, these points—which at best complicate or qualify the more familiar picture of TNC/MNC iniquity—are not as important as the more general point that such iniquitous behavior is most often a product of a structural situation over which these companies, despite the size and massive wealth of many of them, have little or no control.

### The Primary Contradiction of Globalization

To see what I mean by this, we have to understand and focus upon perhaps the most important single factor that makes MNCs so universally unpopular. This factor is, simply, that they *are* MNCs, that is, that they *are* supranational (let us call them that to get around this "multi" versus "trans" issue) economic organizations operating in what we might call a "nationalized" political universe. To be more precise, they are organizations that operate, physically and economically, in a large number of geopolitical spaces (conventionally called nation-states) where the normal requirement of political legitimacy and acceptance is that an individual or organization belongs—and belongs *exclusively*—to that space. But this is the one criterion of legitimacy that a supranational organization *cannot*, by its very nature, fulfill. So multinational corporations, simply by virtue of their multinationality, find themselves occupying a kind of pariah political status everywhere. Of course they occupy that status, most immediately and most deeply, when they move into any geopolitical space that is not historically their home space, or state, of origin. But they can easily find themselves attaining pariah status, even in their home states, if they behave, or are seen to behave, in ways that damage that state or its citizens ("exporting" American jobs, etc.).

It is also interesting that most of the more critical literature on multinationals assumes that MNCs only exult, as it were, in their escape from national political constraints. Thus it is frequently argued that once an MNC is operating in a large number of states, or once (to be more exact) a large number of MNCs are operating in a large number of different states, then they can play off states against each other to obtain the lowest possible profit or corporate tax rates and the maximum possible tax breaks and other subsidies to their operations. Also, as noted above, they can use the threat of relocation to drive down or keep down wages, to nullify or weaken environmental and other controls on their activities, or to seek locations where such controls are nonexistent or unenforced (the Maquiladores case).

MNCs can do all these things, and some do, as we have seen. But in a sense, their ability to do all these things is just the up side, as it were, of a situation that also has a marked down side as far as they are concerned. This down side is the lack of any globally consistent regime of regulation or governance (to use the currently fashionable term) that can provide a stable and predictable global *political* environment in which to operate. It is clear in fact, at least to me, that the recent well-publicized, and much criticized, attempt in Paris to negotiate a Multilateral Agreement on Investment (MAI)[16] was a kind of first attempt to try and create such a

16. The MAI was the focus of an enormous amount of public attention in 1997, when news of the "secret" OECD-sponsored negotiations in Paris was first leaked to the media. In fact the MAI negotiations and the response to them is a perfect example of all the contradictions marking this globalizing phase in the history of capitalism. For on the one hand the MAI was clearly a U.S.-sponsored attempt to substantially reduce nationalist political and economic barriers to the globalization of capital, and on terms that were likely to be highly prejudicial to almost all interests other than those of profit-maximizing companies. But on the other hand, the internet and the global mass media ensured that these negotiations never had any hope of remaining secret, and the internet in particular acted as a powerful tool for a global political mobilization against them. In early 1998 my own bookmark files had a list of no fewer than twenty-one web sites concerned wholly or partially with the MAI, many of which were still active in 2000. For its part the OECD's response to the "outing" of the negotiations has been to hide different parts of the MAI agenda in discussions being carried on since 1998 in a variety of different forums (the WTO, Group of 8, IMF, etc.). But I am sure that this tactic will be no more effective in producing an actual agreement than the original OECD mechanism was. For it is clear, even now, that no formal agreement *can* be reached without its being watered down to meet the demands of globally mobilized interest groups other than MNCs and ideologically neoliberal rich-country governments. And that this is so means, I suspect, that all attempts to negotiate a formal multilateral agreement will be abandoned, at least for the foreseeable future, and reliance placed on a continuation of *ad hoc* deal making. But, by definition, *ad hoc* deal making does not solve the problem MNCs confront—the absence of a consistent, "across the board" global political and juridical environment in which to conduct global economic activities.

regime. For the lack of such a regime has a large number of negative consequences for MNCs or TNCs. These include:

1. The need to "pay off" or "keep sweet" a large number of different political regimes around the world. Where attempts to do this are open (through pressure group politics in democratic states), they make MNCs unpopular. When they are covert or corrupt, as in many nondemocratic states, and they get found out (which they usually do sooner or later), they make MNCs even more unpopular.
2. The danger (oft realized) of regime change, whereby the enemies of those previously "paid off" or "kept sweet" come into power (either by democratic or other means). Such changes usually require much expensive fence-mending with the new regime, new "pay offs" or "sweeteners" to new people, new or renegotiated tax and subsidy arrangements, and so on.
3. The danger of being seduced into some location by a set of highly advantageous tax or other arrangements, investing substantially in the new location, and then finding oneself facing a change of regime with a more (as they would say) "antibusiness" outlook or ideology. Here again there are risks of considerable asset losses, or (at the very least) of considerable expenditure—bribery, subversion—in the attempt to avoid such losses.

More generally and generically, and certainly more importantly, non-national economic agents acting in a nationalist political world often find themselves in a situation in which political uncertainty leads to a semi-permanent strategy of *maximizing short-term profits* (especially in very risky locations), rather than long-term growth of enterprise. But as in so many cases, this strategy, while economically rational for the companies in question, is itself an inevitable source of suspicion and resentment, especially among those who find themselves pillaged in this way. Also, and more generally, the most unscrupulous multinational users of the competitive spaces in a politically fragmented globe put competitive pressure on all other companies (in that sector or industry) to be equally unscrupulous. Thus, to use the well-known example, if one relocating American chemical company ignores the health of its workers and the local environment in the Mexican Maquiladores, then, simply in order to keep costs down and remain competitive, other relocating American chemical companies will be forced to do the same. And, just like the cotton-manufacturing lords of nineteenth-century England, not one of the companies involved will feel able to behave differently until some political authority (whether this be the Mexican government, or the U.S. government, or some new political NAFTA regulator) forces them *all* to do so.

In other words then, political pluralism in an economically globalizing world gives competitive advantages to the least scrupulous of the multinational economic agents, who thus lead behavioral standards downward in many sectors and industries. Other global economic players in those sectors or industries know this, but can do nothing about it, either politically or economically. Thus the level of unpopularity and resentment of *all* MNCs increases (and in a sense justifiably) as a result of the behavior of the most predatory.

In short then, MNCs or TNCs are so universally unpopular in our globalizing world because of the considerable, and ever increasing, lack of fit between the economics and politics of that world. Multinational economic enterprises simply do not fit into our still strongly nationalist global politics, and the precise ways in which they do not fit give them (the MNCs/TNCs) both advantages and disadvantages. But (and I would insist on this, against the conventional radical account) the costs and the risks faced by TNCs in operating in a globalizing economy without a globalizing or globalized polity are at least as great as the opportunities. (In fact they are often one and the same.)

But whether this is true or not, one thing is indubitably true. Neither the opportunities nor the risks, neither the costs nor the benefits, of multinational operation can or will be removed by multinational corporations themselves, either individually or as a collective. On the contrary, since the origins of both costs and benefits, risks and opportunities, are ultimately *political,* they can only be removed or changed by the political reorganization of our globe. And until that reorganization occurs, we can say, equally indubitably, both that MNCs/TNCs will continue to be universally unpopular, and that some will continue (because they will be enabled/forced by politically unregulated competition to continue) to behave in the ways that make them so.

# CHAPTER FIVE

# Globalization as a Monetary Phenomenon

In their book *The Global Trap,* Martin and Schumann write the following:

> In their work the profit chasers move at the speed of light in a global data network with many branches, an electronic Utopia still more intricate than the complex mathematics which underlies individual transactions. From dollars to yen, then into Swiss francs and finally back to dollars—in just a few minutes, currency dealers can jump from one market to the next, from one trading partner in New York to another in London or Hong Kong, and end up with deals worth millions in three different places. In the same way fund managers often shift their clients' billions in a few hours between completely different investments and markets. A telephone call or a press on a key is enough to convert U.S. federal bonds for example into British bonds, Japanese shares, or Turkish government obligations denominated in Deutschmarks. Apart from currency, more than 70,000 different securities are already freely traded across frontiers—a fantastic market with infinite chances and risks.[1]

Martin and Schumann are journalists. On the positive side, this means that, unlike many academics, they write well and arrestingly, so that their

1. Martin and Schumann, *Global Trap,* 49–50.

book is enjoyable to read—even exciting at times—while still being informative. On the negative side, however, they do have the common journalistic tendency—of which, I think, the passage I have just quoted is a perfect example—of describing things in ways which sometimes substitute powerful impressions for clear descriptions. One is awed by a passage such as this. It is a stunning vision of powerful young men in luxurious air-conditioned offices moving squillions of money around the globe without moving from their computer terminals. But at the same time, precisely what it is these global "profit chasers" are doing, and how they are enabled to do it, is left rather unclear (a lack of clarity which perhaps only acts to reinforce the awesome impression).

So in this chapter I will try to redress the balance of an account like this (the reader can find many similar on the Net or on the finance and business pages of any newspaper) by explaining, as exactly as I can, how the supposedly new global financial markets actually work. More importantly, I will also assess the extent to which such markets do act to globalize economic relationships in a variety of ways and with a variety of consequences and (indeed) risks, for us all.

As is nearly always the case, however, getting clear about the present requires knowing a little about the past, because the rapid expansion of world capital and financial markets since the 1970s has been made possible because of events that preceded it, and in particular, by events between the end of the Second World War and the mid 1970s. Two events in particular were crucial. These were the postwar long boom and the collapse of the Bretton Woods system.

### The Postwar Long Boom

Readers will remember that in Chapter 3 I claimed that the most humanly important effect of this boom was to raise mass standards of living (in particular in the United States, Western Europe, and Japan) more dramatically and more sustainedly than at any other period in human history. This in turn had one important financial implication. For the first time in human history hundreds of millions of people (rather than a few million elites, which had been the case previously) had incomes well in excess of their immediate expenditure needs. Another way of putting this is to say that, for the first time, those hundreds of millions of people had money to save and invest—some ability to accumulate capital sums of money. The question, however, was what were they to do with this money, and the answer to this question was not singular, but multiple. For example, many of these newly prosperous middle- and working-class people bought their own homes for the first time, homes that then appreciated rapidly in value, especially in the inflationary period of the late 1970s and early 1980s. In addition, many of these same people saved money for their retirement through employment-related pension plans, and they also bought a variety of life and other insurance policies, also as a form of saving. Some of the more prosperous, or daring (always a minority), even bought shares on the stock market in their own right. Now individually each of these people may not have saved or invested a great deal (perhaps U.S.$400,000 on average over a lifetime). But if such a sum is multiplied by hundreds of millions of individuals in the United States, Europe, and Japan, it comes to billions, even trillions, of dollars. Most of this money is invested, not by those hundreds of millions of people individually, but by the managers of pension funds, insurance funds, and banks in which those newly prosperous masses had their savings invested.

So this is the first point to grasp. We often hear of the doings of "speculators" on international currency markets, but usually only in iniquitous circumstances when "they" are "causing a run" on this or that currency, or are "melting down" the Tiger economies of Asia, or when they are being "reassured" or failing to be "reassured" by the doings of some government or central bank. On the whole then, speculators do not enjoy a good press or image and they also have a remote and mysterious air to them. So if tomorrow you see a prosperous-looking elderly couple walking hand in hand through your local park, you will probably not be tempted to yell "filthy speculators! You have the poverty of the Indonesian unemployed on your conscience!" But actually such an allegation might be justified, not because sweet old Mr. and Mrs. Brown did anything themselves to the Indonesian unemployed, but because Mr. Brown is in receipt of a pension from (say) the Railway Workers Super Fund of Australia. For this Fund (probably unknown to him) was one of thousands of pension funds that invested heavily in Asian stock markets in the late 1980s and early 1990s, and then abandoned those same markets when the meltdown occurred (an act that was *part of* the meltdown as much as it was a *response to* the meltdown).

Thus, global financial markets have existed (albeit in rather different forms) since the early part of the nineteenth century—and individual people and financial institutions have been able to make money from investing around the globe for a similarly long time. But the difference between now, and the situation a hundred years ago, or even fifty years ago (at the end of the Second World War) is that financial markets can now make use, not just of the large amounts of spare cash of the very rich (because they have always done that and still do), but of the much smaller individual amounts of spare cash of the prosperous majority of the population in the world's rich countries. To reiterate, taken as one these small individual amounts actually dwarf the investments even of the world's millionaires and billionaires. (The world's largest investor is not Ted Turner or even Bill Gates, but the California Public Employees Retirement System—CALPERS—a pension fund.)[2] So the next time readers hear of some other iniquitous doings by financial speculators and wonder who is to blame, they might think of looking in the mirror. Or, if they are young readers not yet in full-time employment, perhaps they might ask their mothers and fathers to look in the mirror (although to say that raises complex issues about the role of personal morality and ethics in this matter, which is something we will come to later).

This then is the first crucial fact we need to understand if we are to understand current globalized capital markets—the world long boom and how it turned hundreds of millions of people whose parents and grandparents would never have been able to think about investing in anything into (albeit only collectively) the biggest financial investors and speculators in the world.

### The Collapse of the Bretton Woods System

In July 1944 a small number of powerful politicians, bankers, and economic advisers (including John Maynard Keynes) from the United States and Europe met in Bretton Woods, a small mountain village in New Hampshire, to work out a set of world financial institutions and regulations for the postwar world. The point of doing this was to try and prevent any repeat of the excessive financial speculation of the 1920s, which had led to the Great Crash of the U.S. stock market in 1929 and thus (or so many believed) to the Great Depression of the 1930s. This little conference of the powerful had many important results, including the setting up of such now famous institutions as the International Monetary Fund (IMF) and the World Bank. But from the point of view of this chapter, its most important outcome was the creation of a system of fixed exchange

2. Ibid., 167.

rates among the major currencies of the world, maintained in place by the power of the postwar U.S. dollar, and by fairly strict capital and exchange controls maintained by all the other major economies of the world, except the United States.

The details of how this system worked are complex, but since it no longer exists (its last vestiges disappeared at the end of the 1970s) and since this is not a textbook in international finance, we do not need to understand them. Suffice it to say that, as a result of the Bretton Woods conference, all the other major currencies then existing—the pound sterling, the French and Swiss francs, and the deutschmark—were set at a certain exchange rate to the U.S. dollar, and in turn the U.S. dollar was set at a certain exchange rate to gold (that is, the system supposedly worked on a modified form of the gold standard). Setting each of the other major currencies at a certain exchange rate to the U.S. dollar, also served (of course) to set them at fixed exchange rates to each other. This fixed system, once set in place, was then maintained by nearly all international trade and financial transactions being carried out in U.S. dollars (the only freely available currency) and exchanges of other currencies for dollars being kept tightly restricted by what are called exchange and capital controls.

What this means is that if a German person or business firm wanted to turn deutschmarks into dollars (to buy something American, or something on the world market priced in dollars), that individual or business had to have the permission of the German central bank to do so. In the case of individuals there was usually a legal upper limit (of a few thousand dollars) on the amount that could be exchanged in any one transaction or in any one year. In the case of businesses or firms, they had to show a *bona fide* business reason why they needed dollars and what they needed them for. The desire to make money by speculating in currency was not considered a *bona fide* business reason by central banks, either in the case of individuals or in the case of companies (including private banks). So, in a sense, the value of the dollar (and hence its utility as the world's dominant trade and investment currency) was protected against speculation. These same controls on the volume of currency transactions (and on the purposes for which they could occur at all) protected the pound, franc, and other currencies from speculation in the same way.

So why did the system break down? The answer to that question is complex, because several factors came together at one time to make the Bretton Woods system effectively unsustainable. These were the very success of the Bretton Woods system, the fact that that success rested on the absolute world-dominating power of the U.S. economy, and the eventual overvaluation of the U.S. dollar.

Again the long boom is central here, for as the boom took hold in the late 1940s and then continued more or less unabated for two decades, the sheer volume of world trade increased enormously and the world was awash in U.S. dollars earned in that trade, but now held by individuals and companies everywhere from San Francisco to London, from Frankfurt to Tokyo. In addition, the buildup of financial investment institutions (pension funds, etc.) fueled by long-boom savings was already beginning. All these companies and institutions began to find the cumbersome and restrictive regimes of exchange controls irksome, and argued in fact that they were increasingly acting as inhibitors of the growth of world trade and investment. All this had mattered far less of course when there was much less trade, and therefore much less money, around.

In addition, the Bretton Woods system had, at bottom, rested on the absolute world-dominating power of the U.S. economy, and hence the U.S. dollar, at the end of the war. Virtually all the other industrial economies of the world, except the United States, had either been seriously damaged in the war, or destroyed altogether. But as the long boom continued, and the other major economies of the capitalist world recovered, the domination of the U.S. economy began to weaken. Thus many banks and other important financial institutions came to regard the fixed dollar exchange rate as too high relative to the now "recovered" pound, deutschmark, or yen.

Moreover, this sense that the dollar was overvalued became even more marked when, in the 1960s and 1970s, the United States began to finance its very expensive war in Vietnam by, as they say, "printing dollars." What this meant, more exactly, was that in the 1960s the Americans abandoned their guarantee to turn dollars into gold at a fixed rate, because there were now simply too many dollars around in the world for this to be possible. The world financial system ceased to be tied even nominally to gold, and became entirely tied to the U.S. dollar just at a time (the mid 1960s) when the dollar was starting to seem overvalued. This in turn increased the pressure to abandon the fixed exchange rate system and to allow the dollar to float downward relative to the world's other major currencies. Since doing this also promised to make American exports more saleable in world markets (at a time when those markets were beginning to become genuinely competitive again), the U.S. government itself now had little real interest in maintaining the Bretton Woods system.

These three then were, together, the major factors leading to the gradual breakdown of the Bretton Woods system and its effective abandonment by the end of the 1970s. Thus from the late 1960s through to the late 1970s, one country after another abandoned capital and exchange controls and then (mainly in the 1980s) also removed, or much weakened, the controls they had placed on both individual and institutional borrowing and lending of money.

The most significant effect of this "deregulation" trend was that it gradually became possible (by the 1980s) for individuals and institutions to borrow as much as they wanted, from whomever or wherever they wanted, for any purpose they saw fit. With this wave of deregulation in the 1980s the scene was finally set for the development of the global capital and financial markets of the 1990s, whose effects and consequences we hear so much about all the time. In essence what the global financial market actually amounts to is a concatenation, or coming together, of three factors:

1. A historically unprecedented absolute amount of money available to be invested around the globe, wherever the "returns" or profits seem most favorable
2. An absence of any real effective national or other controls or regulations on the use of this money
3. The development (really since the 1970s) of an ever more sophisticated computer and telecommunications technology by which more sophisticated monetary calculations can be made, and made on a vaster scale and at a higher speed, than ever before, and by which money may be moved more rapidly than ever before (at the speed of light in fact).

We have not dealt with this particular dimension of globalization yet (we might call it the internet dimension), but we shall come to it in Chapter 7. I just note here, however, that this third factor has led a lot of people to think that the old Bretton Woods system of capital and exchange controls could not be reintroduced now, even if states wished to do so. The argument is that if all that is needed to move millions or even billions of dollars in a few seconds is a laptop, a mobile phone, and a modem, then, in effect, capital and exchange controls, even if they were reintroduced, could never be effectively enforced. Not everyone agrees with this view,[3]

3. Martin and Schumann, for example, argue that far more could be done to block capital flight to tax havens than is currently being done, and that the failure to act effectively

but it seems to be the predominant view of most contemporary analysts of financial markets.

## The Global Financial Market

That is how global financial market of the 1990s developed. But how does it work, and, more importantly, why do so many people worry about how it works, and see it as a potentially destabilizing factor in the world economy, a factor that may prove, in the end, to have far more costs than benefits?

I think that the best way to understand this issue (an issue that can seem mind-numbingly complex in detail but is in fact very simple in essence, as is much of economics) is by imagining a "real" producer of some "real" good or service somewhere in the world. Arbitrarily, let us take the Hyundai car manufacturing company of Korea. This company makes and sells cars and to do this it has real equipment stored and used in its real factories. It has real workers employed in its factory and offices, and it sells real palpable physical objects (called motor vehicles) around the world.

However—and this is the essential fact which inevitably connects it to financial markets—it needs money to do all these things. Thus:

1. Its factories and offices and the plant and equipment in them were bought for money and (more important) have a certain monetary value, known in the trade as their "asset value."
2. It has to buy new plant and equipment with money, it has to buy components and raw materials with money, and it has to pay its workers in money.
3. It sells its cars for money—its earnings or revenue is in the form of money.

It therefore follows from this that the operations of Hyundai (or of any other economic enterprise making or selling real goods and services anywhere in the world) can be affected by financial markets if they can influence the monetary value of its assets in some way and/or they can influence the value of the money it either spends or receives.

---

here is a failure of political will, not technological capacity. See Martin and Schumann, *Global Trap*, 63–64.

In fact they can do both. How?

Well, in the case of the value of the company itself—its asset value—this is determined not (as one might naively imagine) by how much it might cost to replace its physical assets if they were all blown up in a war or destroyed in a fire. Rather, the asset value of Hyundai is determined by the aggregate value of the shares in the company, which (these days) are traded not only on the Korean stock exchange but on stock exchanges around the world. Simply, the higher the price of these shares, the higher the value of the company (called its capitalized worth in the business jargon); and the lower the value of the shares, the lower its value as a company. This figure (and its movement up and down) is vital to Hyundai (and to all other public companies—companies whose shares are traded on stock exchanges) mainly because they deeply affect the creditworthiness of such companies. So if, for example, Hyundai wants to borrow $500 million from a bank to build a new manufacturing plant in Belgium (and it may well borrow this money from a Belgian bank, not a Korean one), the bank will look at the value of Hyundai's assets to assess whether the loan is a good risk or not. If Hyundai is borrowing, say, $500 million but has earnings every year of $1 billion and an asset value of $200 billion, then it looks like a very good risk. If, however, its earnings suddenly drop to $500 million a year and its asset value to $100 billion, it may "suddenly" look like a bigger risk and the bank may either refuse the loan or decide to charge a higher interest rate to cover the extra risk.

Now as this example clearly indicates, Hyundai can become suddenly less creditworthy either because its asset value suddenly falls, or because its earnings do. And the important thing to note is that both of these things could happen to Hyundai for reasons that have nothing to do with what we might call the physical economy of the company. Thus, if non-Koreans have bought Hyundai shares with dollars at a given dollar-*won* exchange rate and then for some reason (for any reason not connected with Hyundai's own car-selling business) the value of the *won* suddenly plummets, then the "dollar" value of those shares (being Korean shares they will be denominated in *won*) will suddenly fall as well. In addition, the dollar value of the dividends paid by Hyundai (also denominated in *won*) will fall in dollar, or deutschmark, or yen, or franc terms. All this in turn may lead non-Korean holders of Hyundai shares to sell those shares (since, for people who are assessing the matter in some currency other than the *won* the company is not as profitable an investment as it was). But if this selling of shares occurs on any large scale, then the company's asset value will decline too, not only making it less creditworthy but also (and perhaps more importantly) making it vulnerable to takeover by another company or companies, who can now buy its shares cheaply. Meanwhile, if the value of the Korean currency has fallen sharply, then the real value of the wages it pays its workers will fall sharply too, and they may experience considerable hardship. In addition, any foreign loans that the company has previously taken out will now be doubly as expensive (in Korean currency terms) to pay off. All this can occur, as we see, without any physical change in what Hyundai is doing.

But the consequences of these purely monetary changes will not end there. If maintained, they will indeed start to affect the physical activity of Hyundai as well. Remember, Hyundai still has to service its loans, buy important raw materials or machinery from abroad, and pay dividends to its remaining shareholders (to try and prevent them from selling their shares and making the situation even worse), but because the foreign-exchange value of its earnings have fallen sharply, it may have to cut costs elsewhere. Perhaps it will lay workers off, or buy fewer components and less raw materials, or shut down some less productive plant and equipment. But if it does any of these things then of course it *will* end up producing fewer vehicles (a physical change) and perhaps selling fewer vehicles (a physical change) and thus end up earning even less money (this time for physical reasons). All that will, at least in the short term, make the situation even worse for the company.[4]

The situation may be even worse than the description suggests. So far we have not considered exactly why or how Hyundai's shares may go up and down, or exactly why or how the Korean currency (the *won*) may go up and down in ways that have such spectacular effects on the value of Hyundai's earnings from selling cars. In the case of shares the conventional account says—roughly—that a company's shares go up when it is earning good profits (which means, roughly, profits at or above the level "the market" expects of it) and they go down when it is earning lower profits

4. Of course, if the foreign exchange value of the *won* falls, this will make Hyundai's cars cheaper to buy for customers using dollars, yen, francs, etc., and after a while, this factor will probably *increase* Hyundai's sales abroad. But generally speaking, the damaging effects of a sharp foreign exchange fall tend to hit earlier than the positive (export-enhancing) effects, and this is particularly true if speculation-induced foreign exchange falls coincide with falls in the value of other assets. On these latter falls, see the following four paragraphs and the section, "Back to Hyundai: Government Bonds, Company Shares, and the Derivatives Market," pages 78–80.

than are expected of it. And as a rough rule of thumb for what we might call normal changes in share values, this is a true enough explanation for Hyundai or any other public company. However, with the huge amounts of investable funds that I referred to earlier "sloshing" or "swilling" (water or sea metaphors are often, and significantly, used in this context) around the world, Hyundai's shares can rise sharply, through mass buying of them, for reasons that have little or nothing to do with Hyundai's *individual* performance as a company at all.

Why is this? In essence it is because investment fund managers (hundreds of thousands of them around the world) are not, and cannot be, experts on the individual performance of each and every company in which they invest. This being the case, it seems that the decisions they make on investing the hundreds of millions of dollars at their disposal are often affected by the decisions of a relatively few top fund managers who are seen as, or obtain a reputation as, smart market leaders. So, to take a real and significant case, a relatively small number of such "leader" fund managers began to invest heavily in stocks and shares in a number of Southeast Asian economies (including Korea) in the late 1970s and early 1980s and made very good returns (profits) on those investments. By the mid 1980s, therefore, thousands of other investment fund managers were following the lead of these pioneers, and this second wave of investors was followed by a third and a fourth wave (in the 1980s and 1990s) as fund managers around the world "climbed on the Asian band wagon" (to use a conventional financial columnist's phrase). In this situation the value of Hyundai's shares (and thus its asset worth as a company) rocketed up, and there was a lot of money to be made by these new shareholders *not* from the profits paid as dividends to Hyundai shareholders from the sales of Hyundai vehicles (its real business) but simply from buying Hyundai shares today and selling them tomorrow, or in a week's time, for a "guaranteed" higher price. So Hyundai's shares went up and up (along with the shares of thousands of other Korean, Taiwanese, Malaysian, and Indonesian companies) simply through the process of continual buying and selling of its shares, quite irrespective of how well (or otherwise) Hyundai's real business was actually going.

As may perhaps now be obvious, the very mechanism that can start a speculative boom of this sort—a boom where the price of something (in this case shares, but it can be virtually anything) rises simply because it is *expected* to rise by the people buying it—can also stop one. By the mid 1990s those same market leader fund managers who had led the boom in the first place were starting to have lower expectations about a number of those same Asian economies and began to sell off their Asian stocks and shares. At first they made large profits from doing so, but as sales continued, other fund managers began to understand that these market leaders were selling in order to "get out," and *not* simply as part of the boom buying and selling pattern. So they in turn sold shares in order to "get out," and thus the same tide or tides of money that had flowed in through the 1980s and 1990s now flowed out, but in this case far more rapidly (in a few months of 1997 in fact) than they had flowed in. As a result, the value of Hyundai's shares (along with the shares of thousands of other East and Southeast Asian companies) now plummeted far faster than they had risen in the 1980s and 1990s, and the company's worth shrank to a small fraction of what it had been even in the 1980s. Moreover, since (for reasons which we shall also go into shortly) the value of the Korean *won* had also plummeted, Hyundai found itself with massive debts (dollar loans which it had taken out on the basis of its previous asset values and high creditworthiness) it could barely service, and costs in dollar terms (for imported raw materials and components) which had also rocketed up when calculated in *won*. Yet, to repeat, as a vehicle maker Hyundai had done nothing wrong. It still possessed all its plant and equipment, which it had in fact been continually improving (hence the loans). Its vehicles were, if anything, even more popular abroad than they were when the boom in its shares began, its workers were just as skilled and productive.

In short then, Hyundai, had simply been taken up like some surfer on a massive "Asian-wide" financial wave, roared forward at breakneck speed, and then dumped (because the reasons that had caused the speculative boom to reverse had nothing to do with the real performance of Hyundai as an individual company or the real performance of thousands of other Asian companies as individual companies).

### Currency Transactions and the Derivatives Market

Let us turn to the currency side of things. A rather similar speculative "buying and selling" logic applies here as well, but in a rather different way. In the Bretton Woods system outlined above, central bank controls on currency transactions made it very difficult for an individuals or companies to get hold of large amounts of a foreign currency unless they were going to do something with it that fell within central bank rules. (This could be anything from taking a foreign holiday, to importing some foreign goods, to buying an asset in a foreign country.) Companies, especially those who were successful exporters, *earned* lots of foreign currency. But the central banks of their various home countries always required them to convert those foreign earnings back into the domestic currency (which meant, in effect, to put it in their home central bank) and then to attain new permission when they wanted to convert those funds into foreign currency again for some business purpose. The essential aim of these rules then was to effectively outlaw, or at any rate restrict, the buying and selling of foreign currency as a form of business in itself, rather than as a means of doing other kinds of business.

But with the end of the Bretton Woods system and the more or less total financial deregulation in the rich countries of the world in the 1980s, the buying and selling of foreign currencies was freed precisely to become a business in itself. And with all that post–long boom money available for such speculation, it quite rapidly became a very big business. The fundamental logic of that business is clear and simple enough.

Let us imagine that I am the fund manager of an investment fund—usually called a "hedge" or arbitrage fund—set up by (let us say) a German chemical company that wants to use some of its profits for speculative purposes—to make more money from speculation on top of the money it earns from chemicals. (There are plenty of such managers, and plenty of such hedge funds—as well as super funds, insurance funds, etc.—in the world.)[5] Since I am managing the fund of a German company, that fund is basically in deutschmarks. I now look around the world (say it is 1990) and my analytical gaze alights on Korea. The Korean economy is doing very well, it is booming in fact, growing at a very rapid rate. More to the point, the *won* has been continually strengthening against other currencies on the back of this boom. It is worth (say) 20 percent more against the U.S. dollar than it was five years ago, and 10 percent more against the deutschmark. I see the possibility of a very good currency "bet." So I buy a lot of *won* (say 500 million deutschmarks worth) using money from my fund. I keep the *won* for six months, and then convert it back into deutschmarks, by which time each *won* is worth 1 pfennig (1 deutschmark "cent") more than it was six months earlier. (I've done very well, the *won* has gained 1 percent in value in deutschmark terms over that six months.)

5. The literature on hedge or arbitrage funds is mainly technical and for professionals in the field. However, Joseph G. Nicholas, *Investing in Hedge Funds* (New York: Blumberg Press, 1998), chaps. 1 and 2, is a clear introductory account for the outsider, and the web site "Hedge Fund Research" ( www.hfr.com) has quite a lot of useful general information.

So, simply from selling those 500 million deutschmarks worth of *won* again, I make a profit of 5 million deutschmarks (1 percent of 500 million)—not a bad return from a simple buy and sell operation. In fact this may be as much or more profit than the chemical company could make in six months by investing the 500 million deutschmarks in chemical production, which is one of the reasons it set up a hedge fund in the first place.

That is the simplest possible case, and as such it is in real-world terms rather unrealistic, and does not show the full profit potential from such trading. For example, instead of simply keeping the *won* in some bank account somewhere (where it will of course earn a little interest of its own), I could lend it, for part of that six-month period, to someone who wants to do some "real" business in Korea. I lend at interest (probably slightly above bank rate) and so make an additional profit above the simple "currency trade" profit.

However, while any financial institution, or any individual or business institution which has large amounts of capital at its disposal, can make money from the fluctuating values of currencies in the way described above, for virtually any business firm engaged in any economic activity anywhere in the world fluctuating currency values constitute a considerable *problem,* as well as a considerable opportunity. The reasons for this may be obvious, and were in fact well illustrated in the Hyundai case above. For if a business (any business, anywhere) contracts debts or liabilities in a currency other than its own, and those currencies then rise in value relative to its own currency, then it may find itself having to pay far more (in terms of its own currency) to service those debts or liabilities than it had anticipated when it contracted them. Or again, if any business has to import anything from a country or countries using a currency other than its own, and if, in the period between ordering such imports and paying for them, the value of that firm's domestic currency falls relative to the value of the currencies of the country or countries from which it is importing, then it will suddenly find the cost of those imports (measured in terms of its own currency) rising above the price that it originally contracted to pay.

For all these reasons (and there are many other variants), the vast majority of businesses operating in the world today usually opt to keep part of their money in currencies other than their own, so as to spread risk. Given the centrality of the American dollar in international trade, this means that the dollar in particular is held in significant quantities by businesses all over the world. But other "hard" internationally negotiable currencies (the deutschmark, the yen, the Swiss franc, and so forth) are also used as hedges in this way. But in addition, such businesses also opt to buy ahead through long-term contracts—in so-called futures markets—goods or services which they need, so that they can be insured—or "hedged"—against sudden changes in currency values. And since anything that can be bought and sold globally (government bonds, company shares and bank loans, as well as industrial metals or agricultural products or car components) can have its price affected by currency fluctuations, there are futures markets for virtually everything (every good or service) that circulates in the global economy, including the currencies themselves. Collectively, these markets are known as "derivatives" markets, because they are secondary or "derived" from markets in goods and services. They are derived or secondary in the sense that they would really be unnecessary did not such real market transactions have to take place in a world of fluctuating exchange rates.

Let us take a hypothetical but realistic case. A British importer of metals may decide to buy Malaysian tin at a time when the pound sterling is strong relative to the Malaysian ringgit. She therefore places an order on the metals futures market to buy a certain quantity of tin in three months' time at a price of $X$ Malaysian ringgits per ton, and she pays the tin "futures dealer" (as he is called) a certain percentage of the price, with a legally binding contract to pay the balance in three months' time. However, for the tin futures dealer there is a risk in this. What happens if either sterling depreciates significantly or the Malaysian ringgit appreciates significantly (relative to sterling) in the intervening three months? He will then be out of pocket, since he is legally contracted *now,* to the importer, to supply $Y$ tons of tin at a price fixed *now* but to be paid in the future (a so-called futures price) of $X$ Malaysian ringgits per ton and no more. To "offset" or "hedge" this risk, the tin dealer may therefore take out a credit contract with a dealer in currency futures to buy with sterling *now,* at the sterling-ringgit exchange rate which the market predicts *now* will hold in three months' time (the Malaysian ringgit "futures price"), an amount of ringgits equal to the sterling value of the tin he is contracted to provide to the importer. If, therefore, in the intervening three months, the value of sterling *does* fall relative to the ringgit by more than the futures price in their contract predicts, the tin futures dealer and the sterling futures dealer will share these losses in some proportion agreed on in the same contract. However, the value of sterling may actually *appreciate* over the intervening three months, relative to the ringgit, by more than this "sterling futures contract" (as it is called) predicts. To cover that eventuality this contract between the tin futures trader and the sterling futures trader will also include an agreement to share the profits of appreciation in some agreed proportion. In other words then, in this particular case, the sterling futures dealer reduces the risk the tin dealer is running (of an unexpectedly large sterling depreciation) by agreeing to share any losses from such a depreciation. But in return he obtains the legal right to a share in the profit from an unexpectedly large sterling appreciation.

However, the crucial word in the last two sentences of the paragraph above is "unexpected"—"unexpectedly large" appreciation or depreciation—for it points to the human reality which is at the center of all these futures transactions—*expectations*. For how is the futures price of anything (remember—the price you have to legally *contract* to pay now, but actually pay at a specified time in the future) actually determined? Well, it is the price which "the market" expects will have to be paid for tin (in sterling or dollars) or for yen (in sterling or dollars) or for Hyundai shares[6] (in sterling or dollars or deutschmarks) in a month's time, or three months' time or six months' time. But what is this "market" that (in a curious quasi-human way) is said to "expect" these prices? It is nothing other than the result in "future price" terms of the continual day-to-day buying and selling, by these same traders, of the physical or financial commodity in question. Thus, when there is heavy buying of tin "today," then it is not just the price you have to pay today to *get* tin today which rises (its so-called spot price) but also the price you have to *contract* to pay today to get tin in the future (its futures price). That is, in the normal course of events a sharp rise (or fall) in the spot price of anything will translate into (generally much smaller) rises (or falls) in its futures price too. In fact, not only do the spot prices of all commodities traded on markets change daily, *so do their futures prices.*

Thus if, for some reason (to continue our earlier example), the present exchange rate of the pound sterling to the ringgit does appreciate by a large amount "today," then today's "three months' sterling futures" price of sterling (for buyers using ringgits) will also appreciate. But if the futures contract for tin was fixed "yesterday" or "last week" at the "sterling-Malaysian ringgit" futures price existing *then,* then both the Malaysian tin

---

6. Markets in share futures are called "stock options" markets. For an introduction to stock options, see P. Ritchken, *Derivative Markets: Theory, Strategy and Applications* (New York: HarperCollins, 1996), chap 4.

futures dealer and the sterling futures dealer have "today" made an "unexpected" extra profit (a profit not "discounted" by yesterday's or last week's futures price at which they made their contract), which they will share. They will do this concretely by splitting this extra gain between their two accounts at the end of "today's" trading in proportions that have been previously specified in their futures contract. Conversely, if for some reason the sterling-ringgit exchange rate suddenly depreciates "today" in a way that also dips the "three month sterling futures price" below the price at which the tin futures and sterling futures made their contract, then both traders have "today" suffered an "unexpected" loss (a loss not "discounted" by yesterday's or last week's futures price) which they also have to share between them, and again this will be done in proportions agreed in the initial contract.

In short we must not think that the futures price of anything is some kind of fixed economic magnitude by which traders can know what the spot price of that thing *will actually be* in three or six months' time or even what it will actually be at any time *during* that three- or six-month period. Rather, futures prices change daily, even hourly, in response to present supply and demand movements in exactly the same way that spot prices do. All that is really "fixed" here is the price at which a *particular* futures contract is made by a *particular* pair or set of traders at a *particular* time. And it is "fixed" for them only in the sense that once they have agreed to sell something or buy something at its "now-existing" futures price, *they are stuck with that price* until the contract has expired. This is the risk that both traders in any futures contract deal take. For in accepting "today's" futures price as the basis of their contract, either or both may have failed to "discount" (as it is said) future "futures price" movements correctly. So they risk making unexpected losses but they also "risk" (if we may put it that way) making unexpected gains. Hence, the calculation of the magnitude of the risk one is running in making any given contract is central to any and all forms of futures (or derivatives) trading. Such calculations are technically complex, but, as one might expect, at their center is (1) the amount of time for which a futures contract is made (all other things being equal, the longer the time the greater the risk obviously) and (2) the historic pattern of movement and volatility in the price of the commodity being traded. Quite clearly, if a commodity, or a currency, or a government bond has a strong history of large fluctuations in price, and especially of large fluctuations *occurring in short time periods* (so-called high volatility in price), then the riskier any futures contract made upon it will be and the higher the risk premium that will be charged for making the contract.

Conversely, however, if a physical commodity or a currency or a block of shares on which a futures contract is being made has a recent history of strong, and indeed accelerating, *appreciation* in price (relative to most other commodities, currencies, shares)—if in short it is a "boom" commodity, or currency, or government bond—then the risk of its actual price in three months' time being below its expected "three months' futures" price will seem small. In fact traders will clamber to make futures deals on such a boom asset and will charge very low risk premiums for doing so, because they (how shall we put it?) expect "unexpected" gains rather than *any* kind of losses, "unexpected" or otherwise. This means of course that futures prices or derivatives prices, just as much as present or spot prices, are vulnerable to speculative booms—to rising constantly simply on the basis that they are *expected* to continue rising by those traders buying and selling them. Therefore, of course, they are equally vulnerable to speculative price slumps—to falling constantly simply because they are *expected* to continue to fall by those traders selling and buying them. Concretely, what this means is that a physical commodity or financial asset whose futures price is *expected* to tumble by traders will only find buyers for its futures "now" at very high risk premiums and in forms of contracts that specify that the costs of all "tomorrow's" or "next week's" drops in the futures price below the contracted futures price will be debited daily, hourly, from the account of the seller *only*. This means, in effect, that the seller is getting a lower and lower price for his or her asset with every hour or day that passes. So much for a "fixed price" contract!

The crucial question, therefore, is what changes traders' expectations? That is, how does a boom asset suddenly (or even gradually) become a slump asset—or an appreciating asset a depreciating one? The answer to that question is that such expectations change partly in response to factors that we might call objective—a surge or fall in demand for a real commodity (tin, wheat, oil, rice) by those individuals or businesses wishing to consume or use those commodities, an improvement or deterioration in the productivity and export performance of an economy, thus increasing or decreasing demand for its currency or its government bonds. But the answer is also that such trader expectations change partly in response to factors that we might call purely subjective—for example, in response to the buying and selling patterns of other traders who are deemed "market leaders" or "hot operators" in the particular futures market in which they operate.

That is, we can say that trader expectations sometimes change because something in "the real world" of economic phenomena changes. But we can also say that (some) traders' expectations change because (other) traders' expectations change. It is that latter answer that most worries people who are concerned about speculatively induced instability in the global financial economy. For it is an answer that suggests that such price movements in such markets are not anchored (or at any rate not completely or securely anchored) to any "real world" economic trends or activities. "Traders' expectations change because traders' expectations change" is, that is to say, the kind of answer that gives many people a somewhat queasy feeling when they are considering how stable this globalizing economy is—this economy on which so many millions and billions of peoples' lives and welfare increasingly depend.

If, however, you wished to defend these derivatives markets, what could you say? All you can say (which is indeed all that defenders of such markets do say) is that because expectations often follow expectations financial markets sometimes do get "out of kilter" with trends or events in the real global economy. In particular, they do have a tendency to exaggerate (through the "expectations" mechanism) both the ups and the downs occurring in that real economy (as they did in the Asian meltdown of 1997). However, these defenders also argue that these markets have built into them correction mechanisms by which these "out of kilter" states do not last very long. That is, if financial expectations (and thus spot *and* futures prices) have been inflated beyond what real-world economic phenomena can justify, then there will be, sooner or later, an "adjustment" downward to take account of this exaggeration. Conversely, if financial expectations (and thus spot *and* futures prices) have been deflated beyond what real-world economic phenomena can justify, then there will be, sooner or later, an "adjustment" upward to take account of this exaggeration.[7] But while this may be true, how reassuring it is as a defense of financial markets is unclear until we know what the costs of these exaggerations and compensating adjustments are to real people working in real economies that have been "exaggerated" and then "adjusted" in this way. Some light was thrown on both these issues by the consideration of the Asian financial crisis of 1997 earlier in this chapter, so I will not repeat those

7. As this chapter was being written, the world stock and futures markets were in the midst of a downward "adjustment" of "e-commerce" stocks, whose earlier values, it was being said, had been "unjustifiably inflated."

points here. Rather, I want to end this discussion of derivatives markets with a few more observations about how they work.

## Derivatives and Credit

It may perhaps be obvious now that futures markets are essentially credit markets. That is—to return again to the hypothetical example we have been using—when the British tin importer places an order with the Malaysian tin futures dealer to buy (let us give it a magnitude) £50 million worth of tin "in three months' time," she enters into a legally binding contract that must be honored—or "settled" as it is said—on a predetermined date, and even at a predetermined hour, in three months' time. It is this legally binding contractual obligation which then allows the tin futures dealer to in turn make a *credit-based* futures contract on £50 million worth of Malaysian ringgit futures with the sterling futures dealer. But the credit chain does not have to end there. For the dealer in sterling futures can use the "same" £50 million worth of credit to make (say) a deal in yen futures, a deal predicated on his view that the yen will actually rise relative to sterling, over the next three months, by more than the current "yen-sterling" futures index suggests. And the dealer in yen futures can in turn make a futures contract in Danish kroners (or in Korean government bonds or in some share futures market) where—again, he or she thinks that the £50 million worth of asset purchased will be worth more at the end of three months than its present futures price predicts. And just as in the case of the initial "sterling-Malaysian ringgit" futures deal, there will be clauses in all these subsequent contracts allowing daily crediting and debiting of traders accounts as daily futures prices rise (or fall) relative to the futures price at which each of these contracts has been made. In this way, a single futures contract can be multiplied over and over again as a single "real" future transaction becomes the basis upon which a whole chain or network of credit transactions are undertaken. It is small wonder then that the nominal value of transactions made annually in derivatives markets (one estimate put the figure at U.S.$65 trillion for 1998 alone) is so astronomical.

It should be clear, however, that since the whole chain of subsequent contracts is secured on the initial contract (indeed all the subsequent contracts will have the same settlement date and time as the initial contract), the only real asset that will actually change hands as a result of all this wheeling and dealing is the 50 million pounds worth of tin, which will be received and purchased in full on the settlement date. At that point too (on the same day and hour) the credit given by the sterling futures dealer to the tin futures dealer will be canceled (as "paid off"); the credit given by the yen futures dealer to the sterling futures trader will in turn be canceled; the credit given to the yen futures dealer by the dealer in Danish kroner or Korean bond futures will in turn be canceled, etc. In effect then, for all futures dealers down the chain from the tin futures dealer, profits or losses on all their contracts will *already have been made* (and be equal to the sum of daily credits—or debits—made to their accounts over the ninety or so days of the contract) *by the time the initial "real" transaction is completed.* This kind of trading—where monetarily real profits or losses are in fact *only* the sum of the small changes or increments in futures prices occurring over the time of a contract—is called trading "on margin." It is given this title because, in effect, the only real money a trader trading on credit in this way needs to have is a sum large enough to cover a "marginal" loss resulting from a bad guess about the movement of a futures price index over the time of that contract. In cases where futures traders get their contract prices "right" and make marginal profits (which of course they are all trying to do), then they will put have to have to put no money of their own into such a deal at all. That is to say, *as long as the initiating contract is honored in full on the settlement date,* none of the traders lower down the chain doing these "50 million pound" deals need actually to *have* £50 million, or indeed £5 million, or indeed £5,000.

All this only works of course if and only if, at the stipulated day and hour, the British importer of tin *does* pay up the entire contracted amount owed. But since, at the beginning of such chains, there is usually somebody in what we might call "the serious business business"—highly profitable firms that actually need tin (or copper, or wheat or oil) to carry on their business, or profitable firms or rich people who are seriously intending to buy shares in a particular company or the bonds of a particular country—then the vast majority of the time such initial contracts *are* honored on the settlement date and (therefore) everybody else down the chain can conclude their own credit deals "safely." However, in the rare case where the initial contract *is* defaulted on for some reason, then of course all the traders down the chain are, or can be, in trouble. For since they are all holding contracts (they are called "positions" in market jargon) which are also legally binding and on which settlement has to be made on the same date and hour as the tin contract, then, in the event that, say, the British tin importer defaults, the Malaysian tin futures dealer will suddenly have to find £50 million *of his own* to pay the sterling futures dealer. If he, in turn, cannot do so, then the sterling futures dealer will suddenly have to find £50 million *of his own* to pay the yen futures dealer, and so on. In short, everybody down the chain is potentially exposed in the event of a default at any point in the chain.

This is why regulations for financial markets require that futures traders should not enter into contracts that taken together exceed by more than a regulated amount the amount of liquidity (the amount of real cash assets) to which they have access through the bank or insurance fund or hedge fund on whose behalf they are trading. These regulations are precisely designed to ensure that a single default in a chain does not lead to a sudden rash of defaults across a market. But the trouble is that these regulations can vary markedly in their "minimum liquidity" demands from futures market to futures market and within a single futures market operating in different states (these still being the major regulators here). More worrisome still, even where regulations are nominally tight and conservative (insist on high liquidity to exposure ratios for traders), they may not enforced or enforceable, either because the state in question does not have a sufficiently strong regulatory body or because the banks or other financial institutions on whose behalf futures traders are acting do not police their activities well enough. (This was the case in the Nick Leeson / Barings Bank scandal.)[8]

The principal complicating and worrying factor here is that futures traders do not in reality, and as hypothesized in our example, hold only a single futures contract as part of a single chain of such contracts. On the contrary, big traders trading on behalf of big financial institutions (banks, insurance or pension funds, company hedge funds) will simultaneously hold tens or hundreds of such contracts secured on a vast array of different credit/contract chains and totaling in nominal value hundreds of millions or even billions of dollars. Moreover, in a financial world moving, literally, at the speed of light (at the speed of computers in fact), the total of these liabilities in a single trader's portfolio (and of the profits and losses flowing from them) changes hour by hour and even minute by minute every day as credits and debits flowing from contracts are instantly made to their trading accounts, contracts are instantly terminated and others are instantly entered into, and so forth.[9] In this situation, the precise exposure

8. For a popular account of this scandal, see N. Leeson, *Rogue Trader: Nick Leeson—His Own Amazing Story* (London: Warner, 1997).

9. Throughout this account it will have been clear, I hope, how the massive development of derivatives markets has been greatly facilitated by the world's revolution in

position of any given trader at any given point in time can be hard to determine, let alone regulate. Also, as the Leeson/Barings case demonstrated, there are electronic ways for traders to hide losses, even from their clients, for a considerable time, while hoping that counteracting profits will come through before their total exposure is discovered. Of course, sophisticated computerized transactions can be monitored and regulated by sophisticated computerized checks and controls built into financial hardware and software by determined clients and regulators. These checks must be working moderately well, since to date the total of irresponsible or unregulated defaulting in futures markets has been tiny in proportion to the huge nominal sums being turned over in such markets. Nonetheless, it is hard to avoid the uneasy sense that we are dealing here with a set of financial activities that, *as a whole,* is not even completely understood by the people and institutions operating in it, let alone effectively regulated *as a whole* in a way that can guarantee its probity and stability.

### Derivatives Markets and Global Economic Stability

Let me, for clarity's sake, summarize the argument of this chapter to this point. The emergence of a world of fluctuating or floating exchange rates after the demise of the Bretton Woods regime, created both problems and opportunities for businesses (and this means virtually all businesses of any scale all over the world) that needed to make foreign exchange transactions. It created problems for the obvious reason that it added another layer of uncertainty (changes in exchange rates) to any business dealing. But it also created opportunities because any individual or business institution (including banks, insurance companies, and other financial institutions as well as nonfinancial business enterprises) holding large amounts of liquid capital assets could play the money markets with those assets, or part of those assets, and thus *make* money from precisely the same processes

---

information technology. The ability to program the computers of traders with "risk assessment" statistical formulas, the ability to link daily or hourly changes in futures price indexes directly into those same computers (so that price-index-induced debits and credits to traders' accounts can instantly and automatically occur), the ability to calculate instantly, and down to a fraction of a cent, the change in the value of a futures contract as a result of some small move in a futures price index—all these things and many more would be impossible without modern information technology. In that sense there is an intimate link between the monetary dimension of globalization analyzed in this chapter and the "internet" and general "information-technological" dimension analyzed in Chapter 7.

that might give them problems or cause them losses in another context or contexts.

The inexorable rise and rise of derivatives markets since the 1980s are, in a sense, the single financial institutional response to both the problems *and* the opportunities provided by unfixed exchange rates. That is, such markets act to reduce the risks to business firms and others arising from fluctuating exchange rates (by providing an enormously complex web of hedges or indemnities against future price uncertainties). But at the same time they allow a whole new class of financial operatives (the "whizz kid" traders so powerfully conjured up all the time on our TV screens and in the Martin and Schumann quotation at the head of this chapter) to make money both for themselves, and for their clients, from informed betting or guessing on present and future currency movements and on present and future price movements of other commodities. Needless to say, many of these institutional clients so making money, are precisely *the same* institutions that can risk losing money in real economic exchanges of goods and services if something goes wrong on the exchange rate front. Indeed, there is not a single multinational company of any size, and in any sector, which does not now have some part of its assets invested in hedge or arbitrage funds to play the world money and financial markets. For individual companies these hedge funds represent company attempts to gain on the speculative swings what they may (in another context) lose on the speculative roundabout. Collectively however, such funds probably do act to stabilize the world financial system as a whole most of the time, even if they can also violently destabilize the real global economy at specific times. The real issue then is to understand in detail both the stabilizing functions and the destabilizing dangers of derivatives markets.

Let us take stabilization first. The stabilizing effect of futures markets, and especially of futures markets in currency, can best be understood, I think, by imagining a hypothetical example in which such markets are absent, or are made redundant, by an alternative form of setting currency exchange rates. Let us imagine, therefore, that the Japanese government, tired of the instability of yen values (and therefore of all import and export deals made in yen) as a result of its floating currency, decides to fix the value of the yen vis-à-vis all other major currencies (all the currencies of the countries with which Japan trades) for a period of two years. On the face of it this may seem to be a good thing. No Japanese business engaged in importing or exporting anything would now have to worry about future values of the yen, and all foreign firms doing business with Japan would now know exactly what any yen deal was worth and would be worth in its own currency.[10] Also, all futures dealers in yen would have to find something else to do for the next two years or would go out of business entirely (not necessarily a bad thing).

The problem with such a stabilizing measure however, lies in what would almost certainly happen at the end of the two-year period. For over a period of two years, of course, a lot would have happened in the immensely dynamic globalizing capitalist economy. Many economies would grown weaker relative to the Japanese economy; at the same time, others would have grown stronger. The net result of all these changes would be that, at the end of the two-year period, the yen will suddenly appreciate significantly against the currencies of the economies that have weakened relative to it, while it simultaneously and suddenly depreciates significantly relative to the currencies of the economies which have strengthened. In a word, the cost of the two years of stability bought by fixing would be a greatly increased shock of instability when the fixing ends. Thus an economy relying heavily on imports from Japan (as Britain does for example) which suddenly found that "today" (the day that the fixed period ends) its currency was worth 10 percent or even 15 percent less in yen terms than it was "yesterday," would also find its balance of payments suddenly worsening rapidly as a result of this violent exchange rate change. Not only that, but individual British firms that made yen-sterling deals would suddenly find those deals 15 percent more expensive "today" than they were "yesterday" with likely disastrous effects on their liquidity and profitability.

This then gives us an insight into the principal stabilizing claim made for futures or derivatives markets. This is the claim that, through the daily, hourly, marginal modifications made in futures contracts as the futures price index of any currency or commodity changes,[11] market prices

10. Actually, in a world of floating exchange rates such as we have now, no single state, not even an economically powerful state like Japan, could unilaterally fix its exchange rate in the way being hypothesized here. Given the way the global economy operates as a whole, either all exchange rates must be fixed (as in the Bretton Woods system) or none can be. However, since this example is included here for purposes of explanatory clarity only, its unreality does not matter. It is true, however, that the same "shock" problems which are postulated as occurring when this partial exchange rate fixing ends would also be a real problem in the real world if any total fixing was attempted and then ended. To that extent the example is realistic.

11. Seen collectively, across the market as a whole, these individual price modifications are of course the *cause* of the general price index change. But, from the point of any

(including the prices of currencies, their exchange rates with other currencies) are allowed to shift *slowly* to reflect the slow changes occurring in all other aspects of the global economy. That is, the effect of futures markets is to turn all price changes into slow incremental or marginal changes that the world economy can cope with without severe exchange rate shocks or disruptions. Moreover (and this is the kind of reflection that makes some people think of markets as quasi-magical), this objective *minimizing* of the rate of change of prices, this objective *stabilization* of prices, is brought about by the combined activities of hundreds of thousands of people around the world (futures traders) who are entirely motivated, subjectively and individually, by the desire to make money out of price *instability*, out of unexpected (and they hope, large) price *changes*. That is, all these futures traders individually seek to make money out of price instability, but the entirely unintended combined effect of their activities is actually to minimize such instability by dispersing it into millions of hourly, minutely, marginal profits and losses, which (taken as a whole, across global markets as a whole) entirely offset one another.[12]

So much for the stabilizing magic. But what about the very unmagical destabilizations caused by such markets? At bottom the principal problem here is a basic, and inescapable human limitation—the actual *inability* of human beings to know (in any hard or definite sense of "know") the future. As we have seen, the point of futures prices and of the changes in such prices is to try and discount future events that may affect those prices. Thus, there is a futures price for American wheat "today" that reflects (among other things) informed expectations about the likely size of the next American wheat harvest. So that if something happens (say a decline in the area sown to wheat in America below what has been the "normal" acreage), then the American wheat futures price "tomorrow," or in an hour's time, will reflect that event by factoring in or discounting this news

---

individual trader or group of traders making futures contracts, these daily price modifications are treated—and rightly treated—as the *effect* of, or as "mere responses to," the change in the general price index.

12. And in fact the net change of the total worth of *all* the world's financial assets as a result of *all* currency fluctuations occurring in any given period must, logically, be zero. That is, the profits of the traders who, in that period, speculate on currency movements correctly must—statistically speaking—be exactly offset by the losses of those who speculate incorrectly or unwisely. This formal statistical fact does *not* mean, however—although it is sometimes taken to mean—that all such speculation is irrelevant to, or harmless to, the real economy of the world.

of the drop through a marginal or relatively small rise in the American wheat futures price[13] compared to what its price is "now" (before that news is received).

Now this kind of incremental price adjustment is all very well (and economically stabilizing one might say); but by definition, it can only occur in regard to future events *which can be expected or predicted or foreseen in some way.* Thus, U.S. Department of Agriculture farm surveys can foresee a decline in wheat acreage before it takes effect on the wheat harvest, but they cannot foresee (say) a major tornado in the American Midwest that destroys 20 percent of the Kansas wheat crop only a week before it was due to be harvested. So in part, and importantly, what destabilizes futures markets is what destabilizes the future—sudden natural disasters (a major storm in an important crop growing area, a major fire or war damage in an important oil field) and the sudden and sharp falls in supply prices or rises in demand prices that can follow from such events. As well as unexpected natural disasters of this type, futures markets can be destabilized by unexpected human-made disasters—wars that "blow up" from nowhere or spread more rapidly than expected; financial scandals involving major institutions that have been well hidden or hushed up but then suddenly come to light; an unexpected change in a political regime with control over one or more globally significant economic assets, and so forth.

All this—the inability of human beings to actually be able to discount or predict *all* future events and the limitation this inability places on the stabilizing role of futures markets—is perhaps what one might predict (as it were!) if one thought about the matter.

But there is another destabilizing factor in futures markets that is almost certainly more significant than this direct "unknowable future" factor; it is less obvious, but also derives, although less directly, from the same fundamental human limitation. This is the tendency of individual human beings, when faced with uncertainty, to engage in a kind of collective behavior (often called "sheep-like" or "herd" behavior) that can have deeply destabilizing implications in itself.

---

13. If the American acreage under wheat falls, then, all things being equal, there will be less wheat on present and immediate future markets and the spot price of wheat in the immediate future period is likely to rise. The futures market in wheat "discounts" this future event by raising *present* "wheat futures" prices as soon as the news of the acreage fall is received. But the question of course is, *by exactly how much* will the harvest fall and *by exactly how much* (therefore) will spot prices rise? Here is where the complex mathematics of "risk assessment," as it is called, enters in.

What do I mean by this? Well, imagine that I am a futures trader who is about to make a contract on Korean short-term bond futures. However, I know nothing about Korea and nothing directly therefore about Korean bonds. Are they likely to rise above today's "six-month Korean bond futures price" during the next six months or not? I do not know. But (professionally as it were) I *have* to know in order to make a good deal on the contract price. Therefore, what do I do? I rely on what "the market is saying" about the Korean economy and its immediate future. That is, more concretely, I rely, perhaps, on what a fellow trader tells me about Korea, or (more likely) on what *he* says "the market is saying" about Korea. He in turn relies, for *his* view of what "the market is saying" on another colleague who is a "Korean expert," and he in turn relies for *his* views on what some specialist "Korean investment analysts" (whose Net newsletter he subscribes to) are saying. Thus, when we follow chains or networks of influence through in this way, we discover that what are called "market" views of the future are very often, in fact, the views of a certain limited number of crucial market leader traders and analysts. For it is these people on whom the majority of other traders depend, both directly and indirectly (through a mass of intermediaries), for their market assessments.

This kind of herd behavior among traders—generated at bottom by uncertainty about the future and by attempts to compensate for that uncertainty psychologically by relying on others supposedly better informed or smarter than oneself—is what can set off and sustain speculative booms and slumps in stock futures and other futures. Such booms and slumps occur because traders buy futures simply because other traders do (and not out of any direct or personal assessment of their objective worth) and sell them because other traders do. It is the same endemic uncertainty factor that can make futures markets in particular unusually vulnerable to (meaning, exaggeratedly unstable in response to) *rumors* about the future— about harvests, or likely OPEC decisions, or about some change of government somewhere, or some change of directors in a large company.

However, since I have dealt with speculative booms and slumps, and their effects, earlier in this chapter, I need say no more about that topic here. Rather, and by way of conclusion to this section on derivative markets, I want to say that the truth concerning their stabilizing or destabilizing effects seems, as so often in life, to be "seldom plain and never simple" (as Oscar Wilde said). On the one hand, they do appear to fulfill important price-stabilizing functions in a world of floating currency exchange rates— rates whose continual but uncertain and unpredictable changes themselves reflect continual and equally uncertain and unpredictable changes in a mass of other economic variables. But they also have a considerable latent capacity for destabilization, simply because, despite their ingenuity, they do not, in the end, allow human beings to overcome their final inability to know what the future will bring.

In addition, the stabilization functions and effects of futures markets are continual and mundane and therefore go largely unnoticed by the rest of humanity, while their destabilization effects are occasional and dramatic and are therefore noticed by everybody. Thus, the ordinary user of a currency (any currency) is likely to notice that over the previous six months it (say) first fell by 3 U.S. cents and then rose again by 2 cents. But she or he is very unlikely to notice that, thanks to the discounting effects of currency futures markets, it did *not* first fall by 30 U.S. cents and then rise by 20 cents. In fact, by definition, nobody notices *an absence*. Nobody observes an event *that does not occur*. But everybody noticed the Mexican peso crisis of 1995 and the Asian meltdown of mid 1997. And many people not only noticed them, they also condemned the "speculators" and "irresponsible financial markets," which were thought to have brought them about. And quite rightly too. After all, all the statistical evidence in the world purporting to show the general safety of air travel compared with other modes of transport will not impress you if you are a passenger on a Jumbo jet falling out of the sky. Similarly, all the econometric evidence in the world concerning the "price and currency stabilization" effects of futures markets is not likely to impress you if you are an Indonesian worker made redundant in a currency meltdown. The problem is the same in both cases. The human cost of what occurs when it occurs more than makes up for the relative infrequency with which it may occur. There is a sense in which probability statistics, no matter how impressive, simply cannot provide humanly effective reassurance here—and for very good reason.

This is all I wish to say about derivatives or futures markets in themselves.[14] I now want to examine how the functioning of these markets, *in*

14. Derivatives markets are a continual subject of comment in such specialist economics and business publications as the Australian *Financial Review,* the British *Financial Times,* the American *Wall Street Journal* and the British *Economist.* I have relied a lot on general reading of these sources, and on the last in particular, in constructing this account. However, among more general academic accounts I found P. Ritchken, *Derivative Markets,* and P. Wilmott, *Derivatives: The Theory and Practice of Financial Engineering* (New York: John Wiley and Sons, 1998), particularly useful. The derivatives bookshop at www.globalinvestor.com also has some useful general information.

*conjunction with* some other factors and forces we analyzed earlier in this chapter, can impact, in a violently destabilizing way, on real economic activity in the world. I will do this by returning, once again, to the case of Hyundai and the impact upon its activities of the financially induced 1997 "meltdown" of the South and East Asian economies.

### Back to Hyundai: Government Bonds, Company Shares, and the Derivatives Market

A government bond or security (whether American or German or South Korean or whatever) is simply a piece of paper issued by a government on which that government writes an undertaking to pay to the owner of that bond a certain fixed amount of interest for a certain period. There are both long- and short-term government bonds, depending on the period for which the government promises to pay the fixed interest. So, if a South Korean government bond is issued by the government at a price of 10,000 *won* and the government agrees to pay interest annually on it of 1000 *won*, it has agreed, in effect, to pay the holder 10 percent interest. When we hear that the government (any government) has "raised interest rates," what this means is that it has agreed to pay holders of its bonds a certain percentage more on all its bonds. But—and here is the catch—government bonds can be bought and sold (by banks and other funds, by individuals) just like any other asset.

If, for example, the South Korean economy looks strong, people (fund managers and others) around the world will think South Korean government bonds a good asset and buy lots of them. This of course raises their price. Now let us say that, as a result of all this buying activity, the price of a 10,000 *won* South Korean government bond actually rises to 20,000 *won*. If this happens the Korean government does not suddenly start paying 2000 *won* in interest to keep the interest rate at 10 percent. On the contrary, the rate is fixed (unless or until the government says otherwise for its own reasons). So, in effect, *a rise in the price of its government bonds is the same as a fall in a country's rate of interest.* What this means is that, in the contemporary world, real (as opposed to official) interest rates in all open economies are determined not just by governments but by buyers and sellers of those bonds and bond futures on the (now global) bond market. And if, in fact, a movement on the bond market for a particular government's bonds is very strong (either positively or negatively), it can have a far greater effect on interest rates in that economy than a central bank's official change in interest rates.

However, a continuous increase in the global demand for a particular bond or bonds (as in the case of the government bonds of all the Asian Tiger states in the 1980s) can seem to be an overwhelmingly positive phenomenon for individuals and for firms and business in those economies. The more capital flows into a particular government's bonds (the more "foreign" money is invested in that government and state, in effect) the lower the rate of interest becomes. This is logical if one thinks about it. Lots of money is coming into a state or economy so the price of money (the interest rate) falls *within* that economy, and it is the workings of the bond market that produces this result.

However, there is now a worldwide speculative market in government bonds and securities too, just as there is a worldwide speculative market in currencies. That is, fund managers now buy and sell large numbers of government bonds of a large number of governments to try and make speculative gains as well as to "hedge" the positions of themselves or clients who have assets held as bonds or as other financial instruments. (Will a South Korean government bond be worth more or less over the next six months than its present "six-month futures price" suggests?) They also bet—among themselves—on movements in bond prices through buying and selling in security and bond derivatives markets. ("I'll make a credit contract with you to purchase 500 million U.S. dollars worth of South Korean short-yield bond futures at today's 'Korean six-month bond futures price.' If each bond is worth more over the six months than its 'today's' futures price suggests, you pay me—daily—the difference from our contracted price. If they are worth less, I pay you—daily—the difference.")

I think, or at any rate I hope, that the reader will now see where this analysis is leading. If the real economy of an area is booming (as the economies of the Asian Tigers from the late 1970s to the mid 1990s were), fund managers do not buy just stocks and shares there, as good bets. They *also* buy the currencies of these countries, *and* they buy large quantities of their government bonds—all as good bets for subsequent trading. (That is, they think that the actual future prices of all these assets will be higher than the futures prices they have to pay "now" to buy them.) However, once all this buying reverses itself (because market leaders, and then the mass of followers, no longer believe that their expectations of future speculative profits will be met, and come in fact to believe that their price falls will be even greater than their "futures prices" predict), then they *sell* not just Asian stocks and shares, but Asian currencies *and* Asian government bonds *all at the same time.* (Thus realizing, as it were, their own fears about future values!) Thus, at more or less one and the same time in mid 1997, Hyundai's asset value as a company not only plummeted, the value of the currency it had to use in its domestic transactions plummeted *and* the Korean interest rate rocketed upward. (Remember as the price of government bonds fall, through selling, this is the same as a rise in interest rates.) This made it more expensive for Hyundai to borrow *won* (as well as U.S. dollars), and it made all Hyundai's existing *won* loans (as well as its dollar loans) much more expensive to service. But, and to reiterate our earlier points in this chapter, Hyundai itself had done nothing, in its actual real business activities, to justify its experiencing this degree of economic pain, just as, during the peak of the speculative boom in Asian stocks, it had done nothing in its actual real business activities to justify its experiencing the degree of economic pleasure that it did then.

This in essence is the risk posed by speculative activity to any real economy (whether this be a particular national economy, a regional economy, or the global economy as a whole). In a word it is the risk posed by the systematic *exaggerating effect* of speculation. This is what this kind of mass "one way" speculative movement of money can do under certain circumstances. It can take real economic trends (the Tiger economies were really doing well from the late 1970s) and then exaggerate those trends massively both upward (the so-called Asian miracle of the 1980s and early 1990s) and downward (the meltdown of 1997). For by the mid 1990s some real problems were beginning to emerge in the economies of Asia as the more astute fund managers saw, but they were not nearly serious enough to warrant the extent of the crash that occurred. The crash was as much a speculative exaggeration of a downturn as the boom had been the speculative exaggeration of an upturn. And in the case of the downturn in particular it was an exaggeration that has caused immense human suffering in those societies for people who (in one sense at least) had done nothing wrong.

## Conclusions

Whatever one may think of the speculation activity described and analyzed in this chapter (and remember that if any reader of this book has money in a pension fund, or their parents have, they have probably benefited, or are benefiting, or will benefit, from it), it is probably the case that most of the time it is "harmless enough," at least from an economic point of view.[15] Moreover, the large bulk of the kind of transactions described above are only significantly profitable because of the very large sums of money that are being "moved" or (in the derivatives case) used as credit instruments for speculation. It has been estimated, for example, that the average margin of profit on the average currency transaction taking place in the world at the moment, is rather less than half of 1 percent. This observation led the American economist James Tobin to suggest that if you wanted to wipe out most of this kind of speculation, you could just place a 1 percent tax on every currency transaction.

However, as well as the massive problems that would almost certainly arise from trying to collect such a tax on a global scale, and/or from trying to distribute its revenues, the wisdom of imposing it can also be doubted. As we have seen, derivatives markets do function, most of the time, to stabilize the real economic transactions of a global economy operating through floating exchange rates. That is, although excessive "one way" speculative buying and selling of government bonds and company shares (as well as currencies) can seriously destabilize, and has indeed actually destabilized, particular parts of the global economy, it is probably the case that that economy as a whole would be even more unstable (indeed its very existence might well be threatened) without the workings of derivatives markets.

In fact, even if you take the Tobin tax seriously as a solution to the

15. What one makes of its social and moral implications is perhaps another matter. The view that money and financial markets are a form of economically unproductive and predatory activity in which "paper pushers" and "coupon clippers" make fortunes by leeching off the honest toil of "really productive" people in the "real" economy is a view that is as old as such markets themselves. It should be clear that I do not agree with it—at least not as an *economic* view. Derivatives and other financial traders do do something economically useful and important in the globalizing capitalist economy, and indeed would not be employed if they did not. In fact I have just argued that they perform an important stabilizing role in that economy and to that extent they positively aid "real" economic production and consumption in the "real" economy. Having said that, however, I do have worries about the broader consequences for social norms and moral values in postmodern capitalist societies of the levels of remuneration attained by many of these traders, and of the kind of example their success sets—especially for young people. But these kinds of worries are of a piece with my worries about the success and associated lifestyles of film stars or professional athletes. They do not relate, that is to say, to the worthwhileness of what finance market traders do for a living, but to what seems to me the "disproportionate" rewards they receive for doing it. But this latter observation itself raises complex philosophical questions (about how we are to determine what rewards are socially "proportionate" and "disproportionate") that are beyond the scope of this book.

problem of excess financial speculation, it is clear that it is, at best, the treatment of a symptom of disorder, rather than of the underlying problem. For that underlying problem is clearly the existence of multiple variant national currencies coexisting with a world of increasingly globalized economic relations. That is, the real solution to the problems posed by derivatives markets (indeed the solution that would make such markets otiose) is the creation of *a single global currency*. Now the problems involved in creating such a currency, especially in a world so massively economically unequal as ours, are formidable. (Many of them are well presaged and indicated in the problems that attended the creation of a single currency in the European Union.) I will consider at least some of those problems in a later chapter.

For now, however, I want the reader simply to note that the problems posed by derivatives and currency markets, indeed the very existence of such markets, are simply different manifestations of a single underlying problem to which I shall return again and again in this text—the coexistence of globalizing economic relations with "national" or "nation-state" forms of political organization of that globe. Indeed, it is clear that, in the present period, the principal manifestation of this contradiction—the contradiction between a rapidly globalizing economics and a still overwhelmingly national politics—is found in the sphere of money. That is, the globalizing capitalist economy already needs—economically needs—a single, stable, universally accepted measure of the value of economic assets and a single, stable, universally accepted unit of account in which transactions can be conducted. It already needs a single, global form of *money* in a word. But money (with the very recent and partial exception of the euro) is still an entirely national economic instrument. Therefore, no such single unit of account and valuation can yet be created, for both economic and political reasons. The complicated machinations of derivatives markets are therefore the ingenious, but necessarily somewhat unstable, interim mitigation of this contradiction. It is, therefore, entirely unsurprising, in retrospect, that such markets have been developed rapidly since the 1970s, and develop further every day, as part of capitalism's globalizing trend. Whether it will be possible to proceed beyond this interim (and unstable) futures market mitigation of this monetary contradiction to its complete and stable resolution (a single global currency) is a question that can only be answered by the further development of global capitalism itself. It is not, that it is to say, a question with *any* purely intellectual answer.

❧

# CHAPTER SIX

# Global Direct Investment
# Since the 1970s

I will deal, in this chapter, with the subject of capital investment by multinational companies and make the connection between the monetary dimensions of globalization dealt with in the previous chapter and the activities of MNCs/TNCs described in Chapter 4. These two subjects (global financial markets and the investment activities of MNCs/TNCs) are so deeply interconnected that, ideally, I should have liked to deal with them in a single integrated chapter. However, the world of global money and stock markets, and of derivatives or futures markets in particular, is a rather complex one (at least on the surface) and takes some amount of explaining. It seemed best, therefore, to accord such markets a chapter of their own. In this chapter, therefore, I first deal with the direct investment activities of multinational companies. I then analyze the relationship of these activities to the workings of global financial and investment markets generally. Finally, and as the analytical culmination and major point of the chapter, I consider the issue that brings out the most humanly significant implications of both these types of global financial trends—the so-called economic restructuring that is currently occurring in both the rich and poor societies of the world as part of the development of this global capitalist economy.

*Foreign Direct Investment*

The first thing to say is that multinational companies (including banks

and insurance and investment companies, as well as multinational manufacturing and service companies) based in North America, Europe, and
Japan accounted for not only an estimated two-thirds of world trade in the
mid 1990s but also nearly 65 percent of the world's stock of foreign investment assets (known as "foreign direct investment," or "FDI"). Since the
total of world FDI in 1995 was over U.S.$2.5 trillion, this means that those
MNCs had over U.S.$1.6 trillion of assets held in countries outside their
own country (usually, but not only, in the form of subsidiary or affiliated
companies based in those countries).[1]

In order, however, to fully grasp the contemporary significance of FDI
we have to understand what it is, and how it differs from indirect, or what
is sometimes called portfolio foreign investment. We also have to understand the relationship between this kind of investment and the forms of
money-market investment and speculation I dealt with in Chapter 5.

Simply, to be a direct investor in an enterprise or company means to
own shares in that company, and not only shares but voting shares (sometimes companies issue both voting and nonvoting shares), which allows
you, the investor, to attend shareholder meetings of that company, and to
vote, as a shareholder, on company policy. And, as you might suppose,
when a multinational company sets up a subsidiary company in another
country (say when Goodyear America builds a factory in a Latin American or Asian country), it usually keeps a controlling block of voting shares
in that subsidiary company in its own hands so that it has the ultimate
power over policymaking in that subsidiary. A company keeping such a
controlling block of shares in its own hands is not incompatible with its
selling other shares in its affiliate or subsidiary, either on Asian or Latin
American stock markets, or on its "home" stock market (on Wall Street or
in the City of London or wherever). But even where this does happen,
control is usually maintained by the mother company, either by restricting the number of voting shares in the subsidiary sold or by selling only
nonvoting shares.

### Indirect or Portfolio Investment: A Brief History

As its name implies, foreign direct investment is to be distinguished from
various forms of foreign indirect investment that carry no powers of legal
ownership over the asset in which investment is made. Thus, for example,

1. Dicken, *Global Shift,* 42.

buying government bonds is a classical and well-established form of foreign indirect investment. If a London bank or insurance company holds U.S.$100 million worth of U.S. government bonds and receives regular interest on those bonds from the U.S. government, this does not mean that it owns the U.S. government or state, or even that it owns a share of the U.S. government or state. Rather, all it actually owns, legally speaking, is a right to a certain *stream of income* (called interest payments) from the U.S. government. In the nineteenth century, and indeed right up to the end of the First World War, the vast majority of foreign investment that took place in the world was of this indirect or "portfolio" sort.

Thus, during the great nineteenth-century boom in railway construction all over the world, a group of private individuals or (quite often) a particular state or government somewhere in the world (everywhere from Venezuela to Vladivostok) would set up a company to build a railway line. The directors of the company and thus its legal owners, would be the private individuals involved or, in the case of governments, nominees of the state involved. That group of individuals, or that particular government, would own all the voting shares, and they would entirely determine the policy of the company. But in many cases these shares would not, initially, have much monetary worth (since they were shares in a railway not yet built and therefore with no passengers, freight, or revenue).

However, having formed a company in this way, the directors would then "float" (as it was said) the company on the London—in the nineteenth century it nearly always *was* the London—stock exchange, and rich English and other individuals and companies would buy nonvoting fixed-interest "stock" in the new company.[2] However, since the people buying this nonvoting stock were making a risky investment of their money (for the railway line did not yet exist and it was, therefore, difficult to know how successful it would be), they usually required and got, a guarantee from the government of the country involved that their fixed interest would be paid from $X$ date, whether or not the railway line was

---

2. This is the origin of the distinction between stocks and shares, and also the reason why stock exchanges are called stock exchanges and not share exchanges—they all mainly dealt in stock when they were started. As a financial term the word "stock," however, has a still more antique origin in the important role played by a split hazel stick in twelfth-century English accounting practices. For a fascinating account, see Edward Rutherford, *London: The Novel* (London: Arrow, 1998), 323, where one can also find an account of the origins of the terms "exchequer," "sterling," and "counterfoil." Even pap novels have their uses sometimes!

functioning or earning any revenue. Since such government guarantees had to be supplied for a railway company to be successfully floated, irrespective of whether the company involved was nominally state owned or a private enterprise, there was a sense in which *all* the railways built around the world in the nineteenth century (including those built in the United States) were state rather than strictly private enterprises, at least in origin.[3]

However, over the decades of the twentieth century the flow of real, asset-building foreign investment in the world has slowly changed from being mainly or overwhelmingly indirect (stock) investment of this type to being direct (share) investment of the modern multinational sort. The main reason why this has happened is that, over this century, a large—very large—proportion of the most successful companies in the advanced capitalist countries have changed from being family companies, owned by single individuals or families, to being public companies, owned by a very large and disparate variety of individual and institutional shareholders who have bought those shares on a share or stock market. The reasons why this change in the typical pattern of ownership of large companies in the world has occurred need not concern us here. All that is important here is that once this shareholder pattern of large company ownership was established in all the advanced industrial or advanced capitalist countries, it also spread across the world through companies initially based in those countries setting up, or buying up, subsidiary or affiliate companies around the world (and hence becoming MNCs/TNCs).

## Multinational Companies and Contemporary Financial Markets

Given this distinction between direct and indirect investment, it becomes relatively easy to clarify the relationship between the direct investment activities of MNCs and the activities of the global money or financial markets more generally, which I reviewed in the previous chapter.

Readers will remember, from that chapter, that finance or money markets basically consist of four activities: (1) buying and selling in world share (or equity) markets, (2) buying and selling in world bond and securities markets, (3) buying and selling in world currency markets, and (4) buying

3. The workings of the London stock exchange and its central role in the financing of nineteenth-century railway construction around the world are well described in E. J. Hobsbawm, *Industry and Empire* (Harmondsworth: Penguin, 1969), 111–19.

and selling in world derivatives markets, which are basically specialist risk indemnification markets derived from these other three basic markets. It should therefore be clear that activity (1) directly relates to FDI. That is, global FDI (U.S.$2.5 trillion in 1995) is a *partial* measure of the buying and selling that goes on in global equity markets. However, global direct investment much exceeds the global FDI figure, since by definition the FDI figure only includes investments made by an MNC/TNC or a financial institution outside its own country of origin or headquarters registration (its "foreign" direct investment). Thus, for example, the Australian insurance company AMP makes share investments in Australian companies and in overseas companies. The latter type of investments would therefore be included in the global FDI figure, but the former type would not be. And since company investments (even the investments of many MNCs) in their home economies still usually exceed those overseas, the global total of all direct investment always much exceeds the global total of FDI. But of course FDI is a good—probably the best—measure of global capital *movement,* and this is why it so frequently appears in discussions of globalization.

It is interesting to note in this context, that between the mid 1980s and mid 1990s the annual rate of growth of world FDI—28 percent—was twice the annual rate of growth of world trade—14 percent. Indeed this has been a continuous and accelerating trend since the 1960s.[4] That is, annual outflows of capital across different economies now much exceed both the growth of world GDP and the growth of world trade in goods and services. In other words, the most rapidly growing export, especially of the most prosperous economies of the world, is now *money itself,* and financial market actors and agents are obviously both important players in that development and have expanded their activities simply because of that development.

Let us now look at those other three activities of world global or financial markets—government bonds, direct currency trading, and derivatives trading. Government bonds, as we have already said, are stocks, not shares (forms of indirect, not direct investment), and so obviously do not appear in that $2.5 trillion FDI total. And this is equally true of the money moved around the world in currency and derivatives trading. That is, *all* these types of global financial transactions are *in excess* of that enormous current

---

4. For details, see Dicken, *Global Shift,* 42–43. See also Hirst and Thompson, *Globalization in Question,* 54–55.

stock of global FDI. The most frequently cited figure for the amount of money being moved annually around the world in derivatives markets alone in 1998—over and above actual global transfers of investment capital—is U.S.$65 trillion.[5]

However, apart from the formidable multiple counting problems mentioned in Chapter 5, which make it difficult to assess the reality of this mind-boggling figure (nominally over thirty times the world total of FDI), the most important observation to make here is just that *none of the squillions of dollars revolving in these global financial markets actually creates a single tangible—nonmonetary—economic asset.*[6] If, therefore, we wish to deal with the expansion of the global economy as the expansion of physical productive and service activity—activity involving the employment of people (in activities other than finance), the building of plant and equipment and other physical infrastructure, the increase of the physical production and consumption of goods and services—then it is global direct investment, and global foreign direct investment in particular, with which

5. This figure was kindly supplied to me by my friend Dick Bryan, whose work focuses strongly on the structure and growth of world financial markets. He also informs me that—according to a December 31, 2001, International Swaps and Derivatives Association media release and page 132 of the June 1999 annual report of the Bank for International Settlements—the total turnover in all world derivatives markets *alone* was about U.S.$78 trillion (up from about U.S.$65 trillion in 1998).

6. That having been said, it has recently been brought to my attention that there is an important connection between the merging of large MNCs into even larger MNCs and the acquisition of smaller companies by MNCs (through takeover bids) and the growth of an ever more important derivatives market known as the *swaps market.* Swaps markets are themselves complex, but their most basic function is to allow companies to reduce the interest rate cost of their debts (debts mainly contracted in order to buy foreign companies) by borrowing in a national money market where they enjoy certain credit advantages and then "swapping" the interest rate payment obligations they incur with the debt with a "co-party" (i.e., another firm or business) operating, with as great or greater credit advantages, in another national money market. However, although the development of financial swaps markets have clearly fueled (and been fueled by) the massive growth of multinational mergers and acquisitions since the 1980s, they affect only the financial valuations of companies, not what might be called their physical investment assets, and to that extent my generalization remains true. Moreover, statistics of direct investment generally, and therefore of foreign direct investment, cover only the initial "face value" of the shares acquired and not their resale value, in order precisely to abstract from the massive financial "inflation" of existing share values usually accompanying takeover bids and mergers. For a pioneering analysis of swaps markets and their effects from a political economy perspective, see N. A. Ackland, "The Role of Swaps in the Development of the International Financial System" (Ph.D. diss., University of Sydney, 2000).

we must be concerned. To that extent, therefore, the conventional focus on FDI—and therefore on the activities of MNCs/TNCs which control the bulk of the assets so created—in the bulk of the literature on globalization is perfectly justified. However, and to repeat, MNCs/TNCs, although dominant, are not the only institutions making such investments. *Any* individual or institution that buys direct equity in public companies abroad is engaging in the expansion of FDI.

## *Economic Restructuring*

I want now to turn to the subject of the profound economic restructuring (as it is usually called) brought about in the advanced industrial or advanced capitalist countries since the 1970s, as part of the process of economic globalization. As I have emphasized, the main and ultimate focus of this book is on the role of the poorer and poorest parts of the world in the globalization process—the part they are playing in that process, the effects it is having upon them and their people—the poorest people of the world. But just because this is so I also wish to devote at least part of one chapter to the effect that this process is having—and may have in the immediate future—on the economies and peoples of the rich parts of the world.

The main reason for my doing so is that, as we shall see, quite a few commentators on the process think that these effects may be predominantly *negative,* at least for a large minority, or possibly even for a majority, of the ordinary people living in those parts of the globe conventionally described as "rich" (North America, Western Europe, Japan, also Australasia). Indeed many commentators on globalization argue that it is *already* having pronounced negative consequences for these societies and has been doing so now for at least the last twenty or twenty-five years. Since my central criterion for assessing the significance or otherwise of globalization is the extent to which it has affected—and is affecting—the lives of ordinary people, it is certainly worth assessing this criterion with reference to the lives of ordinary Americans, Germans, Spaniards, or Australians, as well as with reference to ordinary Africans or Indians or Latin Americans. If globalization is having as much effect in Ontario as it is in Orissa, as much effect in London as it is in Lahore (even if the nature of those effects is rather different), this fact itself is a very good reason to call the process "globalization."

If we approach the process of contemporary economic restructuring in the advanced capitalist countries through a kind of historical contrast method, we can begin at least to grasp its essential features reasonably clearly. So let us imaginatively cast our eyes back to the world economy as it was thirty years ago, in 1970. In that year, and indeed for many years previously, it was really quite easy to say how the world economy worked. If one left aside the complicating issue of the communist world (as most people did), it basically consisted of two parts. There was a small group of industrialized countries who supplied themselves and the rest of the world with all the manufactured goods which then existed, and there was the rest of the world—Asia, Africa, and Latin America—which supplied the core group of industrialized countries with some food and a lot of industrial raw materials in exchange for such manufactured goods as they could afford.

Now, if we look at this 1970 situation more closely from the point of view of the countries and economies in the privileged group—a group basically made up of the United States, Canada, Australia and New Zealand, the EU countries of Western Europe, and Japan—what this world economic structure implied was that *considered as a group,* the populations of these countries basically supplied for themselves nearly everything of importance they consumed. It was true that, even in 1970, these countries were becoming increasingly dependent on foreign supplies of some crucial raw materials (most notably oil). But so far as the ordinary person—the ordinary worker/citizen/consumer—in those countries was concerned, nearly everything they bought, as finished goods, was made either within their own economy, or if not, came from one or more of the other privileged or advanced economies in the group. Another way of thinking of this is to say that, as a whole, the peoples of this small privileged group of countries supplied nearly all the demand that supported their own employment. That is, they neither consumed much that was supplied from outside that group, nor did they have any considerable amount of employment dependent on demand coming from outside that group (from Asia, Africa, or Latin America, in short).

We can therefore begin to grasp what the economic restructuring of the advanced economies over the last thirty years or so has meant for the ordinary people of those economies. For now, in the year 2000, it is no longer true that those people "supply for themselves nearly everything of importance which they consume." This means not only that the ordinary people of Australia (to take my own case) depend much more for their standard of living on products produced outside of Australia than they did in 1970, but also that they depend for that standard of living on more products not produced in North America, Europe, or Japan either. And it also means that far more of them than in 1970 depend for their employment on demand for goods and services coming not only from outside Australia, but from outside North America, Europe, and Japan. In particular—and this is the great change since 1970—many Australians, Americans, and Europeans now consume or use *manufactured goods* not produced in Australia or in America or in Europe, but produced in a wider group of countries. This wider group includes, most notably, the "Tiger" or "NIC" economies of Southeast Asia, but also includes China, India, and some of the larger economies of Latin America (like Mexico and Argentina).[7]

In other words, the simple, mutually exclusive division of the world into a rich "manufacturing" "North" or "West" and a poor "raw material producing" "South" or "Third World," which was still almost totally intact in 1970 has more or less disappeared. Manufacturing as an economic activity—or certain kinds of manufacturing—has spread and is spreading to other parts of the world, and this is one of the key aspects of globalization for the rich countries and populations of the world.

One of the effects of such spread has undoubtedly been the decline of certain types of manufacturing employment in Northern economies. In particular employment in certain forms of light manufacturing industry (clothing and textiles, shoes, sporting goods, toys) has declined markedly in the Northern economies as factories and industries based there have been unable to compete with imports coming from factories located in, or relocated to, parts of the globe where labor is cheaper.[8]

7. Thus, for example, in the period from 1981 to 1998 the shares of the United States, the European Union, and Japan in Australia's export and import trade fell, while the shares of China, the ASEAN countries—Brunei, Indonesia, Laos, Malaysia, Myanmar, Philippines, Singapore, Thailand, and Vietnam—and Korea all rose. The net result was that, whereas in 1981 these East and Southeast Asian countries had accounted for only 15 percent of Australia's export trade and 9 percent of its imports, by 1998 they accounted for nearly 25 percent of its exports and nearly 22 percent of its imports. The growth of imports from China over this period was particularly spectacular—from just 1.2 percent of Australia's total imports in 1981 to 5.8 percent in 1998, or in absolute terms from a little less than $300 million in 1981 to over $5 billion in 1998. Australian exports to China grew from $550 million to over $3.8 billion in the same period. Australian Bureau of Statistics, *Australian Economic Indicators* (Canberra: Commonwealth of Australia, 1991 and 1999), February 1991, tables 3.5 and 3.6, and August 1999, tables 2.12 and 2.13.

8. OECD statistics show that whereas in 1960 some 26 percent of the civilian population of all OECD countries were employed in manufacturing, by 1994 the proportion was

To this point my analysis of the implications of globalization for the ordinary people of the North or West might seem perfectly in accord with the prejudices of Australia's right-wing nationalist "One Nation" party. "Our people" cannot get or keep jobs, or are having their wages forced down, because of all those "cheap imports" coming from abroad. We need more economic protectionism for "our" industries, and we need to stop exporting "Aussie" jobs!

But unfortunately for One Nation (and for politicians and parties of a similar ilk in the United States or Europe), there is a lot more to the story than this. Virtually every serious economist who has examined the matter has come to the conclusion that while the spread of some manufacturing industry outside the Northern economies (we will call this "factor 1" in the economic restructuring of the globe) has had some impact on employment and wages in the former "manufacturing monopoly" economies, this impact has been quantitatively much less than the impact of two other factors. These are increases in competition between industrial and manufacturing firms based in different Northern economies (we shall call this "factor 2"), and changes in technology within those Northern economies eliminating a whole range of manufacturing and now, many nonmanufacturing jobs ("factor 3").

In other words, most economic analysts agree that for every one job that has been lost over the last thirty years in the United States, Europe, or Japan as a result of competition from the newly industrializing cheap-labor economies of the world, three have been lost either as a result of competition from some other part of the United States, Europe, or Japan, or as a result of technological change.[9]

However, talk about separate causal factors and of their separate quantifiable effects is economists' kind of talk, and there is reason to think that economists' talk may be misleading here. For these separate factors *may not be separate at all*, but closely interrelated. They may indeed be better conceptualized in fact, not as separate factors at all, but as just different

down to 18 percent. (The fall in Australia over the same period was sharper—from 30.7 percent to 13.2 percent.) The same data also show that for all these countries, the fall was particularly marked from 1976 onward. OECD, *Historical Statistics, 1960–1994*, table 2.11. However, as noted below, the sharp fall in manufacturing employment in Northern economies is as much a result of *labor-displacing technical change* occurring in manufacturing enterprises that remain within those economies as it is of relocation of those enterprises to Third World or Southern economies.

9. On this, see Dicken, *Global Shift*, 436–40.

aspects of a single process, or, to put it another way, as just a single process (global economic restructuring) looked at in different ways. Thus, one of the ways that a textile firm based in (say) Australia or the United States or Europe can respond to competition from a cheap-labor producer based in China or the Philippines (factor 1) is to *automate* their production technology to reduce higher labor costs in the home economy to a minimum (factor 2). Or when a producer of computer chips in Italy has to cope with competition from a U.S. or a Japanese producer of similar chips (factor 2) who has reorganized its production in ways that both cut labor costs and increase productivity, then that Italian producer will have to make the same employment-reducing technological change (factor 3) as well.

In short, locating or relocating manufacturing plants in cheaper-labor locations outside the traditional manufacturing countries; finding new production, distribution, or marketing techniques to capture markets from another producer within other traditional manufacturing countries or markets, or to generate new markets for so-called niche products; and introducing information and other technologies to increase output and lower labor costs generally in the face of all competitors (wherever they are); are *all* just different competitive strategies forced upon firms wanting to survive or prosper in a global capitalist system that is becoming ever more competitive in all of these dimensions all the time. Which one of these strategies, or which weighted combination of these strategies, any particular firm or company will adopt in order to compete, depends a lot on the particular commodity or commodities that a firm produces, the kind of competition it faces, and the different technological possibilities which are abroad in different sectors of production at any one time. But that all this is so means that it is not very sensible—at least as long as there is a relatively open global economy in which competition can be ever more fierce—to imagine that any *single* country within that global economy can protect itself from the effects of any of these competitive strategies. And it is especially not very sensible for any country or any interest group to pick out one of these competitive strategies as particularly politically unacceptable (cheap-labor production and imports), and try to protect themselves from that *alone*. It is not very sensible because the processes increasing unemployment and (in some cases) reducing real wages in the former "manufacturing monopoly" economies are so many-sided, that preventing plant relocations to low-wage economies around the globe (even if one could do it) would not stop more generalized processes of manufacturing job loss, plant closures, and so forth within the advanced capitalist countries.

*Import Substitution Industrialization: A "Third World"*
*Development Strategy and the Implications of Its Abandonment*

Nonetheless, and having said that, there is one aspect of the globalization process that *is* particularly worrying from the point of view of the ordinary people, of the ordinary workers, of the richer countries of the world. This is that, from the end of the Second World War right up to the 1980s, the predominant economic development strategy pursued in most of the poor countries of the world was something called import substitution industrialization (ISI in the development economist's jargon). Now, as its name implies, the main objective of ISI was to industrialize a particular national economy (the economy of Brazil or Argentina or India or China) by setting up local or national factories to make industrial and manufactured goods that had previously been imported from the industrialized or developed economies.

Sometimes countries did this by setting up their own nationalized or state industries, more often they did it by inviting MNCs or TNCs to come and set up subsidiary or branch plants in their countries. (This indeed was one of the main reasons MNC/TNC subsidiaries multiplied so rapidly in the world between the 1960s and the 1980s.) But whichever of these strategies was used, ISI as a development strategy was *always* highly protectionist. That is, tariffs or quotas or other customs barriers were erected by governments to prevent import competition with these new national industries and such industries concentrated on capturing or monopolizing the home market for their products (the market *within* Brazil or India or wherever) rather than making any serious effort to export what they produced.[10] This implies that in this period of ISI domination in development strategy (a domination that ended no more than ten or fifteen years ago) the labor-rich, low-wage countries of the world—the poor countries— "kept their labor to themselves," as it were. That is, their main objective was to use that labor to build up their own national industrialized economies behind protectionist barriers to trade.

But since the 1980s most of these poor countries have concluded that ISI was a mistake all along. Or rather, even they hold that if it was not a mistake originally, they had come by the 1980s to think that it had exhausted its capacity to help them to develop further. As a result most of

10. For just one of innumerable accounts of ISI and its effects, see, for example, M. P. Todaro, *Economics for a Developing World* (London: Longman, 1977), 325–29.

these countries' economies have now gone over to a strategy generally referred to as export oriented industrialization (EOI in the jargon), which means that they are now placing much more emphasis on creating or expanding industries that can increase their *exports* of industrialized or manufactured goods (rather than raw materials). Now, insofar as there is reasonably free trade in manufactured goods worldwide, and insofar as these new EOI industries in Brazil or Argentina or India or China or wherever—can export their products to the rich industrialized countries of the world, then they are no longer "keeping their labor to themselves." Rather, that labor is now competing directly with the labor of workers in the industrialized countries. Thus a totally unintended, but important, side effect of most of the poor countries of the world adopting ISI as their preferred development strategy for nearly forty years after the Second World War, was that Western workers had their real wages and standards of living protected from competition with what Marx would have termed the Third World's "reserve army of labor." But now that unintended protection is being—indeed has been—withdrawn.[11]

And it is not difficult to draw very alarmist conclusions from this fact. For example, according to Ankie Hoogvelt:

> The distinguished historian Paul Kennedy recently has warned [*sic*] of "global gales ahead."... he argues that the move to "market-oriented" production in South America, Indonesia, India, parts of China and the rest of S. E. Asia which is taking place today is likely to place 1.2 billion Third World workers into world-wide product and labour markets over the next generation. The vast majority of them earn less than $3 ... [U.S.] ... a day. As a consequence wages in the traditional advanced countries are set to fall by as much as 50 per cent.[12]

Now I do not believe in these kinds of cataclysmic predictions for a variety of reasons. In my opinion, to the extent that they ignore the demand factor, they are based on a naive economics. That is, if a free trade regime remains, the rising consumption of the new industrial workers of the poor

11. Thurow, *Future of Capitalism,* has some interesting comments on the worldwide growth in popularity of EOI and its likely implications for rich-country labor forces. See in particular pp. 58–59 and 183–84.

12. Ankie Hoogvelt, *Globalisation and the Postcolonial World: The New Political Economy of Development* (London: Macmillan, 1997), 240.

countries will itself provide demand that can provide sources of employment and wages (in tourism and other services for example) for people in
the rich countries. But, in addition, there is no doubt that if they were
faced with a sudden decline in real wages of this magnitude for the majority of their populations (as against for minorities), the rich countries of the
world would respond to this by increasing the protection of their be-
sieged industries. And they would probably now do this on a bloc (EU or
NAFTA) basis rather than on a national basis. That is, they would not
only exclude the poor from their regional labor markets, they would also
exclude the products of the poor from their product markets. Indeed, even
as it is, there are still considerable amounts of (generally nontariff) protection of the markets for manufactured goods from Third World competition in both North American and Europe.

However, having said that (that I do not believe that "wages in traditional advanced countries are ... [imminently] ... set to fall by as much
as 50 per cent"), I do not think it is at all impossible that something much
less cataclysmic, but quite difficult enough, could happen to real wages in
the rich countries. The long slow fall in real wages (which has in fact been
going on in virtually all Western economies since the 1970s) could continue for a lengthy period into the future. Such a fall would never be dramatic in any one year (probably less than 1 percent on average), but over
time it would substantially lower the standard of living of many people,
both over their own lifetimes, and in comparison with that of their parents or grandparents.

This would occur, as I have said, not simply as a result of "cheap-labor"
competition from the poor people of the world, but also as a result of this
factor *combined with* an increasing general competitiveness in all markets
of the world and with labor-displacing technological change (such as information technology), concentrated especially in the higher-wage economies of the world. However, the entry of millions of poorly paid skilled and
unskilled Southern workers into direct and indirect wage competition with
the workers of the advanced countries is only now beginning to "kick in"
as a significant competitive factor in the global economy (the shift from ISI
to EOI strategies being still a very recent phenomenon). It is therefore quite
likely that its significance as a real-wage-reducing factor for many more categories of Western workers will grow as the twenty-first century advances.

It should be noted, incidentally, that this slow decline of mass living
standards in the rich countries of the world need not necessarily be a result
of, or be accompanied by, mass unemployment in those countries. In fact

it could occur in conjunction with full or near full employment, if wages in most of the jobs that continue to exist themselves fall in real terms over time, or if new jobs (probably service jobs of a variety of types) are created to replace jobs lost, but these new jobs do not pay as well as the jobs they replace.[13] And since both these tendencies are at work in all the advanced industrial economies of the world already, and have been at work for at least the last ten years, this seems quite a reasonable scenario to expect for the foreseeable future.

However (and this is the predictive joker in the pack as it were), this slow *decline* in the real wages and standards of living of many ordinary people in the Western world could be accompanied by a slow, but equally significant, cumulative *rise* in the real wages and standards of living of many more ordinary people in the non-Western world. And since the economic magnitude of rising wages will probably exceed (in global aggregate terms) the economic aggregate of falling wages, this contradictory process could still result, overall, in a continued expansion of the global market and of global production and demand. If this happens, then the relative standard of living of different population groups or classes (whether within the United States or within Brazil or China or within the EU) will depend on their differential capacity to take advantage of the opportunities in the still expanding global market place. And this capacity is likely to be extremely differentiated, both between different firms and between different groups of workers. Therefore, in the short to medium term at least, one can expect a continuation, and even an intensification, of that growing inequality among different social classes and population groups which was already a feature of all the advanced industrialized societies of the world in the 1990s.

### Intensified Global Labor Competition and Real Wages in the Advanced Capitalist Countries

In this context (the inequalities that are emerging and are likely to emerge among different groups of workers in the Western economies) a more

---

13. In economic logic a closed economy with full employment should experience upward pressure on real wages as a result of the relative shortage of labor within it. However, none of the worlds' economies are entirely "closed" economies for labor now, and the combination of continuous labor displacement "internally" (through technological change) and immigration (albeit restricted) from "external" labor surplus economies around the globe should be more than enough to prevent "across the board" upward pressure on wages in advanced capitalist countries even with near full employment.

specific and very interesting, issue arises. The British development economist Adrian Wood[14] and a number of other authorities on this issue are
of the view that it is only unskilled workers in the West to date who have
lost jobs to, or are threatened with job loss by, cheap-labor manufactured
imports from the South. This may or may not be the case empirically up
to now (and Wood's findings are disputed).[15] But in a more general sense
it is difficult to know what Wood's thesis actually means, principally
because he defines "skilled" and "unskilled" workers primarily in terms of
the formal level of *education* possessed by those workers. His thesis therefore is that it is unskilled Western workers (= workers not possessing any
postsecondary educational qualifications) whose jobs are most at risk from
the competition of cheap imported manufactures from the South.

But there are two major problems with this equation of "skilled" with
"educated" (and of both these categories with "low paid"):

1. First, many of the low-paid workers of the South or the Third World
   have in fact *high* formal levels of education, including varying forms of
   higher or advanced postsecondary education. (This is especially true in
   communist or ex-communist countries like Russia, China, and Vietnam, where during the communist period, mass education levels rose
   spectacularly.[16] But there are also university and technical college grad-
   uates working in clothing factories in India for example.)
2. Second, and more important, there does not seem to be any necessary
   relationship, either in Western economies now, or in many of the newly
   industrializing economies of the world, between the substantive skill
   level actually required to do a job and the level of formal educational
   requirements or credentials required to obtain such a job.[17]

14. A. Wood, *North-South Trade, Employment and Equality: Changing Fortunes in a
Skill-Driven World* (Oxford: Clarendon Press, 1994).
    15. On some of the disputes, see Dicken, *Global Shift*, 439–40.
    16. See Thurow, *Future of Capitalism*, 55–59.
    17. The importance of this ever increasing discrepancy between the level of skill sub-
stantively required to do many jobs and the "inflation" of paper credentials required to
obtain them was first highlighted by Harry Braverman in his extraordinary book *Labor and
Monopoly Capital* (New York: Monthly Review Press, 1974). Braverman's book led to a massive commentary literature—mostly critical—concerned with his so-called deskilling
hypothesis. But a lot of this literature was vitiated from the start by a continuous confla-
tion of the substantive skill levels of workers with their formal educational levels. That is,
continually rising levels of formal education among Western workers was advanced as
"proof" of their rising skill levels, and as "disproof" of the deskilling hypothesis. But since

In other words, it does not follow that because a person who is soldering microchips onto computer motherboards in (say) Turin has a postsecondary electronics qualification that a postsecondary electronics qualification is actually substantively required to do such a job, or that it could not be done just as well by someone entirely without such qualifications in Malaysia. Also, and perhaps more importantly, it does not follow that, because computer programmers in Bangalore in India or in St. Petersburg in Russia are paid a tiny fraction of the wages of such programmers in Paris or California, they are in any way either less well educated or less substantively skilled as programmers than their Western counterparts.

In other words then, the skill of a Western worker is only a genuine protection from wage-lowering competitive pressures in a global labor market if that skill is (a) *genuine* and *substantive* and closely tied to the more effective carrying out of a job or task, and *not* just a form of paper credentialism, and (b) if that skill is *not* one also possessed, somewhere in the world, by people who (for whatever reason) are prepared to use or deploy it for lower wages than their Western counterparts.

Now it seems to me that, first, a lot of skilled work carried out in Western economies now does not meet the first test above. Therefore, it is both potentially and actually vulnerable to competition from people who are just as well credentialed or who, even if they are not, can still do the supposedly skilled (but substantively low-skill) job involved. But second, and in the long run far more importantly, there does not seem to be *any* kind of skilled work—or at any rate any kind of skilled work that is embodied in tradable commodities—which any human beings can do that other human beings cannot teach themselves, or be taught, to do. Hence,

---

Braverman precisely allowed that workers' formal educational levels *had* risen, but claimed that these paper qualifications were simply functionally redundant for the substantively "deskilled" jobs most of them were actually doing, his critics' equation of rising educational levels with rising skill levels simply begged the question he had been trying to raise. For a rather different application of the idea that the inflation of paper credentials, rather than being a reliable indicator of increasing skill, is rather a symptom either of generally overstocked labor markets or of excessive demand for specific occupations even in generally "tight" markets, see also Ron Dore, *The Diploma Disease: Education, Qualification and Development* (London: Allen and Unwin, 1976). The central theme of Dore's book is that, in developing countries in particular, where supply of labor greatly exceeds demand in many sectors, paper credentials inflate rapidly as a way for employers to "sieve" or "filter" masses of job applicants. But it is clear that this phenomenon of "credential inflation," though perhaps not occurring as rapidly in the labor markets of developed countries, is present there as well.

as I have said, even the most skilled Californian computer programmers can be matched by just as skilled and able Indian computer programmers who are still (despite their skill equality) willing to work at a fraction of California wages. And what is true of the spread of programming skills is presumably true, in the long run, of the spread of any other kind of skills.

### Labor and Capital

At this point we can make a connection between the first and second parts of this chapter—between the discussion of the spread of capital investment through FDI and the problems of economic restructuring in the advanced capitalist countries. The connection is, essentially, that in the modern capitalist world—and indeed since the industrial revolution of the late eighteenth and early nineteenth centuries—the productivity of human labor, and thus the real wages and standard of living of workers has depended a very great deal on the stock of capital with which that labor has been supplied. Or to put it more simply, the greater the productivity of the plant and equipment with which workers work, then (all things being equal) the greater the output produced by those workers and the greater the real wage they can earn.

Up to the time of the industrial revolution the physical productivity of human labor on any part of this planet was basically determined by people themselves—by how hard and assiduously they worked—and (to a lesser extent) by the natural conditions in which they worked. And since, up to that time, the vast majority of people who lived on earth were engaged in agricultural activities of one kind or another, then the natural conditions referred to mainly involved such things as differences in soil productivity, rainfall, incidence of pests and diseases, and so forth. However, since the industrial revolution differences in productivity of human labor across the globe have had less and less to do with differences in human endeavor, or with differences in natural conditions or endowments (although the latter can still play an important role in agriculture), and more and more to do with the technology—the plant, equipment, machinery—available to different workers in different parts of the globe. These differences have in their turn led, slowly, to a more generalized pattern of cumulative material privilege for a minority of the earth's population living in some (restricted) parts of the planet and cumulative material disadvantage or underprivilege for a majority[18] of that population generally living in other parts.

Let us take "cumulative material privilege" first. This refers to the situation enjoyed by workers in advanced industrial or advanced capitalist societies, who have generally had high levels of productivity (per hour or per day or per week worked) because they have been equipped with more and more advanced technology. As a result of this high productivity they have also been able to receive high real wages (as their share of that technologically produced productivity), which have allowed them to have high material standards of living. On the other hand, however, the cost of these high wages has been spread across a large number of goods or services (given high Western labor productivity). As a result these high-paid workers have often been able to produce products that could outcompete on world markets (in terms of both cost *and* quality) products produced by workers working with more limited or inferior technology, even when those latter workers were earning much lower wages.

The situation of "cumulative underprivilege" is of course just the reverse of the above. It refers to the situation endured by workers, mainly in the non-European or non-Western parts of the world, who have had to work with much inferior technology, both in agriculture and in various forms of nonagricultural manufacturing production. Thus, despite the low wages they receive for their work, they could not, *given the technology they have been supplied with to date,* produce products that could compete on world markets with the cheaper and better-quality products produced by much better paid Western workers.

It is, however, just this historical situation—just this historical pattern of cumulative privilege and underprivilege—which the process of globalization may now be beginning to disrupt. Such disruption takes two forms:

---

18. According to the World Bank, there were, in 1998, some 2.85 billion people in the world's labor force. Of these nearly 3 billion people, 2.42 billion—or nearly 85 percent—were in the low and middle income countries of the world, and 1.77 billion (62 percent) were in low income countries, and of those, no less than 1.2 billion (67 percent) were in India and China alone. When I speak, therefore, of the "privileged minority" of the world's workers in the rich capitalist countries of the world, I am referring to about 430 million workers in North America, Western Europe, and the Asia-Pacific, who make up, as it might be said, the world's labor aristocracy. World Bank, *World Development Indicators* (Washington, D.C.: World Bank, 2000), table 2.3, p. 48.

1. First, the globalization of production means, as we have already seen, that Western and non-Western workers are now linked together in single integrated production processes. As a result of this growing global integration of production processes neither Western nor non-Western workers are producing complete usable products at all, but just parts or components of products. Western workers had, of course, been involved in such highly specialized technical divisions of labor long before the globalization period. They have in fact been an ever more prominent feature of manufacturing since the onset of the industrial revolution itself. But until the onset of the globalization period, these specialist divisions of labor, and the technical interdependencies between different groups of workers to which they led, had generally only involved different groups of *Western* workers. Now, however, they have spread to involve significant groups of non-Western workers in genuinely globalized chains of interdependency.

2. Second, and more important however, these globalized chains of interdependency—whether they occur within single vertically integrated MNCs or involve whole groups of independent companies in open exchange relationships—*increasingly involve supplying non-Western workers with forms of technology productively identical to that supplied to Western workers.* That is, in order to produce radiators in Thailand to the technical specifications required by General Motors, workers in Thailand must be supplied with radiator production technology as advanced as that supplied to workers in Detroit or Birmingham or Munich or wherever. In order to provide software programs to the technical specifications laid down by IBM, programmers in Bangalore must work with hardware and software comparable to that being used in California or Scotland or Finland. In order to produce toys in China to the technical and safety standards laid down in the United States or EU, toy manufacturing workers in China must work with a technology identical to that used in the United States or Germany or wherever.

However, once this begins to happen (and so far the process has involved only a few groups of manufacturing workers in some poor countries, and hardly, as yet, impacted on agricultural production at all),[19] then the groups of poor non-Western workers who are supplied with globally competitive or globally cutting-edge technology, will suddenly find themselves

19. See Chapter 10, where Third World agriculture is discussed in detail.

at a considerable competitive *advantage* in the global capitalist labor market. That is, their levels of productivity will have become fully equivalent to that of U.S., Japanese, European, and other workers in the advanced capitalist countries, but the cost of their labor (meaning, the cost of maintaining their material standard of living) will still be a fraction of that of Western workers. Or, to put it another way, with the onset of globalization, workers in advanced capitalist countries begin to lose (only *begin* to lose) their "ace in the hole," which they have been able to play up to now in global labor market competition—their much higher levels of technologically produced productivity as a result of their historically much higher levels of capital stock per worker.

Moreover, once this begins to happen—once as it were the technological "genie" escapes the Western/Japanese "bottle" in which it has hitherto been trapped—it will become almost impossible to reverse the process and reintroduce forms of geographically and socially confined technological monopoly. This is partly because many Western and Japanese MNCs/ TNCs will have no economic interest in doing this. On the contrary, they now have considerable increases in profitability to gain from combining cheap workers with advanced technology, rather than combining expensive workers with advanced technology. But it is also because, in a world of increasingly rapid and efficient global information flows (including technical and scientific information flows), government agencies in poor countries, and indeed business firms in poor countries *who have the necessary technical expertise "in house"* can find ways of obtaining or developing cutting-edge technologies. They can either do this legally (on license from the companies which originally develop them) or—if they have to—they can steal or "pirate" the technologies they need, and put them rapidly to productive work. Rapid licensing of technology users (partly in order to preempt pirating) is already a marked feature of life in both the computer hardware and software industries and in biotechnology. And the continual failure in both industries, despite such licensing agreements, to prevent pirating of technologies, accounts for the obsession of a number of Western governments and MNCs with the issue of so-called intellectual property rights.[20] In a globalizing world, in short, competitive advantages deriving from technical or technological advances are likely to be more and more fragile and short-lived. Certainly, they are likely to be harder and harder for anybody (any company, country, or group of companies

20. See Thurow, *Future of Capitalism,* 135 and 206.

or countries, any group or population of workers) to monopolize for any significant length of time.

## Conclusions

For all the reasons given above I cannot accept Adrian Wood's optimistic thesis that it is only unskilled workers in the North whose wages and standards of living are under threat from the Southern reserve army of labor in an open global economy. Or at any rate I see no reason to think this will be so in the longer term, whatever the current situation may be. It seems to me in fact that those Northern workers and employees who do maintain, or even raise, their wages and standards of living in a global economy will do so mainly *because that global economy continues to grow* (and therefore increases aggregate demand for their goods or services) rather than because they maintain forever a monopoly over some skill or other. And as I have noted, it is very difficult to know now which Northern or Western workers will be lucky in the future in this way, and be able to take advantage of particular global demand growth areas, and which ones will not. All that one can say with certainty is that not all will be equally lucky in this respect, and so inequalities between workers are likely to increase.

Therefore, and in short, the inequality *within* the advanced capitalist societies of the world, which has been growing markedly and continuously for the last twenty or so years, is only set, so far as I can see, to continue and probably to further intensify. But it will do so only as part of an ever growing *global* inequality, a global inequality which will take ever more marked and complex forms, both within the poor or formerly poor societies of the world and between one geographical region or part of the globe and another. What the social, political, even cultural and psychological implications of all this growing inequality and polarization will be is by no means clear, although I will try to say something more about it in later chapters. It is difficult to imagine, however, that it will be easily compatible with the creation of a harmonious and tolerant global society.

# CHAPTER SEVEN

# Globalization as a
# Communications Phenomenon

To this point the focus of this book has been very strongly and narrowly economic. But it would be a grossly one-sided introduction to the globalization phenomenon that did not acknowledge that it also has important noneconomic dimensions. Indeed some authors and theorists think that it is these noneconomic aspects and dimensions that are the most important ones—the ones that are reshaping the world most fundamentally— because they are doing nothing less than reshaping human consciousness. These noneconomic dimensions of globalization, particularly in the realm of communications, are much the most significant, some commentators believe, because they are profoundly affecting the ways in which billions of people across the world think both about themselves and about the world around them.

## The "Global Village"

Emphasis on the "consciousness-changing" dimension of globalization is a particular hallmark of those who have an interest in the electronic media that have developed since the 1960s. Thus we are fairly frequently told that we are now living, or will shortly live, in a "global village" in which the previous barriers to human communication posed by time and space—by geographical distance—have been swept away or annulled by technologies that operate, literally, at the speed of light. We are also told, at least by the

more naively enthusiastic of commentators, that differences and misunder-
standings deriving from variations in human culture and ways of life are
melting—or will melt—away, as the new global media allow a speed and
intensity of cross-cultural global communication never before seen. Those
same commentators tell us that the internet, for example, is a perfectly
democratic world of free information and knowledge, where all who are
on-line are equal, and information and discussion can no longer be controlled or censored by oppressive governments, multinational corporations, or other power holders of the non-cyberspace world, and so on and
so forth.[1]

Now there is little doubt, I think, that a lot of this kind of talk is, and
is widely recognized to be, what is now commonly called hype, hyperbolic
overstatement often employed by those with a direct commercial interest
in personal computers, telecommunications technology, the internet, and
so forth.[2] Interestingly, however, this kind of hyperbolic talk about the

1. "We now live in a global village ... a simultaneous happening. We are back in
acoustic space. We have begun again to structure the primordial feeling, the tribal emo-
tions from which a few centuries of literacy divorced us.... Electric circuitry profoundly
involves men with one another. Information pours upon us, instantaneously and continuously. As soon as information is acquired, it is very rapidly replaced by still newer information. Our electrically-configured world has forced us to move from the habit of data
classification to the mode of pattern recognition. We can no longer build serially, block-
by-block, step-by-step because instant communication insures that all factors of the environment and experience co-exist in a state of active interplay." Marshall McLuhan and
Quentin Fiore, *The Medium Is the Massage: An Inventory of Effects* (Harmondsworth:
Penguin, 1967), 63.

2. For contemporary hyperbolic writing on the "Global Village," the internet, and
cyberspace, the reader is simply advised to pump the phrase "internet hype" into any search
engine. When I did so, my search returned four pages of results, including the following:
"Internet needs clarity not hype," "Multimedia Hype Productions," "Hype Back Issues"
(which included a massive amount of the said hyperbole), "Hype Media: Professional
Internet Services," and "Big Hype Digital Studio Web Services." Most fascinating of
all, the list also included the report of a speech made in late 1998 by "the President and
Chief Executive of IBM unit Lotus Development," which began with the grammatically
dubious claim that "the Internet and Web are concurrently the world's most over-hyped
topics to some extent," but ended with some strong factual claims of its own, to include
the following: "At the end of this year ... we will see 160 million people connected. It took
50 years for radio, 14 years for television, but just 3 years for the Internet to reach an audi-
ence of this significance"; "In 1998, we will have more electronic traffic—e-mail—going
over our networks than we will have paper deliveries on a worldwide basis"; and "This
year, for the first time in history, shipments of PCs will exceed by 20% shipments of television sets."

global communications revolution has its direct counterpart in equally hyped condemnations of the same revolution, which seem to endorse its most inflated claims while at the same time expressing fear and trepidation about what it might bring.

This is especially true of those many radical critics of globalization, both in the West and in the non-Western world, who fear that, through the global media in particular, a single dominant "imperialist" culture (Western and specifically American culture) is being spread around the world and imposed upon others whether they want it or like it or not. This fear of, and condemnation of, Western cultural imperialism is a major theme—in fact the major theme—in a lot of recent so-called postcolonial literature,[3] and it is also frequently articulated by Islamic fundamentalist groups and politicians in many parts of the world. For such people, global satellite TV channels, the mass marketing of Western CDs and videos around the world, and the internet itself are all just new weapons in the arsenal of Western cultural imperialism. They are weapons by which a single individualist, atheistic, competitive, and (above all) materialistic and consumptionist culture becomes universalized and kills or drowns out all other cultures, values, and ways of living. And such fears are not expressed simply by non-Westerners. The French government, for example, recently attacked the American dominance of the internet as yet one more factor threatening the existence and viability of non-Anglophone (and in particular, of course, Francophone) mass media and the cultural values they carry.[4]

But if—as I seem to be saying—both the claims of its enthusiasts and the fears of its enemies are hyperbolic, what can be said, truthfully, about the major changes in global means of communication which have occurred over the last thirty or so years? In what have such changes actually consisted, and what kind of future might they hold in store?

3. For some typical contributions along these lines, see B. Ashcroft, G. Griffith, and H. Tiffin, eds., *The Post-Colonial Studies Reader* (London: Routledge, 1996), especially part 3, "Representation and Resistance."

4. Once again the MAI provided a perfect focus for this sort of anxiety. The French government in particular strongly and publicly objected to any provisions that would have prevented state subsidization of French language film or mass media, and followed this up with more general accusations that the internet was one more American-sponsored mechanism for the Anglophone subversion of Francophone culture around the world. For all this, see the best of the MAI "watching" sites, the "Preamble Center on Globalization" at www.preamble.org/mai.

## Global Communications and the Speed of Light

It is my aim in the second part of this book to examine, in a fairly systematic way, the historical background to globalization, a history that some authors trace back as far as the fourteenth century! Indeed, we have already seen that one skeptical response to the globalization phenomenon, even among writers concerned with it purely as a contemporary matter, is to question the originality or genuine newness of many of its characteristics.

We have already seen such questioning with regard to the movement of capital and populations ("there was more of both—by some criteria— in the nineteenth century"), and one can find a similar response in the literature to contemporary communications developments. A number of writers have pointed out, for example, that the globe has been linked by steamship lines since the mid nineteenth century, by telegraph wires since the late nineteenth century, and by worldwide telephone links since the 1920s and 1930s. So again, what is so new? Some historians would even claim the nineteenth century saw more quickening of international communications—and with more socially revolutionary implications—than anything that has been done in the twentieth century. For at the beginning of the nineteenth century the only form of international communication was through the handwritten letter delivered by postal services that relied entirely on horses and ponies on land and sailing ships on water. (It took months, for example, for letters and dispatches from British colonial civil servants in India to reach home.) But by the end of that century the electric telegraph was already linking many parts of the world by messages sent at the speed of light.[5] (Granted, those messages—which were in morse— had to be short and simple and, at first, had to be transcribed by hand at either end.)

So even if what makes the current (meaning post-1960s) revolution in global communications so innovative is the ability to transmit a whole array of data, in a whole array of ways, at the speed of light, the claim that this change *is* revolutionary cannot rest on the notion that, as physical communications phenomena, satellite TV and phone transmission, or the internet, or electronic multimedia, are absolutely unique in history. For

5. For the development of electrical telegraphy and its social and economic effects, see, for example, E. J. Hobsbawm, *The Age of Capital, 1848–1875* (London: Abacus, 1977), 64– 78. See also Hobsbawm's *Industry and Empire,* chap. 6 and the diagrams numbered 16–19 at the end of the book.

they have in common with both the telegraph and the landline telephone the harnessing of light waves. Rather such an argument must rest on the claim that *the variety of ways* in which those light waves have now been harnessed—for visual as well as aural communication, for communication in color as well as monochrome, for computation as well as data transmission, for mobile as well as fixed point transmission and reception—now allow the speed of light to be put to a much greater range of uses for human beings than ever before in history. Such uses include mathematical and statistical calculation at a speed never before attained, either by the human brain itself, or by the brain aided by any nonelectronic device, and the production and communication of any information that can be encoded digitally at speeds never previously attained, either by human beings unaided, or by human beings aided by any previous forms of data production and transmission.

In addition of course, the new information technology can be put to a variety of new uses, not simply by the use of these technologies individually but by *combining* them in ever more complex and elaborate ways. Thus the personal computer plus the satellite phone, plus some technical improvements in land-based phone communications, gives one the internet. The TV plus the communications satellite gives one global satellite and cable TV. The power of mainframe and (now) personal computers, plus the internet, plus the mobile radio phone, gives one a geographically boundless electronic means of creating and transmitting financial and other numerical data at a speed and on a scale never before seen. And this is not to mention, the numerous *recreational possibilities* of these technologies for the entertainment and edification of both adults and children.

Now all this is well enough known. But what are its implications for our central theme—globalization? Well, the implication is the obvious one. The new information technologies and their combinations (both those currently existing and those still being developed) make it possible to move to any part of our planet, at the speed of light, *anything that can be moved at the speed of light.* To date that means *sounds* (including speech and music), *pictures* (still and moving), and *text* (both numbers and letters). But it also means that anything which is made up entirely of sounds and/or pictures and/or text—newspapers, magazines, radio and television programs, informational and technical reports of all kinds, financial information—can be moved at the same speed.

## Light Waves and Heavy Realities

The converse of the above is that the new global communications revolution leaves behind *anything that cannot be moved at the speed of light*—that is to say, anything that has mass. It is important to make this obvious, but frequently neglected point because it has two implications of great importance. One of these implications tends to minimize the economic and political significance of the revolution in information technology and the other (paradoxically) tends to maximize or stress its human significance. Let us take these two implications in order.

### The Heaviness of Matter

A lot of global economic relations *still* involves moving heavy physical things (including people). Global politics also involves moving such things (everything from military equipment to people—politicians, diplomats, soldiers) and therefore these type of activities remain untouched by the so-called communications revolution *at least directly*, and have, therefore, to proceed at speeds much much slower than light.

It is important however to add this last qualification—"at least directly"—because even these heavier forms of global interaction may be *indirectly* affected or facilitated by speed of light communication. For example, to move thousands of shoes or dresses from Brazil or India you will generally require a ship of some sort. However, to *order* shoes from Brazil or dresses from India, you may only have to make a phone call or send an e-mail.[6] Thus the ability to communicate rapidly, even instantly, about global commerce in heavy physical objects may in turn make it more cost effective to engage in global commerce in such things than it was before such communication was possible.

Nonetheless, and despite this, it is important to note one point. To move people physically, to move crude or refined oil, to move dresses, or shoes, or even silicon chips around the world, requires an expenditure of *energy* vastly greater than the energy now required to move an e-mail message or even a satellite TV program.[7] Therefore, if one wished to see

6. And this is not to mention the fact, for example, that said ships navigate their voyages more accurately or using less fuel per kilometer traveled because of electronic and computational aids of various kinds.

7. I was recently amused to hear, on a radio news program, that the British Navy had had to lay up a considerable part of its fleet in port, because of a lack of funds to purchase fuel. This budget shortfall was blamed on, among other things, the unexpectedly heavy

the globalization of economic relations slowed down or even reversed, an effective way to do this would be *to raise energy prices massively.* To put it crudely, if oil prices were raised to the point where it cost (say) four times as much as it currently does to move dresses from India to Australia or VCRs from Japan to Australia, then it might—might—become more profitable to make those dresses in Australia or those VCRs in Australia than to import them. I do not wish readers to conclude from this observation that I would actually support vast energy cost hikes as an antiglobalization policy. But I do wish to note the possibility, just as a way of helping readers to understand the importance for global economic relations generally and for international trade specifically, of the fact that there are still a great many things that cannot be moved around the globe at the speed of light.

## The Speed of Thought

Not everything can be moved at the speed of light. Indeed, most things are not, and probably never will be, moved at the speed of light. But, on the other hand, the things that are now moved globally and in almost unlimited quantities at the speed of light (sounds, pictures, text) are the things—or the main things—that human beings use to *influence* one another.

Suppose I want to influence somebody in some way. I want this person to think differently about something—perhaps about me, perhaps about something else. How would I, how would anybody, typically do this? Well, I would talk to her or perhaps give or send her information (words or pictures) that I think might influence her. Or perhaps I would show her some sights or sounds that I think might influence her in the way I want. Well, it is obvious, is it not, that since the information revolution I have been able to do all of this (I can talk to her, I can give her information, I can show her sights and sounds) without going physically anywhere near her, while in fact being hundreds or even thousands of miles away from her? In other words then what the information revolution has done is to globalize the most commonly used *means of persuasion or influence.* That is obviously one of the major reasons (perhaps the major reason) why its enthusiasts are so enthusiastic about it, and why, on the other hand, those who fear it fear it most. That is, the enthusiasts are typically those who, for one reason or another, want to do some influencing or persuading on

---

fuel costs involved in getting some British ships to East Timor to support the landing of peace-keeping "Interfet" troops there.

a global scale and the most apprehensive or hostile are those who, for one reason or another, fear being influenced or persuaded.

It is important to note that quite often if we are seeking to persuade or influence somebody in some way we may find that simply talking over the phone, or sending information or pictures, no matter how speedily or beautifully, will not do the trick. I may decide that to really get my message across I have to see that person "in the flesh." Once I have made this decision, I have dropped to sublight speeds. I have now to get in a car or on a bus or a plane and move myself physically to her. This suggests that speed of light media *may have their limits as means of persuasion*— especially perhaps between people who are markedly socially or culturally different in some way. At the very least it may suggest that these media may have to be supported by other forms of influence if they are to be successful in their persuasive task, and whether that task be economic and commercial (as in advertising) or political and cultural.

### Global Distribution of the New Media

Up to this point, we have directed our attention at what the new global means of communication actually are, and what they can typically do and not do, given what they are (speed of light *information* technologies). But of course in assessing the power or efficacy of this technology as a globalizing force, we have to assess not only what it is but how it is distributed globally. Here, therefore, are some simple statistics on the global distribution of what I consider two of the most important communications media—the internet and satellite and cable TV.

I need not spend a lot of time justifying these choices. The global distribution of internet access and use is important for globalization insofar as the internet is the newest and most rapidly growing of the global information technologies. The internet is also vital for globalization because it is the medium in which the interface between telecommunications as a technology and as a business in itself, and other forms of global business— the sale of goods and services, global movements of finance and capital, new management and accounting practices for all kinds of businesses being adopted globally[8]—is developing most rapidly.

8. This is the so-called e-business or e-commerce. For some statistics on its growth and development, emphasizing that this growth has been, and will continue to be, concentrated in North America, Europe, and the Asia-Pacific region, see "Ecommerce Bypasses

On the other hand, the global distribution of satellite and cable TV is important for globalization in that it is often the medium that is accused of being at the heart of modern Western cultural imperialism. Rupert Murdoch's News Corporation in particular, which dominates the production and marketing of global Pay TV, is oft condemned for beaming the same (Western) sitcoms and game shows, the same sports events and (Western) movies, into hundreds of millions of households right across Asia (including both India and China), the Middle East, and Latin America (as well of course as into hundreds of millions of European and North American homes).

## The Internet

Internet statistics are notoriously difficult to decode in social or geographical terms, because surveys of net use and growth typically count either the number of internet hosts (the number of web sites on the Net) or the number of hits (log-ons) on a particular site or all sites at a particular time. They also survey the growth of both these indicators—hosts and hits—over time. Thus, for example, the number of hosts on the Net grew, according to one survey, from less than 1.5 million in 1993 to over 43 million by January 1999.[9] But both these conventional methods can be difficult to decode socially or geographically, because neither an individual nor a business enterprise need be physically located where its computer domain address is registered. In addition a web site may be hit by a log-on from a particular computer, but the actual initiator of that log-on can be another computer far removed (on a net chain) from the hitting computer. However, despite these well-known difficulties, it is equally well known that the vast majority of both Net sites and Net users are American, and the bulk of the rest are European. In Table 1 I have assembled what NUA Internet[10] Surveys presented in June 1999 as their best "educated guess" of the numbers of *people* actually on line and their geographical distribution.

---

Developing World" (NUA InternetSurvey, www.nua.ie/surveys). This same source suggests that "the total ecommerce market should grow from US$2.9 trillion this year [2000] to US$9.5 trillion by 2003."

9. Internet Software Consortium, Internet Domain Survey, January 1999. The survey results can be viewed at http://www.isc.org/dsview.cgi?domainsurvey/report.html.

10. One of a large number of Net surveying companies that have themselves but recently sprung into being, and which are themselves increasingly important and profitable businesses. NUA Internet Surveys can be viewed at www.nua.ie/surveys.

TABLE I  World Total of Net Users, June 1999

| Region | Users (in millions) | Percentage |
|---|---|---|
| United States and Canada | 102.03 | 57 |
| Europe | 42.69 | 24 |
| Asia/Pacific (including Australasia) | 26.97 | 15 |
| Latin America | 5.29 | 3 |
| Africa (including South Africa) | 1.14 | 0.6 |
| Middle East | 0.88 | 0.5 |
| Total | 179 | |

In other words then, the United States, Canada, and Europe alone account for over 80 percent of web users, and if the Asia/Pacific area (Australasia, Singapore, Hong Kong) is included, the figure rises to over 95 percent, leaving the rest of the world (Africa, the Middle East, Latin America, and the largest part of Asia) with barely 5 percent. This distribution is, of course, scarcely surprising. One cannot log on to the internet unless one has, or has access to, a computer. And since, according to the UNDP, only 6.5 out of every thousand people living in developing countries had such access in 1995 (the figure for industrialized countries was 156.3 per thousand), these disparities are much as one would expect. In fact the same UNDP report found that whereas 17.9 out of every thousand people in the industrialized countries (not including Russia or the former Eastern Europe) were internet users, the average for all developing countries was 0.5 per thousand and was below one for every region of the South save Latin America (where it rose to the dizzying heights of 1.3 persons per thousand).[11]

11. UNDP, *Human Development Report 1996*, appendix table 4, p. 144. The World Bank's *World Development Report* for the year 2000 provides an update on these statistics. According to its tables the figure for personal computer ownership for all developing countries in 1998 was 15.6 (per thousand inhabitants) compared with 311.2 for the industrialized countries. (The figure for the poorest developing countries was just 3.2.) And thus while there were just over 777 internet hosts per 10,000 people in all industrialized countries in January 2000, the figure for all developing countries was 5.40 and for the poorest developing countries 0.37. *World Development Report*, 2000, Selected World Development Indicators, p. 311. One should be careful about all of these data, both because personal computer ownership and internet access are clearly highly dynamic trends that are almost defeating

However, one might also reflect that fewer than eighteen people out of every thousand on the Net in Western countries (in 1995) is hardly an overly impressive figure. Indeed, what *all* these numbers suggest is that personal computer ownership and (even more) internet access is a mark of considerable relative privilege everywhere in the world at the moment and a mark of extraordinary privilege in the poorest parts of the world. It is no exaggeration to say that, at present at least, the internet is a means of communication reserved only to the privileged of the world. It is a way in which the middle and upper classes of the world communicate with each other, and the geographical differences in the distribution of internet access is more a reflection of the size of those privileged classes in different areas of the world than of anything else.[12] Hence the main reason why there are significantly more internet users in (say) the United States than in Latin America is just that the middle- and upper-class groups, as a proportion of the population, are so much greater in the United States than in Brazil, Argentina, or Colombia. Conversely, where the number of people enjoying a "world-level" middle- or upper-class lifestyle is tiny as a proportion of the whole population (Africa), figures for internet use hardly register. But in a region of Africa where that proportion is much greater (South Africa) the figures rise sharply and are indeed largely responsible for Africa as a region having any statistical internet presence at all.

---

accurate statistical plotting at the moment, and because of comparability problems in the statistics. Nonetheless, one cannot help but be impressed by the rapid growth of PC ownership in both developed and developing countries currently (an effective doubling in the four years 1995–98 if these data are even approximately correct), even if, as one would expect, the increase in the developing countries is most marked in the more prosperous "middle income" group. Yet despite this dynamism, in 1998 only a third of the population even in the richest countries of the world had internet access (and that on the assumption that all PC owners have such access), and the figure for all developing countries—the most prosperous included—was just 1.5 percent! So my generalizations about the "class privilege" nature of this technology still stand.

12. For much the same structural reasons one would expect computer ownership and internet access to spread much more quickly down the class structure of the rich countries of the world, and a much slower pace of its democratization in poor countries. That is, as the real costs of PCs fall, and internet access costs also fall, even less well off people in rich countries can gain access to the net, but there is clearly an "absolute poverty" limit to such spread that is likely to leave many more people in poor countries out in the cold. And indeed such data as we have on the dynamics of PC and internet spread in the later 1990s (see note 11 above) confirm this "class-geographical" hypothesis.

## Satellite and Cable Television

The most comprehensive statistics on global distribution of satellite and cable TV are those collected by the ITU (the International Telecommunications Union) and published in its annual *Yearbook Of Statistics*. Table 2 shows the growth in the number of households having cable or satellite TV access in eight major countries of the world between 1988 and 1996.

TABLE 2   Number and Percentage of Households Having Access to Cable or Satellite TV in 1988 and 1996 by Country (ITU Statistics)[13]

| | 1988 | | 1996 | |
|---|---|---|---|---|
| Country | Number (in millions) | Percentage | Number (in millions) | Percentage |
| Argentina | 0 | 0 | 5.3 | 56.3 |
| Brazil | 0 | 0 | 6.2 | 15.4 |
| China | 0 | 0 | 45 | 13.6 |
| India | 0 | 0 | 17 | 10.1 |
| Indonesia | 0 | 0 | 3 | 6.6 |
| Iran | 0 | 0 | 0 | 0 |
| Mexico | 0.409 | 2.7 | 1.4 | 7.5 |
| Russia | 0 | 0 | 11.6 | 24.0 |

However, the ITU figures do not reveal the program supplier for these subscribers, so they do not tell us (for example) how many of these households are in receipt of programs through Rupert Murdoch's Star TV (in Asia) or Sky Latin America (in Brazil, Argentina, or Mexico). However, the author was supplied (by Foxtel Australia) with some figures on cable and satellite TV "penetration" for a selected group of countries for 1998. Unfortunately, the countries do not match with the list above, nor (oddly enough) are they figures simply for News Corporation affiliated suppliers either. However, for what they are worth, here they are.

13. International Telecommunications Union (ITU), *Yearbook of Statistics 1998* (Geneva: ITU, 1999), 17, 32, 44, 78, 79, 80, 109, and 137.

TABLE 3   Satellite or Cable TV Penetration for Eleven Selected
Countries, 1998[14]

| Country | Percentage of households with satellite or cable |
|---|---|
| Australia | 16 |
| Canada | 75 |
| Denmark | 60 |
| Hong Kong | 28 |
| Ireland | 47 |
| Japan | 6 |
| NewZealand | 21 |
| Sweden | 59 |
| Taiwan | 76 |
| UK | 28 |
| United States | 77 |

Together, however, these two sets of statistics suggest the following:

1. Cable and satellite TV use, just like internet use, is most developed in the United States and Canada, but is growing rapidly all over Western Europe. In both North American and Western Europe News Corporation is in competition with a number of other commercial providers of these services, but in Asia and in Latin America it appears to have a monopoly position.

2. Cable and satellite penetration of TV broadcasting throughout the South and in Eastern Europe is just beginning. (There were no cable TV subscribers in Russia until 1994, none in Brazil until the same year or in Argentina until 1993, none in China until 1990, none in India until 1993.) But the rate of growth of all these markets is astronomical. Over five million cable TV subscribers appeared in Argentina in just three years (1994–96). Forty-five million such subscribers appeared in China in just seven years (1990–96), and 17 million in India in just four years (1993–96).

3. Moreover, if the scope for further penetration of these Southern markets is measured by the number of households there who already possess a

14. Source: Research Department, Foxtel, Australia.

television set, then that scope is enormous. According to the same ITU tables, virtually all households in Argentina, Brazil, Mexico, and Russia had a TV set in 1996, as did some 97 percent of Chinese households. Even in India some 36 percent of households had a TV set in 1996, as did 55 percent of Indonesian households.[15]

This point alone reminds us that the extent of Western program penetration of Southern or non-European broadcasting media is severely understated if that penetration is assessed *only* by reference to cable or satellite TV dominated by Western (and especially American) MNCs. Many of the programs shown by terrestrial national TV stations in Latin America, Asia, and the Middle East are purchased from Western production and television distribution companies (including the American network giants like ABC and CBS and the British BBC and commercial TV companies).[16] In short, a Southern household does not have to have cable or satellite TV access to have its viewing hours dominated by Western-originated sitcoms, soaps or drama series, game shows and sports broadcasts, and so on (not to mention commercials for Western MNC or other products). Thus while Iran may have succeeded to date in keeping out Western cable and satellite programs, it is unclear how much Western programming its citizens still receive through its own terrestrial TV stations. From personal experience, however, I can testify that Russian TV (all of which is now commercial) is indeed dominated by such programming.

It is perhaps significant that the only part of the planet in which News Corp does not have any presence at all in mass media (whether print or TV) is sub-Saharan Africa. With the exception of South Africa, the continent as a whole simply does not have the volume of middle- and upper-income people to provide cable and satellite TV subscribers. Moreover, it now has the lowest rates of literacy, the lowest overall rates of dwelling electrification, and therefore the lowest rates even of terrestrial TV viewing, in the world.[17] Indeed, in these, as in many other respects, Africa

15. ITU, *Yearbook of Statistics 1998,* 17, 32, 109, 137, 44, 78, and 79.

16. I have failed to find any global or even regional statistics for the sources and distribution of terrestrial TV programs. However, some insight into the extent of Western domination of that programming and the global repetition to which it leads can be obtained by accessing "Worldwide television," a web site providing worldwide program guides for viewers (presumably laptop-toting globe-trotters) for both terrestrial and satellite channels. The site is at www.tvshow.com/tv/sheds.

17. According to the UNDP's *Human Development Report* for 1995, appendix table 2,

(and particularly sub-Saharan Africa) is now becoming the continent most excluded from the globalization process.

## Implications: The Creation of a Single Global Culture?

So much for the new technology and its coverage of the world. But these data, however interesting, are really just preliminaries to the big question. That question, of course, is whether the globalization of media under the dominance of Western media production and distribution companies is leading, in its turn, to the creation of a single global culture—a Western, materialist, individualist, consumerist culture—poised to marginalize or displace all other human cultures and impose a uniformity of tastes, preferences, and lifestyles across the globe.

This question is very easy to ask, but extremely difficult to answer. Indeed, I happen to think that it is far more difficult to answer than either the enthusiasts for globalization or its most strident opponents appear to think. For both of these groups agree in saying that the answer to the above question is yes. Where they disagree is only in how they evaluate this "yes," one side approving of it, the other violently disapproving.

However, to know the answer to this question we need to know far more than how many people across the globe watch *Friends* or *Wheel of Fortune* or *Baywatch* every week, or how many of them watch these programs thanks to some affiliate of Murdoch's News Corp conglomerate, or even how many of them buy Omo or Sony Walkmen or Daewoo cars, or surf the internet using the Yahoo search engine. What we really need to know is how far these practices (where they are engaged in) lead to fundamental changes in how the people involved think about themselves and the world around them. More particularly, we need to know how far exposure to such media also leads people to behave differently in their own lives—whether that be in regard to their family or sexual patterns, their mode of dress, the religious convictions and practices, their career aspirations and activities.

One of the major problems here is clearly the word and concept "culture" itself. When someone asks whether a single global culture has formed or is in the process of forming, they are using the word "culture" in its

---

p. 159, for example, of forty-nine countries in the world in which television ownership was at levels of five or fewer per hundred people, no fewer than thirty-six (73 percent) were in Africa.

most general sense. Now "culture" in its most general sense can embrace just about *anything and everything* that human beings do—everything from their most private of beliefs and practices (sexuality/religion) to their most public forms of behavior (occupational structures, sports activities, ways of shopping). Trying to assess whether cultural change is happening in any human community (let alone why it is happening) can be a task of awesome complexity and difficulty.

In my opinion, the best way to define this question down somewhat so that we might even attempt an answer is to ask what it is that worries most people who are concerned with this question. What specific aspect or aspects of this question worries or agitates them most? And when we do this, an answer is not too far to seek. It seems clear that most people (whether Westerners or non-Westerners) who worry about this question worry about whether a single conception of the good life is now coming to dominate in the world. That is, they are concerned that hundreds of millions, or even billions, of people, whether they are Westerners or Chinese or Indian or Malaysian or Indonesian or African or Brazilian, are coming to share the same set of aspirations or ambitions, based upon essentially the same vision of what the good life is. Those who are worried about this, or who are even angered by it, are so because they see a world of aspirational pluralism (= cultural pluralism) slowly being destroyed or marginalized in the process. That is, in certain parts or cultures of the world, a life of religious purity, or of scholarly devotion, or of military or spartan honor, may once have dominated the aspirations of men and women, may have entered importantly into their conceptions of the good life and, therefore, into their personal or group ambitions. But now (or so it is feared), all such alternative conceptions of the good life are being marginalized or cast aside. In their place, it is feared, a pursuit of what is essentially a single or unitary vision is emerging globally, in which Western patterns of material consumption dominate. Furthermore, it is feared, the coming hegemony of these Western patterns of material consumption may bring in its wake the marginalization of religious belief; the prioritization of physical pleasure over intellectual or spiritual fulfillment; and the public celebration of sexuality and of (an essentially uniform) notion of physical and sexual attractiveness.[18] Along with the exaltation of this way

18. Two nineteenth-century thinkers who express such anxieties when capitalism was still in its infancy were John Ruskin and William Morris. For Ruskin, see P. D. Antony, *John Ruskin's Labour: A Study of Ruskin's Social Theory* (Cambridge: Cambridge University Press, 1983). For Morris, see E. P. Thompson, *William Morris: Romantic to Revolutionary*

of life as the only good life, comes, it is claimed, an increasing perception of other conceptions as "old fashioned," "backward," "superstition ridden," and so on.

This is what is feared. But is it happening? And if it is happening, is it happening on a global scale? I am tempted to say, at this point, that the reader's answer to this question is as good as mine, so vast and complex a question does it seem. But perhaps that is too much of an evasion for somebody having the temerity to write and publish a book on globalization. I will, therefore, say that insofar as I think there is a general, global answer to this question at all, it is that something along these lines *is* happening to varying degrees in all parts of the world, but that it is happening to very varying degrees to different groups of people, in all parts of the world. That is, *this is not a question to which there is a single answer,* whether one is seeking such an answer in Brazil, or China, or Africa, or Indonesia. In all these cases and places different groups of people are being Westernized in their aspirations and ambitions to very varying degrees depending upon—among other factors—their level of education, urban or rural residence, gender (men are probably experiencing Westernization more strongly than women), and age (younger people are probably more prone to cultural Westernization than older people).

Nevertheless, I think it is possible to make one further point, a point that is a little more specific and perhaps more important and insightful than the foregoing, and something that probably *is* globally applicable. I said earlier that interpersonal persuasion "at a distance"—even using all the new electronic media—may not work. A person may decide that to be successful in their persuasive task they will have to meet personally (physically) with the person they are trying to persuade. I also said that if they do that, they immediately step outside the purview of lightspeed media. Well, I think something analogous to this is also important in the analysis of general cultural change as well as in the analysis of particular acts of

---

(London: Merlin Press, 1977), especially part 4. Among more modern thinkers, similar themes can be found in Karl Polanyi in *The Great Transformation: The Political and Economic Origins of Our Time* (Boston: Beacon Press, 1957), see especially chapters 5, 14, and 15; in Herbert Marcuse, *One-Dimensional Man: Studies in the Ideology of Advanced Industrial Society* (London: Sphere, 1968); in E. F. Schumacher, *Small Is Beautiful: Economics as if People Mattered* (New York: Harper and Row, 1973); in A. Gorz, *Ecology as Politics* (Boston: South End Press, 1980); and in almost the entire work of Jeremy Seabrook. See especially *The Race for Riches* (Basingstoke: Green Print, 1989) and *The Myth of the Market* (Bideford: Green Books, 1990).

persuasion by particular people. There seems to me to be quite a lot of evidence that exposure to mass media alone—even quite intense or frequent exposure—has little effect on aspiration formation, unless the people being so exposed can see the way of life they are being shown as *possible* for them. For so long as they do not see it as a possible way of life for them, they are apt to treat it as a kind of remote dream or reverie, perhaps amazing or amusing to watch or listen to but basically irrelevant. Further, there also seems to be a lot of evidence that *a local cultural reference group* is particularly important in effecting this sense of cultural change as a real personal or social possibility for any given group or society of people.[19]

Thus, to be more precise, people in the highlands of New Guinea can watch *Dallas* or some other similar soap opera through satellite TV. Indeed I have seen them doing so. But this is unlikely to affect their personal aspirations very much unless they know that there are Papua New Guineans "like themselves" who enjoy lifestyles at least approximating those they see on the foreign TV program or videos. But conversely, once they *do* know that such local reference groups (elite groups) exist, then mass media exposure, along with exposure to the existence and lifestyle of that local reference group, does seem to change their aspirations very rapidly, especially among young people. However, these effects are, at least at first, likely to be more focused on the obvious material components of a Western lifestyle (houses, consumer durables, clothes, and cars) than on other aspects of that lifestyle, which may or may not be embraced, or which may only be embraced later by later generations of the Westernized.

What this really amounts to is that mass media exposure in itself is unlikely to lead to a uniformity of global culture unless it feeds into—supports and is supported by—*structural social and economic change* occurring within the societies being exposed to such media. For of course the creation of what I have called local reference groups—of particular non-Western groups who adopt this global culture (or at least elements of it)—is itself part of, or an expression of, such economic and social change. Such groups—elite groups enjoying higher real incomes, being exposed to Western-style education, changing their housing, their ways of dress, buying and using cars—only emerge as the processes of economic modernization, industrialization, urbanization, bite into the societies of which

19. One of the best discussions of this phenomenon is W. B. Runciman, *Relative Deprivation and Social Justice* (London: Routledge and Kegan Paul, 1966), especially chaps. 2, 12, and 13. See also Barrington Moore, *Injustice: The Social Bases of Obedience and Revolt* (London: Macmillan, 1978), especially chaps. 1, 2, 3, 13, and 14.

these groups are a part. In fact it is clear that the creation of such groups is itself simply a part of the broader social processes of change which we gesture at by using words like "modernization," "urbanization," and so on.

In my view then, changed patterns of behavior only spread downward to the mass of people in any group or society as they emulate a local reference group. Therefore, those who worry about, or are even opposed to, these processes of global cultural change, may have to grasp that stopping it or reversing it involves more than blocking the satellite signals of Star TV, or removing Western programming from local TV stations, or Western magazines from newsstands. For the mass media, while they may be the most spectacular and obvious manifestations of global cultural change, may only be "behavior change effective" as part of a much broader social and economic process in which Chinese, Brazilian, Javanese, or Indian cultural leaders are as much involved as Rupert Murdoch or Madonna.

PART THREE

# Globalization
# and World Poverty

# CHAPTER EIGHT

# Globalization and the World's Poor

Most of the contemporary literature on globalization and the Third World, or globalization and developing countries, or globalization and the South (the terminology varies by author) focuses on one—very predictable— issue: *Is globalization, on balance, damaging or enhancing the situation of the poorest countries and peoples of the world?* An important question, a morally and politically loaded question, and a very interesting question in all kinds of ways. But before we can even attempt to answer it, we must first recognize that—as is so often the case in social science—the question itself hides a myriad of complexities.

If we are to assess the impact of globalization on the poorer regions and peoples of the world, we will have to assess each of its dimensions (production, trade, labor migration, finance, and communications) separately. We must also bear in mind that, not only may its impact be different in these different dimensions, but the significance of each of these dimensions or aspects of the globalization process may itself vary from poor region to poor region, or even from poor country to poor country within regions.

We have already noted, for example, how little the supposed global revolution in electronic communications media has touched the continent of Africa. We could also add that Africa is the continent of the South that has also been least affected by the globalization of production, the spread of manufacturing production to the South, and the new global financial and investment flows.[1] On the other hand, however, Africa has become a major source of transnational labor migrants (moving to Western Europe and to the Middle East in particular). In fact, Africa has been more powerfully affected by this "labor export" aspect of globalization than, for example, most of Latin America or Asia, although *within* Africa, the same generalizations do not hold for South Africa. There are similar patterns of differentiation and complexity in the impact of globalization within Latin America, within the Middle East, and within Asia as well (as well as differentiation and complexity *among* these regions treated as wholes).

In the question that opens this chapter, Is globalization, on balance, damaging or enhancing the situation of the poorest countries and peoples of the world? it is also crucial to understand what is meant by the extremely vague terms "damaging" and "enhancing." "Damaging" in what ways or in what sense? "Enhancing" in what ways or in what sense? Clearly there are a whole myriad of possible complexities here. But I want to give attention here to one in particular, partly because it comes up over and over again in the literature, and in a whole variety of different contexts, and partly because it will be central to the third and final part of this book itself. It is this. In social science in general and in economics in particular there are two ways of measuring almost any variable, and two ways of comparing almost any variable. In the case of measurement we can measure a variable *at a given moment in time* (its level in a given month, quarter, year, five-year period, decade, and so on). In the jargon this is known as *synchronic* measurement. But also you can measure *change* in a variable *over time*—how much some variable has increased or decreased over a month, a quarter, a year, a five-year period, and so on. This is known as *diachronic* measurement. When comparing two or more variables, one can compare their relative sizes *at a given moment in time* (e.g., per capita income in the United States in 1999 with per capita income in Senegal or Brazil in 1999), or one can compare the *rate of change* of two or more variables over time (for example, the rate of growth of per capita income in the United States in the 1990s with the rate of growth of per capita income in Senegal or Brazil over the same period).

Now the reason that these technicalities matter is that one can often get very different results—and results that may seem to have very different implications—depending upon which of these measurements and comparisons one uses. For example, if I compare the average per capita

---

1. On this, see, for example, Hoogvelt, *Globalisation and the Postcolonial World,* chap. 8.

income of all developed countries now ($19,283) with the average per capita income of all developing countries now ($908), the gap is obviously enormous. The gap, I can say, "shows the poverty" of the developing countries "now" compared with the rich countries. But if I compare the average rate of growth of per capita income in developing countries between 1981 and 1995 (6.2 percent) with the average rate of growth of per capita income in the developed countries in the same period (3.5 percent), then I can draw the conclusion that "the gap is closing." The developing countries as a whole are getting richer faster than the developed countries as a whole. Of course (I might say) "it will take them a long time to catch up," even if the developing countries can maintain this disparity in growth rates in the future. But I might nonetheless conclude that "the poverty gap is closing." "Things are not so bad" I might say, or not as bad as they looked in the simpler static measures and comparisons.

Or again, if I compare the GNP per capita of China now ($568.1) with that of the United States now ($23,760), I get a massive disparity. All Chinese people, I might conclude, are terribly poor in comparison with Americans. But if I note that in 1987 the per capita GNP in China was less than $200, I can conclude that the Chinese people, although still poor, are "getting richer" quite fast. In fact by this measure (per capita income growth, 1987–97) they are actually getting richer almost twice as rapidly as Americans are! So again I could conclude that "things are not quite as bad as they seem at first sight," or something like that.

Nor are the complexities here exhausted simply by synchronic versus diachronic measurements and comparisons. A lot also turns on exactly what I choose to measure or compare. For example, I got the "optimistic" result on rich country versus poor country per capita income growth rates above by comparing the growth rate of all rich countries with the growth rate of all developing countries between 1981 and 1995. But had I opted to compare, not the "all rich country" average growth rate with the "all developing countries" average growth rate, but the "all rich country" average growth rate with the growth rate of per capita incomes in the *poorest* developing countries (which averaged only 1.7 percent in the same period), I would have gotten a very different result. "Not only is the income gap between the richest and poorest people in the world massive" (I would have concluded) "but the gap is growing all the time."[2]

2. All the figures quoted here are from the UNDP's *Human Development Reports* for 1996 and 1999.

So not only are terms like "damaging" and "enhancing" terribly vague and slippery, but so are apparently more specific terms like "poverty," "poverty gaps," "getting poorer," "getting richer," "richest," "poorest," and so on. Above all, it is vital to grasp that it is in general easier to draw optimistic conclusions about globalization's impact on poor countries and peoples by focusing on absolute magnitudes and their growth.[3] Conversely, it is in general easier to draw pessimistic conclusions about such impacts by focusing either on synchronic comparisons between rich and poor countries and peoples or on comparisons of growth rates between rich and poor countries and peoples—in other words, relative magnitudes and their growth.[4] The reason for this is that, in general terms, we live in a world where almost everybody (not quite everybody as we shall see) is getting *absolutely* better off over time by a variety of measures. But we also live in a world in which (again in general, there are some significant exceptions) the better-off are improving their material welfare at least as fast, and quite often faster, than the worse-off are. Hence it seems to be far harder to close relative gaps in welfare (whether within countries or between different parts of the globe) than it is to raise absolute measures of material welfare over time.

The complications with "damaging" and "enhancing" do not end there. For example, according to Peter Dicken, between 1980 and 1994 the number of workers employed in manufacturing in Southern or Third World countries grew by 44.8 million, of whom no fewer than 37.5 million were in China.[5] Now, since we know that, in general, workers employed in manufacturing earn in money terms far more than peasant farmers or workers employed in agriculture, and since many Third World workers in manufacturing will have had a peasant or rural background, this growth in manufacturing employment would seem to be, on the face of it, a clear case of globalization enhancing the situation of at least some people in some Third World countries.

3. For a perfect example of the optimistic utilization of this absolutist methodology, see Bill Warren, *Imperialism, Pioneer of Capitalism* (London: Verso, 1980), especially chap. 8.

4. For a perfect example of a pessimistic utilization of this relativist methodology, see Andre Gundar Frank, "The Thirdworldization of Russia and Eastern Europe," in *The Aftermath of "Real Existing Socialism" in Eastern Europe,* vol. 1, *Between Western Europe and East Asia,* ed. J. Hersh and J. D. Schmidt (London: Macmillan, 1996), 39–61. But in fact all of Frank's work treats poverty or impoverishment in relative diachronic or synchronic terms, rather than in absolute diachronic or synchronic terms.

5. Dicken, *Global Shift,* table 2.3, p. 30.

However, increases of employment in manufacturing generally only occur because of an expansion of urban industry, and the environmental costs of such expansion (including air and water pollution, increased health risks to workers and others, etc.) can be considerable.[6] Therefore, other environmentally focused forms of statistical measurement can treat what (in employment and income terms) might be considered as "enhancement" as (environmental) "damage." So then the question becomes, how do we weigh or evaluate the employment or income enhancement effects of greater industrialization of an economy against its environmental damages effects (or costs)? Quite simply there is no simple statistical way of answering that question, because the weights one assigns here (positive and negative) depend so much on the values that the observer brings to the observations. So that, what one observer or author might treat as "on balance" enhancement, another can, with equal plausibility, treat as "on balance" damage.

So much for the concepts "damage" and "enhancement" in our question. But that is not the end of the complexities posed by the apparently simple but in fact devilishly complex question with which this chapter began. The question finishes by speaking of the "situation of the poorest countries and peoples of the world." Now we have already seen what a slippery concept "poorest" (along with "poor" and "poorer") can be, so we do not need to say anything more about that at this point. Rather, I want to focus on the complications hidden in running together, "countries and peoples" in this apparently simple way. For running them together in this way can risk obscuring a set of most important (in the contemporary world ever more important) facts.

First, we must not forget that in all countries of the world—including the very poorest—there are *always* richer or better-off people to be found. In very general terms the poorer a country is overall, the smaller this prosperous class or stratum will be *as a proportion* of the total population. But nonetheless, where the population of a country is large (as in the case of India or Brazil, for example), that small proportion of the prosperous can still amount absolutely to a great many people. Thus it is estimated that between 150 and 200 million people in India live in households with real incomes that allow them to consume on a scale commensurate with a

6. See J. E. Hardoy, D. Mitlin, and D. Satterthwaite, *Environmental Problems in Third World Cities* (London: Earthscan, 1992), chap. 3.

statistically average Western household.[7] Proportionately these (let us be conservative) 150 million people constitute only about 12 percent of the current Indian population, but absolutely they constitute a market for consumer goods and services ten times the entire size of the Australian market! So again we have another example of absolute magnitudes and relative magnitudes and the complexities to which their relationship can give rise.

In addition, all countries, including the richest, may have substantial populations of comparatively poor people (the United States is a famous case), and in addition, and probably more importantly, *countries* can get richer, by a number of conventional measures, without considerable numbers of their *people* (citizens) getting richer. Thus, to take a very well known case, Brazil's GNP per capita more than doubled between 1965 and 1980, and grew (much more slowly) by a further 10 percent between 1980 and 1997. But since, in the latter period, over 80 percent of the income increase that did occur went to the richest 20 percent of households in Brazil, the real income and consumption of the poorest 40 percent of households actually fell absolutely between 1980 and 1997, and the incomes of the middle 20 percent only remained stable in real terms over this seventeen-year period.[8]

Many writers and authors on globalization and development give considerable prominence to this distribution issue—and quite rightly, since it comes into play in almost every measure of "damage" or "enhancement" we may apply in assessing the welfare of a society. Thus, for example, not only is it possible for richer people in both rich and poor countries to secure a disproportionate share of the benefits of economic growth in a narrow sense, it is also possible for them to avoid disproportionately the wider social or environmental costs of that growth. Thus, as industrialization and economic development proceed, rivers may become more polluted, but it is the poor not the rich who drink, bathe, or wash in those polluted waters. Thus, as industrialization and urbanization accelerate, urban air and atmosphere may become more polluted and give rise to a large increase in respiratory diseases, but the rich will contrive to live in places where they can avoid the worst of this pollution, if not all of

7. See Australian Department of Foreign Affairs and Trade: East Asia Analytical Unit, *The Indian Economy at the Midnight Hour* (Canberra: Commonwealth of Australia, 1994), 3 and 32–36.

8. UNDP, *Human Development Reports* for 1996 (table 17, p. 170) and 1999 (appendix table 6).

it.[9] Or again, some government austerity program may lead to cuts in health expenditure, but if the rich have access to private hospital and other medical care, their health may suffer much less than that of the poor from such cuts.[10]

To repeat, all this is, in general terms, very well known, and stressed by many authors and in many statistical surveys of economic, social, and environmental conditions in both rich and poor countries. But, in general, I find that this awareness is often not consistently maintained through analyses of the consequences of economic development and globalization. And this is perhaps particularly true of the globalization literature, in which, perhaps just because of the enormous geographical scale of the subject, there is a tendency, as accounts develop, for authors to fall into conflating rich countries with rich people, poor countries with poor people; countries getting richer or poorer with people getting richer or poorer; income or wealth gaps between countries opening or closing with income or wealth gaps between people opening or closing. But it is important to remember the complex ways in which such conflations can confuse. For example, the fact that China is currently closing the per capita income gap on (say) the United States, because it is growing economically almost twice as fast as the United States, does not imply that the majority of Chinese *people* are closing the income gap on the majority of American *people*, because (again) the benefits of growth are being very unequally distributed in China.

The socioeconomic or class-inequality dimension is enormously important in assessing the welfare effects of globalization in any and all countries and regions of the world (rich and poor, Western and non-Western). But this is often not given the emphasis it should be in many analyses. In

9. For some good empirical data on this, see Hardoy, Mitlin, and Satterthwaite, *Environmental Problems,* especially 100–108.

10. Virtually all the literature on the effect of World Bank "structural adjustment" programs, in Africa or elsewhere, and whether violently hostile to such programs or more generally supportive, notes the disastrous effects such programs almost invariably have in the short to medium term on health care provision and on health conditions, especially among the poorest and most vulnerable. However, the "class specific" impact of these cuts is more seldom highlighted. See, however, C. Lowe Morna, "Surviving Structural Adjustment," *Africa Report* 35, no. 5 (1989): 45–48. For one of many overviews of the social effects of structural adjustment generally, see UNRISD (United Nations Research Institute for Social Development), *States of Disarray: The Social Effects of Globalization* (Geneva: UNRISD, 1995), chap. 2.

particular it is not given nearly as much weight as it should be in many Western and non-Western treatments of poor or poorer countries. In particular, I think that Western authors are often embarrassed by (and hence unwilling to draw attention to) class differences in poor countries (and in non-Western countries in general).[11] This is so even though—perhaps just because—such differences are very often more extreme, by almost any measure, than they are in rich or richer countries.[12] And at the same time, authors and analysts from the Third World are often similarly silent on the topic of class differences within the Third World, or tend to downplay them and their implications (in comparison with the differences between rich and poor countries) even when they do mention them.[13]

This hypersensitive silence about class differences within the Third World has, as we shall see, deep and subtle connections with one of the major themes of this book—the theme of *nationalism* and of nationalist approaches to the understanding of global capitalism and of its history. For the moment, however, it is important simply to stress that even making a present-day or contemporary assessment of the human welfare implications of globalization is a fraught and complex business precisely because issues of conceptualization, of measurement, of values (and hence of the judgments made about what various measures "show") all enter into this assessment in enormously deep and profoundly interrelated ways.

11. Virtually all the well-known books on contemporary Africa by Basil Davison tend to downplay this dimension, as do most (but not all) of the equally well known books on Third World development problems by Susan George. And even where such divisions are mentioned—as they are in George's *How the Other Half Dies* (Harmondsworth: Penguin, 1976), chap. 3—Third World elites or ruling classes are always presented in ways that reduce their moral culpability by treating them as "puppets" of the West rather than as autonomous agents pursuing their own self interests.

12. This is an extremely well known and often reiterated finding. See, for example, H. Chenery et al., *Redistribution with Growth* (London: Oxford University Press, 1974) chap. 1, and for more recent data and analyses to the same effect, see UNDP, *Human Development Report 1996*.

13. Two cases in point are Walter Rodney's *How Europe Underdeveloped Africa* (London: Bogle-L'Ouverture, 1972) and Eduard Galeano, *The Open Veins of Latin America: Five Centuries of the Pillage of a Continent* (New York: Monthly Review Press, 1973).

CHAPTER NINE

# Industrialization and the Alleviation of Poverty

Having considered the conceptual complexities that surround the apparently simple notion of poverty, we can now turn to the question of what causes poverty and to the closely related question of how mass poverty in any human society can be alleviated or ended.

What is it that makes a person materially poor? At an individual level there is in fact no single or generalizable answer to this question. The poverty of any given individual, that is to say, can be related to a whole variety of factors, from where they live (either on the planet as a whole or within any particular country), to the state of their physical or mental health, to their level of education or skills, to their age, to their gender, to their subjection to various forms of oppression or exploitation.[1]

Thus if we attempt to answer the question at an individual level, we can find a wide variety of factors that may account for the poverty of any given human being; however, it is nonetheless true that if we look at the world—the globe—as a whole, the materially richer human populations of the world tend to be found in industrialized countries and the poorer populations in nonindustrialized countries.

---

1. For a good descriptive discussion of the main factors giving rise to severe poverty in the Third World, see the World Bank's *World Development Reports* for 1990 and 2000, both of which are explicitly devoted to the causality and measurement of poverty in the world. See also UNDP, *Human Development Report 1997.*

*Explaining World Poverty (1): Abstract Economic Logic*

Economists, of all kinds, have long had an explanation for this powerfully obvious general correlation, an explanation that focuses on the relationship between "social" wealth (the wealth of a whole mass or group of people) and the mechanical supplementation of human labor power, and social poverty and the general lack of such supplementation. That is, when we examine the matter at a social or "macro" scale, it is clear that human populations that have managed to increase their physical productivity by harnessing inanimate sources of energy to supplement, or even replace, the expenditure of human bodily energy, are always (without exception) materially more prosperous than human populations that have not managed to do this, or have done so only partially or incompletely.[2] This observation has, in turn, the interesting implication that many—probably most—of the poorest people of the world, are poor not (as we may put it rhetorically) *despite* the fact that they labor—manually labor—so hard. Rather, they are poor *because* they labor—manually labor—so hard. We touched on this point earlier in a tangential way when we were discussing the possible effects of globalization on the welfare of workers in the Western or advanced capitalist countries. However, the specific points made there relate to a much more general economic logic, which because of its considerable importance for the entire train of analysis in this book, needs now to be made more explicit.

Economists (and I mean here economists of virtually every theoretical tendency and ideological allegiance) are generally agreed on how—historically—this difference in the physical productivity of human populations came about. That is, human populations whose labor is now massively assisted by widespread use of "inanimate energy using" capital equipment are generally populations that have a long history of what is conventionally called *capital accumulation*. In other words, they have a long history of inventing and/or applying more and more technically advanced methods of physical production. These are methods that generally increase the

---

2. David Landes is perhaps the scholar whose life's work has focused most insistently and brilliantly on this point and on its many implications. See, in particular, *The Unbound Prometheus: Technological Change and Industrial Development in Western Europe from 1750 to the Present* (Cambridge: Cambridge University Press, 1969) and *The Wealth and Poverty of Nations* (London: Little, Brown, 1998), especially chaps. 13 and 14. For a briefer popular account, see Carlo M. Cipolla, *The Economic History of World Population* (Harmondsworth: Penguin, 1975), chap. 2.

physical output of goods produced in a given period of time (per hour, day, week, and so on) while at the same time reducing the amount of human labor involved in that production. But more "inanimate energy using" forms of production are also more mechanized or machine-dependent forms of production. That is, gradually over time, in specific human societies on this planet, human beings working with hand tools have been replaced, as the dominant form of production, by more and more automated and/or mechanical systems of production in which the use of manual human labor is radically reduced or marginalized. In a word, and as noted earlier, the more materially prosperous human beings on this planet generally live in industrialized societies, and the less prosperous generally live in nonindustrialized societies of various types.

However, as it is described by economists at any rate, the historical process of capital accumulation is a double-sided or dual process. On the one hand it is, as noted above, a process of *physical* accumulation. It is a process involving the accumulation of machinery, of plant and equipment, of inanimate energy storage and transmission systems (oil refineries, electrical power stations, electrical grids, etc.) on the physical landscape of parts of our planet. On the other hand, however, it is also an economic process of *the accumulation of money,* or (more exactly) of money invested in the physical assets described above. Historically, industrialization occurred first in societies (like Britain) that operated on a capitalist or market-economics basis. Since that time it has mainly (not wholly) spread to and through other human societies that have worked on the same basis. Therefore, things like machines, factories, energy generation and transmission systems (and other forms of economic infrastructure), have all generally been *commodities*. That is, they have been goods that had to be created or manufactured by using money and which had, therefore, also to be bought using money.

When we consider the process of capital accumulation, questions arise about the source or sources of *the money* that was used for this accumulation as well as about the technical or physical forms of this accumulation and its results. And it is at this point of course that economists and economic historians leave consensus behind and begin to indulge in intense theoretical and ideological debates. Some scholars hold that the process of capital accumulation is adequately explained simply as a process of the investment and reinvestment of the "profits of enterprise."[3] Others,

3. This tends to be Landes's view. See, for example, *Wealth and Poverty,* especially chapter 12.

however, think that some process of exploitation is necessarily involved in such accumulation—either the exploitation of workers by the capitalists who employ them or the "imperialist" exploitation of the nonindustrialized parts of the world by the industrialized societies. In the latter case in particular it is claimed that, historically, Britain and other European imperialist societies engaged in the "primitive accumulation" necessary to commence the process of industrialization by the pillaging of the labor and resources of their colonies and client states.[4]

Although I will touch on these contentious issues in later chapters of this book, and although I have commented on them extensively elsewhere, I do not wish to explore them here, in the context of discussing the causes of world poverty. I wish to emphasize rather that if a human population—any human population—is to generally escape material poverty (if this escape is not to be restricted to some small or privileged upper class of political rulers or others), then that population has to find some way of initiating and continuing a process of capital accumulation. In monetary terms this means that it has to find some way of initiating and continuing a process of saving and investment. It has to save a significant part of the money earned by that population in the present and invest it systematically in ways that will massively raise the physical and economic productivity of that population in the future. There are a number of ways this can be done in any human society. It can be done by a "private" class of

4. It is still my view that the most convincing review of the whole issue—stressing the fertile interaction of external and domestic factors in the complex pattern of Britain's economic development in the two centuries prior to the industrial revolution itself—is to be found in Hobsbawm's *Industry and Empire,* chap. 2. Hobsbawm concurs with Landes, and many other scholars, that the majority of capital used for the expansion of manufacturing industry in Britain, narrowly considered, came from profits reinvested by the factory owners in question. But he stresses the importance of the investment of merchant profits from the colonial trade of the seventeenth and eighteenth centuries (including the slave and sugar trade) in land. This purchase of landed estates in Britain (and, not infrequently, of the aristocratic and gentry titles that went with them) by former merchants led to the "embourgeoisment" of Britain's landowning class. It encouraged, that is to say, an orientation of that class toward commercial profit making—an orientation not found among other European aristocracies of the period. It therefore created the crucial social and attitudinal conditions for the investment of large amounts of capital by that class in *large-scale economic infrastructure* in Britain (turnpike roads, canals, ports, railways) at the end of the eighteenth century and in the early part of the nineteenth century. Hobsbawm stresses that without these "lumpy" capital investments (which the new factory owners could not have made on their own) the development of manufacturing industry, narrowly considered, would not have been possible at all.

"capitalists" or "bourgeois," by the government or state, or by a combination of capitalist and state action; and all of these ways can be found in the history of actual industrialized societies on this planet. But—and logically—there are also a number of ways in which capital accumulation by any human society can be prevented or impeded and a population remain in poverty. Since it is poverty with which I am specifically concerned in this chapter, it is these on which I now wish to focus.

Such "poverty-maintaining" patterns of human action include the following:

1. Failure of a population to save—the squandering or dissipating of a society's current income by a wasteful government or state and/or by a political or economic elite oriented to maximizing its own consumption rather than the long-term growth prospects of its economy as a whole.[5]
2. Failure to turn savings into productive investments. Here the problem may be not so much that savings are squandered or dissipated on consumption, as that they are invested in economically inappropriate ways that do not leads to long-term productivity growth. Thus savings may be invested in expensive urban real estate or on military hardware, or in various forms of prestige projects that may be passingly impressive but lead to no long-term productivity growth.[6]
3. Transfer of savings and other economic resources from the human population possessing and/or producing them to other human societies or populations. Here savings may be turned into productive investments, but they are turned into such investments outside the society generating them. Many authors have seen imperialist exploitation of non-Western

5. For excellent case studies of just such phenomena, see Tony Killick, *Development Economics in Action: A Study of Economic Policies in Ghana* (London: Heinemann, 1978); Goren Hyden, *Beyond Ujamaa in Tanzania: Underdevelopment and an Uncaptured Peasantry* (London: Heinemann, 1980) and *No Shortcuts to Progress: African Development Management in Perspective* (London: Heinemann, 1983); and above all, Robert Bates, *Markets and States in Tropical Africa: The Political Basis of Agricultural Policies* (Berkeley and Los Angeles: University of California Press, 1981).

6. For an analysis of Latin American economic history emphasizing these kind of phenomena, see F. H. Cardoso and E. Faletto, *Dependency and Development in Latin America* (Berkeley and Los Angeles: University of California Press, 1979). It must be emphasized, however, that though factors (1) and (2) are distinguished here for analytical purposes, they are often found closely conjoined in reality. That is, ruling classes or elites that engage in excessive personal conspicuous consumption often also (though, interestingly, not always) engage in economically wasteful forms of investment or capital expenditure.

by Western societies as operating this way from as far back as the sixteenth century or even earlier. Certainly it is the case that where the "actual economic surplus"—as Paul Baran called it—of any human society is less than its "potential economic surplus" as a result of the forced transfer of investable resources abroad, the potential economic growth of that society has been diminished by the amount of the resources transferred.[7]

It is my view, however, that, whatever may have been the case historically, in the contemporary period (that is, in the period since the end of the various European colonial empires in the non-European world), factors (1) and (2) have been at least as important, and probably more important, in explaining the continuance of mass human poverty on this globe, than the "imperialist" factor (3).[8]

*Explaining World Poverty (2):*
*From Economic Abstraction to Social and Political Reality*

It is abstractly the case then that the mass of more prosperous human beings on this planet have been those whose labor has been made infinitely more productive through the mechanical harnessing of inanimate energy resources. And it is equally abstractly the case that the mass of a poor or poorer people on the planet are, and have been since the industrial revolution, those whose labor remains "simple" and unaided by the inanimate energy sources first successfully tapped by that revolution. Nonetheless, this juxtaposition is also one that, by its very abstraction, hides as much as it reveals. In particular:

7. Paul Baran, *The Political Economy of Growth* (New York: Monthly Review Press, 1959). Showing indubitably that this transfer has occurred and (even more) measuring its size, is trickier, both conceptually and technically, than many people appear to suppose. But where it can be shown to have occurred Baran's logic certainly holds.

8. See, for example, Landes, *Wealth and Poverty,* chaps. 20, 21, and 28. See also the works by Killick, Hyden, and Bates referred to in note 5 of this chapter. For a briefer essay focused explicitly on this theoretical issue, see Goren Hyden, "Capital Accumulation, Resource Distribution, and Governance in Kenya: The Role of the Economy of Affection," in *The Political Economy of Kenya,* ed. M. G. Schatsberg (New York: Praeger, 1987), 117–36. For an overview of the issue for Africa as a whole by two outstanding scholars of the continent, see C. Leys and M. Mamdani, *Crises and Reconstruction, African Perspectives: Two Lectures* (Stockholm: Nordiska Afrikainstitutet, 1998).

1. Historically, the former type of people have generally been what we call *industrial workers* and the latter type of people have generally been what we call *peasants or agricultural workers*. And thus the turning of the latter into the former has often been a more or less coercive process of dispossession and socioeconomic displacement. I discuss this point, and its immense implications, in Chapter 10.

2. However, it has by no means been the case that once peasants or agricultural laborers were forcibly turned into industrial workers they thereby, automatically, got rich or even richer. On the contrary, in the initial phase of industrialization, in which the labor productivity of the working class certainly rises massively, the historically most common result of this has simply been that the owners of capital get generally richer (through greatly enhanced earnings and profits) while the workers increase their real incomes very little, if at all.[9]

3. In fact, the working classes of the industrialized countries of the world (and this is as true of contemporary Korea or Malaysia as it is of nineteenth-century Germany or the United States or early twentieth-century Japan) only begin to benefit from the wealth they produce when one or both of two conditions are satisfied: the creation by the workers of effective means of *wage bargaining* (usually through trade unions) to ensure that some proportion of the increase in their labor productivity accrues to them as substantial wage increases, the intervention by a government or state on behalf of workers (through taxation and government expenditure policies) to ensure that increases in productivity and wealth are *redistributed* to them by a variety of political means and measures.[10]

9. On this, see, for example, Hobsbawm, *Industry and Empire,* chap. 4. Also, Arthur J. Taylor, ed., *The Standard of Living in Britain in the Industrial Revolution* (London: Methuen, 1975), especially the contributions by Hobsbawm, Hartwell, and Thompson. For a more general overview, see the classical statistical essay by Simon Kuznets, "Economic Growth and Income Inequality," in *American Economics Review* 45 (March 1955): 18–19.

10. On this, see, for example, Nicholas Deakin, *The Politics of Welfare* (London: Methuen, 1987), especially chap. 1. It is also the case that much can be done to alleviate the worst forms of poverty among human beings through various forms of social expenditure (on housing, heath care, public health and sanitation, etc.) *alone,* even in societies—such as Cuba or the state of Kerala in India—where the process of capital accumulation and industrialization has, for various reasons, been rather limited. A lot of the work of Amartya Sen stresses this point strongly. See, for example, his *Development as Freedom* (New York: Knopf, 1999), chap. 1. Moreover, it is a central aim of the "Human Development Index," produced by the UNDP since 1990 and presented in its annual *Human Development*

There are yet further complications about the pattern of poverty in the world, once the realm of simplified economic abstraction is left behind. For example, it has never been the case, even at the height of any country's industrial revolution, that its population has been simply and exclusively divided between a tiny minority of capitalists or owners of capital on the one hand, and a mass of industrial workers—or what Karl Marx called the proletariat—on the other. Indeed, nowhere in the world, even at the height of the heavy industrial period in world capitalism, have industrial or factory workers, narrowly defined, ever even been an absolute majority of the working population of any of the countries involved.[11]

This fact has many implications, but from the point of view of our current theme (poverty and its causes) its main implication has been that many of the poor people, even of industrial capitalist societies, have not been industrial or factory workers at all. Rather they have been *service*

_Reports,_ to bring out the point that the health, education, and material well-being of a population can be enhanced by focusing on these matters directly and not leaving them to improve as an incidental "side effect" of economic growth. It does, however, appear to be the case that this process of direct "social" poverty alleviation does reach a certain limit if it is not accompanied by a wider and longer-term process of capital accumulation and economic development.

11. For example, in the year 1881, when Britain was probably at the peak of its world industrial dominance, workers employed in manufacturing constituted just 32.6 percent of the total workforce. Moreover, even when workers in mining and quarrying, building and construction, gas, electricity and water supply, and transport and communication are added to the total (thus counting all "industrial" workers in the most extended sense), the proportion is still less than half (48.6 percent). The main reason for this is that, right up to the First World War and beyond, there were over 2 million British workers (the majority of them women) still employed in agriculture and nearly another 2 million (overwhelmingly women) employed in private domestic service. B. R. Mitchell, _British Historical Statistics_ (Cambridge: Cambridge University Press, 1988); these percentages were calculated from data on p. 111. Moreover, even when, in the interwar period, employment in agriculture and in domestic service fell sharply, this was not accompanied by a massive expansion in manufacturing employment. On the contrary, employment growth in the interwar period was concentrated overwhelmingly in white-collar work in the public and private sectors. As a result, in the entire period from 1955 to 1971 (i.e., even before it had begun its long-term decline) manufacturing employment in the United Kingdom still accounted for just 35.7 percent of total civilian employment on average, and never exceeded 38.3 percent even at its twentieth-century peak. OECD Statistics Directorate, _Main Economic Indicators, 1955–71_ (Paris: OECD, 1972), 468 and 469. I have chosen to cite the U.K. statistics because Marx happened to focus his own study of capitalism and class on that country. However, consulting the same OECD source will show that a similar generalization holds for all advanced capitalist countries.

*workers* of all types—domestic servants, retail and distributional workers, small-scale artisans, and poorly paid clerical workers in both the state and private sector.

Moreover, it has been a hallmark of such workers, at all times, and all over the world, that they have much more often been *women,* than have workers in the industrial sectors. That is, the service workforce is, in general, and across many countries and regions, much more feminized than its industrial counterpart.[12] Also, poorly paid service workers have generally found it much more difficult, than have industrial workers, to form effective trade unions to bargain for better wages and conditions. Therefore, they have generally been much more dependent—even than industrial workers—on various forms of government regulation of their wages and conditions (minimum wage legislation, maximum hours of work legislation) and on direct government subsidies to their standard of living (health care, education, child care) to escape from poverty. Indeed, despite this kind of state assistance, the majority of service workers in advanced capitalist societies (there is a significant minority who are much better off) generally still enjoy lower average standards of living than industrial workers.[13] Moreover, many of the poorest workers, even in the nonindustrialized societies of the contemporary world, are also service workers.[14]

*Governments* have therefore played a crucial role in turning the accumulation of wealth under capitalism into the effective reduction or alleviation of mass poverty. Moreover, these forms of poverty-alleviating governmental or state action have also been a crucial political means by which forms of national social solidarity in capitalist societies have been created and

12. For a general overview, using statistical data bases from forty-one countries, see R. Anker, *Gender and Jobs: Sex Segregation of Occupations in the World* (Geneva: ILO, 1997).

13. See, for example, Keith Middlemas, *Politics in Industrial Society: The Experience of the British System Since 1911* (London: Andre Deutsch, 1979), 137–41 and 286–87.

14. Many of the very poorest people in the South or the Third World are people who work in the so-called informal sector, an entirely unrecognized and unregulated sector of informal employment existing in both the urban and rural areas of Third World societies. Workers in this sector (which is predominantly a service sector) generally have the lowest incomes; have no form of sickness, injury or other insurance; and are often the object of considerable governmental harassment, since many of the activities in which they engage are formally illegal or semilegal. Many urban informal sector activities are carried out in the slums and shantytowns of the Third World where so many of the world's poorest people live. For a general survey, see R. Bromley and C. Gerry, eds., *Casual Work and Poverty in Third World Cities* (Chichester: Wiley, 1979).

maintained. Indeed, they have long been recognized as such, as much by conservative as by radical politicians in those societies.[15]

However, such reflections also raise questions about the difficult ideological position of many contemporary Third World states and governments, who often find themselves popularly pressured to engage in such political forms of poverty alleviation or wealth redistribution *before* any significant degree of wealth or capital accumulation has occurred in the societies they superintend.[16] But also, and more importantly, such reflections on the historically most important forms of poverty alleviation in capitalist societies also raise severe questions about whether or not such national political mechanisms of wealth redistribution have much of a future in a world of global or globalizing capitalism.

This question takes a different form in the cases of developed and underdeveloped capitalist societies. In the case of developed capitalist societies it is a question about the difficulties of *maintaining* state regulation of labor markets and state forms of poverty-reducing or poverty-alleviating welfare in a situation of ever more intense competition on global labor and capital markets and in a situation of intense competitive pressures on states to keep tax levels (and thus public expenditure levels) down.[17]

---

15. For an excellent general discussion of this phenomenon in Europe, see Charles S. Maier, *Recasting Bourgeois Europe: Stabilization in France, Germany and Italy in the Decade After World War I* (Princeton: Princeton University Press, 1975), especially chap. 8 and conclusion. See also the documents presented in J. R. Hay, *The Development of the British Welfare State, 1880–1975* (London: Edward Arnold, 1978), especially chap. 2.

16. East and Southeast Asian states have proved rather more effective than many other Third World states in resisting these pressures, especially through an ideological mobilization around family sources of social security as part of the "Asian way." See, for example, G. White, ed., *Developmental States in East Asia* (New York: St. Martin's Press, 1988), chap. 1. But my own guess is that this ideological resistance is not going to hold much longer against popular pressures from below. Furthermore, I believe that they should not hold. That is, I believe that an effective state-funded system of social security simply becomes a technical economic and social necessity as the process of capitalist industrialization advances. However, there is no doubt that many other Third World states, outside East and Southeast Asia, have faced severe problems of political legitimacy stemming from the fact that they are rhetorically or formally committed to a "human rights" or "welfare" agenda in a situation in which they simply do not possess the economic resources necessary to realize that agenda. At the equivalent stage of their economic development many Western governments and ruling groups were in a much sounder ideological position in that human rights and welfare conceptions simply did not have the political salience or influence (in the nineteenth century, for example) that they have at the end of the second millennium.

17. This issue is well discussed in Martin and Schuman, *Global Trap*, chap. 8.

In the case of underdeveloped capitalist societies, however, it is about the greatly increased difficulty—again in a situation of ever more intense global competition—of *moving toward* state-initiated systems of income and wealth redistribution, even after a considerable degree of success in national industrialization has been attained. Indeed, in a situation of such competition, it may be argued, at least by the ruling classes of such societies (in Thailand, Malaysia, Korea, or wherever) that the adoption of such systems will only lead to the loss of whatever competitive success or "edge" their state has attained in the world capitalist economy.

Aside from this, it cannot be denied that the willingness of ruling groups in capitalist societies to countenance serious redistributional policies—such as those put into effect in many Western societies—seems to be importantly affected by cultural factors. Thus, for example, the ruling classes of Brazil or Argentina or Chile, in the more prosperous southern cone of Latin America, have a long history of resisting either the adoption, or the serious implementation of such policies. This is so, despite the fact that it can and has been argued that, in a narrowly economic sense, these economies could well afford effective redistributional and state welfare policies.[18] And similar remarks apply *a fortiori* to ruling groups in the United States, who have certainly long been more resistant to such policies than their European counterparts.[19]

*Conclusions*

All these considerations to do with productivity and poverty under capitalism, seem to point once again to the same dilemma on which we have remarked in other contexts—the increasing disjunction between the economic globalization of the world and the still overwhelmingly national focus of politics and forms of social solidarity.

For it does now seem that relatively poor people, all over the world, will be able to look less and less to the governments of their national states for effective protection from the economically polarizing or impoverishing effects of free market capitalism. In the rich parts of the world this is because such forms of effective protection are being dismantled, or just becoming less practically effective. In the poor parts of the world,

18. See, for example, Marshall Wolfe, *Elusive Development* (Geneva: UNRISD, 1981).

19. For a rather suggestive discussion of the roots of this phenomenon in the United States, see Paul Krugman, *The Accidental Theorist: And Other Dispatches from the Dismal Science* (New York: Norton, 1998), especially 63–74.

however—in the majority of states in the world—it is because there seems less and less chance of such national state forms of protection being put in place. This is either because the states in question are simply too absolutely poor to afford them, or because, even where they are not, they fear loss of a competitive edge in an increasingly intense global capitalist competition. So then, at least in formal logic, the only way out seems to be a globalization—or partial globalization—of forms of political or social *regulation* of capitalism to match its ever more global scale of functioning. We shall discuss at length in later chapters the possibility of these forms of global regulation of capitalism becoming a reality. For the moment, however, there is still more to say about the forms of mass poverty still remaining in a globalizing world.

# CHAPTER TEN

# Poverty and
# Peasant Agriculture

When it comes to poverty, or rather to the notion of relieving or ending human material poverty on a mass scale, peasant agriculture has generally been viewed—in conventional development theory at least—almost entirely as a *problem* or an *obstacle* to be overcome. That is, from the perspective of the energetic economic reasoning I rehearsed in the previous chapter, peasant agriculture has traditionally been viewed as a form of economic activity that is incapable of yielding high, or even relatively high, material standards of living for the vast majority of people engaging in it. Human beings tilling small patches of the earth's surface using only a primitive animal or hand technology of cultivation are, in this perspective, the historically classical case of poverty induced by low levels of labor productivity. Peasants, that is to say, are seen as the historically classical and demographically dominant example of people who are poor *because* they work so hard—because they are without any really effective mechanical or industrial means to lift that productivity dramatically. And this is quite apart of from other social characteristics which often distinguish peasant agricultural systems and further exacerbate problems of mass poverty within them. These include predatory landlords taking a large part of what little the peasants do produce in rent or debt payments; inequality of landholdings among peasant households or families (often causing the most "land short" to hire themselves out as poorly paid part-time agricultural laborers to those families with more land); poor sanitary and health conditions in rural areas (further lowering levels of labor productivity); mass illiteracy among many peasant populations; and so forth.

For all these reasons, as we have already observed, states or nations commencing on the process of industrialization or (in the preferred terminology of the twentieth century) on the process of economic development, have usually envisaged this as involving the effective *elimination* of peasant agriculture as a mass form of economic activity. That is to say, such states have envisaged the peasants themselves, or their children and grandchildren, being transferred, more or less rapidly, to more productive urban industrial and service occupations. This does not have to mean, of course, that agricultural production disappears as part of a modern industrial society. Rather, agriculture becomes—or is envisaged as becoming—precisely a modern commercial sector of economic activity based on the same economic imperatives of output and profit maximization as operate in modern urban capitalist industry. That is, economic development is seen as involving the replacement of a mass subsistence oriented *peasant* agriculture with a demographically very small scale but highly productive *commercial* agriculture conducted precisely as a commercial business, rather than as a direct source of subsistence. To use yet another terminology, economic development is seen to involve the gradual replacement, throughout the rural areas of the nation or state concerned, of a mass of small-scale *peasant* producers by a much smaller number of large-scale commercial *farmers*, conducting agriculture on the basis of scientific agronomy and as a profit-maximizing business.

Very broadly it can be said that this "peasant elimination" strategy of agricultural development, conducted as part of a broader structural transformation process of industrialization, took place in the United Kingdom, throughout all of mainland Western Europe, in Japan, and (under rather different institutional conditions) in the USSR and Eastern Europe over the two centuries between about 1780 and 1980.[1]

1. For some classical accounts of this process in Europe, described and assessed from a variety of ideological perspectives, see Barrington Moore, *The Social Origins of Dictatorship and Democracy: Lord and Peasant in the Making of the Modern World* (Harmondsworth: Penguin, 1967); John Hammond and Barbara Hammond, *The Village Labourer* (London: Longman, 1978); Eugen Weber, *Peasants into Frenchmen: The Modernisation of Rural France, 1870–1914* (London: Chatto and Windus, 1977); Karl Kautsky, *The Agrarian Question* (London: Zwan Publishers, 1988); Dieter Senghaas, *The European Experience: A Historical Critique of Development Theory* (Leamington Spa/Dover: Berg Publishers, 1985), chaps. 1–3; David Mitrany, *Marx Against the Peasant: A Study in Social Dogamatism*

Note, however, that there are also several major modern agricultural economies (including the very largest, the United States, but also Australia, New Zealand, Canada, and Argentina) which did not go through this peasant elimination strategy at all, for the very simple reason that they never had any peasantries. That is, in these countries, a modern commercial or capitalist agriculture was directly transplanted onto the rural terrain of these states through a process of alien farming "settlement." In all these cases the settlement or colonization process dispossessed, not a mass of small-scale peasant producers, but a generally more sparse population of pastoral nomadic or hunter-gatherer peoples whose traditional way of life, prior to the arrival of the colonists or settlers, had generally not included using this terrain for the purposes of permanently settled or sedentary agricultural production.[2]

Whether it is simply coincidental that many of today's largest commercial agricultural economies are found in countries that did not have to undergo the peasant elimination process in order to create a capitalist agricultural sector, or whether there is something more than coincidence to this, is an interesting question.[3] But it is not a question that I am going to address here. I am not going to address it because—as it happens—all of the poorest countries of the world today *are* peasant economies. That is, they are economies with large peasant agricultural sectors, and therefore (and again speaking conventionally—from the point of view of conventional development theory) they are economies that still face the task of eliminating, or radically reducing, those sectors as part of their process of economic development. Some of these countries (including Korea, Brazil, Mexico, and—to a lesser extent—Algeria and Iran) have succeeded in

---

(London: Weidenfeld and Nicolson, 1951); Moshe Lewin, *Russian Peasants and Soviet Power: A Study of Collectivization* (London: Allen and Unwin, 1968); and Ron Dore, *Land Reform in Japan* (Oxford: Clarendon Press, 1959).

2. For Australia, Argentina, and Canada, see, for example, D.C.M. Platt and Guido di Tella, eds., *Argentina, Australia and Canada: Studies in Comparative Development, 1870–1965* (London: Macmillan, 1985); and for the early history of New Zealand's economic development, C.G.F. Simkin, *The Instability of a Dependent Economy: Economic Fluctuations in New Zealand, 1890–1914* (London: Oxford University Press, 1951), is very good.

3. Much light is thrown on this question, however, by Herman Schwartz's brilliant analysis of the "outward" geographical displacement of food and raw material production from Europe to the non-European world (through a series of "von Thunen rings") as a central part of the development of a global economy in the nineteenth century. See his *States Versus Markets,* especially chaps. 5 and 6.

reducing those sectors wholly or in part.[4] But the majority of them (the countries of Central America, all of sub-Saharan Africa, and above all, India and China) are still societies in which peasant producers are in the large majority and in which, therefore, the peasant elimination process has just begun. On the face of it, therefore, it is the history of agricultural development in peasant Europe and Japan that should be relevant to the future of these countries, and not the non-peasant history of North America or Australasia.

## Limits of the Conventional View

However, as soon as one looks more closely at the history of peasant elimination in Europe and Japan and compares it to the contemporary situation of the peasant Third World one observes deep and disquieting differences. And they are differences that very strongly suggest that the former experience cannot hold any simple developmental lessons for the latter.

First, the demographically largest peasant elimination exercise in world history to date occurred in the USSR. In that country between the late 1920s and the 1980s nearly 100 million peasant people were turned either into urban industrial or service workers or into rural agricultural and other workers.[5] This may sound impressive, until one recalls that there are still some 750 million peasants in China and somewhat more than this (800 million) in India, not to mention the 500 million or so peasants of sub-Saharan Africa. That is, India and China are each faced with a peasant elimination task that is seven to eight times larger than has ever been achieved in human history.

Second, peasant elimination in Europe and Japan occurred at a time when industrial technologies were typically much more labor intensive

4. All these countries now have less (in some cases much less) than 40 percent of their populations now directly employed in agriculture. See UNDP, *Human Development Report 1996*, table 16, p. 168, for the percentage falls in their labor forces employed in agriculture between 1960 and 1990. Among the more spectacular reductions were those in Brazil (from 52 to 23 percent), Libya (from 53 to 11 percent), Saudi Arabia (from 71 to 11 percent), Jordan (from 45 to 15 percent), Algeria (from 67 to 26 percent), the Dominican Republic (from 64 to 25 percent), Korea (from 64 to 38 percent), and Nicaragua (from 62 to 28 percent) For an excellent general discussion of the rapidly disappearing peasantries of Latin American and the Middle East in particular, see Hobsbawm, *Age of Extremes*, 289–93.

5. For the most precise figures currently available, see Stephen K. Wegren, "Rural Migration and Agrarian Reform in Russia: A Research Note" *Europe-Asia Studies* 47, no. 5 (1995): 887–88.

than they are now. That is, it occurred at a time when even new factories and industries typically employed far more people per deutschmark or franc or yen invested, than they do today. In a word, it occurred at a time when industry could much more effectively absorb the labor of or generate employment for peasants and ex-peasants than it can now.

Third, peasant elimination in Europe and Japan also occurred at a time and in places where the population growth rates were typically much lower (very roughly between 1.5–2 percent per annum at the peak) than they are now (2.5 percent or 3 percent and over).[6] That is, not only were urban industrial structures better at absorbing labor than they are now—under current technological conditions—but they had proportionately fewer people to absorb.

Fourth, peasant elimination in mainland Europe at least, also began at a time when, generally speaking, prices for agricultural commodities were much higher in real terms than they are today.[7] This means is that the so-called terms of trade between agricultural and nonagricultural commodities generally favored agriculture up to the beginning of the twentieth century, but that since that time they have generally turned in favor of nonagricultural goods. It is a very interesting question both how and why this change has occurred, but for the moment it is only important to know that it has occurred and the implications of its occurring for the present prospects of peasant elimination. And, as one might expect, these implications are generally negative. For buoyant prices for what peasants produce, if they are also accompanied by attractive real wages in nonpeasant occupations, tend to mean that peasant elimination can be carried out at

6. On this, see, for example, Carlo M. Cipolla, *The Economic History of World Population* (Harmondsworth: Penguin, 1975), chap. 4.

7. Hobsbawm, *Industry and Empire,* 140–44, has the relevant terms of trade data for the nineteenth century. For the twentieth century, Pasquale L. Scandizzo and Dimitris Diakosawas, *Instability in the Terms of Trade of Primary Commodities, 1900–1982* (Rome: FAO, 1987), is the most careful analysis known to me of the long and tortuous debate over whether there has been a "secular" tendency for the terms of trade of primary commodities to decline in the twentieth century. See especially their chapter 1 for a review of the debate, and chapter 2 for their own data and statistical conclusions. Their own conclusions are that "there is evidence of a long-term decline in the barter terms of trade" but that this is more likely to be a product of a long-term economic cycle "whose detection is made impossible by the insufficient length of the time series available" than a secular trend (54). One can, however, certainly say, on the basis of all the data provided and surveyed by Scandizzo and Diakosawas, that primary product producers were in a consistently better trade position in the nineteenth century than they were in most of the twentieth century, and certainly since the Second World War.

a moderate pace and in a way that generally minimizes the need for coercion. That is, good agricultural prices mean that peasants can be attracted off the land by better economic prospects in the town and cities. Yet, and at the same time, those who chose to stay on the land can earn a reasonable living just because prices for their produce are good.[8] This is very different from what occurs in a situation where earnings from peasant crops are so low that they can provide only a life of grinding poverty, but in which prospects for urban employment, while possibly holding out some hope for a better life than remaining in the village, are themselves both ill-paid and limited in quantity.

And fifth and finally, whereas the peasant producers of Europe and Japan produced so-called temperate-climate grain, vegetable, and fruit crops, most (not all) of the peasant producers of the contemporary non-European world produce tropical or subtropical grains, vegetables, and fruit crops, in addition to subtropical beverages like coffee and tea. In short, it may be significant that the central or essential crops in the diet of the peoples of the rich countries of the world are mainly temperate crops, which many of the peasant producers of the tropical and subtropical world could not, for climatic reasons, produce even if they wished.[9]

However, in thinking about the practical feasibility of peasant elimination as a development strategy for the contemporary non-European world, it is probably the first four points taken together that give one most pause for thought, for together they suggest that the demographic scale of the task is massive, indeed unprecedentedly large, *and* that neither the contemporary industrial technology context, nor the population growth context, nor the price or terms of trade context, is anywhere near as conducive to peasant elimination as it was when the European world accomplished its (demographically much smaller) transformation. In short, a much bigger boulder to move, a much steeper hill up which to move it,

8. F. Skrubbeltrang, *Agricultural Development and Rural Reform in Denmark* (Rome: FAO, 1953), 183–206 and 282–300, is very good on this, as are P. K. O'Brien and K. Chaglar, *Economic Growth in Britain and France, 1780–1914: Two Paths to the Modern World* (London: Allen and Unwin, 1978), especially chaps. 4 and 5 and the conclusion.

9. The role of climatic factors in creating a more or less propitious natural environment for human habitation and for economic development, although readily acknowledged in some of the early classical writing on development—see, for example, Gunnar Myrdal, *Asian Drama: An Inquiry into the Poverty of Nations* (Harmondsworth: Penguin, 1968), vol. 1, chap. 14—hardly get a mention in more recent literature. This, however, does not prevent them having important and real effects, as David Landes (*Wealth and Poverty*, chap. 1) has recently reminded us.

and fewer tools to accomplish the task. Not a promising scenario on the face of things.

## *Peasants and Economic Development: Less Conventional Views*

It is against this sort of background then that many people have been forced to consider whether the contemporary non-European world could, or should, adopt development strategies that do not emphasize urban industrialization and peasant elimination. Many thinkers and policymakers concerned with the issue have been forced to wonder whether or not it might be possible to produce forms of economic development in which small-scale agricultural producers remain as a significant minority, or even as a majority, of a country or region's population. That is, could material standards of living of peasants be raised *in situ* (with peasants still on the land and in the village) through a combination of appropriate improvements in their technology of production, specialization of their output, and improvements in their housing, their health care, and their levels of education?[10] In a word, the sheer scale and difficulty of peasant elimination as a contemporary development strategy raises the issue of whether forms of agricultural or rural development can be found that circumvent, or at least reduce, the need for mass industrialization and urbanization as the one and only route to widespread material prosperity.

There are many dimensions involved in considering the practicality or feasibility of this rural development alternative. Many of these dimensions have as much to do with the economic and political interests of the ruling elites of the developing world as they have with the economic rationality or viability of such solutions more narrowly considered. But let me at any rate concentrate on some economic questions surrounding such a strategy that—in accordance with the central theme of these this book—have explicitly *global* implications.

## *Peasants, Industrialization, and Globalization*

To focus on these questions we need to return to the fourth difference noted above between the history of peasant elimination in Europe and

10. For discussions of this issue, see, for example, Michael Lipton, *Why Poor People Stay Poor: Urban Bias in World Development* (London: Temple Smith, 1977), chaps. 5 and 6, and Robert Chambers, *Rural Development: Putting the Last First* (London: Longman, 1983), chap. 3.

Japan and the contemporary situation of the peasant Third World—the generally negative terms of trade for agricultural products prevailing in the contemporary world, as opposed to the generally positive terms prevailing from about 1780 until about fifty years ago. Why has this sharp change in the terms of trade between agricultural goods and manufactured goods in the last half century or so occurred? The answer to this question is fascinating and has to do with what economists call changing "elasticities of demand" for different products as standards of living rise. I will explain.

The majority of people who formed the first working classes of Britain and Europe in the nineteenth century (and indeed of Japan in the late nineteenth and early twentieth centuries) were, of course, poor. Many were peasants or ex-peasants who had been used to a low material standard of living. Also, and as noted in the previous chapter, in the first phase of industrialization they remained dreadfully poor—suffering from overwork, malnutrition, appalling housing conditions, and so forth.

However, as the process of industrialization advanced, and as they won higher real wages for themselves, so their standards of living slowly began to rise. And the predominant way this rise expressed itself—or the predominant form that it took—for many years was an increase in both the quantity and quality of food these new industrial masses demanded and consumed. The process usually began with such people consuming more of some staple grain product (wheat and maize in Europe, rice in Japan). But it soon led on to enhanced demand for a larger range of both vegetable and animal products (including meat and dairy products). In short then, the medium to long term process of urbanization and industrialization itself *set off a demand boom for farm products.* It was this boom, together with a general tendency for productivity improvements in agriculture to lag behind those in urban manufacturing industry, which lay behind the persistent movement of the terms of trade in favor of agriculture all over North America, Europe, and Japan right through the nineteenth century and indeed up to the First World War or just after.[11] And, generally speaking, it was local farmers who benefited from this boom or these booms—farmers in Europe from the European boom, farmers in North America from the North American boom, farmers in Japan from the Japanese boom, and so on, although, from the end of the nineteenth

11. For an excellent general account, see Hobsbawm, *Industry and Empire,* 140–45.

century onward, more distant producers of temperate food crops—like farmers in Australia, New Zealand, and Argentina—also became involved in supplying these industrial food and raw material markets.

However, from 1945 or 1950 onward—in fact with the enormous, upward push to Western living standards by the long boom—most ordinary consumer-workers in North American, Europe, and (then) Japan reached the limits of their demand for food. So as their standards of living rose further, they spent more of every additional dollar or pound or deutschmark or yen, not on food, but on more and more "exotic" or "complex" *manufactured goods* (furniture, fridges, home or house ownership, TVs, hi-fi equipment, cars, computers, and so on). So it was that the prices of these goods began to rise—under the impact of this prosperity demand—relative to the prices of food. That is, the terms of trade turned sharply against agricultural commodities and in favor of manufactured goods for the first time since the industrial revolution. Moreover, this turn has not proved merely conjunctural or short term, as were previous terms of trade movements against agriculture. Rather, it has remained in being for the last fifty or so years with real market prices for most (not all) agricultural commodities falling more or less continuously.[12]

Now, whatever else a successful rural development strategy (or even "rural plus urban" development strategy) in the non-European world may require, one of its essential prerequisite is prices for agricultural products that give small-scale agricultural producers a reasonable chance of themselves enjoying rising material living standards from the sale of crop and animal products. But as I have just argued, that is the one thing that the rich people of the already industrialized world cannot and will not provide for them. In fact they cannot even reliably provide it for "their own" farmers now, which is why agriculture in North America, Europe, and Japan is now kept in being by highly artificial (subsidized) prices.[13] To put it simply, in the United States and the EU in particular, but in Canada, Australia, and New Zealand too (albeit to a much lesser degree) the prices paid for farm products are not market prices, but so-called administered

12. That is, I think, a fair summation of the argument and data presented by Scandizzo and Diakosawas, *Instability*. See note 7.

13. Lauchlin Currie, *Taming the Megalopolis: A Design for Urban Growth* (Oxford: Pergamon, 1976), has a very good discussion of the logic of the agricultural subsidization process in the West and Japan and of some of its more important social and economic consequences.

prices paid out of taxes. That is, they are prices that are well above the level that would prevail in these markets if market forces of supply and demand were allowed to freely determine them.

However, all is not quite as black as it may seem. Peasant farmers in China or in India or in sub-Saharan Africa would have a moderately buoyant domestic demand for their crop and animal products if a large urban industrial population with rising real incomes appeared in their country or region. Such a population would spend a lot of the initial increase in its income on food, and would probably do so for several generations. (The slower the rise in real incomes, the greater the number of generations who will be "food fixated" in this way.) However, local peasant farmers will only benefit from this, *if they can keep this rising demand to themselves*—if, that is to say, Chinese or Indian or Indonesian urban workers do not end up buying (or at any rate entirely or predominantly buying) American wheat or rice or meat, or Australian wheat or rice or meat.

But that is only half the problem. To keep the rate and scale of urbanization in India or China or Africa "within bounds" as it were (which means, within limits that do not lead to levels of urban unemployment or social distress that are likely to be politically explosive or massively humanly degrading) we have to envisage forms of rural development that will keep (say) 500 million Chinese peasants, about the same number of Indian peasants, and some 500 million or so African and Central American peasants on the land. To put it simply, I do not see how this can be done, even in principle, unless at least a considerable part of the existing Western demand for food products is also being supplied by farmers from these regions. That is, it seems to me that the only conceivable strategy that might produce this result would be a policy of *global free trade in food stuffs*—an international agricultural trade regime that placed no barriers in the way of Australian or American farmers supplying Chinese or Indian demand, but equally, no barriers in the way of Chinese or Indian or African farmers supplying European or North American or Australasian demand. And when I say "no barriers," I mean of course no explicit barriers to trade (tariffs, quotas, etc.), but also no implicit barriers such as derive from state and other domestic subsidies to farmers. I mean, in short, the total abandonment of the Common Agricultural Policy of the EU, and the similar total abandonment of farm protection and subsidization as it currently operates in the United States, Canada, and Australia.

Moreover, I believe that this is the only policy that can, over the long run, command global support. For, on the one hand, Western farmers and governments can hardly be expected to tolerate free access to their markets if the markets of China or India or Africa are protected. And at the same time Indian, Chinese, and African peasants *cannot* have their domestic food markets entirely reserved to them if—as they certainly require—they are given free access to Western markets. Also, global free trade in agricultural produce is the only way to produce a pattern of producer survival either in agriculture generally, or in any particular product line or lines, that is not *politically* produced by state policy or policies.[14]

In all honesty, however, I should say that I believe that a regime of global agricultural free trade would produce a shrinkage of the agricultural sector both in North America and in Europe, and (perhaps) in Australasia as well, at least in the long run, although how great this shrinkage would be, and in what products it would be most marked, it is impossible to say in the abstract. Nevertheless, it is my view that most Western societies could only benefit, environmentally speaking, from such a shrinkage and that they could probably also manage such a shrinkage reasonably well politically. That is to say, the farming population in all Western societies is too small to have any great electoral force, and the large non-farm majority of the population in all Western societies would undoubtedly benefit greatly from global agricultural free trade. For they would almost certainly enjoy decreasing food prices on the one hand and tax reductions on the other (as a result of the cessation of expensive farm subsidies). In considering how great the shrinkage of the Western farm sector would be, however, the point about many non-European farmers being unable to produce temperate climate food stuffs should also be borne in mind.[15]

14. It may seem that my analysis is self-contradictory in that I have previously suggested that Third World agricultural producers need to keep the bulk of their domestic food demand to themselves, and it may be wondered how this could happen if Western farmers have free access to those markets. However, I believe that local producers *could* keep the bulk of domestic food demand to themselves if global trade in food crops and commodities were genuinely free—i.e., provided that Western producers were *not* in receipt of explicit or implicit export subsidies (which is the prime way in which they "crack" export markets in poor countries at the moment).

15. One implication of this point is that, in a regime of global agricultural free trade, the acreage under (say) wheat or maize in Europe or the United States would probably be more significantly affected by the outcome of competition with Australian, Argentinian, or South African producers of such crops (i.e., by competition among advanced capitalist producers) than it would be by competition with Southern or Third World peasant producers, as such. It is important to note, however, that part of China *is* capable of producing a large range of temperate food crops, as are the rural areas of the former USSR and other

*Global Agricultural Free Trade and Third World Rural Development*

Even a regime of global agricultural free trade would not, in itself, be of much assistance in adding a significant rural development dimension to the economic trajectory of Third World societies unless certain other conditions are satisfied. To take advantage of such expanded market opportunities, Southern or Third World peasant producers would have to be able to produce plant and animal products of a comparable quality and at a comparable cost to that of Western capitalist producers. In a word, they would have to modernize their production, processing, and marketing procedures in a way that would allow them to compete, in terms of both quality and price, with capitalist farmers in the West. What are the chances of this happening?

In my earlier book *Development and Underdevelopment in Historical Perspective,* I outlined the history of a long-running debate, both in Europe and in the non-European world, about the economic feasibility of forms of modernization of peasant agriculture that do *not* involve the destruction (gradual or rapid) of small-scale peasant agriculture and its effective replacement by large-scale capitalist or state farms.[16] Very broadly, those who were and are skeptical about such a possibility, tend to focus on the advantages that flow in agriculture, as well as in manufacturing industry, from so-called economies of scale—from producing a large volume of output of a single crop or small number of crops on a large-scale farm. Those, on the other hand, who think this peasant route to agricultural modernization is a feasible option, tend to stress the way in which economies of scale in agriculture only operate for certain types of crop (most notably grain crops of all kinds). They also explore the possibility of attaining economies of scale in peasant agriculture (where this is necessary) by unifying peasant farms as productive entities while not unifying them as juridical or "ownership" entities. Thus one hundred peasant farms of say ten hectares each producing wheat, could be unified into a single thousand-hectare

---

Eastern and Central European economies, the "southern cone" zone of South America, and the upland eastern and southern zones of Africa. And it is also important to note, on the other hand, that farmers in the southern United States and in the Mediterranean and Black Sea littoral of Europe *would* be in direct competition, over a large range of crops, with a mass of peasant producers in the tropical and subtropical zones of the world.

16. G. Kitching, *Development and Underdevelopment in Historical Perspective: Populism, Nationalism and Industrialisation,* 2d ed. (London: Methuen, 1989), especially chaps. 3 and 4.

grain farm with each of the peasant farmers obtaining one percent of the revenue and profits accruing from the sale of the wheat.

In addition, there is some evidence that small-scale peasant producers of labor-intensive crops such as coffee or tea, or of specialized horticultural flowers and fruits, or of specialized animal products can, if supplied with the right technical inputs, and given a proper agronomic training, produce both a volume and quality of output fully competitive with that from "large-scale" capitalist or commercial farms.[17]

As one might expect, definitive historical evidence on the merits of the arguments of the two sides in this debate is difficult to come by. This is partly because the picture is very empirically varied both from crop to crop and even from one period to another in the history of the same crop. Judgment is also made difficult by the fact that peasant commercial farmers have seldom been allowed the luxury of "level-playing-field" competition with large-scale capitalist farmers anywhere in the world.[18] But most important of all perhaps, a number of states, especially in Europe, have pushed ahead with policies that promote large-scale farming (in imitation of the success, as they saw it, of both British and American farming practices) irrespective of the performance of their peasant sectors, and in blithe indifference to the merits of any of the pro-peasant arguments considered above.

However, if the debate mentioned above has been inconclusive, it is possible to make several more widely agreed points that need to be borne in mind when assessing the feasibility of such a strategy of peasant agricultural modernization in the non-European world. First, capitalist farmers in the United States, Europe, and Australasia have much higher real incomes and standards of living than Third World peasant farmers. Indeed, Western farmers are nearly always among the most prosperous occupational groups in their respective societies. This means, therefore and obviously, that their per capita labor costs are much higher than that of Third World peasant producers. Western farmers make up for this competitive disadvantage by being much fewer in number. Like Western industrial workers, they also compensate for the much higher cost of their labor by spreading higher labor costs across a much higher volume of output. In other words then, an hour or day of a Western farmer's labor costs

17. The small-scale peasant production of high-quality coffee, tea, and dairy products in Kenya is often adduced as an example of just this. See, for example, Judith Heyer et al., *Agricultural Development in Kenya* (Nairobi: Oxford University Press, 1978), especially 1–31.

18. On this, see Lipton, *Why Poor People Stay Poor,* especially chap. 4.

much more than an hour or day of a Third World peasant's labor, but like the Western industrial worker in competition with a cheaper non-European counterpart, in that hour or day the Western capitalist or commercial farmer produces much more "stuff" than the peasant farmer. This is because, once again, the Western farmer's labor is aided by a large amount of machinery and other agricultural technology (herbicides, pesticides, higher-yielding seeds)—agricultural capital in a phrase—that the typical peasant farmer usually does not have. In order, therefore, for non-European peasant farmers to be able to globally compete they must have machinery and other technical inputs made available to them that will assist their labor power in a way analogous to the assistance that the Western capitalist farmer obtains. For it is only when they have such equivalent assistance that the much lower cost of their labor becomes their competitive trump card.

Second, global market competitiveness in agricultural commodities is not just a matter of the technical conditions of production of such commodities on the farm. It is also importantly determined by the quality of agricultural processing, and of the storage, distribution, and marketing of the processed commodities. To put it simply, even if peasant farmers in Kenya (say) could produce milk of a quality and price comparable to European production (in a situation of open competition), it would make no difference if that milk is then turned into only mediocre yogurt or cheese, or is delivered to the European retailer in a state unfit for human consumption or (even) in a packaging unattractive to the eye. In short, there are a whole range of "off-farm" conditions that must be satisfied if an agricultural sector or particular sort of peasant-produced output is to be globally competitive. And needless to say, satisfying these conditions (whether they be processing or storage conditions or marketing strategies) requires a considerable volume of capital investment, and a considerable amount of managerial and worker expertise, off the farm as well as on it. Cooperative forms of organization among peasant producers can sometimes supply the volume of capital required for the creation or improvement of processing plants and factories.[19] But even so, all of the other off-farm conditions for competitiveness in agricultural commodities markets can seldom be satisfied without considerable direct or indirect support to peasants from the state.

19. For an excellent example of this phenomenon, see Skrubbeltrang, *Agricultural Development*, 191–206.

And finally, even if these two conditions are satisfied, this may still not be enough to keep rural peasant populations stable (or even to markedly slow down the rate of rural-urban migration—which is probably a more realistic goal) if other, still wider conditions, are not satisfied. That is, there is a lot of evidence that young people in particular leave the rural areas of the Third World, not just because they are attracted to the possibility of higher-income urban occupations, but because they find rural life dull and unstimulating.[20] That is, a modernized peasant agriculture, to constitute a genuine alternative future for masses of people in the Third World, will need to be set in a context of much richer social and cultural life, and of the institutions necessary to support that life (sporting, educational, and recreational facilities of all kinds, for example) than they generally possess now.

So, having laid out these three minimum necessary conditions for making Third World agriculture globally competitive, we gain some sense of the magnitude of the task involved. We also gain an insight into the main reason for the general failure (or at any rate very disappointing performance) of rural development efforts in the Third World to date. To put it simply, to make rural development work as a mass development strategy in China or India or Africa requires a *massive* investment of money, labor power, and expertise, both on the farm and off it. It requires, that is to say, not only investments in peasant agronomic education, or in the production and supply of modern farm inputs. It also requires (for example) enormous investments in rural electrification and clean water supply and in the building, running, and maintenance of everything from agricultural processing plants to rural discos, sports centers, and internet cafes. But, at the same time, Third World peasant agriculture, shut out from Western markets by agricultural protectionism, and with even its own domestic food markets invaded by artificially subsidized food exports from Western nations, is not in a position to justify such massive investments by its existing economic performance or even by its potential performance. To put it brutally, it is hardly worth turning subsistence producers of low-quality milk, maize, or wheat in East Africa into small-scale high-quality commercial producers, if the only result of this is that EU producers of the same crops only obtain more protection to fend off the African competition in

20. On this, see, for example, N. Carynnyk-Sinclair, "Rural to Urban Migration in Developing Countries, 1950–1970: A Survey of the Literature," International Labour Organisation Working Paper WEP2-19, Geneva, 1974.

their own markets, and/or obtain yet more subsidies to compete in East African markets!

In short, it is difficult not to conclude from the logic of this analysis that the creation of a global free trade regime in agricultural commodities is a *prerequisite* of most Third World states "getting serious" about rural development. Conversely, the *absence* of such a regime (or rather of the economic opportunities it would immediately present to Third World states and peasant farmers) is a principal cause of the highly partial and half-hearted policies that have been pursued in the name of rural development in the Third World to date.[21]

I have believed for a long time now that agricultural protectionism and subsidization is the item of Western governmental policy that is most damaging to the poorest people of the world. It is also—and not coincidentally—the policy that is most economically distorting both of world commerce and of the economic structure of development efforts in the Third World. The vast majority of Third World states have put their development eggs almost entirely in the urban industrial basket, not just because they have learned, from Western experience and history, that development = industrialization. They have also done it because the protectionist agricultural policies of the rich countries of the world ensure that the poorest people of this planet are prevented from doing what they are naturally best equipped to do—to supply its relatively cheapest commodities (food stuffs and other agricultural raw materials) profitably at market prices determined only by the cost of their labor and other necessary inputs. They are best equipped to do this partly because agriculture is what the vast majority of the poorest people on this planet do anyway. But more importantly, they are best equipped to do it because, even in a world in which agricultural terms of trade are negative and declining, the low labor costs of peasant producers could (in the right institutional conditions) make agriculture still a profitable activity for them, *and without subsidies,* in a way that it can never, now, be profitable for many Western farmers. "Let the poor of the world feed the world and they will become less poor thereby" is both a very good slogan in itself and a perfectly valid inference from the analysis above.[22]

21. For a distinctly gloomy assessment of the real effects of such policies to date, see Chambers, *Rural Development,* chap. 1.

22. I have put the case here as strongly and polemically as possible because I feel so strongly about it. I am perfectly aware, however, that a global regime of free trade in

Another perfectly valid inference from the same analysis is that, as already noted, a regime of global free trade in agricultural commodities would certainly result in some shrinkage of the farm sector in all Western countries. This in turn means that some considerable part of what is now agricultural land would simply go out of production and could revert to forest or woodland or open grassland, and be put to a variety of recreational or other uses in those forms.[23] In addition, use of fertilizers and pesticides on that land would cease (with some positive environmental effects, especially for the cleanliness of aquifers, for example). This would not mean—or not necessarily mean—that *global* levels of use of such chemicals would decline. The most probable result, in fact, is that their use would simply be redistributed from one geographical region of the world to another or others. However, and also, shrinkage of the Western agricultural sector is not the same thing as its total disappearance. Almost certainly some forms of agricultural production in the West could compete even in a regime of global free trade. In particular, it seems very likely that Western farmers would move into niche markets for organic produce, with Third World producers coming to dominate the production of cheaper, nonorganic crop and animal products.

---

agriculture, even should it come about, might at first benefit the landlord, merchant, and other dominant classes in the countryside of the Third World more than peasant producers or (especially) landless agricultural laborers. However, even though many rural sociological studies of the Third World—from India to Indonesia, from Brazil to Burma—give us every reason to believe this may well be so, I still do not resile from my position that the establishment of such a regime would represent a massive step forward for many of the poorest people of the world. This is partly because many are so poor that even a small share in massively increased revenues would make a considerable difference to their material welfare. More important, however, once flows of export earnings into the rural areas of the Third World increased markedly so (I think) would social and political *struggles* over the distribution of their benefits. A globalizing world does not reduce the incidence of some people "ripping off" (as it is said) other people. Perhaps it even has the reverse effect initially. But the "information explosion" that is so integral to the globalizing process does make it harder and harder to hide from the ripped off that they *are* being ripped off. That may make its medium- to longer-term distributional effects more progressive than its initial effects.

23. Perhaps the buffalo would once more come to roam in the U.S. and Canadian prairies for example, which would also provide enormous space for several huge "West World" theme parks with thousands of cowboys and Indians, etc. "doing their thing" for the tourists of the world (including newly prosperous Chinese peasant farmers!)—a classical postmodernist fantasy come true!

## Conclusions

In the development of capitalism to date peasant agriculture has—generally speaking—enjoyed neither a positive reputation in theory nor a very desirable fate in practice. That is, it has been seen, ideologically, as the principal expression of a country or state's economic backwardness or underdevelopment. In addition, in most conventional development strategy and practice at any rate, it has been treated only as a source of labor and of capital for the urban industrial revolution. And this revolution has in turn been designed to eliminate—sooner or later—peasant agriculture and the peasant way of life entirely, and to replace it with "proper" large-scale commercial or capitalist agriculture. However, this account of the "anti-peasant" nature of capitalist development is accurate only as an account of what we might call *national* capitalist development—of capitalist development carried out within the framework of the nation-state and designed to produce, or rather reproduce, a national modern economy or modern capitalist system in every state of the world.

However, it is very possible that the heyday of such national forms of capitalist development is over, and that, from now on, human beings will have to make, and take, their economic opportunities within the context of a genuinely *global* capitalist system. And if that is true, it becomes possible to see a way—a global way—in which a form of peasant (or at any rate small-scale family or household) agriculture might be able to fit into such a global system and even modernize and prosper within it, rather than simply perishing as the price of capitalist industrialization.

However, as I have strongly and repeatedly emphasized, it is only possible to even conceive such a possibility within a context of global free trade in agricultural commodities. I therefore commend such free trade as a genuinely progressive economic, social, and (indeed) environmental policy, from which a large proportion of the poorest people of the world can only benefit—both directly and indirectly. Of course a small group of humanity—Western farmers, or some significant section of them—would also lose from such policies. And I would therefore wish to see social and economic measures put in place by Western states, and by Japan, to cushion in various ways the losses that those farmers would undoubtedly suffer. However, it is only realistic to recognize that the identification—indeed creation—of winners and losers is a necessary feature of any real world (as against utopian) policymaking. And once we abandon the national perspective in our thinking about possible global futures, there is simply no reason to weight the losses of a (globally tiny) number of American or European farmers higher than the gains of the (globally dominant) mass of Chinese or Indian or African peasants. This is especially so if, once allowed to feed the world, such peasant people were also able raise their own standards of living, breathe fresh air, stay out of the misery of urban slums, and avoid the experience of what we still call in the development discourse (in a classical piece of misery occlusion) the "informal sector" of Third World economies.

PART FOUR

∾

# *Globalization*
# *and Imperialism*

# CHAPTER ELEVEN

# Globalization
# and Imperialism

## *Introduction: More on Words*

In the first chapter I noted that it is usually a sign that something—something important—is going on in the world when a new word appears and proliferates as the word "globalization" has done in the last five to ten years. Logically then, it is equally a sign that something important is going on when words that have been widely used become markedly *less* popular—*less* widely used. In this context I want now to discuss one word in particular—"imperialism." The word "global" and its derivatives (including "globalization") have, over the last five to ten years, been used to discuss and analyze empirical features of the world that, prior to the 1990s, were usually discussed and analyzed using the word "imperialism" and some of its derivatives. So again, are we merely dealing here with some trivial change of intellectual fashion? Or is this linguistic change both a sign of, and part of, some more substantive change in the world?

I shall concentrate in this chapter on the word "imperialism," because the phenomena it is used to discuss (though not the word itself) are older than the phenomena the word "nation" and its derivatives (including "international") are used to describe and analyze. But I also want to concentrate on "imperialism" here, because since the 1960s or so, the very use of this word has been politically and ideologically contested. In fact, since the 1960s, willingness to discuss *contemporary* political and economic events and trends using the term "imperialism" has itself been a kind of mark of political allegiance—usually of allegiance to the political left. And conversely, refusing to use the word, or contending that the phenomena to which the word properly applies are purely "past" or "historical" phenomena has usually been a sign of a political allegiance to the center or right, or (indeed) of overt hostility to the left.

But some history first, and history in a double sense; history of the world and history of language. There is an uncontested historical use of the word "empire" and its derivatives (including, nowadays "imperialism").[1] This use, of course, is to describe situations in which one state or people *formally rules over or governs* another set of states or another set of people. It is in this sense that historians of the ancient world speak of the Roman, of the Chinese, or of the Incan empire, and in which historians of the modern world speak of the Portuguese, Spanish, French, or British empire. There are, of course, important differences between ancient and modern empires. But what they had in common (and what justifies the use of the same term to refer to both of them) was *the fact of political conquest.* Empires, ancient and modern, were formed by the conquering of a state, or territory, or people, by another state or people, and by the formal inclusion of the conquered in a form of political rule (called "empire") imposed upon them by the conquerors. Thus the people of Judea or Carthage or Egypt, having been conquered by the Romans, were all formally subjects of the Roman emperor. The peoples of India or of the colonies of Africa or of the West Indies, having been conquered by Britain, were all subjects of the British monarch. In this sense an empire is a formal political or governmental entity formed by conquest. Therefore we can tell clearly and easily, not only when an empire of this kind exists, but when it comes to an end. It comes to an end when the subjected or ruled or governed people or peoples throw off that rule and gain, or regain, some form of political independence—some form of government "of their

---

1. I add the qualifier "nowadays" because in fact the word "imperialism" was not widely used in the English language or in other European languages at all until the 1890s and was used at that time entirely in reference to the "new" colonial empires of the European states. It was really only in the later twentieth century that it leaked over into academic discussions of ancient empires. On the origins of the word and its use (it appears nowhere in Marx's own work, for example, although it is often thought of as a Marxist term), see E. J. Hobsbawm, *The Age of Empire, 1875–1914* (London: Abacus Publishers, 1994), 60, and Raymond Williams, *Keywords: A Vocabulary of Culture and Society* (London: Fontana, 1976), 131–32.

own" in place of government by the imperial conqueror.[2] In a word, since empires are essentially political phenomena, they come to an end in political ways—by a change of formal government or rulership among the conquered or colonized peoples.

This then opens up the question of whether there are any empires—understood in this political way—still existing in the world today. In the 1980s it was said that the answer to this question was no and that the "last" formal empires in the world—the British, French, Dutch, and Portuguese colonial empires—had ended with the political independence of their colonies gained, at intervals, in the years between 1945 and 1975. In 1991, however, historians discovered or rediscovered another modern empire—the Russian empire—which came to an end simultaneously with the disintegration of communism. For with the end of communism came, not only the freeing of Eastern Europe from Soviet informal dominance, but also the actual formal political independence of areas of southern Europe and of Central Asia that had been part of the Russian empire of the tsars even before the Revolution of October 1917.

So here we see an ambiguity even in the traditional concept of empire. The coming into existence of political independence movements can, retrospectively as it were, lead to the reclassification of what had previously been treated as a state, as an empire of this traditional type. Let us take an example on the doorstep of my own country, Australia. Since the people of East Timor have succeeded in gaining political independence from Indonesia, this may lead other peoples of the archipelago to seek such independence. And if that happens on a large enough scale we may be tempted, in retrospect, to view Indonesia as having been, not a single state at all, but a kind of Javanese empire.

That is, we may be tempted to say that what we now call the Indonesian independence movement of the 1940s and 1950s did not really create an integrated nation-state at all. We might come to say that it was merely a "Javanese imperial coup"—a political means by which a multiethnic,

---

2. I put the phrase "of their own" in quotation marks because I do not wish to imply that, in the case of ancient empires at least, their political breakdown led to any form of democratic or popular local rule. On the contrary, in the ancient world imperial breakdown or collapse nearly always led to some other, more localized form of authoritarian government (by a local dynasty, warlord, feudal lord, etc.). Indeed, the demand for "national democratic" forms of rule to replace imperial rule is a unique hallmark of the breakdown of *modern* empires specifically (and one of the crucial features differentiating those empires from their ancient predecessors).

multireligious, multicultural empire was marginally reconstituted, with the Javanese replacing the Dutch as imperial rulers. Similarly, one can conceive future situations in which the "imperialist" nature of states such as India or China might retrospectively be discovered in the same way—by the emergence of political independence movements defining themselves precisely as "anti-imperialist" movements. In the case of China the movement for Tibetan independence defines itself against "Han" China in just these terms.[3] But in the "right" (or "wrong"?) circumstances it could be only the first of many such movements in China. And so could the movement for the independence of Kashmir in India.

So then even the formal political understanding of empire and imperialism is not without its ambiguities. But these ambiguities do not, on the whole, lead to debate about the appropriateness or legitimacy of the use of the terminology itself. That is, despite these ambiguities, neither historians nor anyone else have much doubt about how formal empires of this type may be identified, or about the legitimacy of calling the Roman empire an empire or the British empire an empire or the Russian empire an empire. And though movements for political independence from Indonesia may not lead immediately to the widespread use of the term "Javanese empire," the description of Indonesia as a Javanese empire would probably not be a widely contested description of Indonesia if, at some time in the future, that state were to disintegrate into a mass of smaller states, of which Java was just one. (The Javanese, however, might take exception to the term even then!)

Still, there is a use of the terms "empire" and (in particular) "imperialism" that *is* highly contested. This, of course, is its Marxist or neo-Marxist use to mean, not "the formal political rule of one state or people by another usually as a result of military conquest," but something like "informal economic, political or cultural dominance of one state or people by another even if not accompanied by formal political or military conquest." This is the use of the term "imperialism" found in phrases such as "American imperialism" or "Western imperialism" and applied, by some people, to the pattern or distribution of power in the contemporary world and in particular to the contemporary world of nation-states and international relations since 1945. Now of course a large number of people, from spokespeople for the U.S. State Department, to historians or political

3. On this, see the majority of the statements appearing on the "Independence Home Page" of the Tibetan independence movement (www.taklamakaa. org).

scientists of a more traditionalist or conservative bent, have indignantly denied that the use of the term "imperialism" (and still less of "empire") is at all appropriate here. One even sometimes hears it said that "America has never had an empire and never will have." This is not actually technically true, even in the traditional sense. (For the United States *has* had a small number of formal colonies at different times in its history—the Philippines and Cuba[4] being the two most notable.) But the point of the denial of course is to say that patterns of informal economic or cultural or even political influence or domination are not to be equated with forms of political or military conquest. And that is quite clearly true. It may be the case that the small Caribbean state of Jamaica, for example, could not pursue a foreign policy, or even a domestic economic policy, strongly disliked by the United States without considerable costs. But even if this is true, it is not the same situation as Jamaica being a formal colony of the United States. Having limited room for maneuver is not the same as having no such room at all. Therefore, to the extent that informal notions of imperialism appear to ignore this difference they can be challenged as illegitimate.[5]

However, a close look at the Marxist or neo-Marxist concept of imperialism shows that those who use it do not—or do not typically—use it to equate formal and informal empires. That is, for them the phrase "the American empire" or "American imperialism" is not a *synonym* for "the British empire" or "British imperialism" or for any other example of formal empire. Rather, what the Marxist use of the term does is to take what were regarded as real but secondary or ancillary characteristics of formal empire and make them the primary or identifying characteristics of informal empire. That is, it has been a persistent allegation of the conquered or colonized, ever since there have been conquered or colonized peoples, that once an imperial power takes control of another population or territory, it

4. Some might take issue with my calling Cuba a U.S. colony. At the end of the Spanish-American War, the United States and Spain signed a treaty in Paris (on December 10, 1898) in which Spain ceded Cuba, Puerto Rico, the Philippines, and Guam to the United States. A clause in the treaty explicitly granted independence to Cuba; however, on independence day, it was the U.S., not the Cuban, flag that was raised in Havana. The United States government annulled the results of the first free election and restricted the franchise. It was only after the second election (1902) produced a government acceptable to the United States that the Cuban flag was allowed to be raised.

5. For a standard challenge relying on this argument among others, see D. K. Fieldhouse, *The Theory of Capitalist Imperialism* (London: Longman, 1967), especially parts 3 and 4.

then exploits that population or territory for its own benefit. The forms that this imperialist exploitation has taken have varied down through the centuries. They have encompassed everything from enslavement of the conquered in the ancient world, through the pillaging of gold, jewels, and other precious metals in both ancient and modern empires, to the capitalist forms of exploitation found in modern empires (for example, and typically, the use of the conquered population as cheap wage labor in mines and plantations owned by the imperialists). But the essence of imperialism, formal or informal, is—or so it is argued in this tradition—always the same; the use of the land and people of the conquered for the enrichment, or further enrichment, of the conquerors.[6]

Hence—or so the Marxist argument goes—if the point, the principal purpose, of formal political conquest, of formal political empire, is always—was always—the exploitation of the conquered for the enrichment of the conquerors, then *any* type of domination that has the same economic point or purpose (whose consequence is exploitative in this general sense) can, equally appropriately, be regarded as a form of imperialism, as a type of informal imperialist conquest. Thus if America or Europe still continues to exploit the peoples and lands of other parts of the world for their own enrichment, then we can speak of "American" or "Western" imperialism continuing. Moreover, we can legitimately do so even if there is no formal American empire in Latin America, or no formal French empire in Africa.

## Imperialism Out, Globalization In

I do not want to consider the validity of this Marxist or neo-Marxist extension of the concept of imperialism here. That is, I neither want to consider systematically whether what it asserts about formal empires is true (that they *were* all merely means to economic exploitation) or whether what it asserts about American or Western dominance in the contemporary world

---

6. Of course, that this is so can itself be challenged either as a generalization, or in regard to any particular case of imperialist conquest. There has been, for example, a long running and methodologically convoluted debate over the question of whether or not, on balance, an economic accounting entity called "Britain" made a profit out of its period of formal imperial rule in India. For an impeccably scholarly assessment of that debate and some of its confusions, see Victor Kiernan, "Development, imperialism and some misconceptions," Centre for Development Studies, University of Wales at Swansea, Occasional Paper No. 13, 1981.

is true (that it *is* just an informal means to the same exploitative ends). Rather, I want to address the question of why, in the last ten years or so, talk about "imperialism," even among leftists or on the left, has been superseded by talk about "globalization."

The answer to this question is clearly *not* that in the last ten or so years the world has become markedly more equal. On the contrary, as I stressed in an earlier chapter, one of the few characteristics of globalization on which virtually all observers agree is that it has been, and is being, accompanied by rapidly increasing inequality in almost all dimensions. Thus, to quote the UNDP's 1996 *Human Development Report*:

> The poorest 20% of the world's people saw their share of global income decline from 2.3% to 1.4% in the past 30 years. Meanwhile, the share of the richest 20% rose from 70% to 85%. That doubled the ratio of the shares of the richest and the poorest from 30:1 to 61:1.
>
> *and*
>
> During the past three decades the proportion of people enjoying per capita income growth of at least 5% a year more than doubled, from 12% to 27%, while the proportion of those experiencing negative growth more than tripled, from 5% to 18%.
>
> *and*
>
> The gap in per capita income between the industrial and developing world tripled, from $5,700 in 1960 to $15,400 in 1993.[7]

However, and significantly, what we might call the globalization phase in the history of the world economy has seen not just an increase in inequality (along a number of dimensions) but also what an increasing *complexity* of that inequality.

7. UNDP, *Human Development Report 1996, An Overview*, p. 2 (viewable at http://www. undp.org/hdro/e96over.htm). The most recent data do not suggest that anything much has changed in any of these respects. See, for example, World Bank, *World Development Report, 2000*, chap. 1, and UNDP, *Human Development Report 1999*, appendix table 6. The latter, for example, shows that whereas between 1980 and 1997 the GDP per capita in the industrialized countries grew from U.S.$14,206 to U.S.$19,283, and the growth in all developing countries was from U.S.$686 to U.S.$908, there was actually an absolute *fall* in GDP per capita over these eighteen years both in sub-Saharan Africa specifically and in all the world's least-developed countries generally (most of which are in Africa). See also the same chapter of the *World Development Report 2000* and appendix table 4 of the *Human Development Report 1999* for the massive levels of inequality that continue to be a feature of most of the world's poorer countries.

Perhaps the most single important aspect of that complexity is in fact signaled in the second of the quotations above. For over the three decades from the mid 1960s to the mid 1990s some of the world's poor peoples actually made considerable gains in material welfare, while at the very same time others were actually getting absolutely worse off. And as this and many other sources show, this is an aggregate reflection of a very important regional differentiation. For most the poor people of the world who got markedly better off in this period were concentrated in Asia, and in particular in Southeast Asia, while most of those who got worse off were concentrated in Africa, and in particular in sub-Saharan Africa. (According to the same report, in 1995 twenty African countries actually had per capita incomes below what they had been in 1975.)[8]

The picture in the rest of the poor world (Latin America, the Caribbean, the Middle East) was rather mixed, but in all, slow to moderate growth from the 1970s to the 1990s was accompanied by rapidly rising internal inequalities, with the income gap between the richest and the poorest growing markedly within all these regions and within all or nearly all of the countries in these regions.

The simple bipolar world of 1970 (to which I referred in an earlier chapter) has been transformed in the last thirty or so years not just economically but *socially* as well. That is, it is no longer accurate economically to see the world as made up simply of a modern, industrialized, developed North and a traditional, peasant agricultural, underdeveloped South. But equally it is no longer accurate socially to see our world as one in which all the rich people of the world are to be found in the European North, and all the poor people are to be found in the non-European South. This stereotypical picture, still broadly accurate in 1970, has now become significantly inaccurate for two reasons: (1) the growth in the number of poor people (both European and non-European) now to be found in living in the "rich" North, and (2) the growth in the number of rich and not-so-poor people now to be found living in the "poor" South, and most especially in East and Southeast Asia and in Latin America.

Now of course the simple bipolarities of the 1960s were not strictly empirically accurate even then. That is, even in the 1960s it was possible to find rich or better-off people all over the South and to find poor people (especially poor immigrant non-European people) all over the North. But—how shall we put it?—these exceptions to the bipolar stereotype

8. UNDP, *Human Development Report 1996, An Overview,* p. 4.

were not significant enough, not on a sufficient scale, to call the stereotype itself into serious question.

But what does all this have to do with the decline in the concept of imperialism and the rise in the popularity of globalization, especially in the last ten or so years? Well, calling the world economy economically imperialist was both easier, and more convincing I believe, as long as the world could be seen as essentially bipolar. It was persuasive, that is to say, as long as the most significant "fracture line" in that economy was seen to run between "Northern" or "First World" exploiters on the one hand and "Southern" or "Third World" exploited on the other. For this simple bipolarity—this simple spatial or regional fracture—made it easy to see the dominant form of exploitation and oppression as essentially spatially and culturally bipolar too. That is, it was possible to build on the simple bipolar forms of inequality in the world a simple bipolar theory of "imperialist exploitation." In this theory the world economy, dominated by the rich countries of the North, continually operated so as to "pillage" resources from the underdeveloped South, and to transfer them or pump them to the already developed North. And thus it was—or so said this theory—that the latter became ever richer and the former ever poorer.[9]

Now the popular and influential theories of imperialist exploitation in the world system that emerged in the 1960s and 1970s (and which are often associated with the "neo-Marxist" or "dependency" school of writing on underdevelopment so fashionable and influential between about 1960 and 1980) varied considerably in their economic and theoretical sophistication and plausibility.[10] But the point was that whatever their theoretical or logical coherence, they often seemed persuasive because they seemed to explain what needed to be explained. That is, they purported

9. For some classical examples of this kind of bipolar theorizing, see A. G. Frank, *Capitalism and Underdevelopment in Latin America* (New York: Monthly Review Press, 1967); Rodney, *How Europe Underdeveloped Africa*; and Galeano, *Open Veins*. In addition, a lot of the work of Samir Amin tends to be of this type. For an overview and critique, see Sheila Smith, "Class Analysis Versus World System: A Critique of Samir Amin's Typology of Development," in *Neo-Marxist Theories of Development*, ed. P. Limqueco and B. McFarlane (London: Croom Helm, 1983), 73–86.

10. For some of the many critiques of dependency thinking, see my *Development and Underdevelopment*, 157–76, and also Warren, *Imperialism*, chap. 7. For two more recent useful overviews, see also David Harrison, *The Sociology of Modernization and Development* (London: Unwin Hyman, 1988), chaps. 3 and 4, and Robert A. Packenham, *The Dependency Movement: Scholarship and Politics in Development Studies* (Cambridge: Harvard University Press, 1992).

to explain why the world was so sharply divided between rich and poor, why that divide had been so long-lived (some theorists traced it back as far as the sixteenth century, others even as far as the fourteenth), and why, despite all liberal development efforts, this gap seemed to grow inexorably wider.

### The End of Bipolarity and the Waning of Imperialism

Now readers might think that, in the latter respect at least, nothing much has changed. For we have just quoted the 1996 *Human Development Report* as saying that between 1960 and 1993 the per capita income gap "between the industrial and developing world tripled" from $5,700 in 1960 to $15,400 in 1993.[11] But in fact, in the very same period in which both the annual *World Development Reports* and *Human Development Reports* showed an ever widening gap between the average per capita incomes of the industrialized countries as a whole and the developing countries as a whole, they also found it necessary to create a new statistical category called (variously) "middle-income developing countries," "more developed countries," or "medium human development countries" to accommodate the ever growing differentiation of economic and social conditions *within* (what used to be called) the "Third World" or "the South." Thus for example the UNDP's category of "medium human development" countries currently encompasses fifty-one countries in the world, which together contain nearly 900 million people and have an average GDP per capita nearly three times that of the countries in the UNDP's "low human development group" (of forty-six countries, thirty-six of which are in Africa).[12]

Now of course it is possible to develop simple bipolar theories of exploitation to take account of this ever more complex socioeconomic

11. More recent data show that the gap continued to grow, albeit rather more slowly— from U.S.$13,520 in 1980 to U.S.$18,295 in 1997—i.e., by over 35 percent over these eighteen years. *Human Development Report 1999*, appendix table 6. In all these comparisons *per capita* GNP or GDP figures for the last year of the comparison are always deflated to those for the base year of the comparison. In this case, therefore, what is being said is that in 1960 the gap was U.S.$5,700 and in 1993 it was U.S.$15,400 *measured in "1960" dollars*, namely, an almost threefold increase in real terms. Were one to compare *per capita* income figures in 1960 with those in 1993 using a "1993" dollar figure then of course the gap would be much larger in nominal terms, but given the massive amount of inflation over the intervening period it would not be an even remotely accurate measure of the growth of the real gap.

12. See, for example, UNDP, *Human Development Report 1995*, appendix table 1, p. 156.

differentiation of the world. One of the first of the dependency theorists to do so was the American Immanuel Wallerstein. He argued that the present world system was not, and had never been, made up of a simple rich and exploiting "center" and a poor and exploited "periphery." On the contrary, it had always been characterized by a rich and exploiting center exploiting a poor periphery with the aid of a half-exploited and half-exploiting "semiperiphery" of countries and regions. This semiperiphery helped—and helps—in the process of siphoning resources from the poor to the rich and is rewarded by receiving a (comparatively small) share of the economic surplus involved. The semiperiphery also performs the important political function of keeping the world system stable by acting as a "buffer" between rich and poor.[13]

Whether this development of the simple bipolar theory of imperialist exploitation is either theoretically or logically plausible when closely examined is not a question I want to go into here. Whatever one might decide about that, the truth is that all theories of exploitation lose a great deal of their moral and political force once they cease to be bipolar—once they can no longer identify unambiguously a single class of exploiters to morally and politically "boo" as it were, and a single class of exploited to "cheer." In fact the very notion of exploitation is *grammatically* bipolar, simply because its most commonly encountered form is a simple transitive sentence—"X exploits Y." So, for that very reason any concept of exploitation has great difficulty accommodating social or economic relationships that are not bipolar. "X-exploits-Y-through-the-mediation-of-Z-who-plays-the-role- of-exploiter-in-relation-to-Y-but-of-the-exploited-in-relation-to-X" does not have the rhetorical force of "X exploits Y." More importantly, at least from a political point of view, it does not fit easily into a Manichaean worldview.

But in any case developing the theory of imperialist exploitation to make it spatially *multi*polar only deals with half of the problem posed by the current complexity of inequality in a globalizing world. Because to do justice to that complexity we need to be able to explain not only why India (for example) has a per capita income of $1230 (compared with the developed-country average of $15,324) but why, *within* India, the top 20 percent of households have an income share five times that of the lowest 20 percent. We need to explain not only why China has a per capita

13. I. Wallerstein, *The Capitalist World Economy* (Cambridge: Cambridge University Press, 1979), especially chap. 5.

income 50 percent higher than India (one of the factors leading the UNDP to categorize it as—unlike India—a country of "medium" rather than "low" human development), but why, *within* China, the top 20 percent of households have an income share six and a half times that of the lowest 20 percent, and so on.

In an article published nearly twenty years ago now, I argued that Marxist or neo-Marxist work on the world economy would be greatly benefited if the category of "imperialism" was dropped altogether, and an attempt made to develop a unified theory of capitalist development and capitalist exploitation to be applied to both developed and underdeveloped societies.[14] Although my views about many things have changed since I published that article, I nonetheless think that it continues to have some merit. One of its greatest merits, oddly enough, is that adopting its recommendations would tend to focus—or rather refocus—Marxist or radical analyses of the world squarely on *class divisions,* both in the world as a whole and in different societies around the world. That is, it would have to take as its first organizing protocol the characterization of economic exploitation as something that some *people* do to other *people.* Exploitation, that is, is not something that a country or nation does to another country or nation. It is not something that one culture does to another culture. It is not something that one region does to another region. Or rather, if we choose to speak in these ways (of "countries" or "states" exploiting other "countries" or "states," of one "culture" exploiting another, of one "region" exploiting another), then at best what we are doing is speaking in rather inexact or vague ways about the exploitation of people by people. Moreover, we are speaking in ways that, being inexact, are likely to lead us to confusions about who is doing what to whom, confusions that can have rather important (and damaging) political consequences. And that being the case there is probably both analytical and political merit in dropping these inexact ways of speaking and writing altogether.

### Politics and Intellectual Fashion

It would be wrong, however, to pretend that the explanatory inadequacies of the theory of imperialism are the only reasons for the disappearance or

---

14. G. Kitching, "The Marxist Theory of Imperialism and the Historical Study of Underdevelopment," in *Middle Eastern Research and Information Project (MERIP),* February 1980, 36–42.

marginalization of this terminology over the last decade. Other more directly political factors are also involved. The most important of these is undoubtedly the collapse of communism as a significant political system, many of the theorists, thinkers, politicians, and political activists, both in the Third World and outside, who thought that imperialism was the central problem of the world, also thought that socialism was the answer to that problem.[15] But as the severe economic and political limitations of "actually existing" socialism were dramatically revealed,[16] so even those who remained convinced that imperialism was still the problem, became unsure what the solution was, or if, indeed, there was any solution at all. Hence these kind of radical analyses of the world system lost certainty and direction and their voices became muted to the point of silence, leaving a large ideological space for advocates (and critics) of "globalization" to fill.

However, and oddly enough, I am not sure that this political factor in the decline of "imperialism" is as important as the more purely intellectual problems with the idea to which I have given more attention. The reason for this is that, as a matter of fact, not all those who condemned "capitalist" or "Western" imperialism and its effects *were* committed to socialism as an alternative. Many at least of the Third World intellectuals and politicians who engaged in this condemnation were in fact more nationalist than socialist in their economic policy beliefs and prescriptions. That is, their alternative to "imperialism" was not socialist revolution (national or international) but "national" economic development. Such "national" development was conceived as requiring either the delinking of their countries' economies entirely from the Western dominated world system or (and far more commonly in practice) at least reducing the level or scale of their involvement in that system.[17] But in general terms, this nationalist

15. See, for example, Clive Thomas, *Dependency and Transformation* (New York: Monthly Review Press, 1973).

16. It is still my view that the best single account of those problems is to be found in Alec Nove's *Economics of Feasible Socialism* (London: Unwin Hyman, 1983) and *Economics of Feasible Socialism Revisited* (London: Unwin Hyman, 1991).

17. Perhaps the classic case here is the "dependency" analysis of the Brazilian intellectual Henrique Cardoso (best known to Anglophone intellectuals as the joint author, with Enzo Faleto, of *Dependency and Development in Latin America,* but in fact the author of a large number of works on dependency in Portuguese, Spanish, and English—see the bibliography in Packenham, *Dependency Movement,* 324–25) for whom the "nationalist" project of creating a rich and socially equable Brazil was always more important than any specifically socialist objective. And this is no doubt why, as finance minister and then president of Brazil, it has not been too difficult for him to drop all dependency nostrums and

alternative to imperialism (ISI most notably) has fared no better than socialism—no better, that is, as an alternative to global capitalism—over the last twenty to thirty years. So these radical nationalist versions of anti-imperialism have become as uncertain and muted in political discourse as the more overtly socialist or Marxist versions. And the consequent retreat of both has left yet more space for the new terminology and discourse of globalization to take over the world.

### A Change in Weltanschauung and Its Implications: The Examples of TNCs and International Investment

In the second part of this book, I presented transnational or multinational corporations and transnational flows of capital as two of the most important characteristics of globalization. But in a lot of radical books on development published even ten years ago they would have figured, equally prominently, as two of the most important dimensions or characteristics of "Western" or "capitalist" imperialism. For TNCs were just as unpopular then as they are now, but instead of being described as the leading force in the globalization of a capitalist economy, they would have been seen as the leading force in Western imperialist domination of the rest of the world, and in particular of the Third World.[18] And as for foreign direct investment—a lot of it carried out by TNCs as we have already seen—this would just have been seen as another imperialist mechanism for exploiting the people and resources of the Third World for the benefit of the West.

Now when things are put that way one might be tempted to conclude that all that has really happened here is a change of terminology consequent upon a change of intellectual and political fashion—that really nothing has changed here except a few words ("globalization" and its derivatives having been substituted for "imperialism" and its derivatives).

---

pursue an avowedly neoliberal economic agenda. The essentially nationalist economic and social objectives remain untouched. Only the choice of means has changed—rather radically! (See, for example, *Human Development Report 1996*, p. 44, in which Cardoso supplies an inset article titled "Humanizing growth—through equity," in which equity objectives are explicitly argued to be enhanced by certain aspects of the neoliberal economic agenda.)

18. For some classical examples, see E. Mandel, *Late Capitalism* (London: New Left Books, 1975); J. Halliday and G. McCormack, *Japanese Imperialism Today: Co-prosperity in Greater East Asia* (Harmondsworth: Penguin, 1973); and H. Radice, ed., *International Firms and Modern Imperialism* (Harmondsworth: Penguin, 1975), not to mention virtually all the dependency literature of the 1960s, 1970s, and 1980s.

But once again things are not quite that simple. Once again, as I have stressed several times in this book, what we have here is actually a change in preferred terminology taking place *as part of* a change in a broader reality.

Let us take the subject of international investment first. Here it is important, historically speaking, to remember that in the nineteenth century (and indeed right up to the First World War) the bulk of Western investment in the non-European world was overwhelmingly indirect or portfolio investment ("stock" investment). This investment occurred mainly in the building of railways and other forms of transport and communications infrastructure—ports, docks, electric telegraph lines, and so forth.

Thus, and as has often been noted by historians of European colonialism, the average European colonial territory in Africa or Asia (and even the average nineteenth-century Latin American ex-colony) typically had a railway system radiating out, like spokes of a wheel, from a capital town or city. This capital city in turn was either a port city or (if the colony or ex-colony happened to be landlocked) a transshipment center for a port located in an adjacent colony or country. And the point of this "spoke" system of transportation was very simple. It acted both as an exit conduit for raw materials (whether from plantations, mines, or oilfields) going to the "mother country" and as an entrance conduit for manufactured goods (both producer and consumer goods) coming from the "mother country." In other words, the communications systems built by foreign portfolio investment in the nineteenth century were a direct physical expression of the bipolar economic structure created by European imperialism across a large part of the non-European world.[19] Up to the First World War then, and indeed beyond, Western investment in the non-European world created and sustained a structurally and conceptually simple system of domination, at once economic and political, which we can properly call imperialist. In this period international investment outside Europe was, unproblematically, a tool of imperialist domination.

Let us now turn to TNCs/MNCs and the "direct" ("share," not "stock") investment in the non-European world with which they have been associated over most of this century. Here the crucial point is that up until the 1960s the bulk of TNC activity in the non-European world (and indeed the bulk of foreign direct investment in Africa, Asia, and Latin America) was *also* in what economists call "primary production activities" rather

19. For a good overview, see Hobsbawm, *Age of Empire*, 62–65.

than in any form of manufacturing.[20] In that sense it was "of a piece," in terms of its economic function, with the infrastructure portfolio investment that had preceded it and which had indeed made it possible. In fact investment in the non-European world by Western trans- or multinational firms began in the late nineteenth century and was for a long time almost entirely concentrated in areas such as the plantation production of rubber, oil seeds, fruit, tea, and coffee, as well as in petroleum production. (Companies such as Standard Oil and Royal Dutch Shell, the United Fruit Company, Unilever, Dunlop, and Brook Bond were among the pioneers here.)[21] So that, out of a century of TNC activity in the non-European world (say 1895 to 1995), manufacturing industry hardly figured for the first sixty or seventy years.[22] However, manufacturing activity, both as a proportion of TNC output and as a proportion of TNC controlled direct investment, has *grown very rapidly* since the 1960s, and by the late 1980s accounted for more than half of all Western TNC investment in the non-European world.[23] And with this rapid expansion of manufacturing activity came also a very rapid increase in both the number and variety of foreign firms operating in non-European areas of the globe, with manufacturing multinationals often bringing in their train finance and service multinational companies as well.

In short then, and in retrospect, we can see the 1960s as representing a historical "fracture line" in MNC/TNC activity in the non-European world. Before that decade the pattern of multinational activity and investment was broadly consonant with the imperialist picture of the world as divided between the industrial exploiters and the raw-material-producing exploited. After that decade, however, TNC activity and investment became an important force *making* the economic structure of the globe gradually more complex, or less bipolar. In particular it was a powerful force in increasing the importance of secondary and tertiary activity (manufacture and services) in the economies of an increasing number of non-European

20. For a good short standard account, see R. Jenkins, *Transnational Corporations and Uneven Development: The Internationalization of Capital and the Third World* (London: Methuen, 1987), chap. 1.

21. Ibid., 5.

22. Latin America, in particular Chile, Argentina, and southern Brazil, represents something of an exception to this generalization. Investment by both U.S. and European manufacturing multinationals actually began in these states before the Second World War. On this, see Jenkins, *Transnational Corporations,* 5. There was also a small amount of investment in India by British manufacturing multinationals in this same period.

23. Ibid., 7–8.

areas and countries. And in the 1970s and 1980s there was a further development in this complexity, as manufacturing industries set up initially as import substitution industries, began to be increasingly successful in generating manufacturing exports. (This was particularly the case in mainland Latin America and in Southeast and East Asia.)[24] This development was important because it made another dent in the imperialist picture of the world economy as one in which Western countries and companies monopolized manufacturing production and trade and the non-European world was consigned to the "under-laborer" role of producing and trading only raw materials. Indeed, in the 1960s, and even 1970s, radical writers in the imperialist tradition could still be found arguing that the emergence of ISI in many areas of the non-European world made no real difference to the essentially bipolar structure of that world. This was so, they argued, because such industries were, and would be, incapable of being export competitive. Thus (or so the argument went) even countries that had an ISI manufacturing base would remain trapped in raw materials exporting, while having to continue to import industrial technology and indeed industrial raw materials and components from the West.[25]

Now it is not that such gloomy prognostications proved entirely false. In fact, they proved almost entirely true for Africa and for small Caribbean or Central American states. It is rather that they proved true for some areas of the non-European world and false for others. Most notably, they proved false for southern Latin America and for Southeast Asia, where as I have already noted, some ISI industries and sectors *did* become export competitive. Indeed they provided a basis for the export oriented industrialization strategies of the 1980s and 1990s.[26] Thus, once again, the world—

24. For data on the rapid expansion of manufactured exports from Southeast Asia since the 1970s, see Dicken, *Global Shift*, 35–40.

25. Arguments of this kind were, for a long time, central to A. G. Frank's continued defense of the relevance of dependency theory. See, for example, his "Dependence Is Dead, Long Live Dependence and the Class Struggle: A Reply to My Critics," *Latin American Perspectives* 1, no. 1 (Spring 1974): 87–106, and also his *Dependent Accumulation and Underdevelopment* (New York: Monthly Review Press, 1979).

26. For some Asian cases studies, see R. Leudde-Neurath, "State Intervention and Export-Oriented Development in South Korea," and R. Wade, "State Intervention and 'Outward-Looking' Development: Neoclassical Theory and Taiwanese Practice," in White, *Developmental States*, 30–67 and 68–113. See also Alice H. Amsden, *Asia's Next Giant: South Korea and Late Industrialization* (New York: Oxford University Press, 1989), and Robert Wade, *Governing the Market: Economic Theory and the Role of Government in East Asian Industrialization* (Princeton: Princeton University Press, 1990).

the globe—became more complex, more differentiated in socioeconomic structure and in global economic role, and the bipolar imperialist picture became harder and harder to sustain as a compelling picture of the world. Moreover, the gap between the imperialist picture and reality grew yet wider in the 1980s, when China and then India moved away from industrialization strategies that had been almost entirely protectionist and internalist in orientation (from the 1950s through the 1970s). During the 1980s both these giant countries became significant exporters of manufactured goods and—especially in the case of China—significant meccas for MNC/ TNC manufacturing and service investment.[27] And finally, from the late 1970s/early 1980s came a development that might have seemed stupefying from the perspective of the 1960s. This was the emergence of TNC/ MNCs with an origin and home base outside the United States, Europe, or Japan—Korean multinationals, Mexican and Brazilian multinationals, and (today) even some Chinese and Indian multinationals.[28] These southern-based MNCs/TNCs are small in number and as yet none can match the asset or sales size of their American or Japanese or European rivals. But they exist (an amazing enough fact in itself when seen from the assumptions of the 1960s) and are both multiplying in number and growing in size individually all the time.

*Conclusions: Language, History, and Politics*

How and why intellectual representations and explanations of the world rise and fall in popularity is one of the most fascinating questions in intellectual history. It is rarely the case, for example, that such representations disappear simply because facts are discovered or emerge in the world they cannot account for. For, as we see in this case, and as is indeed very common, it is possible to make any representation more complex (to add new elements to the picture in effect) in order to take account of these new facts. It is also possible to protect the initial picture by saying that the new facts are not really new, or that they are not really significant, or (indeed)

27. In 1994 foreign investment in China was equal to nearly 18 percent of its GDP. Dicken, *Global Shift*, table 2.10, p. 48. See also Dicken's chapter 9 (on the global textile and clothing industry) and chapter 11 (on the electronics industries).

28. Sanjaya Lall, *The New Multinationals: The Spread of Third World Enterprises* (Chichester: John Wiley and Sons, 1983), and Louis T. Wells Jr., *Third World Multinationals: The Rise of Foreign Investment from Developing Countries* (Cambridge: MIT Press, 1983).

that they are not facts at all.[29] But it is equally clear, both from the case we are considering here, and from intellectual history generally, that at some point these tactics or strategies no longer seem convincing, even to those who have been employing them. That is, the gap between a preferred picture and what it purports to represent becomes so large that none of these tactics seem adequate to bridge it or account for it. At this point, as historians of ideas also stress, it is rather rare for defenders of the old representation to make any high-profile public recantation of their previous views or theories. Rather, they simply fall silent.[30] And at that point, and in that silence, there is space for purveyors of new pictures, new explanations, to make their voices heard more and more loudly. And in social sciences in particular there is not infrequently a further twist. For having fallen silent for a minimally decent period, purveyors of the old pictures and explanations often "reappear," are "reborn," as purveyors of the new picture or even as critics of the new picture (but using nonetheless the new vocabulary—of "globalization" in this case—rather than the old).

So readers may think then that the globalization picture of the world economy has largely replaced the imperialism picture of the world economy (even among people who consider themselves on the left) for one of two reasons. The imperialist picture, one may think, was most plausible as a simple bipolar picture, and just became less and less *intellectually* convincing as the forms of differentiation and unevenness in the world economy became too complex to be accommodated to that bipolar structure. On the other hand, one may think that the intellectual collapse of imperialism was due as much to more directly *political* factors (the end of communism for example) as to these more purely intellectual reasons.

However, even entertaining the notion that there is a "choice" of different explanations here would be to demonstrate a complete misunderstanding of the argument I am trying to develop both in this chapter and in this book as a whole. Asking whether the discourse of imperialism has ended, or become unfashionable, for "intellectual" or for "political" reasons is to ask a question based precisely in the traditional or commonsense view of

29. I suppose the first modern writer, and certainly the most influential writer, to make these kinds of insights central to his philosophy of science was Thomas Kuhn in his *The Structure of Scientific Revolutions* (Chicago: University of Chicago Press, 1962), especially chaps. 4–8.

30. H. Stretton, *The Political Sciences: General Principles of Selection in Social Science and History* (London: Routledge and Kegan Paul, 1972), is rather good on this for the social sciences.

the relationship between language and the world which it is the central aim of this entire book to challenge. For in both cases it is being assumed that the discourse (the language) of imperialism has gone out of fashion *because* something called "the real world" has changed. In this conception the only real debate is about which aspects of this "real-world" change— its economic or political aspects—were more important in "causing" the change of language. But on the contrary, I am arguing that the replacement of the language of imperialism by the language of globalization, the rise to significance of manufacturing exports for some parts of the non-European world, *and* the collapse of Russian and East European communism are all just different *aspects* of a single process—a process we can quite properly call *globalization.* Or (to put it in other words) they are all just different aspects of what we "see" when we look at the same process from—as we say—different perspectives. (And which, for shorthand, we call "intellectual," "linguistic," "economic," "political," etc.). In my preferred vocabulary, *all* these phenomena are just different *aspects* of the development of *a single global capitalist economy.* For the development of this economy has a myriad linguistic, economic, political, cultural, and psychological aspects, all and each of which are always and everywhere uneven in their incidence.[31]

So, in short, rather than saying that it was changes in the real world economy that "caused" the language of imperialism to be replaced by the language of globalization, I want to say that the phrase "changes in the real world economy" has, *as part of its meaning,* a change in the language used to describe that economy. Ultimately the reason for this is that in acting *en masse* to bring about the process we call a change in the world

31. Formulated in this way the argument is reasonably clear I think. But there is yet another confusion or misunderstanding to which it can lead. For I can be interpreted as saying that the development of something called a single global capitalist economy *caused* all these other things—linguistic change, collapse of communism, greater global spread of manufacturing, and so forth—but that is *not* what I am saying. Rather, as I hope the immediately following paragraph in the text makes clear, I am saying that these more specific things are just different *parts* or *aspects* of a more general phenomenon that we can characterize, roughly, as the development of a single global capitalist economy. And if I am asked what *did* cause that—the development of this global economy—my answer would be "the highly varied activities of millions of people." Actually, I increasingly think that the use of causal vocabulary in the study of human society should be avoided all together on the grounds that it causes (!) more confusion than clarity about how such societies work and change. However, these are complex philosophical issues the in-depth discussion of which certainly does not belong in this book.

economy, and *as part of* that acting, human beings also change the language that (variously) accompanies, describes, justifies, and criticizes that action. If one wanted to use the language of causality at all here, one would have to say that a change in language use is both caused by changes in (non-linguistic) action, and is itself, in turn, a cause of further changes in (non-linguistic) action. And one would also have to say that this "causally dialectical" relationship between linguistic and nonlinguistic action is itself always a part of any process of structural economic and social change.

One final point. In saying that we are now in a globalizing world capitalist economy, rather than in an imperialist economy, I am not of course claiming that we have moved, in the last thirty or so years, from a world of exploitation and inequality to a world of mutualism and equality. Of course not. As I have stressed over and over again, by some criteria at least, the world can be said to be markedly *more* unequal now than it was thirty years ago. It is rather that the *patterns* of inequality and differentiation in the world have become markedly more complex than they were thirty years ago. We might say that we have moved from a world in which virtually all the economic winners were in one part of the globe and virtually all the losers in another, to a world in which winners and losers are to be found everywhere around the globe, even if there are still bigger concentrations of winners (and of losers) in particular parts of the globe.

The implication of all this is not only that essentially bipolar exploitation theories are no longer adequate to describe or explain the workings of global capitalism. It is also that it now makes more sense to go about describing and explaining inequality in (say) China in essentially the same way (using more or less the same concepts and process logics) as you would go about describing and explaining inequality in (say) the United States. That is, what we now need is a way of explaining both how the global capitalist system works as a single system *and* the varied inequality outcomes it has in different parts of that system. But the point is that it *is* a single system ("capitalism"), globalizing itself rapidly. And just because it is globalizing rapidly it is understandable, now, in an essentially unitary way rather than as two systems ("Western" capitalism and "non-Western" imperialism) to be understood in more-or-less bifurcated ways.

So yes, we *are* all now in the same boat. But the accommodations on the boat range all the way from the most sumptuous of first-class cabins to the most fetid of steerage bunks. In addition there are also people (many of them in Africa) whom we have to conceive as either having missed the boat entirely or (perhaps) as being dragged in its wake on homemade rafts. And (to push the analogy to its absolute limit) if I am advocating renaming the boat the *HMS Global Capitalism* rather than the *HMS Imperialism,* I am neither claiming that all the passengers are equal nor, in any way, denying the reality of certain forms of exploitation of the steerage passengers by those in first class. Rather I am claiming (to abandon the analogy) that capitalism is not an economic system that can be endlessly monopolized by one ethnic or cultural group of the world's population, or by one geographical region of the globe. And thus the "imperialist" view of the world, which suggested that it could or might be so endlessly monopolized, was simply misrepresenting a contingent feature of the history of capitalism as a sort of essential cultural attribute of the system. Capitalism as an economic system, one might say, can be mastered by *any* group of human beings on this planet who are prepared to be as ruthless (usually with their fellow citizens), as organized, as determined, as its processes of accumulation require. In that sense capitalism has not merely no nationality, it has no (one) essential culture, no (one) essential ethnicity, and no (one) essential geographical location either.

# CHAPTER TWELVE

# The Psychological Dimensions
# of Globalization

In the previous chapter I observed that the language of globalization has, in the last ten years or so, largely replaced the language of imperialism as the dominant way of describing and analyzing world-level economic relations, even on the left. I also argued, much more contentiously, that this replacement is justified. It is justified, not because the world has become a markedly more equal place socioeconomically in the last thirty or so years, but because global patterns of differentiation and inequality have become too complex for the simple conceptual bipolarities of imperialist discourse to explain. I went on to suggest that it is now more illuminating for us to think of the world as a single global capitalist system that functions as a single system, but has markedly varied distributional consequences in different parts of the world. However, these different consequences are themselves, or so I argued, understandable in terms of a single set of fundamental determinants impacting in differently weighted ways in different institutional and cultural environments.

However, I should be wary, and everyone should be wary, of passing off ethnocentrism as apparent universalism. Who is the "us" for whom it is more illuminating to think in this essentially unitary way about the world? One possible answer is "Westerners" or "Western scholars." This is a possible answer because my characterization of imperialist discourse as now outmoded—as made outmoded by changes in global capitalism (or perhaps more accurately by changes *toward* a genuinely global capitalism)—

could itself be accused of being psychologically and culturally ethnocentric, whatever its narrowly economic merits.

The argument here would be that the appeal of imperialist discourse to masses of people throughout the non-European world (and not just to orthodoxly, or even unorthodoxly "leftist" people) has never been based primarily in economics or sociology, but in psychology and culture. That is, its primary political appeal in the non-European world is not based and has never been based, primarily on the explanatory or descriptive adequacy of imperialism as a way of characterizing global *economic* relations, but on its felt appropriateness as a way of expressing what we might call a profound *historico-cultural* insight. And what is that insight? It is the insight that for the last (it is difficult to be precise, but let us say) four hundred years or so the people of the non-European world have had to live a history of which they are not—or at any rate do not feel themselves to be—the prime movers. Or to put it another way, they have felt themselves to be living a history in which their role is only or mainly *reactive* rather than active.

It is possible, for example, to argue endlessly over the question of the precise economic importance of the African slave trade or of Latin American silver in the "primary" or "primitive" accumulation of capital (as Marx called it) in Europe. But whatever one might conclude about the economics of the matter, it is hardly to be disputed that the transatlantic trade in African slaves and the mining of Potosi silver by Native American serfs, represent *violent incursions* into the history of the indigenous peoples of Africa and Central America. Nor is it possible to deny that it was a violent incursion that took the personal, social, and cultural fate of the people affected out of their own hands and placed it in the hands of people largely indifferent to anything save their own enrichment.

Or again, it is possible to argue endlessly over whether or not Britain (as an economic accounting entity) made a profit out of India (as an economic accounting entity) during the Raj.[1] But whatever one might conclude about that, it is hardly to be disputed that throughout the Raj the indigenous peoples of India were forced to adjust to patterns of economic, social, and cultural change of which the British rulers (rather than those indigenous people) were the prime instigators. Of course the degree and type of historical disturbance wrought by European impact upon the peoples of the world varied enormously both from one area of the non-European world to another and from one historical period to another. Indeed that

---

1. For an excellent assessment of this debate, see Kiernan, "Development."

disturbance could vary from more or less deliberate policies of cultural and physical genocide at one extreme (the Caribs and Arawaks of the Caribbean, the aboriginal people of Tasmania) to the creation or importation of "European-style" schooling or health services at another. But whatever the form of the disturbance it was always felt as *intrusion,* at worst a culturally and physically destructive intrusion of the most violent kind, at best a possibly well motivated paternalistic intrusion of a developmental sort (schools, roads, health services) that nonetheless always had important social and cultural implications for the indigenous people. And again, whether the colonialists fully understood or intended those implications or not, and however indigenous people assessed those implications (either at the time or subsequently), they were always seen, and still are seen, as the consequences of "the Other's" actions, intentions, and initiatives. That is, such incursions are always seen, and surely rightly, as patterns of events to which indigenous people had to adjust as best they could, rather than products of their activity and history.

If this is the aspect of imperialism that seems most truthful, most profound, then one can also see the supposed change from imperialism to globalization as no change at all. Because again, however one assesses the contemporary economic or welfare impact of TNC activity and investment in any part of the non-European world, the fact is that it is a Western initiative, instigated for Western reasons, to which non-European peoples (be they workers for such TNCs or local entrepreneurs/capitalists trying to compete with them) have to react/respond as best they may. Similarly, whether or not one holds that Indian people viewing Rupert Murdoch's "Star TV" or reading one or other of the News Corporation's magazines are being profoundly psychologically and culturally affected by Western "cultural imperialism," the fact is that they are being affected by global forms of mass media created outside the Indian cultural context and being globalized for reasons entirely to do with the profit imperatives of News Corporation and similar companies, rather than for any reason or purpose to do with India. So once again then, Western individuals and institutions initiate and Indian (or Chinese or Malaysian or Indonesian) people must respond to those initiatives as best they can. Once again they appear as appended to the (in this case) communications history of the cultural "Other," rather than making their own.

So then, anyone who takes this sort of view of things is likely to say *either* that there has been no change from imperialism to globalization— that imperialism remains, in this respect, as valid a way of understanding the world now as it has been for the past four hundred years. Or if they are inclined to be more linguistically permissive, they might say that one can talk about "globalization" or "the global system" if you want, but that this global system remains as much a Western show as it was when we called it imperialism. But either way they will be inclined to see historical continuities in fundamental patterns of world cultural relations that transcend any more narrowly economic discontinuities that others (like myself) might wish to identify over the last thirty or so years.

So what might we (what might I?) reply to this sort of view? I will say that it is a generally powerful and convincing view of matters, but that there are, nonetheless, questions that one might ask about it. Perhaps the most fundamental of these questions concerns the conceptual contrast that always underlies this sort of view—the contrast between an "indigenous" or "authentic" history and a culturally "alien" or "inauthentic" history imposed on it. Because this sort of view always postulates—always *has* to postulate—that there was an authentic or indigenous Inca history going on before the Spanish conquerors disrupted it; that there was an authentic or indigenous Indian history going on before the British conquerors disrupted it; that there was an authentic or indigenous African history going on before the British, French, Portuguese, Germans, Belgians, disrupted it, and so forth. Perhaps this assumption seems no more than commonsensical. But it becomes rather less so if found in conjunction (as it nearly always is) with another assumption, that the future to which this authentic history was leading was a *better* future than the future to which the imperialist imposition actually did lead. That the people who lived in the Inca empire would have had a better future if that empire had continued than they actually had under the Spanish; that the people who lived in the various preconquest states and societies of the Indian subcontinent would have had a better future if those states and societies had continued unconquered, than the future they actually had under the British Raj; that the peoples who lived in the various states and societies of preconquest Africa would have had a better future if these states and societies had continued unconquered than they did under colonialism.

What can one say about this assumption? Well, one can say that it seems pretty well justified in *one* context—any context in which European colonial conquest led to the total or near total *physical extermination* of the people involved. The reason for this of course is that a people who are physically exterminated (like the Caribs or the Tasmanians or—in fact— the majority of the Inca and Maya peoples of Central America) have (had), by definition, no future. So it is difficult to see how any future that they faced untouched by Europeans *could* have been worse.

However, in any situation short of this genocidal extreme the matter becomes much murkier. As I remarked in *Development and Underdevelopment in Historical Perspective,* in any situation short of genocide, we are dealing in effect with questions of *hypothetical history.* What would have happened to all the different peoples of the Indian subcontinent if they had not been conquered by the British? What would have happened to all the peoples of Africa if there had been no European slave trade and no European colonial conquest? What would have happened to the peoples of Indochina if there had been no French conquest? And surely the only intellectually honest answer to any of these questions is (variously) "Who knows? who can say? it is impossible to say." Hypothetical history is, by definition, history *that never happened,* and so, logically speaking, it is impossible to compare it with history that did happen, so as to judge it better or worse.

But—and this is very interesting—it may not *seem* that this is the case. It may seem, that is to say, that one could answer these sorts of unanswerable questions if one adds one further assumption to the argument. This is the culturalist assumption that Indian history untouched by British (or other European) conquest would have been a "better" history *just because* it would have been culturally indigenous or authentic; that African history untouched by European impacts of any sort would have been "better" history *just because* it would have been culturally indigenous or authentic; that Vietnamese history untouched by French conquest would have been a "better" history *just because* it would have been culturally indigenous or authentic. In other words then, this view says that, in effect, any history that the peoples of the Indian subcontinent had made for themselves between (say) 1750 and 1947 would have been "better" than the history they did have just because—for the simple reason that—they (rather than the British) would have made it.[2]

2. This sort of assumption seems to me central to most of the Indian "subaltern studies" literature. See, for example, the debate over the merits of that literature which took place in the journal *Comparative Studies in Society and History* in the early 1990s, and which tended to focus on just this issue. See Gyan Prakash, "Writing Post-Orientalist Histories of the Third World: Perspectives from Indian Historiography," *Comparative Studies in Society and History* 32 (1990): 383–408; Rosalind O'Hanlon and David Washbrook, "After Orientalism: Culture, Criticism and Politics in the Third World," ibid., 34:141–67; and Gyan Prakash, "Can the Subaltern Ride? A Reply to O'Hanlon and Washbrook," ibid., 34:168–84.

Well now what are we (no, what am I) to make of this culturalist assumption, this further culturalist step in the argument? Well, I would first note that it is indeed a "culturalist" argument in very strong sense indeed. That is to say, it places a very strong weight on cultural similarity or membership in a single cultural community as a sort of principle of ethical judgment. It says, in effect, that if there is a landlord who exploits a peasant or peasants, if there is a merchant who cheats her customers, if there is a man who beats his wife, if there is a ruler who squanders her subjects' taxes, if there is an employer who abuses his employees, then such things are bad, but that they are nonetheless "better" (morally better) if the landlord shares a culture with the peasants, the merchants with her customers, the man with his wife, the ruler with her subjects, the employer with the employees, than if the same relations pertain and in addition each of these pairs is made up of culturally different people.

I do not, on the face of it, find such an argument convincing. An exploitative landlord, a corrupt ruler, an abusive husband, an oppressive capitalist employer, are such, I want to say, whether or not they share a cultural/linguistic/religious identity with those they variously abuse or not. And if I find what they do morally opprobrious or politically enraging, then I find it so regardless of the cultural or linguistic identity of the actors involved. In fact I can think of only one further assumption that might give this argument even a reasonable amount of plausibility. And that is an empirical rather than cultural assumption. It is the assumption that *in fact*—empirically—landlords who share a cultural identity with their peasants, rulers who share a cultural identity with their subjects, employers who share a cultural identity with their employees, and so on, are less likely to be abusive in these various ways than are culturally alien landlords, rulers, employers, and so on.

If this latter assumption were true—factually true—it would strengthen the culturalist argument, and strengthen it quite considerably. Unfortunately, however, I do not think that it *is* true. Or rather, the reasonably large swathe of world history with which I am familiar does not suggest to me that such a view can hold even as a predominant generalization, although it might hold in some cases. That is to say, while cases can be found of foreign oppressors who were, at any rate arguably, worse than the indigenous oppressors they replaced (the Spanish in Central America would be such a case),[3] there seem to be just as many, if not more, cases

---

3. Although even here the judgment of a Solomon is required to make a decision.

where the foreign conquerors—precisely because they felt their rule to be in some sense culturally illegitimate—were actually, or at any rate arguably, less oppressive than the indigenous oppressors they replaced (the British in India vis-à-vis the Moghuls might be such a case). The history of Africa, on the other hand, is deeply ambiguous in this regard. But there is at least as much evidence from African history that could be brought forward to support the "indigenous rulers more oppressive" opinion, as could be brought forth for the opposite point of view.[4] Certainly when we turn to the contemporary world it would be difficult to argue, at least as a generalization, that the contemporary indigenous rulers of Africa, or Indonesia, or Latin America, or the indigenous capitalists of these regions are, *as a rule,* less oppressive or exploitative either than the colonial rulers they replaced or than the "foreign" TNC/MNCs, which also employ local people.

In short then, I cannot accept the "indigenous-is-better-just-because-it-*is*-indigenous" *conceptual* argument, and there does not seem to be enough evidence to support the "indigenous-is-actually (*factually*)-better" argument either, at least as a universal, transcultural, or transhistorical generalization. Indeed such arguments seem to me to be nothing more than thin rationalizations of an attitude very aptly expressed in the oft-heard sentiment "he may be a bastard but at least he's *our* bastard."[5] Such

Compare, for example, the account of the Spanish conquest of Central America in, say, Galeano's *Open Veins* with the account in chapters 7, 8, and 20 of Landes's *Wealth and Poverty.*

4. See, for example, the long-running and bitter debate among historians of Africa over the causes and consequences of the Atlantic slave trade. The literature is huge but the most important contributions are probably J. D. Fage, "Slavery and the Slave Trade in the Context of West African History," *Journal of African History* 10, no. 3 (1969): 393–404; Philip D. Curtin, *The Atlantic Slave Trade: A Census* (Madison: University of Wisconsin Press, 1969); Walter Rodney, "African Slavery and Other Forms of Oppression in the Upper Guinea Coast," *Journal of African History* 7, no. 3 (1966): 431–43, and chap. 4, 103–12, of his *How Europe Underdeveloped Africa;* and Philip Manning, "Notes Toward a Theory of Ideology in Historical Writing on Modern Africa," *Canadian Journal of African Studies* 8, no. 2 (1974): 235–53. An excellent collection of the leading pieces on the African slave trade and its impact on Africa is H. A. Gemery and Jan S. Hogendorn, eds., *The Uncommon Market: Essays on the Economic History of the Atlantic Slave Trade* (New York: Academic Press, 1979).

5. In this context I remember being in Nairobi in the early 1970s, at a time when Idi Amin had just become the ruler of neighboring Uganda. I was shocked to find that Amin had attained something of a hero status among many "left" students and teachers at the University of Nairobi because of his supposedly "radical" actions in expelling Asians from the country and "nationalizing" their economic assets. Amin's (mercifully brief) hero

a sentiment does not, in fact, excuse (morally speaking) the bastardy of the bastard, it rather includes him in an identity universe ("us"—"our" bastard) and exalts him insofar as he is part of that universe and for no other reason. But though I understand such sentiments (and have occasionally felt and expressed them myself), they still do not intellectually persuade me that bastards are not bastards simply because they are "our" bastards. And if I interpret this expression aright, it is not meant to intellectually persuade me, or anybody else, of such a truth. Rather, its function is expressive—to express an identity and (thus) a loyalty. Insofar as we all—all human beings—have identities and loyalties, such expression is fair enough. Only it is not an *argument* for anything.

So if I am not impressed by any or all of the arguments that might justify a view of indigenous history (even hypothetical history) as *always* better for the indigenes than a history imposed by culturally alien imperialists—then why did I say earlier that I found the culturalist concept of imperialism "powerful and convincing"? I said it because what seems to me "powerful and convincing" is simply the notion that for four hundred years or so the majority of people on this planet have had to live a history imposed upon them (to varying, but always significant degrees) by a minority—a minority we normally refer to as culturally "Western" or "European." I think this general observation is factually correct and that it is so irrespective of what we might or might not be able to say about hypothetical alternatives to this imperialist state of affairs, which state of affairs I also agree still exists in all essentials. And just because I think that this factual generalization is true—obviously true—I also agree with the aspiration that flows from it among so many non-European people. This is the aspiration to bring about a changed global balance of power in which the making of history is not nearly so culturally partial or one-sided as it has been for the last four hundred years. That is to say, I agree with the aspiration to bring about a situation in which *all* the peoples and cultures of the world contribute, if not equally (perhaps that is impossible), at least a lot more equally than they have done for a good part of the

---

status among African students and intellectuals in Nairobi, however, contrasted markedly with the views held of him by the peasant people of Kenya's Central Province. Here, even in the 1970s, he was still well remembered, by an older generation at least, as one of the colonial government's more brutal interrogators in its counterinsurgency campaign against the protonationalist "Mau-Mau" uprising of the 1950s.

modern period, to the making of global history. And note: endorsing this aspiration—this political goal or objective—does not require, any more than does endorsing the factual generalization from which it flows, believing *any* hypothetical stories about what the last four hundred years of history would have been like if such cultural equality had existed then.

### *So Back to Globalization*

Taking the last remarks above particularly into account, we now have a new question to ask about globalization: are there any signs that as capitalism becomes a genuinely global system the world is becoming any less "culturally partial or one-sided" than it has been for the last four hundred years? The first answer to that seems fairly obviously to be no. That is, if the Western imperialist period of world history has been marked by a pattern in which Western societies and cultures initiate historical change and non-Western societies and cultures are forced to react to that change as best they can, then that pattern seems to be more or less intact. For whether we think of technological changes in the production and distribution of goods and services, or the predominant pattern and flow of capital and money across the world, or human-induced changes in the physical and communications landscape of the planet (urbanization, infrastructure development), or the direction and flow of all kinds of electronic media and communications, we see essentially the same pattern now as a hundred or even two hundred years ago—namely, the West initiates and the non-Western world responds.

It is true that there have been occasional important inputs into modern culture from the non-European world. (The tremendous influence of the Afro-American musical tradition on U.S. popular music and thus on global popular musical culture comes immediately to mind, as indeed do other—albeit rather less important—contributions to global music from other non-European parts of the world.) Indeed music and dance, along with food and drink, are perhaps the most successful transcultural human artifacts, in the sense that they are the artifacts that seem most readily to permeate across human cultural differences. But apart from this and some significant inputs of the non-European world into global fine art culture—of painting, sculpture, architecture (inputs embracing the entire non-European world)—any observer must readily admit, I think, that Western hegemony over what one might call the socioeconomic fundamentals of the modern world (and thus, in effect over the culture of modernity itself) is as marked now as it has ever been.

So a first answer to the question is no. A second answer, however, based on a somewhat closer look at the historical evidence, suggests, not that the answer is yes, but that the meaning of the no we gave above may be open to further interpretation. For the meaning of the no answer depends heavily, if we think about it, on what we mean by "West" and "Western" or (alternatively) by "European." Both these terms appear prominently in all "global" talk and writing and indeed in all "international relations" talk and writing. But when we look more closely at their use, whether in talk or writing about history or about the contemporary world, we see some complex patterns of change and disjunction which the very generality of the terms themselves can serve to obscure. Here are some important examples of these disjunctures and changes.

The concept of "Western" or "European" dominance of the world tends to run together (as one "thing" as it were) such historically varied phenomena as the Portuguese and Spanish empires of the fifteenth and sixteenth centuries, the Dutch empire of the seventeenth century, the British and French formal empires of the eighteenth and nineteenth centuries, and the U.S. informal empire of the twentieth century. But it should be remembered that for a large part of modern European history the British and Dutch were on one side and the Spanish, French, and Portuguese on the other side of an enormous religious and cultural divide in Europe (the Catholic/Protestant divide) which led to numerous wars. In addition, all these Western imperialist powers saw themselves as rivals (often bitter rivals) and not allies in the conquest of the non-European world and its resources. "Small" wars between European countries over imperialist squabbles were commonplace from the sixteenth to the nineteenth centuries, and many historians, like many contemporary observers, still refer to the First World War as an "imperialist" war—a war whose roots lay in intra-European imperialist rivalries (especially the rivalry between Britain and Germany).

An overgeneralized notion of "Western" culture can obscure the extent to which "non-Westerners" have had an important input into the making of that culture. I have already mentioned the importance of Afro-American influences on American popular culture (and especially musical culture), but similar remarks could now be made about the influence of Hispanic (mainly Latin American) people in the United States, of Afro-Caribbean people in the United Kingdom, and of people of African origin

in France. But above all this equation of historical and contemporary capitalist domination of modern world history with "Western" domination
has to ignore, and to assiduously ignore (as I indeed have done to this
point) one massively discrepant example—Japan. For Japan, one might
say, breaks all the rules of conventional anti-imperialist discourse. That is
to say, it is most clearly not a Western nation or culture by any criterion.
It is now one of the most successful and powerful capitalist economies
in the world (usually ranked second after the United States by most
observers, but some would put it first, certainly by some narrow economic
criteria), and to a considerable degree it has succeeded in keeping its own
cultural and historical fate in its own hands, rather than having that fate
dictated by Western economic and cultural hegemony. But note that while
it is true that Japan is all these exceptional things and has done all these
exceptional things, this exceptionalism is not reflected in global and especially "global non-European" perceptions of the world. That is to say,
although when a Latin American, or African or Indian or Middle Eastern
person is reminded of this Japanese exceptionalism, they will of course
acknowledge it, they still have to be reminded of it. It hardly springs spontaneously to mind. And why? Because despite Japan's enormous wealth
and the genuinely global power and range of its famous transnational
corporations, it never figures, or hardly figures, certainly in comparison
with the United States, in global popular perceptions of the cultural and
geographical location of power in the world. And if one asks, in turn,
why that is, there is I think no single answer, but rather a combination of
answers. These include, that Japan, because of the terms of the peace
treaty with the Allies which ended the war in Asia, does not possess a
global military capacity to match its economic strength. This in turn tends
to mean that Japan's diplomatic role in the world also fails to match its
economic strength. But in addition, and perhaps more important, at least
since the failure of its own imperialist efforts in China and Korea in the
1930s, Japan's political leadership seems to have reverted to the view that
playing an essentially supporting role to the United States in global economic, diplomatic, and military management is the price she has to pay
for maintaining a significant degree of economic and cultural autonomy
in a Western-dominated world. So, in short, Japanese exceptionalism
makes little or no dent in perceptions of "Western imperialism" or of
Western domination of global capitalism because since the end of the Second World War at any rate, Japan has fallen into an almost invisible support role behind that domination. This support role, which is particularly

vital economically,[6] is seen by the rulers of Japan as the necessary price she must pay to maintain a genuine cultural autonomy from the West. If one wanted to be particularly provocative, one might say that since 1945 Japan has almost become an honorary Western nation, at least economically speaking! So perhaps this might lead us to conclude, that Japanese exceptionalism is really no exceptionalism at all. Japan is the one non-Western country and culture that managed to avoid the fate that befell most others. But if it has not (yet) fallen under Western cultural domination, this is only because it was astonishingly successful in adopting and developing the capitalist mode of production pioneered by the West to "fend off," as it were, Western economic domination. In addition, since Japan's defeat in the Second World War, it has used its economic success at least as much for the benefit of the West (and especially for the benefit of the United States) as for its own people.

However, I think that the conclusion that Japanese exceptionalism is really no exceptionalism at all is simply incorrect. I contend that what Japanese exceptionalism absolutely and unequivocally demonstrates is that capitalism is not a culturally Western form of the organization of economy and society in any essential sense. That is, to put it more simply, the example of Japan absolutely and unequivocally demonstrates that human beings do not have to be Western to be "good" at capitalism. That capitalism historically developed in the cultural West and spread around the world (in the form, initially, of imperialism) from that Western epicenter is simply a contingent historical fact. This in turn means that there is no essential cultural reason (note: no cultural reason) why other non-European peoples cannot, or could not in the future, do what the Japanese have done.[7]

6. Just how vital is powerfully argued in Thurow, *Future of Capitalism*, chap. 10. In sum, the exchange value of the U.S. dollar would be much lower than it currently is (with, almost certainly, immensely disruptive implications for world trade), were it not for the Central Bank of Japan acting, in effect, as a second Federal Reserve in its support. That is, through its continual support for the dollar, Japan uses its massive trade surpluses as much in the defense of the standard of living of Americans as it does for the benefit of its own people. Thurow explains very well why it chooses to do so.

7. It is possible to argue that the culture of Japan was, somehow, uniquely fitted to the development of capitalism, just as it is possible to argue, now, that the cultures of the "Tiger" economies of East Asia are so uniquely fitted. The problem, however, is to say *what* it is about these cultures that so uniquely fits them for capitalist development, and unfortunately, the one thing that scholars are apt to pick on in this context—the so-called Confucian tradition or heritage—happens to be what, in earlier days, was picked on to explain

This also implies that recapturing control over one's own culture and people, even partially, has, as its necessary price, the development of capitalism. That is, the paradox of a globalizing world is (as the Japanese ruling class perceived, with astonishing farsightedness more than a century ago)[8] is that the price of any kind of cultural autonomy within it is a whole-hearted economic identification with it. In a word, the price of even relative cultural autonomy in a world of capitalism is the development of capitalism.

Nevertheless, there is, now, some doubt that even the Japanese solution to the riddle of "cultural imperialism" is adoptable by other non-European societies and cultures. The reason for this is that for a variety of contingent historical reasons, Japan was able to develop a form of national capitalism that maximized its export role in the world economy (most especially of course in the export of manufactured goods) while minimizing its import role as a consumer of Western manufactured or cultural goods (through various forms of economic and cultural protectionism).[9] But this is a very lopsided form of involvement in the global capitalist system. Moreover, it

---

the cultural roots of Asian underdevelopment or backwardness! Compare, for example, Ron Dore, *Taking Japan Seriously: A Confucian Perspective on Leading Economic Issues* (Stanford: Stanford University Press, 1987), with the classical pieces by Max Weber, "The Social Psychology of the World Religions" and "The Chinese Literati," chapters 11 and 27 of H. H. Gerth and C. Wright Mills, eds., *From Max Weber: Essays in Sociology* (London: Routledge and Kegan Paul, 1970), 267–301 and 416–44. One should be aware in this context of how easy it is to write *post hoc* narrative accounts of what has occurred, which make it sound, retrospectively, as if what has happened was what somehow *had* to happen, could not help but happen. But in the end of course, what makes such accounts convincing is just the simple fact that what they purport to explain is what (in fact) happened. This can make us forget that a historical event or set of events having occurred is not in fact a *proof* of the correctness of any explanation of those events if there is (as there always is in the case of human history) more than one explanation that could be offered of that occurrence or set of occurrences. This is my one major intellectual reservation about the explanations of both the "wealth" and the "poverty" of nations found in Landes's monumental work, *The Wealth and Poverty of Nations*. His wonderful book does seem to provide powerful explanations of both why the world's presently wealthy nations are wealthy and why the world's presently poor nations are poor, but undoubtedly part of that persuasive power derives from the fact that he is "explaining" what one already knows to be the case even before one has read his "explanations."

8. For just one of many accounts of the Meiji restoration and the thinking behind it, see Moore, *Social Origins,* 243–54.

9. On this, see, for example, R. Storry, *A History of Modern Japan* (Harmondsworth: Penguin, 1968), especially chap. 7.

is a form or type of involvement that is having considerable economic costs for Japan now[10] and which is unlikely to be available to other non-European countries and peoples (given a world of global free trade enforced by the West) in the future.

## Conclusions

When one looks closely at the whole notion of capitalism and imperialism as a culturally Western phenomena, one sees a whole variety of empirical complexities and disjunctions both at the Western end (intra-Western cultural differences) and at the non-Western end (the exceptional case of Japan's role in global capitalism). These complexities seem to me to be reducible to one important observation. This is that the economic and political epicenter of capitalism has continually shifted historically both within the West (from Portugal to Spain to Holland to France to Britain to the United States) and then—at least in part—outside the West entirely (to Japan). There is therefore no reason, in logic, why it cannot shift again in the next hundred or two hundred years to any other part of the globe, Western or non-Western. Of course, that this is a logical possibility does not mean that it will happen. What is logically possible may be impeded by political, military, economic or other means. But if it does not happen— if the epicenter of global capitalism does not move again, and to some part of the non-Western world—it will either be because it has been deliberately impeded or because non-European peoples and cultures of the world fail, for one reason or another, to make it happen. It will *not* be because capitalism is somehow, of its essence, always and forever linked—like some Siamese twin—to Western or occidental forms of society and culture.

And one final point. On the basis of reflection on the first of our observations one might be led to ask the question, is the West one culture or several? I hope that it is now clear that the answer to this question depends entirely on one's perspective. That is, looking at seventeenth-century England as a seventeenth-century Spaniard, one would be likely to see massive cultural differences. However, through the eyes of a seventeenth-century Chinese or Japanese or Arab, Spain and England might have been seen as "basically" similar.

And what applies historically also applies to the contemporary world. That is, an English migrant who settles in the United States may find it

10. See, for example, Thurow, *Future of Capitalism*, 203–10.

culturally quite strange, while a Taiwanese visitor to both countries may see little difference (after all they both speak English!). Throughout European history most Europeans have been far more aware of the differences among them (often extreme and quite often leading to war) than of their cultural commonalities. A migrant African worker, however, may be more struck by what all Europeans have in common than by what divides them.[11] (And think, on the other hand, of European stereotypes of "Africans" or "Asians" applied to people whose only commonality perhaps is that they *are* stamped with the same stereotype.)

So, the question, is the global capitalist system Western? or is imperialism Western? is a question, it must be stressed, with no absolute answer. But the answer, from the point of view of most non-European people it certainly is! is perfectly proper. Indeed, it may be the "right" answer—from their point of view.

And yet even this answer generates one more paradox. For if I (a European) write what I have just written above, then am I (a European) adopting—or at any rate endorsing—a point of view that I have just characterized as non-European? But in that case in what sense is this non-European answer actually "non-European"? Or rather what does it *mean*—what can it *mean*—to characterize such an answer as "non-European"? Perhaps this question is most instructive if it is posed, and left, as a genuine question to be answered by the reader. So I leave it as such.

11. For some contemporary insights on this matter, see some of the e-mail exchanges at the web site of the European Africa Center for Success and Self-Reliance at www.africasuccess.com.

❧

# CHAPTER THIRTEEN

# Industrialization and Historical Compulsion

*Introduction: More Thoughts on Imperialism*

In the previous chapter I suggested that the lasting truth the notion of imperialism expressed for non-European people was the sense that for the last four hundred years or so they have had to live a history—or live in a history—whose most fundamental parameters were laid down for them by Europeans or Westerners. And as a result of this, I said, they had experienced their own history over that period as essentially reactive rather than active, as something done to them, rather than made by them. Moreover, this sense of being the objects rather than the active subjects of global history continues to this day. For many non-European people, therefore, not only does the notion of "Western imperialism" still retain meaning and importance, but the anti-imperialist struggle (understood, at bottom, as the struggle to retake control of their own history, their own fate) is also still very much alive, even in, perhaps especially in, this new period of globalization.

Although in the previous chapter I offered some qualifications of this continuing "Western imperialist" view of the global capitalist system (to do, mostly, with the curious role of Japan in that system), these qualifications did not lead me to deny the basic truth about the modern history of the world contained in it—that that history has been, broadly, a history of Western dominance or hegemony over the rest of the world. However, at this point I do want, not so much to deny that truth, as to *reconceptualize* it in a certain way, that is, to set it in a still broader context in which it will perhaps appear as a somewhat different truth, or as having a somewhat different meaning or significance, from that given it in orthodox anti-imperialist discourse.

For there is a question which one can ask not merely about modern history, and not merely about modern global history, but about all history, ancient and modern, parochial or global. It is this. Is the making of history *ever* democratic? Or perhaps more exactly, has the making of structural historical *change* ever been a democratic process anywhere on the surface of this globe? That is to say, can we find any example in human history of major economic, social, or political change occurring as a result of a consensual process of democratic agreement? Or, on the contrary, have such changes always been imposed on majorities by powerful minorities of one sort or another? Because if the answer to the latter question is that, in fact, structural change is *always* imposed or enforced (so far as the majority of people affected by it are concerned), then the last four hundred years of Western imperialist global history are not anomalous or extraordinary, in this regard at least. On the contrary, they are merely of a piece with human history as a whole.

Actually I am convinced that this is so. I am convinced that, for example, the creation of all the empires of the ancient world (from the Greek to the Roman to the Inca to the Chinese) were experienced as impositions by those conquered in their creation, just as much as the creation of any modern empire (British, French, Dutch, Spanish, German) was so experienced. And it is not merely the creation of political empires that are testimony to this. The ancient Egyptian, Inca, Chinese, and Roman rulers altered the physical landscape around them by the enforced mobilization and brutalization of millions and millions of slaves and serfs, as did the medieval builders of feudal castles, cathedrals, and temples all over Europe and in Japan. There is scarcely a major architectural feature or set of features (town- or cityscape) created on this planet between the beginning of recorded human history and (say) the nineteenth century that was *not* the product of coerced mass labor of some form—including every one of those features (from Roman aqua- and viaducts, to Egyptian pyramids, to ancient Chinese temples) now revered by cultural historians and "culture-vulture" tourists around the world. And even that is not all there is to it. In Eurasia, Africa, and large parts of preconquest North and South America, societies of hunter-gatherers were often forcibly dispossessed of their land by nomadic pastoralists, who, in their turn, were forcibly dispossessed by sedentary agriculturalists. Sometimes (often) this dispossession went along with enforced cultural incorporation of the preexisting societies into new social and economic forms; always it was accompanied by some amount of killing and forcible expulsion.[1]

So then, if the modern period of human history (say from the sixteenth century to the present) is to be distinguished from an earlier period it is *not* the brutal facts of conquest or imposition that distinguish it, or even the facts of what we would now call "cultural imperialism." (Slaves in the ancient and early modern period often had their culture—religion, language—forcibly altered by their masters, certainly over a period of several generations.[2] The imposition of pastoral nomadism on hunter-gatherer peoples was often a cultural as much as—what we moderns would call—an "economic" imposition. It affected language, marriage, and kinship patterns as much as it affected ways of utilizing natural resources.) Rather it is, or so I would argue, the *extent, variety, and speed of the coerced or imposed change* that distinguishes the modern period of world history from its ancient and medieval predecessors.

There is nothing new in modern human history in the brutal facts of imposition and conquest. Rather, it is the geographical and demographic scale of this imposition and conquest that is new, together with the variety and speed of change imposed on the peoples so conquered or dominated.

But why were the subjects of modern empires required to adapt to far more change than the subjects of ancient empires or the people of the medieval or early modern world? Quite simply, they were required to do so because modern empires (including in this term the U.S. informal empire of the twentieth century) were the creation of *industrial capitalist*

1. For preconquest Latin America, see Landes, *Wealth and Poverty,* chap. 7. For Africa, see S. Marks and A. Atmore, eds., *Economy and Society in Pre-Industrial South Africa* (London: Longman, 1980), especially chaps. 1–4, and I. N. Kimambo and A. J. Temu, eds., *A History of Tanzania* (Nairobi: East African Publishing House, 1969), chaps. 1 and 2. For Eurasia, see J. Blum, *Lord and Peasant in Russia: From the Ninth to the Nineteenth Century* (Princeton: Princeton University Press, 1961), especially chaps. 2 and 4.

2. For the ancient world, see G.E.M. de St. Croix, *The Class Struggle in the Ancient Greek World* (London: Duckworth, 1981), chap. 3, pt. 4; chap. 4, pt. 3; and chap. 7, pt. 2. See also M. I. Finlay, *The Ancient Economy* (London: Chatto and Windus, 1973), chap. 3. For the cultural effects of modern slavery, see, among a mass of possible references, Eugene D. Genovese, *Roll Jordan Roll: The World the Slaves Made* (New York: Random House, 1974), and Giberto Freyre, *The Masters and the Slaves: A Study in the Development of Brazilian Civilization* (New York: Knopf, 1956), especially chaps. 4 and 5.

states and societies. Therefore, they imposed such changes on the peoples and territories they dominated as were required by the capitalist economy and society of the mother country. Such changes generally did not include the creation of industrial capitalism in the conquered territories, but they did include such changes in those territories as the introduction of those types of *food or raw materials production* as could find a market in the mother country; the introduction of *transport and other modern means of communication* required to facilitate such production; and the introduction or deliberate encouragement of forms *of material consumption* by the colonized peoples that could be supplied by the industries of the mother country.[3] These latter could involve everything from changed forms of food, clothing, and domestic utensils—to provide demand for mother country light industry—to steam engines, electrification equipment, and road construction machinery—to provide demand for mother country heavy industry.

The really important point, however, is that in these as in some other respects, the experience of capitalist imperialism was closely analogous to the experience of capitalism "at home," in the mother country. That is, the experience of the creation of an industrial capitalist economic system itself, at first in Britain, and then in the rest of Europe (including of course in the home countries of other European imperialist states—France, Germany, Belgium, Holland, Italy) was itself just as socially and psychologically traumatic—perhaps, by some criteria, more traumatic—than its imperialist extension to the rest of the world.

## Capitalism and Industrial Revolution

The broad parameters of structural economic and social change brought about by the process of industrialization in Europe, North America, and Japan are well enough known and have been rehearsed by scores of historians. They include the destruction, more or less rapidly, of peasant agriculture; rapid and unplanned urbanization with all the social and

3. On this, see, among a mass of possible references, Hobsbawm, *Industry and Empire,* especially chaps. 7 and 9; my *Class and Economic Change in Kenya: The Making of an African Petite-Bourgeoisie* (London: Yale University Press, 1980), chaps. 6–8; and R. D. Wolff, *The Economics of Colonialism* (New Haven: Yale University Press, 1974), especially chap. 1; A. Maddison, *Class Structure and Economic Growth: India and Pakistan Since the Moghuls* (London: Allen and Unwin, 1971), chap. 3; and M. Cowen and R. Shenton, *Doctrines of Development* (London: Routledge, 1996), chaps. 4 and 6.

environmental problems (overcrowding, lack of sanitation or clean water) usually associated with such urban explosions; the imposition of new "time-bound' work disciplines in the rapidly spreading factories; the destruction of various forms of artisan and handicraft production unable to compete with factory output (this destruction bringing with it, in Britain at least, perhaps the most horrific of all the forms of human impoverishment and degradation caused by the industrial revolution); and the use and abuse of child and adult labor, in factories, mines, and elsewhere. The story, to repeat, is a well-known one and one that forces even the most sanguine or optimistic historians of the long-term social benefits of capitalist industrialization to acknowledge its short-term costs.[4]

And yet, though the story itself is well known, it is rare for professional students of the industrial revolution in Britain and Europe to draw a wider, and obvious, implication from it. This is that the story of the industrial revolution in Europe, quite as much as the story of imperialism itself, is a story of historical change initiated by a powerful minority (of landlords, factory owners, political governors, etc.) and suffered by an overwhelming majority. And this European majority (of dispossessed peasants, artisans, new factory workers) had, just as much as their peers in the colonies, to react to changes imposed upon them. They too were forced, often violently, to fit in to a history being made for them from above and being made (at least initially) without any regard for their welfare or well-being.

In fact, there is a further paradox here. For as I remarked in the previous chapter, the central intellectual motif of the history of world capitalism as a history of imperialism is the notion (which I endorsed as profoundly and lastingly true) that, for the imperialized or colonized peoples, imperialism is experienced as a kind of "theft" of history, as the loss of control of one's own destiny to the power of a culturally alien "Other." And yet, if we leave aside certain very spectacular counterexamples (serf mining of

4. For the British experience, E. P. Thompson's *The Making of the English Working Class* (Harmondsworth: Penguin, 1968) is still perhaps the single most important secondary source one can recommend, along with John Hammond and Barbara Hammond, *The Village Labourer* and *The Town Labourer* (London: Longman, 1978), and perhaps John Foster, *Class Struggle and the Industrial Revolution* (London: Methuen, 1974). For France, Eugen Weber's *Peasants into Frenchmen*, is eloquent, and Moore, *Injustice*, has much to say about one area of Germany (the Ruhr). For some of the social consequences of the industrialization of Italy, Gwyn A. Williams, *Proletarian Order: Antonio Gramsci, Factory Councils and the Origins of Communism in Italy, 1911–21* (London: Pluto Press, 1975), is very useful, especially chaps. 1–3. For Russia, Orlando Figes, *A People's Tragedy: The Russian Revolution, 1891–1924* (London: Pimlico, 1996), chap. 3, is a powerful recent account.

precious metals in colonial Latin America, the Atlantic slave trade, the creation of mining capitalism in South Africa), we can say that, in general, European imperialism did not lead to the same intensity of social uprooting of the societies affected as did the capitalist industrial revolution in Europe. By this I mean that, for example, when the British conquered India the majority of the subcontinent's people were peasants; and when the British left, they were still peasants.[5] When the British, French, Portuguese, and Belgians colonized sub-Saharan Africa the majority of its peoples were nomadic or sedentary pastoralists, hunter-gatherers, or peasant producers; and when all these colonial masters left, this was still the case.[6] When the French conquered Indochina, the majority of the people were rice-growing peasant producers; and when they left, this was still the case.[7]

In short, as a whole generation of dependency theorists stressed, the hallmark of European capitalist imperialism is that it generally did *not* lead to the creation of fully fledged industrial capitalist societies in any of its conquered territories.[8] And this implies that whatever forms of social disruption the colonized peoples of the non-European world suffered, they were not (or overwhelmingly not) the classical forms associated with the full-blown development of capitalism—mass urbanization, proletarianization, restructuring of gender and family relations consequent upon urbanization and proletarianization, and so forth.[9]

And yet, and yet, while the sense of having been robbed of a certain historical autonomy remains very much alive throughout the non-European world, it has largely disappeared in the European world itself, even among the descendants of those people who experienced all the traumas and

5. See, for example, E. Stokes, *The Peasant and the Raj: Studies in Agrarian Society and Peasant Rebellion in India* (Cambridge: Cambridge University Press, 1978).

6. Although the demographic proportions among these different rural groups of the population had altered markedly as a result of colonial patterns of agricultural development. On this, see my *Class and Economic Change,* especially chaps. 7 and 11. See also Ken Post, "Peasantization in West Africa," in *African Social Studies: A Radical Reader,* ed. P.C.W. Gutkind and P. Waterman (London: Heinemann, 1977), 241–50.

7. See, for example, E. R. Wolf, *Peasant Wars of the Twentieth Century* (London: Faber and Faber, 1971), chap. 4 (on Vietnam).

8. Samir Amin was perhaps the dependency theorist who was the most insistent on this point. See, for example, his *Unequal Development: Essays on the Social Formations of Peripheral Capitalism* (Hassocks: Harvester, 1976).

9. Which is not to say that there was no restructuring of family or gender relations, but just that the experience of proletarianization was not as central to such restructuring as occurred as it was in nineteenth-century Europe.

upheavals of industrialization. That is to say, the social dislocations and upheavals consequent upon capitalist industrialization have somehow been normalized or naturalized in popular perceptions of European history (including the history of the United States). Even the social dislocations of the "earthquake" period of industrialization have somehow been reclaimed, become somehow non-alien features of a history understood as inclusively "ours" (as just an unfortunate part or episode in the "national" history of Britain, France, Germany, the United States, Italy, etc.). But the social dislocation consequent upon imperial conquest have never been reclaimed, or reclaimable in the same way, in the popular consciousness of the people of the non-European world. And this is despite the fact that, by some criteria at least, those "imperialist" dislocations were socially *less* deep, *less* volcanic, *less* totally destructive of the preexisting economic and social structure than was the experience of capitalist industrialization proper. What explains this paradox?

### Capitalism, Imperialism, and Historical Memory

I know of only two possible candidates for such an explanation. The first candidate—the "culturalist" candidate—in effect denies what I have said above. That is, it claims that the experience of imperialist conquest made up—more than made up—in its *cultural* trauma for what it may have lacked in socioeconomic depth (in comparison with European industrialization). In this conception the central trauma of imperialist conquest (and one which has no parallel in European history, or certainly in modern European history) is precisely *the fact of conquest itself and the cultural humiliation which it imposes.* For modern capitalist imperialism is precisely distinguished from the imperialism of the ancient world in being legitimized, not by the gross fact of superior power itself, but by a claim to cultural superiority.

Thus, the British came to India and Africa, the French came to Africa and Indochina, the Dutch came to the East Indies, not simply as military conquerors. Rather they came, in their own eyes at least, as bearers of a superior culture and civilization to that of (in that ubiquitous colonial expression) "the natives." And hence the aim and objective of their rule was not, or not simply, to exercise the normal imperialist prerogative of pillaging desired resources (humanly created or natural) but to bestow their superior culture and civilization on the benighted locals not possessed of it. In a word, the distinguishing feature of modern European imperialism is that the imperialists regarded themselves as the cultural superiors of those they had conquered and made this apparent in everything they said and did.[10] And hence, on the side of the colonized, the experience of imperialism is necessarily an experience of *humiliation,* in the way that the experience of capitalist industrialization in Europe (however traumatic in other respects) was not. And that is why (on this account) the history of imperialism is never reclaimable by the colonized or the descendants of the colonized in the way that the history of industrialization is reclaimable by the proletarianized or the descendants of the proletarianized.

What are the merits of this argument? There is no doubt that what it states of modern imperialists (that they justified imperialist conquest by claims of cultural superiority) is true, at least from the nineteenth century onward.[11] However, it is also true that the landed aristocrats and factory bourgeoisie who dominated Britain throughout the period of the industrial revolution had a view of their own lower- or working-classes almost indistinguishable from their view of the "natives" and "savages" in their imperial territories. Indeed, when, in the later nineteenth century, a form of social Darwinism was the preferred justifying ideology of the powerful in Britain and Europe, terminology derived from that perspective was applied, with little discrimination, to both cases. That is, the inhabitants of the slums of London or Manchester were perceived as, at best, only a few rungs further up the ladder of evolutionary development from the natives of Africa or Asia.[12] In short, contempt for inferiors was as much a

10. This is the aspect of imperialism most insistently stressed in the work of Frantz Fanon. See, for example, his *Black Skins, White Masks* (New York: Grove Press, 1967) and above all his *Wretched of the Earth* (Harmondsworth: Penguin, 1967). Such insistence is also a central motif in the more recent and very influential work of Edward W. Said, most notably in his works *Orientalism* (London: Routledge and Kegan Paul, 1978) and *Culture and Imperialism* (London: Vintage, 1994), especially chap. 1 of the latter.

11. The situation before that is somewhat less clear. The Spanish and Portuguese conquests of the fifteenth and sixteenth centuries had an explicitly religious ideology of legitimization, but it is unclear how far this was an ideology of cultural superiority as such. Moreover, the British East India Company, the forerunner of British colonial rule in India, was first formed (in the early seventeenth century) for the purposes of monopolizing trade with a society explicitly considered, by those traders and merchants involved, to be at least the material *superior* of Britain. On this, see, for example, G. Moorhouse, *India Britannica* (London: Harvill Press, 1983), chaps. 1 and 2, and P. Spear, *A History of India* (Harmondsworth: Penguin, 1966), 65–69.

12. On this, see, for example, Weber, *Peasants into Frenchmen,* chap. 1, and Gareth Stedman Jones, *Outcast London: A Study of the Relationship between Classes in Victorian Society* (Oxford: Clarendon Press, 1971), especially chaps. 6, 16, and 18.

part of the weft and warp of capitalist social organization in Europe as it was of imperial domination abroad. In fact, in the British case at least, the same public school boys who had been steeped in contempt for domestic class inferiors at home, experienced little difficulty in transferring the same contempt to their racial and cultural inferiors abroad (in their role as district officers and so forth).[13]

However (and this is vital) contempt and humiliation are not the same thing. That is, the upper classes in any society may regard other social classes with open or thinly disguised contempt, and imperial conquerors may regard those they have conquered in the same way. But as Frantz Fanon brilliantly observed many years ago, to experience *humiliation* those held in contempt must echo that contempt in their own psyche.[14] That is to say, for contempt to be turned into humiliation, those held in contempt must be convinced, or at least half convinced, that the contempt is justified. They must be convinced, or come somehow to convince themselves, that their superiors are indeed superior and that they are rightly considered (and must consider *themselves)* inferior. So, is it perhaps true then that the new working classes of Europe only experienced contempt but not humiliation, while the colonized peoples of the non-European world experienced both?

Quite frankly I do not know how to answer this question in general terms. In fact it seems to me that the answer is probably so varied both from individual to individual (both in Europe and the non-European world) and from one conquered culture to another (in the non-European world) that no general answer can be given. Only one general remark does occur to me. It is that, as Fanon also emphasized, the best psychological antidote to a sense of humiliation is *anger* at the display of contempt by one's putative superiors, along with attempts (individual or collective) to organize *resistance* to it.[15] And in this context we might say that nationalist and protonationalist movements in the colonized world played much

13. On this, Charles Allen, ed., *Plain Tales from the Raj: Images of British India in the Twentieth Century,* with an introduction by Philip Mason (London: Futura, 1976), has much to say, albeit mostly by implication. So too does Philip Woodruff [Philip Mason], *The Men Who Ruled India,* vol. 2, *The Guardians* (London: Jonathan Cape, 1954), especially pt. 1, chap. 4, and pt. 2, chap. 1. David C. Potter, *India's Political Administrators* (Oxford: Clarendon Press, 1986), is also informative in a more modern academic/analytic style.

14. Fanon, *Black Skins, White Masks,* especially 17–40 and 141–49.

15. Fanon expressed this view most famously and notoriously in his essay "On Violence," chapter 1 of his *Wretched of the Earth.*

the same role as did the organization of trade union movements in Europe. They acted, that is to say, as mechanisms by which self-respect and self-esteem could be built among those stigmatized as inferior, as well as being mechanisms by which the colonized could press for particular social or political reforms.[16]

So in sum we can say that this first candidate for the explanation of why imperialist conquest created such enduring resentment in a way that the trauma of capitalist industrialization did not—that it was an experience of unparalleled cultural *humiliation*—does not seem to hold much water. This is not because imperialism was *not* such an experience, but because the experience of class contempt associated with the rise of industrial capitalism was probably just as humiliating, at least for some people in some places. In fact the difference between the one experience and the other is just that in the one case we have contempt and humiliation *that has been forgotten* (at least by the descendants of the humiliated).[17] In the other case, however, we have contempt and humiliation that has not been forgotten, that indeed is perceived as still continuing to this day.

So that allows us to focus the question a little more sharply. *Why*, we may ask, has the class contempt/humiliation of the European industrialization experience been forgotten (or at least largely so) and *why*, on the contrary, does the contempt/humiliation of the imperial experience remain alive as a potent psychological and political force in the world? As it happens, my second candidate for an explanation can answer this more focused question as well as the broader one. For my second answer says, quite simply, that it is the experience of widespread *material prosperity* in Europe and the North that has allowed the violent dislocations and humiliations of capitalist industrialization to be forgotten. Conversely, it is the absence of such prosperity in most of the ex-colonial world which makes

16. In making this remark I am reminded how often nationalist movements and trade union movements have cross-fertilized and interweaved in various ways. Thus colonial nationalist movements often had their roots in trade union movements, and even when they did not, usually organized trade unions as one of their "wings." Also, the case of the Irish in Britain is just one of many European cases in which trade union militancy has provided an outlet for nationalist aspirations or for resistance to discrimination perceived as much in national or ethnic as in class terms. On this latter point, see, for example, Emret O'Connor "A Historiography of Irish Labor," *Labour History Review* 60, pt. 1 (Spring 1995): 21–34.

17. Whether it has been forgotten by the descendants of the contemptuous, I am not quite so sure. As an Englishman of working-class background, meeting Englishmen of upper-class background sometimes makes me wonder.

it impossible for such forgetting to occur. That is to say, the horrors of the capitalist industrialization experience (insofar as these are still remembered or known about), can be seen, by the bulk of Europeans, as the horrendous but necessary price that had to be paid by previous generations for the prosperity of their present-day successors. But lacking such prosperity, the vast majority of the peoples of the postcolonial or postimperialist world cannot view their present or their past in such complacent terms.

In short, feeling oneself to be the object rather than the subject of history, or feeling that one's history has been largely a reaction to changes imposed exogenously or externally (whether that exogeneity be class or cultural) is a feeling that is only oppressive when the outcome of that history is seen to be less than satisfactory. Such a history continues to be felt as oppressive, that is to say, when it cannot be seen to be leading or have led somewhere (to some state of affairs) of which one approves. To put the matter more pungently. If the average Indian today were as materially prosperous as the average Briton today, then perhaps the architectural monuments of the British Raj would be preserved in contemporary India with the same measure of affectionate indifference as the cotton mills or coal mines or ironworks of the industrial revolution are preserved in the social history museums of contemporary Britain. But it is difficult to apply the cheerful realism of "dreadful but necessary cost" to one's reactive history, unless you have a clear sense of what that history was a necessary cost of. And it is far harder to have such a sense in postimperialist India or Africa or Indonesia than in contemporary Italy or Germany or the United States or Britain.

And that is particularly so of course if you are still living in a world in which the formerly imperialist parts of the world are still economically and culturally dominant *and* incomparably richer than your part of the world. For then, as I said in the last chapter, the sense that one's history is being made by others—that one's fate is not in one's own hands, that one's role is only to react to what others initiate—continues in the present. A sense that one is living a reality importantly determined by others is not merely (as it is, or at least appears to be,[18] in the European or Northern case) a matter of history, it is a dominating fact of the present and indeed of the foreseeable future.

---

18. A lot is hidden behind this phrase "appears to be." See the next section of this chapter.

But if this second explanation of the uniqueness of the imperialist humiliation is indeed the correct one—that it is not a humiliation which can be rationalized, and then forgotten, as the necessary cost of a desirable present, but one that, on the contrary, is still seen as a dreadful histori-cal *cause*[19] of an undesirable present—then we have (at least logically) an answer to how its uniqueness may be terminated. It may be—or will be—terminated when the non-European peoples of the world are living a pre-sent they consider desirable.

## Globalizing Capitalism and Its Ironies

So the wound of imperial conquest and domination will heal only when the colonized, or formerly colonized, peoples of the world are living a present they can consider desirable. What kind of present would that be? I think that, given the world in which we live, it can only be a present in which those peoples enjoy a material standard of living they can regard as satisfactory or acceptable. That does not mean (as the case of Japan affirms) that they have to be living in a present which is culturally West-ern. But it does mean that they have to be living a present in which hunger and malnutrition have disappeared, in which infant mortality and life expectancy levels are comparable with those in the richest countries, in which all children and adults have access to a level and type of education also comparable to those in the richest countries, and in which at least the majority of the population possess such consumer durable and nondur-able goods as, within that cultural tradition, are considered necessary and proper for a good life.

19. This is a particular example of what may be a more general phenomenon—the tendency of human beings to treat antecedent history as *causal* only when their present realities are unhappy in some way, but not when their present is regarded as more or less acceptable. In the latter case, however, it is not so much that historical events are *not* treated, in popular consciousness, as causal, as that history simply becomes totally mar-ginalized in that consciousness. In happy, or more or less contented societies, history becomes, that is to say, the concern—or at any rate the serious concern—only of a small band of professional *savants*. The popular concern with history in presently unhappy places (Northern Ireland comes to mind, but so do the Balkans) provides at least some *a priori* support to this hypothesis. Incidentally, this historical amnesia of prosperous capitalist societies has been seized upon in postmodernist writing, where much is made of the space it provides for reinventing history as sentimentalized pastiche. On this, see, for example, David Harvey, *The Condition of Post-Modernity: An Enquiry into the Origins of Cultural Change* (Oxford: Basil Blackwell, 1989), 85–88 and 97.

All this seems to imply, in turn, that the material benefits of capitalism (or such benefits as any particular group of people consider necessary and desirable) should be made available to the entire population of the world. The really important question about globalization therefore (to return to our leading theme) is whether it marks the beginning of a process that may lead to the achievement of such a goal. This is an enormously complex question. For example, I now think that a situation in which "the material benefits of capitalism [are] made available to the entire population of the world" does *not* (or does not necessarily) imply that the entire population of the world has to live in a form of industrial capitalist society comparable to that now existing in North America, the EU, or Japan. Logically at least, it may only require that a part of the world's population (albeit a large part)[20] lives in such forms of society, while the rest of the world lives in somewhat differently structured societies which nonetheless are materially prosperous through the provision of goods and (more especially) services for the industrialized part. However, these are complexities which I cannot go into here. For the moment I only want to focus on one deeply ironical implication of this vision of a genuinely globalized capitalism which could, I have suggested, finally heal the festering wound of imperialism.

I have said that the experience of industrialization, wherever it has occurred, has, quite as much as imperialist conquest itself, been experienced by the vast majority of people who have lived through it as a deeply repugnant, forcing upon them of far-reaching changes in their lives initiated by others. I have said, in effect, that if the central fact of imperial conquest is the theft of one's history by others, then *all* those peoples of the world who have experienced the transition from precapitalism to capitalism have also experienced that theft. And the theft of history that was the forcible creation of industrial capitalism was quite as violently disruptive, in its own way, as the experience of imperial conquest itself. In the former case, however, that theft, and the disruption, has been forgotten and forgiven, because it can be conceptualized as a "necessary cost" of a state of affairs deemed by later generation to be desirable.

However—and vitally—it is *not* the case that once the mass of any people, of any human population, are living in a materially prosperous capitalist societies, control over their history is returned to them by that

---

20. I think that "large part" would, for example, have to include a goodly proportion of the population of India and China.

prosperity. On the contrary, *the permanent price of material prosperity under capitalism is a kind of endemic insecurity*[21]—a sense that at any time that prosperity may be severely compromised or even ended, by factors and forces (as we revealingly say) "beyond our control." Indeed the permanent price, even of maintaining the prosperity an individual or social group or whole society possesses under capitalism, is a permanent willingness to accept and adjust to a continual stream of economic and social changes—changes the vast majority of people rarely if ever willingly initiate or (even) desire.

The founding father of systematic reflection on capitalism—Adam Smith—grasped this "endless insecurity" aspect of capitalism very firmly, and with the insight of one who had personal knowledge of precapitalist forms of human social organization as well as of their disruption by capitalism. Book I of the *Wealth of Nations*[22] begins with a revealing juxtaposition of what he terms the "market society" with a form of village agrarian society (in this case in the Scottish Highlands) untouched, or little touched, by such forces.

In the case of the former—a market society—a growth in the specialized division of labor is simultaneously, Smith says, an "extension of the market." That is to say, in such a society each individual is at once highly productive in his or her specialized economic activity but ever more dependent on market sale and purchase (to and from other individuals at ever greater social and geographical distances) for their material standard of living. In other words, the individual in a market society is ever more economically dependent on a world of social strangers whom s/he does not know and will never know personally, but whose decisions (to buy or sell, to cease buying or selling, to buy or sell to/from others) may affect his/her material welfare profoundly.

On the other hand, the Highland villagers in their precapitalist world enjoy close social and human relations with neighbors on whom, however, they are actually *less* economically dependent than is the specialized

21. Recognition of this fact and examination of its social and psychological implications is an increasingly common theme in both the mass media of advanced capitalist societies (endless magazine articles on problems of "stress" and various nostrums for dealing with same) and in the scholarly sociological literature on those societies. See, for example, and most brilliantly, Marshall Berman, *All that Is Solid Melts into Air: The Experience of Modernity* (London: Verso, 1983).

22. Adam Smith, *The Wealth of Nations, Books I–III* (Harmondsworth: Penguin, 1982), bk. 1, chap. 3.

individual in a market society. They are less dependent because, in the classical peasant village, each individual household strives for the largest possible degree of economic autonomy. Each individual, or rather each individual peasant household, attempts to produce as much as it possibly can of its own means of production and consumption. through its own labor. Of course, in times of scarcity or trouble the precapitalist peasant family may rely heavily on its village kin and neighbors for its very survival. But this does not alter the paradoxical fact—emphasized by Smith— that the precapitalist peasant individual lived in a world of close social relations founded upon an underlying premise of economic autonomy or independence, while the individual in a capitalist or market society lives in a world of much looser (though perhaps more freely chosen) social relations founded upon an underlying premise of intense and uncontrollable economic dependence.[23]

Generalizing beyond Smith's original insight, we might say that, under capitalism, individuals gain a kind of social freedom at the price of a sort of economic captivity to that which they can only understand abstractly (in abstraction)—as "market forces." They can only understand or describe that captivity abstractly or in abstractions ("'A sharp rise in oil prices threatens a down turn in world trade growth with damaging implications for employment and incomes' says today's *Wall Street Journal*") precisely because the pattern of human economic activity in a market context is too demographically massive and too individually and socially diverse to be understood in any personal or concrete way. Conversely, the precapitalist individual lives in a world in which, far from needing to deal in abstractions, their economic prosperity is in the most concrete and personal sense "in their own hands." But the price of this economic independence is a kind of social bondage to (generally unchosen) village and kin relations.

23. This "ideal type" juxtaposition was to become a feature of a whole mass of nineteenth-century writings on the themes of industrialization and modernization, including, famously, Sir Henry Maine's *Ancient Law: Its Connection with the Early History of Society and Its Relation to Modern Ideas* (London: John Murray, 1906) and Ferdinand Tönnies, *Community and Society* (East Lansing: Michigan State University Press, 1957). It was also a powerful theme in the so-called populist and neopopulist literature of nineteenth-century Russia. On the latter, see A. Walicki, *The Controversy over Capitalism: Studies in the Social Philosophy of the Russian Populists* (London: Oxford University Press, 1969), especially chap. 2, and chapter 2 of my *Development and Underdevelopment*.

## The Ultimate Irony Located

Thus, if a globalizing capitalism finally replaces the simple bipolarities of an imperialist world economy, and even if "in the end" (whatever that means) it were to produce a generalized material prosperity for this entire planet's population of human beings, it would not—*not*—thereby create a world in which the colonized or formerly colonized peoples of the globe had gained, or regained, control of their own destiny. On the contrary, it would only have expanded to its planetary limits an economic system whose predominant characteristic is that, within it, everybody's (individual economic) destiny depends on everybody else's. And another way of putting that—an equally accurate way—is to say that the price of exiting the imperialist world, in which one's destiny is controlled by cultural strangers, is to enter a capitalist world in which one's destiny is controlled by everybody and nobody. Thus, if the British are ruling India and there is a major famine, it is right and proper to blame the British for that. But if all Indian people are living in a world of global capitalism and they experience some meltdown in the value of their currency as a result of global speculative movements out of the rupee, it makes equal sense, in such a context, to blame "ourselves," "the speculators," the "Indian Central Bank," "the IMF"—anyone, everyone, no one.[24]

But, and to repeat, whomever they might choose to blame in such a context, in a world of globalized capitalism Indians will not—*not*—have moved from a situation in which their destiny was in the hands of others to one in which their destiny is in their own hands. They will only have

---

24. There is actually a sense in which the concept of blame, and the very activity of blaming, becomes radically misplaced in this sort of context. One might say that precisely because capitalism is a system, its systematic functioning (and malfunctioning) cannot meaningfully be blamed on any (specific) body. But I note that it seems to be almost impossible for human beings (even those who have lived within capitalist societies for many generations) to accept this—especially, of course, in cases of severe systemic malfunction (depressions, recessions, etc.). But even when the system is functioning well, this is rarely understood in systemic terms. Thus when my business is booming, this is because of "my" entrepreneurial skills. But when it has gone bankrupt in a recession, this is because of "those bastard big boys" or "the bank" or "the government." In either case (success or failure, booms or recessions) "the system" does not figure in popular or participant causal accounts. The reason for this is perhaps that to give up all notions of blame is to give up all notions of control or responsibility, and that we live in a system whose very principle of functioning almost completely attenuates such notions (of control or responsibility) is perhaps the one fact about capitalism that we all—all human beings—cannot face.

moved from a situation in which their destiny was in the hands of a single known Other to one in which it is in the hands of a countless unknowable Others (including rich and powerful *Indian* Others). But (and this may be important) in the latter situation the Indian people would simply be on a par, as it were, with all other peoples of the world. For capitalism is democratic in a way imperialism can never be. Under imperialism, that is to say, the formal situation at least[25] is that the imperialists are powerful and control the destinies of others and the colonized are powerless and have their destinies controlled. Under a truly globalized capitalism, however (which I must emphasize we do not have yet and are a long way from having still), there is a sense in which all would be equally powerful and all equally powerless. And that may actually be a great deal more acceptable situation to all human beings, including Indians. Moreover, if my arguments above are right, it would be particularly acceptable—indeed hardly noticed—if it were accompanied by genuinely global economic prosperity. Certainly in the West or in Japan, to live a permanently insecure and economically dependent life now, as a citizen of a prosperous capitalist society, seems, somehow, to be a great deal more acceptable than it was when the ancestors of the presently prosperous experienced the same insecurity and dependence accompanied by the horrors of industrialization and proletarianization.

25. This qualification is important. In any real situation of imperialism the imperialists are never all-powerful and the conquered or colonized are never utterly powerless. Indeed, in all kinds of subtle ways the imperialists may be as culturally influenced by those over whom they rule as the latter are by the rulers.

However, certainly at high periods of nationalist resistance to imperialism it is rarely politik to draw attention to these complexities, and even after formal independence has been gained there may still be a great deal of emotional or psychological comfort to be got, at least for the formerly colonized, from portraying the history of imperialism in "hapless victim" terms.

PART FIVE

❧

*Globalization and
the Nation-State*

# CHAPTER FOURTEEN

# Nationalism
# and Capitalism

The subject of nationalism is a particularly fraught one in the study of human society. There is little agreement among scholars about how and when nationalism originated, about its relationship to the (equally difficult) phenomenon of human ethnicity, and even about how the term itself should be defined or understood.[1]

However, it is not my aim here to go into this complex issue (about what nationalism "is"). Rather, I want to make things easier for myself by restricting this chapter to a discussion of the relationship between nationalism and capitalism. This discussion is necessary as a prerequisite of my coming to deal—in the last part of this book—with the "overwhelming question" to which the entire text has been tending—the question of the role and future of the nation-state in a world of globalized capitalism. In examining, in this chapter, the conceptual fundamentals that underlie this question, I shall *not* be assuming or arguing (as some scholars have) that nationalism is itself a product of capitalism. Rather, I am simply going to argue that, whatever its origins, nationalism has enjoyed a close relationship

---

1. Some outstanding contributions to these debates include E. J. Hobsbawm, *Nations and Nationalism Since 1780: Programme, Myth, Reality* (Cambridge: Cambridge University Press, 1992); E. Gellner, *Nations and Nationalism* (Oxford: Basil Blackwell, 1983); B. Anderson, *Imagined Communities: Reflections on the Origin and Spread of Nationalism* (London: Verso, 1983); and the voluminous work of A. D. Smith, especially his *Theories of Nationalism* (London: Duckworth, 1971) and his important edited collection, *Ethnicity and Nationalism* (Leiden: E. J. Brill, 1992).

with capitalism since the nineteenth century. In particular nationalism, or at any rate the making of nation-state or nationalist economic policy, has performed two important historical functions in relation to capitalism: (1) it has made *the creation of industrial capitalist economies an object of national policy*, and thus (in effect) made the spatial boundaries of capitalist economies coterminous with the boundaries of nation-states; and (2) it has provided *forms of political influence or control over capitalism*, forms which helped to attenuate the alarming or even terrifying sense (referred to in the previous chapter) that individuals living under capitalism can have of possessing no control over their own destinies.

That is, one of the promises of nationalism, historically speaking, has been to provide a particular form of collective action—action taken by the state in the name of the nation—which can tame capitalism on behalf of the otherwise powerless individual. In this respect then, as in some others, the individual gains power as a member of a politically organized collectivity (the nation-state) that they cannot have alone or even as a member of smaller or more sectional social groupings, such as occupational associations or trade unions.

Now that nation-states have performed these functions vis-à-vis capitalism is something that is hardly disputed by scholars of nationalism, whatever their disagreements over other matters, so neither of the points above is very original or contentious. However, both points attain a new significance if we are now entering a new phase of the development of capitalism—the globalization phase—one of the most marked features of which is the increasing inability of nation-states (or at least of the vast majority of such states) to perform either of these functions any longer. That is, if it is the case that, in its globalization phase, capitalism as an economic system has now simply outgrown the boundaries of even the largest, most populous nation-states, then it becomes increasingly difficult for such states to influence either the general developmental trajectory of that system or to control its social and political effects. But in addition, and perhaps more importantly, this inability then leaves the individual (meaning here both the individual worker and consumer and the individual firm or business enterprise) "alone again"—just a hapless atom or molecule tossed around in a globalized or globalizing economic universe.

If it turns out that this is the case, then we would indeed have an interesting example of history repeating itself, but—as is in fact nearly always the case—in a transformed context which makes it not a simple repetition at all.

## Capitalism and Nationalism in Europe and the North

The creation of the first industrial capitalist economy in the world (in the United Kingdom at the end of the eighteenth and beginning of the nineteenth centuries) was distinguished by the fact that both these features of contemporary globalization applied to that historical case as well. That is, the British industrial revolution was not the planned product of any kind of governmental or state action. Moreover, in its initial, most socially disruptive and destructive phase at least, no attempt was made by the British state to provide any protection (to workers or consumers anyway) from its more pernicious effects on human welfare.

Now this second feature of British industrialization (lack of any kind of state welfare intervention or protection) did not last. That is, from the late nineteenth century onward the British state did move (hesitantly and slowly and with much ideological resistance) into the provision of gradually increasing amounts of consumer protection and social welfare.[2] But its first and unique feature—the "spontaneous" "non-state" character of the initial industrialization process in Britain—did not change. Indeed it could not change (having already happened), and proved subsequently to be an absolutely unique feature. That is, because capitalist industrialization occurred for the first time in world history in Britain it could not, by definition, have been a planned process, whether by the state or any other individual or social body. There was a sense, therefore, in which nobody really knew what was happening in Britain between (say) 1780 and 1840, and this bewilderment comes out very powerfully in contemporary accounts of the British industrial revolution.[3] And there was also a strong sense in which they (contemporaries I mean) experienced it much more as precisely something that was *happening to them* and their society rather than as something that anybody was consciously *doing*.

In fact, while we call these sixty or seventy years the years of the British "industrial revolution," that is of course a description given by hindsight.

2. For two standard accounts of that movement, see M. Bruce, *The Coming of the British Welfare State* (London: Batsford, 1961), and D. Fraser, *The Evolution of the British Welfare State: A History of Social Policy Since the Industrial Revolution* (London: Macmillan, 1974).

3. I think the secondary text that brings this out best is H. Perkin, *The Origins of Modern English Society, 1780–1880* (London: Routledge and Kegan Paul, 1969), especially chaps. 3–5. But perhaps the best single exemplar of this confusion in a primary source is William Cobbett's *Rural Rides* (1830). I have read the Penguin edition of the latter (Harmondsworth, 1981) with an introduction by George Woodcock.

Most contemporaries had no clear sense that Britain was doing something called "industrializing" in this period. They certainly did not have any idea that they were experiencing a set of changes that would prove to be irreversible and lead to the creation of a qualitatively new form of economy and society.[4] Indeed, and very interestingly, all they really had was a clear sense that a number of very rapid and socially disruptive *changes* were taking place. And significantly, they often characterized these changes using language ("gales," "plagues," "tides," "earthquakes," "growths," "cists," "warts") that emphasized precisely their spontaneous and uncontrollable character.[5]

But this, as many economic historians have noted, was indeed a unique feature of the British industrial revolution. Because, albeit to varying degrees, every industrialization experience that has occurred since *has* been a consciously planned project in which the state has played a leading role. That is, it is possible to say of industrialization in France, or in Germany, or in Italy, or (even) in the United States, that it was something that the rulers or governors of those states set out to *do* (and they even called what they were doing "industrialization") rather than something that, as it were, just happened to them. And from the very beginning of industrialization as a planned national project, it is very clear that fear of falling prey to British economic dominance was a prime motivating force behind such state industrialization efforts.[6] That is, once Britain had spontaneously industrialized, the increased economic, military, and indeed diplomatic power that other governments and rulers saw Britain as possessing as a

4. In fact a great many of the earliest "communitarian" experiments with the socialism or communism so scornfully dismissed by Marx and (through him) by posterity as "utopian" were precisely predicated on the notion that such changes might be reversible and some (rather more egalitarian) version of a preindustrial world be created. N. W. Thompson, *The Market and Its Critics: Socialist Political Economy in Nineteenth Century Britain* (London: Routledge, 1988), chaps. 2–4, is very good on this.

5. Despite being mired in the fashionable Althusserian jargon of its time, Keith Tribe, *Land, Labour and Economic Discourse* (London: Routledge and Kegan Paul, 1978), is very good on the crucial changes taking place in economic terminology at this time, see especially his chapters 4–6. For changes in broader social terminology in late eighteenth- and early nineteenth-century Britain, Raymond Williams's *Keywords* is especially useful. See, for example, his entries for "Society" (243–47), "Culture" (76–82), "Nationalist" (178–80), and "Class" (51–59), but the whole book is fascinating.

6. On this, see A. Gershenkron, *Economic Backwardness in Historical Perspective: A Book of Essays* (Cambridge: Belknap Press of Harvard University Press, 1962); Tom Kemp, *Industrialization in Nineteenth Century Europe* (London: Longman, 1969), especially chap. 1; and Landes, *Wealth and Poverty*, chaps. 15 and 16.

result of this industrialization led them, in turn, to seek to do in a planned and conscious way what Britain had done in an unplanned and unconscious fashion. The justification for state involvement in this process (and in particular for state sponsorship of infrastructure projects and state protection of domestic markets) was that without such involvement the industrialization process could not be speeded up, and it needed to be speeded up in order to catch up with Britain as soon as possible, and also that without protectionism in particular new French, American, or German industries would not be able to compete with imports from Britain. Thus Britain would simply expand its role as the only industrialized economy, with everybody else reduced to the role of supplying Britain with food and raw materials forever. It is this kind of argument we hear in Alexander Hamilton's *Report on Manufactures* of 1791 (a founding policy document of American industrialization) and in Friedrich List's *National System of Political Economy* of 1841, a very influential book written by the principal architect of German economic protectionism.[7]

Now the fact that, in Europe and the United States at least, industrialization was undertaken for explicitly nationalist reasons and by explicitly state-nationalist means from the very beginning suggests to many authors that nationalism must, in some sense, predate industrial capitalism. If people like Hamilton or List (or the numerous other French, Italian, or Russian statesmen who visited the wondrous factories and ironworks of nineteenth-century Britain in order to admire and copy) embarked on capitalist industrialization for explicitly nationalist reasons well *before* their own countries were remotely industrialized, then, logically, capitalist industrialization cannot have been a cause of nationalism.

On the other hand, however, writers like Eugen Weber[8] have precisely suggested that it *was* the state-sponsored development of modern communications infrastructure (roads, railways, telegraph), and of a modern mass state education system, as well as the growth of industrial cities and factory labor forces in France which, over the course of the nineteenth century, "turned peasants into Frenchmen." Weber suggests that it was these economic processes which had the social effect of turning a mass of peasant people who had never previously thought of themselves as French at all, and many of whom had not even spoken the language we now call French, into self-conscious, literate, educated French citizens. And one can

7. Kitching, *Development and Underdevelopment,* chap. 6.
8. Weber, *Peasants into Frenchmen,* especially chaps. 12 and 16–18.

find similar accounts of changes in the self-identification of peasants living in the politically organized territory now called Germany or in the one now called Italy as a result of the state-sponsored social and economic modernization of those territories later in the nineteenth century. So all these accounts then suggest that it is nationalism which *follows* industrial modernization, rather than the other way round.

It is possible, however, that these two arguments are not quite as point-blank contradictory as they look. If, for example, national self-consciousness tends to spread from the top down in any and all societies, it would be perfectly possible for there to be upper-class French, or American, or Italian nationalists *before* the industrialization of France, America, or Italy, but only a mass nationalist consciousness in such countries *after* they have industrialized and modernized. And if that is the case, then it is possible to see elite-inspired industrialization and modernization as a state policy to spread national consciousness downward in a society as well as to increase its nation-state economic power. Indeed that is the way many theorists of nationalism (and most especially Ernest Gellner) do see it.[9] Even if that is so, it still leaves open the question of how these preindustrial nationalist elites originated, of how they acquired *their* nationalist outlook. But since that question is rather remote from my concerns here, I shall not even try to address it now. Rather, I now want to turn from the European nationalism of the nineteenth century (and its disputed relationship to the development of industrial capitalism in Europe), to the non-European nationalism of the twentieth century (and its relationship to the spread of industrial capitalism beyond Europe and the North in general).

## *Capitalism and Nationalism in the Non-European World*

In one sense, once we know even a little about the nationalist economic history of Europe, what we see in most of the non-European world since the end of European colonialism there seems very much a repetition of classical patterns. That is to say, whether we look at postcolonial India, or any of the states of postcolonial Africa, or even at China since the Communist takeover of 1949, what we see is a classically nationalist economic pattern. The new nationalist rulers of India, or Pakistan, or Kenya, or Jamaica, or Indonesia, or wherever, almost invariably proclaim that domination and exploitation by the imperial mother country has left their country

9. Gellner, *Nations and Nationalism,* chap. 6.

economically backward and poor, and trapped in the production of a few low-priced primary products or raw materials. They then state that the only way out of this backwardness is industrialization and modernization, and that, in pursuit of this, the newly independent government of [*wherever*] is immediately putting in place a massive program of industrialization and modernization. This program, they further say, will make full use of various forms of economic protectionism, state construction of infrastructure, massive state expansion of education, and various forms of state subsidy to industrial and capital investment.

In other words, seen in historical context, the postindependence speeches and programs of the first generation of Indian, African, or Asian nationalist leaders and rulers seem little more than reruns of the speeches of Alexander Hamilton, or the books and articles of Friedrich List, or the speeches of Count Witte (a leading architect of the beginning of Russian industrialization).

And the same conceptual or causal puzzle therefore arises in the non-European as in the European case. That is, on the one hand the creation of greatly improved transport and communications infrastructure, of mass education systems, of new industrial and service cities, seem to be, in important respects a means to *create* new national identities (the same first generation of nationalist leaders often explicitly called it "nation-building")[10] in place of older tribal, regional, or "particularistic" identities in ex-colonial territories. But, on the other hand, the "new states" (as they used to be called) of the postwar non-European world were created after, and partially as a result of, the emergence of mass movements of nationalist opposition to European imperialism. So again, there were clearly Indian nationalists in India *before* India even started to industrialize or modernize. And there were clearly African nationalists all over Africa *before* the bulk of that continent had made any serious movement out of the economic backwardness associated with European colonialism. Once again, however, it is possible to resolve this apparent contradiction by making a distinction between elite and mass nationalism, a distinction that is as important in the non-European world as it was in the European.[11] In the

10. For a standard account of the ideology of postcolonial "nation-building," see, for example, K. W. Deutsch and W. J. Folz, eds., *Nation-Building* (New York: Atherton, 1963).

11. A brilliant and deservedly influential account of the sociological origins of nationalism in the non-European world is to be found in Anderson, *Imagined Communities*. See also my review of Anderson (and of Gellner's *Nations and Nationalism*), "Nationalism: The Instrumental Passion," *Capital and Class*, no. 25 (1985): 98–116.

non-European case, however, we must also note the extreme fragility and incompleteness of the latter (mass national consciousness) in many of the new nation-states, and most especially in Africa. In fact there is, I believe, a clear link between performance in nation-building and performance in economic development right across the non-European world. That is, the nation-states that are doing worst at economic development are also the states that are doing worst at winning the loyalties of the mass of their citizens to the new "nations" of which they are supposedly a part. But again, to follow this trail of the argument would be to risk losing the main point of this chapter.

## Nationalism, Globalization, and Development

In fact the issue to which that point now leads us may be put as follows. If state-led nationalist attempts at industrialization in America and Western Europe were undertaken out of "nationalist elite" fear of endless dominance by spontaneously industrialized Britain, then we must say, at least in retrospect, that they were very—indeed completely—successful. For Britain is not now and has not been for a long time, the major industrial economy in the world. She was long ago overtaken by the United States, by Germany, by Japan (another "state-sponsored" industrializer), and indeed by most other Western European states. Moreover, the period of catch up and overtake was, comparatively speaking, very short. If Britain is regarded as having completed at least the initial stage of her own industrial revolution by (say) 1840, then her period of undisputed world industrial dominance can be said to have lasted roughly sixty years (both the United States and Germany had overtaken her by 1900). Moreover, in the century since she has continued to plummet down the world league table of average per capita income, being passed by nearly all of Western Europe, including such previously despised rivals as Italy, Finland, and even Ireland. Moreover, whereas in 1970 the GDP per capita of Britain had been more than five times that of South Korea, by 1996 it was only 27 percent higher and this most spectacularly successful of the Asian Tigers was closing the gap all the time.[12]

12. OECD Statistics Directorate, *National Accounts, 1960–1996: Main Aggregates Volume 1* (Paris: OECD, 1998), table 2, p. 162. For the debate on the causes of Britain's relative economic decline, see, among a host of possible sources, Hobsbawm, *Industry and Empire,* chap. 9, and Glyn and Harrison, *The British Economic Disaster,* chap. 2. The most interesting issue surrounding Britain's relative economic decline is how far it has been a "natural"

So on that logic, and given this kind of historical timetable, might we not expect the non-European industrializing economies, beginning their own industrialization drives only after 1945 (and many much later), to start gaining real ground on the Northern economies by about now, and a number of them to have surpassed those economies by—say—2060 or so? Well we might, as long as nothing of real significance has changed since the nineteenth century. That is to say, if general Western or Northern dominance of the world industrial capitalist economy is not significantly or structurally different from British dominance of the world industrial economy in the nineteenth century, then (at least in economic logic) there is nothing to stop at least some of the nations of the South catching and overtaking the industrial nations of the North, just as the United States and Germany overtook Britain. (That is, of course, provided that these states/nations in their turn made or make a reasonably competent "go" of their own industrialization.)

However, it is just this *ceteris paribus* condition that (as so often in the study of the social world) seems not to be satisfied. That is, there is a lot of evidence to suggest that the dominance of the North in the contemporary world capitalist economy is significantly different—different in kind—from the dominance exercised by British industrial capitalism in the nineteenth century. This difference appears to resides precisely in the globalization or "transnationalization" of productive capital in the twentieth century and in the far greater difficulty now, of successfully copying or reproducing the most advanced forms of that capital on a national basis.

That is to say, if in the nineteenth century Germany (say) wanted to set up, on its own territory cotton or woolen factories or ironworks to compete with preexisting British factories or works, it was relatively easy, technically speaking, for German engineers and artisans to do this (perhaps with some advice from British engineers or advisers hired for that very purpose). Moreover, once such factories and plants had been set up, they

---

phenomenon, deriving, essentially, from the loss of industrial monopoly status—a loss which was "inevitable" given time—and how far that relative decline has been greater than was "inevitable" as a result of either structural weaknesses in British capitalism or mistakes of domestic economic policy. Texts advocating the latter, more pessimistic view, include Colin Leys, *Politics in Britain: An Introduction* (London: Heinemann, 1983), chaps. 2, 7, and 13, and Martin J. Wiener, *English Culture and the Decline of the Industrial Spirit, 1850–1980* (Cambridge: Cambridge University Press, 1981). A more recent text arguing the former view and disparaging more alarmist accounts (especially that of Wiener), is W. D. Rubinstein, *Capitalism, Culture and Decline in Britain, 1750–1990* (London: Routledge, 1993).

could generally operate, almost immediately, on a scale that would enable them to compete with British products both on the domestic and on export markets.[13] In the late twentieth century, however, the setting up of modern vehicle or electronics or petrochemicals plants is a much more technically demanding business. Moreover, even when they are set up, it is much more difficult for such plants (if they are purely national plants relying on a purely national market) to obtain the economies of scale that will allow them ever to successfully compete (at least on export markets) with the products of massive transnational companies from the North already dominating those markets.

In fact these differences are precisely why so many of the non-European world's ISI experiments have taken the form (almost unknown in nineteenth-century Europe) of inviting MNCs/TNCs to set up so-called turnkey or preprepared branch plants or subsidiary plants within a state-protected market, rather than having the state itself or local capitalist entrepreneurs set up such plants (as was almost always the practice in nineteenth-century Europe). For through such licensing arrangements the difficult late-twentieth-century technology is supplied ready-made rather than having to be locally reinvented. But the cost of this is that, on the one hand, there is not much advance made in indigenous technological expertise through the construction or operation of such plants, and on the other, the MNC subsidiary or branch plant tends to produce just for the local market, and makes no attempt to penetrate export markets.[14] And all this is quite apart from other problems with industrialization as an economic development strategy under late-twentieth-century technical conditions—most notably that such industries often do not employ many people anyway, so that they do little, at least directly, to lift mass living standards in poor countries that have an abundance of labor.

To sum up the argument to this point. The predominant form of state-directed economic development strategy pursued in both the European and the non-European worlds since the nineteenth century has come down

13. Once again, David Landes is excellent on this. See *Wealth and Poverty*, chap. 18, and also his *Unbound Prometheus*, chap. 2.

14. For a standard general account, see Jenkins, *Transnational Corporations*, and also his *Dependent Industrialization in Latin America: The Automotive Industry in Argentina, Chile and Mexico* (New York: Praeger, 1977). For more specific case studies, see S. Langdon, *Multinational Corporations in the Political Economy of Kenya* (London: Macmillan, 1980); Killick, *Development Economics in Action*, on Ghana; and A. Coulson, *Tanzania: A Political Economy* (Oxford: Clarendon Press, 1982), especially chap. 23, for much the same story in a supposedly "socialist" developing country of the 1970s and 1980s.

to little more than a kind of sophisticated *imitation*. At any given point in time, leaders pursuing a nationalist form of economic development (generally = industrialization) have simply looked at the national economy deemed to be the most advanced at that time. (In the nineteenth century it was Britain, in the twentieth century it has generally been the United States and/or Japan and/or Germany.) They have then treated that example as a kind of blueprint, attempting to reproduce that blueprint more or less *in toto* within their own states. And such a procedure, one might say, made sense, indeed eminent sense, for as long as the term "British industry" meant (as in generally did in the nineteenth century) "industry on the territory of Britain" or the term "British capitalism" meant (as it generally did in the nineteenth century) "capitalism as it operates on the territory of Britain."[15] But whatever the phrases "American capitalism" or "American industry" or "Japanese capitalism" or "Japanese industry" mean now, in the late twentieth century, they do *not* mean (or do not mean simply) "industry and/or capitalism as it operates on the territory of the United States or Japan." In other words then, the problem with copycat national-development strategies now is that they are still attempting to treat as national blueprints for reproduction forms of economic organization that have ceased to be national in this sense. And that is quite apart of course from the problems of this kind of "blueprint reproduction" strategy in the case of demographically small and poor states. That is, it might still make some sense, at least in principle, for a nationalist leadership of Brazil or India to try and reproduce the American economy on its soil. It makes no sense at all, even in principle, for a nationalist leadership of Jamaica or Samoa or Fiji to try to do so.

For the vast majority of small and poor states in the world, in fact, an altogether more sensible approach might be to drop the "national blueprint reproduction" strategy of development altogether, and to pursue a development strategy or strategies not based on the nationalist premise "how can we be like ... [national entity] ... as quickly as possible?" but on the globalist premise "how can we fit into the world capitalist economy on the most advantageous possible terms?" And this means that instead of thinking of the world economy as consisting of a series of national entities engaged in a never ending competitive race, they would think of it as a *single economic entity* in which they have to try and find a specialized niche

15. As noted, from the 1890s on, "left" analyses of British foreign investment, trade, etc., tended to be analyses of British *imperialism,* seen of course as an outgrowth of British capitalism, but not as identical with it.

or niches that will benefit as many as possible of their people as much as possible. This niche may be ecotourism or specialized forms of labor export, or niche production of some specific set of manufactured or artisan products, or some combination of all of these. But in any event it will *not* consist of trying to become a United States in miniature or a Japan in miniature.

## Conclusions

There is still a lively debate among scholars about the precise causal relationship between capitalism and nationalism. But whatever the outcome of that debate, there is no doubt that, up until the middle of the twentieth century, forms of state economic policymaking based on the desire for national prestige, or (at least) on the desire to avoid domination by more economically advanced nations, acted as a powerful stimulus for the development of industry generally and of industrial capitalism particularly, in many parts of the world. We might say that in this period (from about 1780 to 1960 or so) economic nationalism and the development of capitalism as a form of economy and society reinforced each other.

In the last forty or so years, however, for a combination of complex reasons, the development of capitalism in the most economically powerful nation-states of the world (the United States, Japan, the states of the EU) has begun to outreach national boundaries, and a genuinely global form of capitalism has begun to emerge. This development has in turn posed considerable problems for economic nationalist ways of thinking and acting, both in the home economies of transnational capital themselves, and (most especially) in the new nation-states of the world trying to pursue their own forms of national economic development and "catch up" (as it used to be said) with the West. The problems posed are rather different in the two cases. In the former case they have to do with problems of the potential loss of existing privileges. In the latter they have to do with finding new strategies to end disprivilege or underprivilege. But in both cases they are problems that lead to one overwhelming question, which is, does the very notion either of a "national" capitalism, or of a "national" economic strategy for the development of capitalism, any longer make sense? Can such notions, that is to say, any longer lead to practically effective policy outcomes for anybody? And clearly if the ultimate answer to that question turns out to be no for everybody—for every state on the planet— then we will have entered a new world indeed.

CHAPTER FIFTEEN

॰ঌ

# Globalization and Modern
# Economic Nationalism

## *The Importance of Free Trade*

Globalization has only happened, and is only happening, because the world has maintained something approximating a free trade regime in goods and services since the Second World War. For, fairly obviously, none of the things that have concerned us in this book up to now—the ever increasing dependence of production upon trade, the spreading of TNCs/MNCs around the globe, the international flows of capital and money to which we have given such attention—could have occurred, or would be occurring, without a international regime of rules and regulations designed to maintain as open a global economy as possible. As is well known, the GATT (the General Agreement on Tariffs and Trade) and its successor organization the WTO (World Trade Organization) had, and have, as their specific legal role and obligation the maintenance and extension of a global regime of free trade. But in addition there is a whole network of what are called bilateral agreements (agreements made between two countries, or between an economic bloc—like the EU—and another country) designed to free up trade between the countries involved.

Note that globalization had depended, and depends, as a process on maintaining "something approximating" a free trade regime. I stress this qualification because the world does not now have, and indeed has never had, a completely free trade regime—a situation in which every country can export to and import from every other country in the world entirely without any restrictions whatsoever. On the contrary, virtually every country in the world operates some forms of protection of at least some sectors of its domestic economy.

Thus, and notoriously, both the EU and the United States still protect their farmers, in various ways, from competition from overseas farmers and agricultural producers,[1] and Japan, equally notoriously, has found ways of protecting both its farmers and many of its domestic industrial producers from foreign competition. And, as I noted in an earlier chapter, many developing countries, as part of their ISI development strategies in the 1960s and 1970s, protected their so-called infant industries from competition from imported manufactured products from the advanced industrial economies, usually through the use of tariffs and quotas. Indeed, as I also said in that same chapter, many Western MNCs and TNCs would probably not have set up, or bought up, subsidiary companies in those countries at all—in Latin America, Asia, and parts of Africa—except as a way of attaining or retaining access to those protected markets for manufactured goods. Moreover, the same could be said of the setting up of both American and Japanese multinational subsidiaries in the EU countries. In this case too non-EU multinationals set up or bought up subsidiary companies within the European Union because if they had not done so, they would have been cut out of the lucrative Western European market by EU protectionist legislation.

However, even though there are those significant qualifications to be made to the idea that we live in a "free trade" world, still, nonetheless, that assertion is valid at least in the minimal sense that since the 1930s none of the major industrial economies in the West has tried to become self-sufficient (none has tried to be or become a closed economy) and since the Second World War there has been, both through the GATT/WTO and through bilateral agreements, a continual process of reducing tariff protection (protection through using customs duties and quotas) of all domestic economies in the world. That process has now gone so far that, except in the case of some agricultural products, there is now very little

1. For an excellent and accessible recent account of the state and level of agricultural protectionism, production subsidies, export subsidies etc., in the contemporary global economy and the forces supporting them, see Robert Wolfe, *Farm Wars: The Political Economy of Agriculture and the International Trade Regime* (New York: St. Martin's Press, 1998).

effective tariff protection left in most economies of the world.[2] This does not mean that states are left entirely without means of protecting their domestic market, since like (most notoriously) the Japanese they can use a number of so-called "non-tariff measures (technical standards, marketing requirements, quarantine regulations) to maintain such protection. But it does mean that, since the Second World War, it has become gradually easier to trade goods and services around the world. And this is undoubtedly one of the reasons why global trade in goods and services has consistently grown faster than global production of goods and services and why (indeed) the growth of the former seems to be accelerating relative to the latter all the time.

Even where states or economic blocs (like the EU) have insisted that MNCs/TNCs establish subsidiaries within their boundaries if they are to have access to their domestic market, they have not stopped such companies repatriating profits made in those markets back to their home economy. Thus, for example, if Nissan builds a factory in the United Kingdom in order to have access, not just to the British market, but to the entire (protected) European market for cars, it is still able (indeed, it has the legally guaranteed right) to repatriate whatever proportion of the profits it chooses from these European sales back to Japan. And the same applies to Volkswagen if it builds a factory in Brazil or Argentina, or to Dow Chemical if it builds a factory in India. Indeed, without such legal guarantees of profit repatriation big companies would not "multinationalize" their operations at all.[3] Similar legal guarantees are given to banks lending money abroad. Thus even where there are impediments to global free trade of *goods and services,* there has generally been less impediment to global free trade in *money.* Indeed, and paradoxically, guarantees of the absolutely free global flow of money have often been a prerequisite of creating, or maintaining, certain forms of protectionism for goods and services.

Now the fact that all this is so—that globalization has depended on the

---

2. See Thurow, *Future of Capitalism,* 132.

3. It was because communist countries did not (indeed could not, as a matter of political principle and ideology) provide such guarantees that they did not receive any FDI and had to rely entirely on their own sources of capital to industrialize. This isolation from capitalism became in turn (as we can now see clearly in hindsight) one of the reasons why communist economies generally became technically and industrially backward in comparison with the West. On this, see, for example, A. Aganbegyan, *The Challenge: Economics of Perestroika* (London: Hutchinson, 1988), chap. 1.

maintenance of a global regime of relatively free trade, and that globalization has accelerated ever faster as that regime has become ever freer—provides (of course) one policy option, or apparent option, for those who do not like globalization or its consequences. For if you are frightened by what globalization appears to be doing to the trend of real wages in the advanced economies, if you think it is having a deleterious effect both on the level of employment generally and on the terms and conditions of employment even of those who retain their jobs (reduced hours, lower hourly wages, fewer benefits), if you think that it is leading to ever worse public services (mainly because of the pressure on states to reduce taxes to a globally competitive level), if you think that it is leading to the global domination of an individualist, consumerist, and (indeed) American capitalist culture, then one policy response to all this might be *to return to a regime of national economic protectionism.* Or, at any rate, you may be tempted to move in a more rather than less protectionist direction, especially for those sectors or areas of your economy or society which you think are being most damaged by globalization.

Now interestingly, this nationalist response to the problems posed by globalization seems to have some appeal on both the left and the right of the political spectrum in the advanced capitalist countries. Thus, to take the Australian case (which is also quite typical of France, or Germany, or the United States in this respect), a strong protectionist thrust can be found both in the manifestoes and propaganda of the right-wing One Nation Party as well as in the ideas of some radical or left-wing economists and other intellectuals.[4]

Now I do not want to express any personal view on the merits of this protectionist approach here. (I think, in any event, that my opinion should have emerged clearly in earlier parts of this book.) Rather my aim in this chapter is to do two things: to outline the major conventional arguments against protectionism as a response to the problems of globalization, and to describe how it is possible, for those who wish to resist any return to protectionism, to provide a nationalist rhetoric in regard to globalization which is nonetheless *anti*-protectionist in thrust. Indeed this rhetoric serves in fact to endorse the process of globalization while still appearing to contain it within a national political frame.

4. See, for example, Frank Stilwell, "From 'Fightback' and 'One Nation' to an Alternative Economic Strategy," in *Beyond the Market: Alternatives to Economic Rationalism,* ed. S. Rhees, G. Rodley, and F. Stilwell (Leichhardt: Pluto Press Australia, 1993), 189–202, and especially 199–200.

*Economic Nationalism and the Fear of Free Trade*

The most common argument deployed by mainstream politicians against both right- and left-wing advocates of a return to protectionism is the simple assertion that if "we" protect ourselves against "them" (whoever "we" and "they" are), then "they" will protect themselves against "us." The net result of this, it is said, is that the total of trade between us will diminish, and we will be set upon the road to the "beggar thy neighbor" policies of general protectionism that will stifle global trade altogether and (just like the protectionist responses to the Great Depression of the 1930s) serve to render all the countries of the world and their peoples worse off. Sometimes this argument is deployed in this general form, sometimes in a more specific form (especially where it is being deployed against a more specific interest group requiring not a general retreat into protectionism but some altogether more limited protectionist measure in regard to one product or sector). Thus, for example, if "we" in Australia try to protect Queensland banana growers from competition with cheap Central American bananas, then "they" will retaliate by getting the United States and Canada (their fellow NAFTA members) to introduce off-setting protection on "our" wool, lamb, or mutton products.

This argument—we might call it the "danger of retaliation" argument—is a persuasive one. It also has the political merit of being both easy to follow and usually correct, both specifically and generally.

However, despite its intellectual simplicity and its political effectiveness, this argument is neither the most important antiprotectionist argument nor, I think, the one that most influences mainstream politicians and their orthodox economic advisers. The antiprotectionist argument that probably *does* influence them most has the marked political disadvantage of being both more intellectually complex (and therefore less easily or readily understood by the ordinary person or voter) and, actually, a lot more debatable and doubtful than the simple "danger of retaliation" argument. It is therefore a lot less well known (to noneconomists) and appears much less frequently in the popular political arena of debate. I will now outline it.

In essence, as a long-term dynamic argument (rather than as a short-term static one) the case in favor of universal free trade and against universal protectionism is a kind of informed bet or wager on the future. This bet or wager is, in essence, that, though at any given point in time there will be winners and losers in a regime of global free trade, since the total of output and demand in the global economy will grow far more rapidly under a regime of free trade than under a regime of protectionism, everybody (including the short-term losers) will be better off under free trade than under protectionism "in the longer run."

Now that is the argument in its most general form, but it can be broken down into more specific variants to deal with each of the worries that a person might have about the economic and social effects of globalization on his or her (national) economy and society. To those who are worried about losing jobs to cheaper labor competition from abroad one might argue that as global output and demand increases (through, for example, gradually rising wages among workers in the competing industries abroad), more jobs will be created in "our" economy too. To those who are worried about losing jobs in both manufacturing and services to other advanced economies as well as to newly industrializing economies as a result of labor-displacing technological change that allows much higher productivity with much less labor employed one might say that this increased productivity will lead to an increase in wealth, wealth which can and will be used, directly and indirectly, to fund the creation of other kinds of jobs in the future, jobs that will most likely more than replace the jobs now being lost. To those who are concerned about the fact that as a result of global movements of money, domestically produced capital is being used to invest in economic enterprises (and thus in jobs) in other countries one might say that as a result of the flow of profits from those enterprises and jobs back to "us" and of the increased output and demand in the global economy created by "our" foreign investments, new future jobs are directly and indirectly being created for "our" workers.[5]

Now, in all these cases, if conventional economists are asked how they know that these future benefits will flow in order to offset, or more than offset, the current costs of the globalization process, the only possible answer is "because it has always been like that in the past." That is, such economists will point to the fact that both within individual capitalist economies (since the onset of the industrial revolution just over two centuries ago) and within the international capitalist economy as a whole (since there has been one) a regime of free trade has *always* generated more wealth and prosperity for everybody "in the long run."

---

5. Arguments of this kind are the staple fare of any conventional textbook on neoclassical trade theory. However, for a pungent and popular expression of them by a distinguished neoclassical theorist, see Paul Krugman, "Is Free Trade Passé?" *Economic Perspectives* 1, no. 2 (1987).

But the problem is that, even if you accept this historical argument as broadly correct (which, as a matter of fact, I do), this does not alter the fact that this is all it is, an argument from history, from past experience. But as Hume argued nearly 250 years ago, the problem with all arguments of the form "*X* has always been the case in the past; therefore, we can know that *X* will always be the case in the future" is that they are "always" logically unsound! According to Hume, we have no warrant, logically speaking, for inferring from the past to the future in this way.[6] Therefore, even though it has been the case *in the past* that labor-displacing techno-logical change has indirectly generated enough jobs to replace, or more than replace, the number of jobs lost, that does not allow us to infer with certainty that labor-displacing change resulting from advances in com-puter and information technologies will have the same effect in the future. It is at least possible that this time we may be dealing with a form of tech-nological change that will simply, and over a long time period, "eat" more jobs directly, than it creates indirectly. It is possible, that is to say, that this is a form of technological change which will simply produce a long-term pattern of "jobless growth"—more and more output produced by fewer and fewer people, thereby creating formidable and long-term problems both of employment and demand in the system.

Or again, while it is true that in the past the absolute increase of out-put and demand produced by growth in an open economy has, in the long run, benefited more people than the restructuring processes accompany-ing it have damaged in the short run, we equally cannot, absolutely safely, infer that this will be so in the future. For example, if that growing wealth is generated, more and more, by productive and service technologies that

6. For Hume's original argument here, see his *Treatise on Human Nature*, bk. 1, sec. 14, in *David Hume: The Philosophical Works*, ed. T. H. Green and T. H. Grose (Aalen: Scien-tia Verlag, 1964), 450–66. On the whole, whatever its logical merits (and they have been contested), Hume's argument to the effect that (for example) the mere fact that all human beings who have put their hand in a fire in the past have been burned does not provide "certain knowledge" that if I put my hand in the fire now it will be burned, has not had much impact in altering everyday human behavior re fires and burning. However, it does have both logical and practical merit in situations where (a) the number of previous obser-vations of any given phenomenon are very limited and (b) the internal complexity of the phenomenon in question (for example "technological change") is so great that one can never be sure that the phenomenon one is observing is sufficiently similar to any past phe-nomenon to constitute a repetition of it. And clearly this is exactly what we are dealing with in the claim that, for example, labor displacing "technological change" under capital-ism "always" generates increased employment in the long run.

employ fewer and fewer people, then the increased demand (which is the logical and inevitable concomitant of that increased wealth) will be demand *placed in the hands of fewer and fewer people*. That is, it will be demand placed the hands of the minority who do retain well-paid jobs and, above all, in the hands of those who own the enterprises—the owners of capital. That is, in this scenario increased wealth and demand may not equate with increased material welfare of the majority of people at all (although generally it has done so in the past).[7]

And this logical problem—of inferring from the past to the future—is not the only problem with this optimistic gamble on the future. There are at least two others. The first problem with this optimistic gamble on the future is that it is a gamble on the *future*, that economists find it notoriously difficult to attach actual durations to the expressions "short term," "medium term," and "long term." But any sensible person of course would want these concepts to have some numbers attached to them, at least of some rough and ready sort. If I am losing—or have lost—my job as a result of technological change in 2000, I am likely (as are my fellow unemployed) to be more reassured if I am told that "the long-term increase of global wealth and demand" will provide me with a job in (say) 2002 than if I am told that there is no chance of this happening before 2075. As Keynes quite properly said, "In the long run we are all dead," and even if we are not dead in 2075, seventy-five years is a long time to be poor and miserable. The second problem with this optimistic gamble on the future is that it is a *gamble*, a gamble on conceptually *endless* economic growth. But with our new environmental knowledge and consciousness does this now even seem like a sensible gamble? Can the environment sustain endless economic growth?[8] And if it cannot, then what becomes of the gamble?

7. Although precisely *how* it has done so in the past is an interesting and contested issue. As indicated in an earlier chapter, I am one of those people who believes that, historically, wealth created in free market economies has had to be redistributed by *political* means in order to bring significant improvements in mass material welfare. That is, I am not a believer in the so-called trickle-down theory—the idea that market economies have some "automatic" market-based mechanism for transferring wealth from the well-off to the less-well-off. Or at any rate I do not believe that such a mechanism works sufficiently well that it can ever eliminate mass poverty on its own.

8. This—the environmentalist objection—is by far the most fundamental objection to the economists' "gamble on the future," since it calls into question the very sustainability of the central phenomenon—continual economic growth—that makes the gamble a rational one. It is small wonder then that it has excited strong rebuttals from economists, since it threatens, not merely the central plank in their whole worldview, but indeed the central

If we suffer today on the promise of jam tomorrow, what happens if tomorrow's jam turns into sludge (to mix an image)? The conventional economist has nothing to say about such a possibility. Having outlined here the most significant arguments on both sides of the protectionist issue, I am dropping the question of whether we shall all in the long run be better off through globalization than under protectionism.

I am dropping the question partly because I don't believe it has a definitive answer. Since the future cannot be known, it must be *made.* But I am also dropping the question because I consider it a waste of the reader's time and my own to consider the hypothetical merits of the case for a return to a world of national economic protectionism. In my opinion, *the matter has no real world practical or policy relevance at all.* That is, I think it extremely unlikely that any of the major capitalist or industrial states of the world will make a concerted move toward full-fledged protectionism in any situation short of catastrophic economic collapse and massive internal social and political upheaval.

I believe this because one of the structural economic characteristics of globalization is, as I stated at the beginning of this book, "an ever tighter integration of formerly national economies into a globalized system of production," the primary expression of which is the fact that much global trade these days (most especially trade carried on within MNCs/TNCs—

---

mechanism which has been relied upon to date to generate mass human material prosperity in a world of huge socioeconomic inequalities among human beings. For two well-known attacks on environmentalism from growth-oriented economists, see Wilfred Beckerman, *Through Green-Colored Glasses: Environmentalism Reconsidered* (Washington, D.C.: Cato Institute, 1996), and Julian L. Simon and H. Kahn, *The Resourceful Earth: A Response to Global 2000* (Oxford: Basil Blackwell, 1984). The issue is so complex as to require a book in itself, but one short remark can be ventured here. Contrary to what is often said on the "Green" side of the argument, it is *not* true that economic growth has to cause, must always cause, environmental damage. Michael Jacobs, *The Green Economy: Economy, Sustainable Development and the Politics of the Future* (Vancouver: University of British Columbia Press, 1993), chap. 5, is very good on why there is no such logical necessity. It is true, however, that the predominant *technological types and forms* of growth pursued in industrialized societies to date *have* (i.e., have in fact) often been environmentally damaging and *are* almost certainly unsustainable on a global scale. The challenge for humankind therefore is to create and adopt (worldwide) environmentally sustainable— and indeed environmentally enhancing—forms of economic growth, and there is no doubt that technically this could be done, even in the present state of human technical and environmental knowledge. The question, however, is whether it will be done before global environmental catastrophe strikes, and this is ultimately a socioeconomic and, above all, a political question, not a technological one.

the so-called intrafirm trade) is not trade in finished goods that could be consumed by any actual people—by final consumers—at all. Rather, it is trade in bits and pieces of such finished commodities. It is trade in semi-finished products or product components, which are being moved around the globe as precisely part of a globalized production network (sometimes under the control of one firm, sometimes involving many firms) with the final assembly of the product simply being the final link in a complex chain of processes.

Now, as I also said earlier, this characteristic of economic globalization alone carries the implication that any economy trying to opt out of this globalizing system totally, or even partially, would undoubtedly pay for attempting such an escape with massive short- to medium-term economic and social disruption. To be more exact, an economy like that of Australia opting out in this way would undoubtedly face massive shortages of many commodities (virtually all complex mechanical, electrical, and electronic products, for example) its people have become accustomed to consuming. Many factories and offices situated in Australia that currently owe their reason for being to the fact that they constitute the Australian "bit" of some global product or service chain would simply shut down, since they could not function cut off from that chain. Hence unemployment would increase massively as an almost immediate result of such opting out. And in addition of course, if Australia wished to invest in new forms of plant and equipment (so that it could make for itself a whole range of products which it had previously obtained from globalized production systems), it would have to raise all the capital to do this internally, since it would also be cut off from global capital markets. However, to raise the huge sums of money required for this reequipping exercise, the people of Australia would suddenly have to do a massive amount of forced saving (whether by taxation or by some other mechanism) just at the time when their real incomes had already fallen sharply as a result of mass unemployment and/or wage reductions.

I think, therefore, that one only has to review the logic of such opting out to see that no responsible Australian government would even contemplate such a course unless it was in a situation in which globalization *itself* was already causing such massive economic and social pain that the costs of protectionism seemed lower. But this is obviously not the situation in Australia at the moment and it is difficult to see it being the situation in the foreseeable future, even if the economic and social costs of globalization do slowly increase over time. And if and when it did find itself in such a desperate situation as a result of globalization, then (presumably) the Australian economy, being so dreadfully weakened, would hardly be in a position to bear the additional economic and social costs imposed by the retreat into protectionism. For example, if there were already mass unemployment as a result of globalization, how would the Australian people respond to massive tax hikes to pay for new Australian industries?

It is very difficult then to resist the conclusion that at least for demographically small but rich economies and societies of the world—like Australia—a point of no return has already been reached, and passed, as far as globalization is concerned. That is, the tactical or strategic protection of some *specific* industry or sector (perhaps as part of bargaining with a global trade partner or partners) is, and will remain, a policy tactic in the arsenal of the Australian government, as it remains as a "specific case" policy tactic for many other states in the world. But a retreat to a kind of "fortress" Australia, attempting total or as-near-total-as-possible economic self-reliance (or "autarchy" as the economists call it) is, and will remain, nothing more than an extremist's delusion.[9] Or, at any rate, that is all it ever will be as long as the bulk of Australian people are not prepared to live a radically simplified economic life ("three acres and a cow" in a totally rural Australia) as the price of such autarchy. That is, economic autarchy is and will remain a nonstarter for Australia and Australians as long as the bulk of them are habituated to, and wish to retain, what we now think of as a normal, Western, consumerist lifestyle.

In fact the only economies remaining in the world today that could even conceivably opt for autarchy and survive the considerable economic and social disruption involved are those of the United States and the EU. This is so because both these economies have internal markets large enough

9. And, to be fair, "left" protectionists, like Stilwell and others (see note 4 above), are far too intellectually sophisticated to be advocating economic autarchy or anything close to it, and in this respect, as in many others, they are light-years from the know-nothing economics which often distinguishes the nationalist right. Rather, such "nationalist" left thinkers tend to advocate limited protectionism as one of a battery of policies to cope with the negative domestic economic and social consequences (unemployment, increasing inequality) of globalization. The problem is, however, that in a globalizing world, even supposedly "limited" or "temporary" increases of *overt* protectionism (increased tariffs, more limited quotas, etc.) tend to provoke retaliation, or threats of retaliation, very quickly. And at that point national governments either have to "back off" or reply to the retaliation with retaliation. In other words, in a globalizing world, it is in practice much more difficult than advocates of such "limited" protectionism seem to think to keep the limits limited!

to carry integrated or reintegrated industrial structures without the outlet of global trade and internal sources of a large number of raw materials necessary to support such a structure. But even in their cases reversion to autarchy would involve considerable economic disruptions and sacrifices (involving sharp falls in the standards of living of a majority of their populations for some considerable period of time), and it is not clear that either of them could bear the likely *political* costs of this, even if they could cope economically. For example, would the fragile unity of the nation-states composing the EU survive the making of desperately difficult decisions on how the economic pain of unemployment and falling living standards was to be shared out among them? (Whose car plants to shut or scale down, how to ration out a large number of now—very restricted—imports of producer and consumer goods between different national producers and consumers.) But if EU unity did not survive these strains, then the constituent small European economies left as the result of its breakdown would be no more able than Australia to function self-reliantly.

So then, short of some barely imaginable environmental or other cataclysm, it is difficult to see any route back from the economic and social problems posed by globalization to some entirely national or preglobal world of economic relationships.[10] And yet many people worry—and I think have good reason to worry—that an economic process that has passed beyond the capacity of any nation-state (even the largest, like the United States) to regulate or control, could, as a result of that very lack of control, generate very considerable economic, social, and (indeed) environmental problems for many people and societies in the world. Moreover, these are problems which may in turn cause those societies considerable political difficulties (rising unemployment, declining wages, and standards of living) but problems that current national political mechanisms and regulations are increasingly unable to solve or even mitigate.

So given such reasoning, logic at least points us in only one direction. If we cannot go back, we must go forward. That is, if we feel that the new globalizing economy requires some forms of economic and political regulation, and this cannot any longer be done effectively within the old

10. Even assuming of course that such a world ever "previously" existed. But one does not have to believe that, since the birth of capitalism, the bulk of economies in the world have *ever* been "completely" independent of world trade and financial movements, to believe that the *degree* to which they are now tied into global economic relationships has increased significantly since the Second World War, and since the 1970s in particular. It is this increased *degree* of economic interdependence which we are calling globalization.

national frameworks, then we must have new global forms of regulation operating on a scale to match the new global market place.

It is my aim, in the final two chapters of this book to suggest, at least in a preliminary way, what these new global forms of the regulation of capitalism might be, and the objectives they might aim to achieve in the short, medium and long term. However, for the moment, and to complete this chapter, I want to examine the most common response of mainstream politicians, at least in Western societies, to the dilemmas posed by the necessity (as they see it) of embracing the economic imperatives of globalization while endeavoring to maintain a degree of political legitimacy among constituents who are still overwhelmingly national (and indeed nationalist) in their economic and social outlook. In a word, this is the solution of "nationalizing" (as one might say) in dominant political rhetoric the process of globalizing capitalist competition.

### Globalization as Competition Among Nations

Here is a lengthy political speech dealing with the phenomenon of globalization and the role that a modern national government must or should play in regard to it. Readers are invited to nominate, in order of likelihood, three contemporary politicians whom they believe to have made this speech. The correct answer can then be located in note 11 below.

Today, the pace of global change is quickening. Whether we like it or not, we are part of an international community whose outlook is becoming increasingly global. As the economic and social map takes shape for the next century, we all fall into two camps. You are either a globaphobe or a globaphile. This is the great dichotomy of our age, as fundamental as the old conflict between capital and labor. The global economy is giving more of our own people and millions around the world the chance to work and live and raise their families with dignity. But the expansion of trade hasn't fully closed the gap between those of us who live on the cutting edge of the global economy and the billions around the world who live on the knife's edge of survival. The globalization of the world economy has had profound effects on work, on workers, and on wages. Open markets mean products come into America that are made by people who work for wages American's can't live on. That can cost some American workers their jobs and keep others from getting a raise. But overall, trade has generally brought benefits to most Americans. We will work toward free trade with the smaller nations of Central America and the Caribbean. We must be flexible because one-size-fits-all negotiations are not always the answer. But the ultimate goal will remain constant, free trade from northernmost Canada to the tip of Cape Horn. Protectionism is the swiftest road to poverty. Only by competing internationally can our companies and our economies grow and succeed. I'll never forget the contrast between what I learned about the free market at Harvard and what I saw in the closed isolation of China. Every bicycle looked the same. People's clothes were the same. A free market frees individuals to make distinct choices and independent decisions. The market gives individuals the opportunity to demand and decide, and entrepreneurs the opportunity to provide. In a global economy, governments have decreased control over the economic levers. Their constituents are all too open to influences from around the globe. But governments are still required to protect and advance the interests of their respective communities and must find new ways of doing so. The point is that liberalization in economic policy and a modern conservatism in social policy are not only appropriate to our national interests as we enter the twenty-first century. They are mutually reinforcing as well.[11]

11. It is not a single speech at all, but a compound of extracts. The first five sentences, from "Today ..." to "... labor," are from a speech, "Globalisation or Globaphobia: Does Australia Have a Choice?" made by the Australian minister for foreign affairs, Alexander Downer, to the National Press Club in Canberra on December 1, 1997. Sentences six through eleven, from "The global economy ..." to "... Americans," are from two speeches by Bill Clinton, "Between Hope and History," made in January 1996, and his farewell address as president, made in January 2001. Sentences twelve to fourteen, from "We will ..." to "Cape Horn," are from a campaign speech by George W. Bush, made in October 2000. Sentences fifteen and sixteen, from "Protectionism ..." to "... succeed," are from a speech by the British prime minister, Tony Blair, to the Economic Club of Chicago in April 1999, and sentences seventeen to twenty-one, from "I'll never forget ..." to "... provide," are from another speech by George W. Bush ("A Charge to Keep"), made in December 1999. Finally, the last four sentences, from "In a global economy..." to "... as well," are from two Australian sources. The penultimate two sentences are from a speech made by the leader of the Australian opposition Labour Party, Kim Beazley, to a CIDA "Vision Asia" Conference held in Melbourne in September 1994, and the final two sentences come from a speech ("Building a Stronger and Fairer Australia"), by the current Australian prime minister, John Howard, also given in Melbourne in May 1999. All these extracts were downloaded from the Web, the speeches by Clinton and Bush from the "Issues 2000" web

This speech, it will be seen, essentially presents globalization as a process of national competition, in which, only by "competing internationally" will "our" companies and "our" economies succeed. This process will be difficult. Jobs may be lost and wage rises may have to be foregone for some workers, but "governments" are, nonetheless, still expected to "advance the interests of their respective communities," and if they do so then those "communities" (= nations) will still benefit from the globalization process.[12] But does it make sense or (more simply) is it even basically empirically accurate, to describe this competition as a competition *between nations* at all? That is, is it really true that in current globalizing capitalism we have ever more intense competition *between nations?* That is, if the Rip Curl company becomes the world's largest producer and seller of surfwear, is it "Australia" that gains as a result of this victory? Or, alternatively, if Ford becomes the world's largest seller of motor cars, is it "America" that gains by this? Or, again, if Sony is the world's largest producer and seller of audiovisual electronics, is it "Japan" that gains by this? The whole point of the kind of nationalist description of global competition that I have provided above is to suggest to us that the obvious answer to all these questions is, in all cases "yes." But surely we now know enough to say that this obvious answer is not nearly as obvious as we are invited to think it is by most of our politicians and commentators. If, for example, Rip Curl's expansion provides as many or more jobs in India or China than it does in Australia, then in what sense is "Australia" a winner if Rip Curl wins? If Ford's shareholders are a complex global mass of American individuals and institutions, European superfunds and banks, and Japanese investment houses, in what sense does "America" win when Ford wins?

Now, note, I do not want you to say that the right answer (therefore) is "No, Australia does not gain *at all* when Rip Curl gains, America does not

---

site (www.issues2000.org), the speech by Tony Blair from the Tony Blair web site (www.dicppi.org/speeches), and the speeches by Kim Beazley and John Howard from the Parliament of Australia web site (www.aph.gov.au).

12. In an address given to the "Politics in the Pub" discussion forum in Sydney in 1998, Leslie Sklair suggested that ideologists of what he called the "transnational capitalist class" could instantly be recognized as such by the frequency and enthusiasm with which they deployed phrases such as "cutting-edge technologies," "world's best practice," "bench-marking," and similar management-speak. See L. Sklair, *Sociology of the Global System,* 2d ed. (Baltimore: Johns Hopkins University Press, 1995). For a much more detailed treatment of what they call the "competitiveness agenda" as it operates in Australia specifically, see D. Bryan and M. Rafferty, *The Global Economy in Australia: Global Integration and National Economic Policy* (St. Leonards, New South Wales: Allen and Unwin, 1999), chap. 3.

gain *at all* when Ford gains . . ." etc. Because that reverse answer may not be true—or simply true—either. Rather, I want to ask the question, what sense does it make (now) to describe global competition as competition *between nations* at all? And if the answer to that question is (as I think it is) "it makes some but not much sense" or "it makes some but less and less sense,"[13] then we can also ask another question, which is, then why do our politicians (and so many other people) describe it in that way and wish us to understand it in that way? Because if this nationalist way is not an accurate way to describe how contemporary global economic competition is structured (or the consequences it has), then, presumably, politicians must employ it for reasons other than its accuracy. But what could those reasons be?

13. Bryan and Rafferty, *Global Economy in Australia,* chaps. 1 and 2, provides an excellent theoretical account of why, in a globalizing world, it makes less and less sense to consider Australia as a single "economy" at all. Their arguments are extremely persuasive, and apply, as they well recognize, very broadly. It is now very clear, for example, that "national" economic accounts now obscure as much as they reveal, not just about Australia, but about every other nation in the world.

❧

# CHAPTER SIXTEEN

# The Ricardian Game

*Introduction: The "Cosmopolitanism" of Classical Economic Theory*

When, in 1841, Friedrich List—architect of the German "Zollverein"[1]—published his *National System of Political Economy,* one of its prime objectives, along with the first overtly theoretical defenses of industrial protectionism, was to attack what List called the "spurious universalism and cosmopolitanism" of Adam Smith's *Wealth of Nations.* The basic thrust of List's attack on Smith's great work was that Smith's supposedly "universal" economic postulates applicable to "producers" and "consumers" everywhere and of benefit to "producers" and "consumers" everywhere were nothing more than a spurious defense of British economic imperialism. List's attack on what he significantly called "British" political economy was many-sided. But his greatest ire, was, as one might expect, reserved for Ricardo's theory of comparative advantage, the classical economic postulate upon which the doctrine of international free trade has been defended from the time of its formulation until today.

For readers who are not familiar with the theory of comparative advantage, its most basic contention is that it is in the interests of all economies

---

1. The early-nineteenth-century "common tariff" free trade area linking Prussia with a number of other German-speaking states which was a precursor of the political unification of Germany later in the century.

to engage in international trade insofar as they all (without exception) must have comparative advantage in the production of some goods and comparative disadvantage in the production of others. Thus, to take Ricardo's own classical example, if *both* Britain and Portugal can produce woolen cloth and wine, but Britain has a comparative advantage in cloth production and Portugal a comparative advantage in wine production, then it will benefit the British economy most to give up wine production and import its wine from Portugal, and it will benefit the Portuguese economy most to give up its cloth production and import its cloth from Britain. And what the phrase "benefit most" means here is that the British economy will get a better return from transferring the land, labor, and money previously invested in wine production for domestic consumption to cloth production for export and that Portugal will get a better return from transferring the land, labor, and money previously invested in cloth production for domestic consumption to wine production for export. That is, for the landowners in both countries the land will yield higher rents in its comparatively advantageous uses, the labor employed in both countries will be paid better, and the capital invested in the comparatively advantageous activity will yield a better return in both countries than the land, labor, and capital did before trade between the two was established in these commodities.[2]

List's critique of the doctrine of comparative advantage is one now very familiar to us, and it seizes on the (for List) very significant choice of commodities in Ricardo's famous example. In essence, said List, Ricardo's theory is a perfect rationalization of the British desire to maintain its effective world monopoly on trade in manufactures ("cloth") and to convert the whole of the rest of the world into a supplier of food and raw materials ("wine") for Britain in perpetuity. Because, said List, while it may well be true that, given its climate and soils, Portugal has a *natural* comparative advantage over Britain in wine production, Britain's comparative advantage over Portugal in cloth production has nothing "natural" about it at all. On the contrary, it is simply the product of an entirely contrived

2. The argument in its original form is in David Ricardo, *Principles of Political Economy and Taxation* (1817; Harmondsworth, Penguin, 1971), especially chap. 7 ("On Foreign Trade"), 152–55. For one of a million popular textbook restatements of the argument in a modernized form, see, for example, Paul Samuelson, *Economics* (Tokyo: McGraw-Hill Kogkusha, 1976), chap. 34. The distinction between comparative and absolute advantage and its importance for the logical coherence of the theory of free trade is particularly well stated by Samuelson. See especially p. 669.

process of industrialization, which is just as much open to Portugal to undertake, as it was to Britain. (Or rather it would be, if Portugal were not coerced into what he called "subordinate" trade relations with Britain justified and rationalized by the comparative advantage doctrine.)[3]

Now this Listian critique of the doctrine of comparative advantage is interesting because it happens to be one of the first formulations of an argument that has been made over and over again. It is also interesting because it is based on a fundamental confusion (between "comparative" and "absolute" advantage) which has equally often been a hallmark of those rejecting of the comparative advantage doctrine from that day to this.

That is, List thinks Ricardo is saying that it is in Britain's and Portugal's interest to trade freely with each other because Britain can produce cloth more cheaply than Portugal and Portugal can produce wine more cheaply than Britain. But that, though true, is not Ricardo's argument. For Ricardo the crucial point is that *Britain* can produce cloth more cheaply than *Britain* can produce wine, and that *Portugal* can produce wine more cheaply than *Portugal* can produce cloth. That is, Ricardo's argument for free trade is an argument based on the relative (comparative) advantages of some types of economic activities over others *within* individual economies, not between or among different ones. (Ricardo calls this latter advantage "absolute advantage" precisely in order to distinguish it from comparative advantage.) And his argument is that, given an unequal distribution of factors of production across the globe as a whole and within individual economies, all economies will have internal *comparative* advantages and disadvantages in production.[4]

Thus, to take a crucial contemporary case, given the unequal distribution of cheap labor across the globe, not only will some economies be more attractive locations, given free trade conditions, for labor-intensive manufacturing than others ("absolute advantage" in labor costs) but *within* any given cheap-labor economy there will be comparative advantages in using that labor, under free trade conditions, in some kinds of activities (for example, clothing or toy manufacture) rather than others (for example, peasant agriculture or large-scale plantation agriculture). And conversely, *within* expensive labor economies there will be, under free trade conditions, comparative advantages in using that labor in some activities (high

3. F. List, *The National System of Political Economy* (London: Longmans Green, 1916). He reiterates this point often. See, for example, his chapters 11, 13, and 15.

4. This point is well made in Krugman, *Accidental Theorist*.

value added manufacturing or services) rather than in others (low value added manufacturing). In other words, and crucially, there can be, and indeed there always are, comparative advantages and disadvantages *within* manufacturing and *within* other sectors (raw material production, services) as well as *within* individual economies, of which countries may take advantage through free trade. Therefore Ricardo's comparative advantage doctrine is *not*—or at any rate not necessarily—an argument that applies only to primary activities (like agriculture). Contrary to many criticisms of it, from List onward, it *can* also be applied to economically secondary or tertiary activities like manufacturing and services as well.[5]

In fact, in retrospect, it is clear that Ricardo's choice of commodity examples (cloth and wine) was rather unfortunate, because it led to an understandable but profound misunderstanding of his doctrine on which rather theoretically facile (if nationalistically appealing) criticisms have been based from Ricardo's day to ours.

### Logical Implications

I have begun this chapter with the most famous theoretical defense of free trade, because although globalization means many things, one of the most fundamental things it means is the advocacy of a global system of unconstrained market economic relations between countries. Advocates of such a system, of course, advocate free trade in goods and services, but these days they also go beyond that to advocate the free movement of capital around the globe, as well as the free movement of people (of labor), of science and technology, and of information generally.

Now enthusiasm for Ricardo's comparative advantage concept and its innumerable developments in modern trade theory—is widespread among "straight" neoclassical economists and can still be found outlined and advocated in innumerable orthodox economics textbooks. But, on the whole, neither it, nor the policy based upon it (global free trade), finds

---

5. Paul Krugman, "Ricardo's Difficult Idea," which I viewed at the "Unofficial Paul Krugman Web Page" (members.home.net/copernicus/ricardo.html) is very good on the often ignorant criticisms of Ricardian free trade theory, and of the comparative advantage concept in particular, which abound among many intellectuals. However, while acute, his defense of free trade is often a little too sanguine for my taste concerning its distributional and welfare implications in the real world, given, in particular, highly imperfect labor markets both nationally and internationally. On this, see both his "Ricardo's Difficult Idea," above and "A Raspberry for Free Trade," the latter also viewable at the same location.

much favor with those whose interest in globalization is mainly focused on its social implications and consequences—on poverty and inequality, for example. Indeed, typically such people either do not know neoclassical trade theory at all, or if they do, they reject it, often with the List-like argument that it is a thin rationalization of, or ideological apology for, Western economic imperialism.

Just for this reason, therefore, I think it is worthwhile making explicit the logical implications of Ricardian comparative advantage theory for the subject often dearest to the hearts of such people—relief of world poverty. And, in order to do that, and to make what I have to say as clear as possible, I think it best to engage in a little hypothetical history. That is, I want, for reasons that will shortly become clear, to construct a hypothetical history of the global economy over the previous (say) three hundred years, based not on the constraints and parameters that did apply to it in fact, but on the organizing assumptions that are built into Ricardian notions of comparative advantage.

### Comparative Advantage and Global Economic History: A Hypothetical Model

I would like the reader to try to imagine a world in (say) the year 1700 in which the following are true:

1. The real cost of the production and reproduction of labor is more or less the same across the globe. That is, the real wages that would need to be paid to buy one hour or day of labor is the same in Europe as in Africa, as in Asia, as in Latin America, etc.[6]

---

6. Ricardo's entire economics is based on the central assumption that the wages of labor everywhere have a tendency to gravitate toward a basic physical subsistence minimum as a result of the continual tendency for the growth of the human population to outrun the growth of food supply. This is the famous, or infamous, "iron law of wages" in Ricardo, which he basically borrowed from Thomas Malthus's *An Essay on the Principles of Population* of 1798, and reproduced in chapter 5 of his *Principles* ("On Wages"). There is of course much debate about how humanity was enabled to escape the workings of this "Malthusian" law and indeed about whether in the long run this escape will prove to be only temporary. However, none of these arguments concerning global population growth and its possible implications are relevant to the argument I am making here. The point, for my purpose, is that on the basis of the "iron law" Ricardo was able to outline a model of the workings of an international free trade regime in which differences in real wage levels were not an important determinant of relative production costs or (therefore) of international

2. A regime of global free trade commences from this starting point—a regime that includes the absolutely free and unhindered global movement of goods, money (capital), and labor, and continues to run continually on this basis to the present.

3. Given the first two conditions, it should be clear that the goods and services that equally paid workers in different parts of the globe would produce would be determined primarily by the natural resource conditions pertaining in their particular part of the globe. That is, workers in one part of China paid $1 an hour would be mining coal if they happened to live where there was coal, workers in another part of China paid $1 an hour would be producing rice because they happened to live in an area suitable for rice. Meanwhile workers in a part of India—also paid $1 an hour—would be producing cotton (because they happened to live in an area suitable for cotton growing). Workers in Europe, also paid $1 an hour, would be producing copper (if they lived in a copper mining area) and beet sugar (if they lived in an area suitable for sugar beet production), and so on.

4. Since (unlike in our actual world) neither expensive nor cheap-labor would, or could, act as an influence on decisions as to where to invest capital in anything or (therefore) on decisions as to where on the globe's surface anything was produced, the *only* thing that could and would determine such decisions would be (by definition) Ricardo's criterion of "comparative advantage." And therefore every labor force in every part of the world would engage in production of what it was best contextually situated to produce, would enter most or all of that production into global trade, and would obtain all other goods and services it needed from that trade. In other words, under these circumstances and assumptions a global division of labor *entirely determined* by the criterion of comparative advantage would come into being. And this in turn is just another way of saying that there would be, in Adam Smith's terms, *the creation and expansion of a global market in all goods and services* because for Ricardo (as for Smith) the expansion and deepening of market relations and the expansion and deepening of the division of

---

capital flows. It then becomes possible to ask what the implications are of having a regime of more or less free movement of capital and of goods (as advocated by Ricardo) in a real world in which, as a result of protectionism and imperialism, real wages *are* markedly unequal in different parts of the globe and *are* therefore an important factor in differing costs of production globally.

labor among human beings are just two alternative descriptions of the same economic phenomenon.[7]

So far so good. But many critics (of whom again List was, again, among the first) of the doctrine of comparative advantage have argued that such a "natural" global division of labor is bound to break down once modern manufacturing production appears in the world This is because there are no "natural conditions" in the world making it more comparatively advantageous to produce PC monitors, or car radiators, or surgical instruments in (say) Southeast Asia or Southeastern Canada, in Central America or Central Europe, in southern Latin America or in southern Africa.[8]

This of course is true. But on the Ricardian assumptions—of absolutely free movement of goods, capital, and labor across the globe—where such industries began or were (initially) situated would be a matter of accident (a question of who, for example, initially invented what and where). However, production of that thing or things—PC monitors, advanced medical equipment, or whatever—could expand either through capital investment in their production in other areas of the globe outside the initial area of development, or by workers coming freely from elsewhere on the globe to further expand production in the initial location, or by some combination of these trends. Moreover, given the Ricardian assumptions—of equal labor of equal skill and training, paid equal wages around the globe—*whatever* global distribution emerged of economic activities *not* determined by comparative advantage this distribution would *not* significantly or lastingly privilege one part of the globe's population against another.

This would be the case because, first, such patterns of invention and development are likely to be roughly equally spread around the globe. That is, in his model Ricardo assumes that human inventive abilities, although individually unequal, are not unequal by human cultures or

7. For Smith's original argument relating the division of labor to the growth of the market, see *The Wealth of Nations*, bk. 1, chap. 3. Ricardo's entire argument in his *Principles* is developed in dialogue with Smith, as any reader of the book may easily see. Indeed it is clear that Ricardo saw himself as simply "internationalizing"—through the "free trade" postulate—this argument. For Ricardo the homology between the growth of the division of labor and the extension of the market was the single most important or significant aspect of Smith's great work precisely because it had implications well beyond the (mainly implicit) "national" or "single country" framework in which Smith developed it.

8. For a sophisticated modern example of such arguments, see Thurow, *Future of Capitalism*, 65–70.

regions.[9] But more importantly, even if these inventions, and the industries they spawn, are *not* equally distributed initially, free movements of capital and/or labor will soon radically reduce or eliminate any advantages. For example, free movements of capital in a sector will tend to equalize prices for the commodities in that sector *wherever* on the globe's surface they are produced, and absolutely free movement of labor will have a similar equalizing effect on wages.

So the ultimate logical result of the Ricardian model is that in a globalized industrial economy a part of the global distribution of differentiated economic activity (that which has climatic or other natural resource constraints) is still determined by comparative advantage. But that which is not (the bulk of modern industrial activity whose location is not constrained by raw material or natural resource factors) does *not* lead to long-lasting inequalities among producers or workers.

*Pure Logic and Impure History*

It can formally—mathematically—be demonstrated that all these desirable consequences would have followed from the consistent application of the principles of comparative advantage to an initial situation in which real cost of labor across the globe was equal or approximately equal. But this demonstration is far more likely to impress the mathematically minded neoclassical economist than anyone else. This is because the formal conditions required for it to operate in this optimizing way (absolutely free movements of goods, services, capital, and labor across the globe) are likely to strike any minimally historically informed person as so grossly unrealistic as to be laughable.

To imagine that the human population occupying this globe in 1700 (or 1600, or 1500, or 1400, or whenever one chooses to start running the model)[10] could have been so organized as to have countenanced such free

---

9. On this point, see Ricardo, *Principles of Political Economy,* especially chap. 1 ("On Value"), 64–65.

10. When one chooses to start running the model depends upon when you think equal, or even approximately equal, costs of production and reproduction of labor power across the globe last pertained. Some historians would say that something like this pertained as late as the eighteenth century, others (like Immanuel Wallerstein) would push the date back at least four centuries earlier than this. The question is interesting historically, but has no bearing on the Ricardian logic, as logic. It just means that to have "worked" the Ricardian world economy might have been able to "begin" as late as 1700 or might have

movement (and most especially the free movement of labor—of people) would strike most people who know anything about the actuality of the medieval or early modern world as absurd.

Leaving aside the fact that conditions permitting the effective and rapid global movement of goods, people, or money simply did not exist then, the early modern world (let alone its medieval predecessor) was a world so steeped in cultural myopia and intolerance that the only significant numbers of culturally alien workers it could tolerate were those bought and brought as slaves. Apart from a small coterie of merchants, artisans, and nobility, the only time that any significant number of people of the medieval and early modern world traveled (what we would now call) "internationally" was in war, when they went to slay enemies equally often regarded, for religious or other reasons, as barely human. These are the centuries of the Inquisition, of the Spanish *conquistadores,* of the Hundred Years' War, of the Thirty Years' War, of the horrific Atlantic slave trade, of continuing Islamic conquests of innumerable "infidels" in Africa, India, and Asia, of the brutal imposition of the Muscovite state on a variety of Eurasian peoples—hardly a conducive environment for the flourishing of pacific, superrationalistic Ricardian principles!

### *Moral Implications in the Real World*

All this is true, and we shall return to some other implications of its truthfulness later. But it is not in itself a conclusive reason for simply writing off the Ricardo's doctrine of comparative advantage as absurd. In fact, it makes a lot of sense to think of our *contemporary* global economic situation as a kind of *incomplete* (and therefore self-contradictory) Ricardian world. That is to say, since the Second World War, we have seen a gradual but consistent movement toward global free trade in a wide variety of goods and services, and—even more spectacularly and rapidly since the 1970s—toward a much freer movement of capital. These two tendencies, along with massive technological improvements in industrial productivity, have created the conditions for the capitalist market economy to increasingly escape the political control of the nation-state and to set in train the process we call globalization.

---

had to be put in place in 1400. Of course I take it as axiomatic that it would not, could not, have been "put in place" in the real world on any of these dates!

However, this globalizing economic process is impacting on a global human population that does *not* have equal—or even remotely comparable—real wages, that does *not,* that is to say, have a single set of global material conditions of production and reproduction. On the contrary, capitalism's actual, real historical creation and growth occurred in the context of various forms of nationalist economic policymaking. In this real situation national "capitals" were routinely protected from competition from foreign goods and services until they had established themselves both on domestic and export markets and national labor forces were routinely protected from massive incursions of foreign workers—incursions that would have served to weaken trade unionism and lower wages. The net result then of this non-Ricardian form of the development of capitalism (however historically unavoidable or inevitable it may have been) is that we now have markedly—massively—unequal real wages among labor forces on different parts of the globe.[11] And the most globally privileged of these working populations are generally found in those parts of the globe which are *also* the most technologically advanced and the most financially prosperous parts. They are, therefore, the parts of the globe that have been the most instrumental in pushing forward the globalization

11. In general terms this is of course very well known, but nonetheless exposure to some specific numbers on the extent of these differences can still amaze one. Thus for example, the Australian government's Industry Commission recently produced a lengthy report on the competitive situation of the "Australian" textile, clothing, and footwear industries, the first volume of which contains a table showing average hourly wage rates in the clothing industries of thirteen different countries in 1992. The numbers ranged from just over U.S.$12 an hour in Italy and between U.S.$8 and U.S.$10 in the United States, Australia, and Japan, to U.S.25 cents an hour in China, U.S.26 cents an hour in Vietnam, U.S.27 cents an hour in India, and U.S.28 cents an hour in Indonesia. In other words, in this particular sector the hourly wages in the highest-paying country (Italy) were nearly *50 times* those in the lowest-paying country (China). When, in addition, one considers that the Italian workers (overwhelmingly women) earning fifty times more than their Chinese counterparts (also predominantly women) are themselves among the lowest-paid workers in their country (as are the American, Japanese, and Australian textile workers), the sheer multiplicity and complexity of the concepts of "poverty" and "inequality," when viewed in a global perspective, becomes palpable. But that sense of complexity is yet further compounded by reflecting on some closely related data presented by Peter Dicken. According to that data, in 1995 China—the cheap labor producer *par excellence*—was indeed the world's largest exporter of garments with 15.2 percent of the world market, but "expensive labor" producer Italy was second with 8.9 percent! Australian Industry Commission, *The Textiles, Clothing and Footwear Industries,* vol. 1, *Report* (Canberra: Commonwealth of Australia, 1997), table 1.6, p. 18; Dicken, *Global Shift,* table 9.5, p. 291.

of capital flows, and of goods and services markets, over the last thirty to forty years.[12]

But the problem is that with markedly unequal real wage levels across the globe, the globalization of capital investment cannot now proceed very far without threatening to undermine the privileged *domestic* labor forces in precisely the parts of the globe from which the globalizing push is coming. Indeed, as we have already seen, the contradictions this incomplete Ricardian situation generates are awesome. They do not just involve capital in (say) the United States or Western Europe making investments in cheap labor abroad—investments that may damage the wages or employment prospects of labor in the regions of advanced capitalism. They also involve those very labor forces (through pension funds, insurance funds, and even direct share ownership) being contributors—however unknowingly or unwittingly—to the global capital movements that may serve to increasingly undermine their real wage privileges. In fact, as we have already observed, it is the privileged workers of the world *en masse,* through pension funds (and not the Western and Japanese capitalist classes) who are, collectively, the biggest players in global financial markets today. And they are so because of the historically unprecedented levels of real wages they enjoyed during and after the long boom of the postwar years. That is, the long boom itself created global financial institutions engaged in massive global capital movements, institutions that may yet prove the most significant means for the undermining of the high real wages that historically produced them!

---

12. Readers who are old enough will recognize that my argument here has some commonalities with that found in Arghiri Emmanuel's *Unequal Exchange: A Study of the Imperialism of Trade* (London: New Left Books, 1972). The commonalities consist in my attempting, like him, to analyze the current global trade system from some (modified) Ricardian premises. More specifically, they consist in my endorsing the argument of that book that, historically, Western workers have been able to garner a part of the massive technologically induced increase rise in their labor productivity as increased real wages. I also believe that, as argued in Emmanuel's text, they have done this through (a) gaining "national" protection from massive inflows of migrant labor from the Third World's reserve army of labor and (b) using trade union wage bargaining power deriving from the relatively "tight" labor markets resulting from (a). My argument here differs from that of *Unequal Exchange,* however, in holding, conventionally, that declining terms of trade for Third World primary products are a function of changing price elasticities of demand for manufactured goods vis-à-vis primary products as real wages rise, rather than a result of the "unequal exchange of labour times." (I understand, however, that Emmanuel himself has now abandoned this latter view.)

We might put it this way. It is right and proper to observe that what we might call the "Ricardian game" of global economic relations could never have been played out consistently over the last three hundred, four hundred, five hundred (choose your own time period, it hardly matters) years on Ricardo's hopelessly abstract and rationalistic principles. We can properly and justifiably say that historico-cultural conditions made such a possibility an absolute nonstarter in the real world. But we can also properly and justifiably say that the human race's failure (if that is what we want to call it) to play the Ricardian game consistently—unfettered movements of goods, money, *and* labor operating continuously from a historical baseline of equally low labor costs everywhere—means that workers in one part of the world *now* (much more than capitalists, or much more than most capitalists, in that part of the world) have a very great deal to lose even from playing it inconsistently.

That is, the standards of living of the real world's prosperous workers are now threatened markedly even by the beginnings (for it is still no more than that) of genuine globalization of *capital,* and they would be entirely and radically undermined by the global movement of *labor* on any significant scale. This latter is so just because, given the vast discrepancies in real wages across the globe, such free movement of people would, initially at least, be overwhelmingly a movement from the poorer to the richer parts of the world. And since, as I observed in an earlier chapter, a lot of that incoming labor would not only be cheap but also well educated and trained, there is probably no part of the domestic labor market in the United States, Western Europe, or Japan that it would leave unaffected. That is, it is a delusion, as I said in an earlier chapter, to imagine that it is only the real wages of unskilled workers that are threatened by free global movements of capital. And it is even more of a delusion to think that it is only the wages of such workers which would be undermined by free global movement of labor.

So historical irony is piled upon historical irony. In 1700, or 1500, or 1400, global historico-cultural conditions made it unthinkable (I believe literally *unthinkable*) to have played the Ricardian comparative advantage game at all, let alone consistently. But nonetheless, one crucial economic condition of its being a beneficial game for everybody to play (a "sum-sum" game as the game theorists say)—broadly equal real production and reproduction costs of labor across the globe—was met at that time. On the other hand, however, *now* many of what one might call the historico-cultural (and technological) conditions for playing the Ricardian game *have been* met.[13] But the crucial economic condition of its being—at least in the short to medium term—a "sum-sum" game for everybody on the globe has long ago disappeared (and as part of the very same process that makes it now at least a historico-cultural possibility). For I personally do not doubt that the short- to medium-term beneficiaries of the genuine globalization of capitalist economic relations commencing *now* would be the presently poor and poorer workers of the world. I have equally have little doubt that the short- to medium-term *losers* from such a process commencing *now* would be the rich and richer workers of the world. That is, a consistent Ricardian game played *now* would necessarily be zero-sum at least for the foreseeable future, *not* (as Ricardo genuinely and sincerely envisaged) a sum-sum game. And it would be a zero-sum game, moreover, that would threaten considerable social dislocation and political upheaval, especially in the currently most prosperous capitalist societies on the globe.

If I might turn a phrase perhaps more purple than technically appropriate, I could say that, as capitalism passes from its imperialist to its globalization phase, it begins to *take revenge* (economic revenge) on that subgroup of the world's workers whose living standards have been artificially raised and sustained by a combination of national economic protectionism and imperial domination. In particular, the free movement of productive capital which is a hallmark of the globalization phase, allows the poor workers of the world to play their economic ace card (the low cost of their labor's production and reproduction). It does so by eliminating the capital stock advantage that enabled the richer workers of the world to compensate—in global competition—for the higher cost of their labor.

And this, at bottom, is why the vocabulary of imperialism is now being jettisoned, and indeed should be jettisoned. For it was a vocabulary appropriate to a stage in the development of capitalism from which the poorest

13. Or, at any rate, the technological conditions for its being played are now met, whether, however, human beings even now have cultures and belief systems that are any more *genuinely* "open" to the cultural "Other" than they were three or four hundred years ago is moot. Indeed, it is probably too abstract a question to be useful or (it amounts to the same thing) answerable. What is clear is that there is no hope at all of that kind of genuine human openness emerging in situations in which the arrival *en masse* of culturally different people is also perceived (and rightly perceived) as a severe economic threat. That is, if human cultural openness is to increase (in other words, if anything like a genuinely shared human or global identity is to emerge among human beings), it can only do so gradually and incrementally in a situation, or long historical sequence of situations, none of which are seen or felt as severely threatening by any of the people involved. Such considerations profoundly influence the broad policy recommendations I make in Chapter 17.

people of the world only or mainly *suffered*. We have now begun, however, to move into a phase of capitalist development in which "the wretched of the earth" can be *beneficiaries,* or at least partial beneficiaries, of the further development of a global capitalism. The policy recommendations that follow, and which take up the final two chapters of this book, take this sea change in the balance of world economic power as a given and seek to preserve and indeed to expand and intensify it. But they also seek to protect humanity as a whole from the most socially conflictual and destructive possibilities inherent within it—inherent within it that is, given the four hundred years of imperialist and non-Ricardian global economic history that have preceded the present globalization phase and so formed the social attitudes and values of the world.

❦

# CHAPTER SEVENTEEN

# Non-Nationalist Economic
# Policies for a Globalizing World

In the previous chapter we analyzed some of the moral and political im-plications that follow from our Ricardian analysis of the economics of globalization. In the light of those implications we must consider, in this chapter, the most desirable set of economic policies vis-à-vis globalization that can be pursued now, in the current economic and social conditions produced by over three hundred years of real, actual capitalist economic development on this planet.

In considering this question I take it as simply axiomatic that it is neither possible nor desirable to reverse the process of globalization and to corral capitalism, once again, into national or nation-state boundaries. I consider it impossible on the familiar grounds that the scale of the pro-ductive forces of which industrial capitalism now disposes make even the largest national markets inadequate as consumption arenas. Therefore, a global marketplace for goods and services is simply a technical require-ment of the productive scale of the system as it now exists. Or, in other simpler words, a return to exclusively or even predominantly national mar-kets would be impossible without a massive global *collapse* of the current capitalist production structure, with ensuing large-scale unemployment, social disruption, impoverishment, and so on. I consider it undesirable, however, to return to such national economic parameters because I believe that globalization has given at least some of the world's poorest people a real opportunity, for the first time in their history, to improve their living standards considerably. In addition, as will become clear shortly, I also happen to be a convinced humanist who believes that a humanly richer life is available for all in a world that is economically, politically and culturally open and cosmopolitan, than in any more parochial or closed set of arrangements.

Given these premises then, the central policy issue becomes one of maintaining the most open possible set of global economic arrangements consistent with maintaining a set of social and political conditions *within the currently most prosperous capitalist societies* conducive to that openness. For we should not be in any doubt that it is in those societies ("our" societies, for what, I suspect, will be the majority of readers of this book) rather than in the poorer societies of the world, that any sustained political threat to the globalization process is likely to emerge. In particular it is, I would say, certain to emerge if those societies are forced to face simultaneously the economic effects of the free global movement of capital *and* of labor. That is, in a world with real wages as unequal as they are in ours, the free global movement of capital alone threatens employment in all sectors of prosperous capitalist economies in which labor costs are a significant part of total production costs. If one added the free movement of labor to that, the necessary result would be (depending on institutional arrangements) either a significant rise in unemployment in prosperous economies or a sharp fall in real wage rates across the board, or (and in practice most likely) some combination of both of these things. Given the appeal of racist and ultranationalist political groups in advanced capitalist countries in current conditions (in which inward movement of labor to such economies is highly restricted), it is not difficult to imagine the likely political consequences of such widespread drops in real wages. In short then, this crucial condition of the full Ricardian game (global free movement of labor) is as much out of the question now as it was three or four hundred years ago, albeit for somewhat different reasons. I therefore conclude, reluctantly, that the creation of an open global labor market is a practical impossibility, at least for the foreseeable future. However, just because that is the case, I believe it is *essential* that the global free movement both of goods and of capital be maintained, and indeed made freer than they currently are for both agricultural and industrial commodities. This should be done by the removal of all remaining formal and informal barriers to such movements.

Quite obviously, I advocate the removal of all remaining formal and informal barriers to the global free movement of agricultural and industrial commodities because I believe such a policy is needed (although in itself not sufficient) to raise mass standards of living in the currently poorer and poorest parts of the world. I hope I have explained why I believe this in earlier chapters. Further, the mass raising of such standards (to levels at least not greatly below those currently enjoyed by the presently most prosperous peoples of the world) is, in turn, a condition of creating a global free market in labor *without* producing a sudden and massive—and politically very dangerous—drop in living standards in the most prosperous societies.

In other words, and logically, if Bangladesh enjoys a standard of living not far below that of Belgium, or if China enjoys a standard of living not far below that of Canada, then allowing free movement of people out of Bangladesh and into Belgium or out of China and into Canada will not then result in a mass migration of Bangladeshis to Belgium or Chinese to Canada. In fact, the essential logic here is the same one we applied earlier to the discussion of rural-urban migration of people *within* poor countries—that given a conducive economic and cultural environment where they are, fewer people will choose to move to an environment with which they are unfamiliar.

In short then, if we accept that a sudden movement toward playing the full Ricardian game is out of the question for reasons to do with the political stability of the advanced capitalist societies of the world, then we must accept (by which I mean that the governments and peoples of the advanced capitalist world must accept) that a full commitment to the free movement of commodities and capital is the price they have to pay for being protected from the consequences of the free movement of labor. More polemically, I must insist that prosperous or advanced capitalist societies should not respond to globalization by rejecting an open global labor market and by opposing or even only half-heartedly supporting the free movement of commodities and capital. In other words, I want to insist, and quite unequivocally, that it is a humanly (not nationalistically but humanly) reactionary policy both to disallow the poor of the world to move *en masse* to where the best jobs are, *and* to protect any and all groups of workers in advanced capitalist societies from the employment or income losses associated with the movement of capital to where the poor of the world live. It is probably inevitable, if sad, that Australia continually returns boatloads of illegal immigrants to China. It is morally outrageous, however, if it does that *and* tries to ratchet up protection to keep (for example) a rump of domestic garment and footwear employment in being in Australia, rather than allowing it to move *in toto* to—say—China! "Let them keep their people where they belong" is an ungenerous human sentiment but one can perhaps stomach it. "Let them keep their people where they belong while we keep forms of employment where they *don't* belong" compounds ungenerosity of spirit with economic irrationality in a way that makes it hard to say which is worse or why!

There is, however, a third policy issue, following from Ricardian principles, that arises for both richer and poorer capitalist countries even in a period, such as the present one, in which there remain significant barriers to free trade in goods and services, as well as to free movement of labor. This concerns Ricardo's classical notion that all economies should specialize in the production and trade of commodities that come at the top of their comparative advantage schedule, and should reduce, or cease, the production of commodities at the bottom of that schedule. Yet one may ask how countries are to know what their schedule is (or, therefore, what commodities are at the top and bottom of it) in the absence of a complete free trade regime. I think there is an answer to that question. It is that in a world in which there are still some formal and significant informal barriers to free trade around the world, countries should specialize in those goods or services with which we can supply both domestic and export markets successfully and profitably *without requiring the use of either subsidies or protection greater than the marginal level prevailing in that industry or sector across the globe.*

This implies, for example, that if Australia can produce a range of wines that can hold their own in its domestic market on the above technical condition, and can also be exported profitably under the same technical condition, then it should expand production and employment in these forms of wine production. However, if it is producing, for example, a range of motor cars domestically that cannot hold their own on its domestic market without levels of protection above the world margin and cannot export at all without levels of subsidy above the world margin, then it should reduce or cease entirely the domestic production of motor cars. And what applies—the logic that applies—to Australia, should be applied in all other countries of the world engaged in the global capitalist economy, both rich and poor.

Moreover, if there is continued progress toward the elimination of all formal and informal barriers to free trade worldwide (a gradual approach of marginal rates of protection and subsidy to zero), then it should become easier and easier—technically more straightforward—for each and every country to know what its comparative advantage schedule is. Conversely, if protective barriers are then reapplied elsewhere for any commodity or commodity which a country knows to come at the top of its schedule, then it also knows where it should spend money on subsidies (to counter-act, say, tariff barriers) or put on diplomatic or other pressures to have informal barriers reduced or eliminated.

### Policy Implications for the Poor Specifically

In this context it is particularly important to understand what the eco-nomic policy implications of this modified Ricardian approach are for the presently poor countries of the world. The most important of these impli-cations, of course, is that they should *not* endeavor through protections or subsidies above world marginal levels to create, or keep in being, domestic economic activities in which they have no comparative advantage.

In the case of poor countries, fairly obviously, their *comparative* advan-tage lies in any and all activities whose labor intensity makes the low repro-duction costs of labor a significant *competitive* advantage. Such activities include many types of agricultural and horticultural production, labor-intensive forms of manufacturing, and labor-intensive service activities, such as tourism. However, and needless to say, labor-cost-based compara-tive advantages in agriculture and manufacturing can only be realized if such countries are given unfettered access to markets in the rich countries. However, this is very far from being the case at the moment, with rich capitalist countries operating high levels of formal and informal protection in agriculture, as well as significant informal levels of protection in man-ufacturing. In this case, however, it represents a far better use of scarce resources for poor countries to concentrate on enhancing exports of labor-intensive products by protection-circumventing subsidies (where they can be afforded) and by diplomatic pressure, in the World Trade Organization and elsewhere. It is far better, that is to say, for poor countries to put their political weight behind the free trade agenda, than to respond to nation-alist economic policies in the rich countries with a "copycat" economic nationalism of their own.

Because, and to repeat, this copycat economic nationalism is what is at the heart of any and all Third World attempts to reproduce entire advanced capitalist economies "internally" by protectionist means. For such attempts involve, in effect, investing resources in a whole range of economic activi-ties deemed modern or developmental, irrespective of whether or not the country in question has any comparative advantage in engaging in such

activities. In a phrase, they involve a policy of import substitution industrialization predicated on the assumption that economic development is
best pursued by trying to reproduce—in Kenya or Ghana or Colombia or
Thailand or wherever—the entire advanced capitalist economy of Germany, or Japan, or the United States or wherever. But the sheer paucity of
the domestic market, especially in countries that are demographically
small as well as poor, means that a whole range of import substitution
industries cannot be established or maintained without levels of effective
protection that are enormously in excess of world marginal rates, and have
little chance of falling, let alone of being eliminated, at least in the short
to medium term. More importantly, domestic real incomes (which along
with demographic size are the principal determinants of domestic market
size) are likely to rise much faster by concentration on labor-intensive
exports and on services that bring in foreign exchange than they are by
squandering scarce resources (and especially scarce foreign exchange) on
small import substitution industrial plants. For the low level and high
cost of output in those leads only to artificially high domestic prices for
the goods they produce, prices that actually reduce the real incomes of an
already poor population.

It should be noted, however, that concentrating developmental efforts
on export-oriented activities—primary, secondary, and tertiary activities—
in which low labor costs can give one a competitive advantage does *not*
mean pursuing a policy of ignoring the educational, health, or housing
needs—the social needs—of one's population. In fact, quite the contrary.
For if a country has a population that, as well as being cheap (on a world
scale) to employ, is also healthy and (above all) *well educated,* this is
likely to make it even more a magnet to globally mobile capital than its
cheapness alone would do. Textile workers who will work for 5 percent of
the Western wage in the same activities are highly attractive to globally
mobile capital in the textile sector. Computer programmers, however, who
will provide programs of a world competitive standard at 10 percent of
the Western labor cost are—in the current "information-technological"
phase of capitalist development—an even more attractive magnet to such
investment.

In short then, I am arguing that in the current globalization phase of
capitalist development, nationalist development strategies of an import
substitution sort are unlikely to be effective. They are unlikely, that is to
say, to be as effective in lifting the standard of living of the mass of any
poor country's population as a strategy based on comparative advantage

would or will be. And this latter strategy, to repeat, is the strategy of identifying the "niches" in the global economy for which the activities at the top of a country's comparative advantage schedule best fit it. This is so, even though ISI strategies have been very popular in Third World countries since the 1960s and even though (indeed) such strategies were followed historically by virtually all the currently advanced capitalist states. The reason this is so is, essentially, that the forces of production of capitalism have now reached a point where they cannot be constrained within national boundaries. Thus the capitalist firms of the United States, Japan, and Western Europe must seek markets, not only in each other's territories, but in other parts of the globe as well. However, these wider global markets (in Asia, Africa, Latin America) cannot be significant markets without sharp rises in the real incomes of their populations. But these rises, in turn, cannot occur without significant investment of capital in the labor of these areas, *and* without allowing the products of their labor and capital access to the prosperous markets of the world. But if this in turn occurs, it must mean some restructuring of economic activity and employment (especially in the agricultural and traditional manufacturing sectors) in the advanced capitalist economies, a restructuring that may *also* be resisted on broadly economic nationalist grounds.

In short then, the globalization phase of capitalist development is marked by an increasing clash between the developmental or expansionary needs of the capitalist system *as a whole* and nationalist political imperatives and outlooks. These latter lead to highly "partial" of "fragmentary" economic policy initiatives, initiatives that, whatever their popular appeal, are no longer consistent with the further development of a globalizing capitalism into a genuinely unitary global system. The nationalist sentiments underlying these policies were tightly bound up with the genesis of capitalism from the beginning, and they continue to be enormously socially and politically influential in the world, even if they are increasingly anachronistic from an economic point of view. This conflict between the expansionary needs of the system as a whole and the increasingly anachronistic nationalist political framework within which that system is still (partially) mired expresses itself in increasingly conflictual and contradictory forms of economic and social policymaking both at the nation-state and at the global levels.[1] In particular, politicians of all nominal ideological

---

1. Those readers who know their Marx will readily recognize this reference to the central idea in Marx's famous 1859 *Preface to a Contribution to a Critique of Political Economy.*

persuasions in advanced capitalist societies now find themselves increasingly caught between long-running, legitimacy-enhancing commitments to (and popular demands for), social protection from the endemic insecurities and vagaries of a market-based capitalist economic system, and their increasing inability to deliver this on a national basis. In effect, as is now being increasingly realized in ever more advanced capitalist societies, such protections can now only be operated and enforced effectively in some *transnational* way. But as yet (and for very good reasons) nobody has any clear idea what such arrangements might be or how indeed they might practically be put in place or enforced.

In this situation, I am arguing, poor or marginal or peripheral capitalist societies have a certain advantage. For, on the one hand, they have never been able to put in place the national forms of social protectionism for the mass of their people found in advanced capitalist societies, so they are not saddled with the costs, or the political difficulties, that arise from trying to maintain such protection in a globalizing system. And on the other hand, they can only benefit from a globalizing system *if* the advanced capitalist countries as a whole can be persuaded to implement the deprotection of their own agricultural and industrial markets. For whatever the political difficulties they encounter from their own citizens in fully carrying through a deprotection of their domestic markets, for the rich capitalist economies of the world such a policy is the logical Ricardian concomitant of the increasing flows of productive capital from those countries to cheap-labor areas of the globe. It is, that is to say, the policy that will lead to the best possible economic returns from that export of capital in the short to medium term, and the policy that will lead to the most rapid growth of incomes in both rich *and* poor capitalist countries in the longer term.

Poor capitalist countries have much to gain then, as a bloc, from pushing the free trade agenda in world forums, and in supporting those political forces in advanced capitalist societies which also push that agenda

---

I continue to think that this central idea—that there can be revolutionary moments in human history produced by conflicts between the technical requirements of what Marx called the growth of the economic "forces of production" and the social and political forms and institutions within which human beings are living at that time—has considerable merit. However, as I have also said elsewhere (see my *Karl Marx,* chap. 2), I think that it has most cogency as a thesis about a profound change mechanism operative in human history *after the development of capitalism* rather than as a thesis about the totality of human history. (If indeed it was ever intended as the latter, which is disputable).

against more protectionist groups (on both the right and the left). But again, the logical concomitant of peripheral capitalist countries doing this (and, in their case a concomitant of giving such a position political force) is a willingness both to abandon their own nationalist import substitution development approaches, and to throw open their own economies to Western capital, goods, and services (but on a fully reciprocal basis only).

I take it as axiomatic, however, as I said earlier, that even if this free trade agenda is pushed by the peripheral capitalist states, and accepted and endorsed by the leaderships of advanced capitalist states too, it will only involve—at least for the foreseeable future—free movement of goods and services and of capital, not of people. That is, I take it that the global free movement of human beings, if it ever occurs, would occur only after a long period of what we might call more restricted Ricardianism. One can perhaps hope (only hope) that a human population that had, after a century or two, grown used to being entirely economically dependent on a highly specialized pattern of production and trade, that had attained at least approximately equal global living standards, and that had become accustomed (through global mass media) to communicating frequently with, and about, "the Other," might (might) get to the point where it could conceive letting all human beings locate themselves anywhere on the planet they liked at any time they liked.

# CHAPTER EIGHTEEN

# Globalization and Imagination: Beyond Economics

I have devoted a lot of space and time in this book—in fact a lot more than I intended—to economics and economic issues. But in retrospect this is unsurprising. For as I have stressed from page one of this book onward, globalization is almost entirely an economic phenomenon, and—more than that—an economic phenomenon that seems to have happened to the world almost entirely against its political will. Just like the "world historical" industrial revolution in Britain, in fact, it seems much more a phenomenon that is *happening to* the people of this planet than as something that they, or even part of them, are *doing*, at least as any consciously planned or singular project. And yet of course, and as always, "it" (globalization) would not be occurring at all without certain forms of human action or activity. In fact, one of the most important uses of the word "globalization" is, clearly to give a name to a perceived *outcome* (mainly unintended) of a mass of different human activities taking place across the planet.

This contrast—so important to Hegel, to Marx, and to many other thinkers—between outcome and will, between effects or results of actions and the intentions of actors, between constraints on human action (created by the actions of others in the past and in the present) and the understanding of those constraints—in a word between "objectivity" and "subjectivity"—is at the center of globalization as a process and of this book as an analysis of that process. One of the persistent themes of all the preceding chapters in fact is—in a classical formulation—that our world is increasingly afflicted by a lag between social being and social consciousness. That is, we increasingly live in a world whose economic institutions and interactions cannot be described adequately, let alone understood, in national or nationalist terms, and yet we (and here "we" means everybody, all human beings on the planet) seem incapable of describing or understanding them except in such terms. Thus, as I stressed in earlier chapters, the beneficiaries of the activities of MNCs or TNCs are, in nearly every case, of varied nationality, and yet we persist in presaging these entities with national adjectives—"American" multinationals, "Japanese" multinationals, "British" multinationals. Also, while the world capitalist economy is indeed, in its globalization phase, becoming ever more intensely competitive, the predominant forms that that competition takes are inter- (or, occasionally, intra-) *firm,* not inter-*national.* But to hear the speeches of Australian or American or European politicians, one would never guess this.

Of course one can say about this—as other authors have done—that in "nationalizing" a global competitive process in this way politicians are enhancing or encouraging the globalization process by legitimizing it with the world's predominant form of political discourse. (So that, in this perspective nationalism and globalization are not simply antithetical. On the contrary a form, or adaptation, of the former is an important facilitator of the latter.)[1] But even if this is true, one may still wonder *why* it is true, why globalization needs to be legitimized by description as an economic competition among nations, rather than among firms.

It may seem, however, that this question barely needs asking, for its answer is so obvious. Globalization needs to be domesticated and legitimized nationalistically precisely *because* national categories and forms of explanation—nationalist forms of consciousness if you like—form the dominant political discourse of the world, and have done so for at least two hundred years. In other words, we do not as yet have a generally accepted globalist discourse of economics, let alone of politics or society. And as long as we do not, the nationalist discourse will continue to be adapted or expanded to fill the globalist role.

But when I hear this "obvious" explanation I feel dissatisfied, and I feel

1. This is one of the central arguments in Richard Bryan, *The Chase Across the Globe: International Capital and the Contradictions for Nation States* (Boulder, Colo.: Westview, 1995), and in Bryan and Rafferty, *Global Economy in Australia,* chap. 3.

dissatisfied for two reasons. First, I *personally* find this explanation disappointing. I feel that this explanation presents a historically contingent feature of the world (the dominance of the nation-state and of nationalist discourse) as a kind of "fixed" or "eternal" feature that, somehow, cannot be or could not have been otherwise. Yet we know it *has* been otherwise. There was once a world without nation-states and nationalism. Presumably there could be one again. Moreover, in eternalizing a contingent reality in this way this explanation begs the normative question "*Ought* the nationalist understanding of the world dominate in this way?" And there are many reasons, which I shall come to shortly, why one might want to ask that question.

But second, this explanation leaves me dissatisfied not just because I feel that nationalist understandings of the globalizing economy are, in important respects, inaccurate or inadequate. It leaves me dissatisfied because I feel that such understandings increasingly act as *impediments* to—to what?—I want to say, to actions that would lead to greater human fulfillment, or to certain kinds of human fulfillment at least. I believe, for example, that if there were global free trade in agricultural and industrial goods, this would not only serve to raise the material standard of living of the masses of poor people on this planet more rapidly than any other single measure. I also believe that—after a period of economic and social dislocation affecting some of them—it would also have only positive results for the majority of people in the rich or richer capitalist states of the world as well. That is, I believe that the application of what, in the last chapter, I called a modified Ricardian game would lead first to something of a "zero-sum" game for some workers in the advanced capitalist countries, and then to a "sum-sum" game for all workers and producers of the world.

There is no doubt, however, that, from the point of view of some of the workers and citizens of the advanced capitalist states, movement further down the road of globalization does entail some risks, dangers, and costs. More importantly, there is even less doubt that so long as one thinks about the matter in a "nationalist" way, the potential risks and dangers, as seen from the perspective of the currently rich countries, will necessarily be given a higher weight than the potential benefits. That is, if a group of textile or metal workers in an advanced capitalist country lose their jobs as a result of the relocation of such production to some lower-wage economy, then the (say) 10,000 jobs lost, appear, from a national perspective, as just that—jobs *lost*—a clear and unequivocal economic minus. The fact that the relocated plants have directly and indirectly produced (say) 20,000 jobs elsewhere (so that there has been a net job gain of 10,000 jobs world-wide) will simply disappear, as it were, in a "job loss" nationalist descrip-tion of what has occurred. Equally, and just as importantly, if, ten years later, 15,000 new jobs are generated in the advanced capitalist economy of (say) Australia in part, at least, because of demand coming from the newly prosperous metal or textile workers of (say) China, this will not appear in nationalist descriptions of what has occurred either. On the contrary, the job losses of 1999 are likely to appear as one discrete, separate description of a "national" economic event ("Textile and metal plants close in ...") and the job gains of 2009 in a discrete description of another, quite sepa-rate, "national" economic event ("Tourist industry expands in Victoria: 8000 new jobs in the last three years says official report").

Moreover, this kind of nationalist discreteness in description can often be accompanied by a similar disconnected discreteness in understanding. That is, when jobs are lost "here" it is not "our fault," but due to cheap-labor competition from "over there." However, when jobs are *gained* "here" it is not "they" who have provided them, but "we" who (quite mys-teriously) have been successful in "generating" them. Whereas, from a genuinely global perspective, this whole *deeply interconnected* set of events can be far more briefly described. That is, there was a global net jobs gain in the textile and metal sector in 1999 leading, directly and indirectly, to an even larger global net jobs gain in the tourism sector in the first decade of the twenty-first century in which Australia (among other places) shared.

So then I want to say that conceptualizing the global economy nation-alistically prolongs the hegemony of a discourse (nationalism) and of an associated political form (the nation-state), both of which one might wish to challenge for normative reasons. But I also want to say that it actually and actively prevents us seeing what we need to see if we are to act aright, and by act aright I mean "do that which is in everybody's long-term (not necessarily in everybody's short-term) interest to do." Putting that more concretely, what thinking nationalistically prevents us doing is weighting one job in China (or Cambodia or Tanzania) as humanly equal to one job in Australia (or Britain, or Germany, or the United States, or wherever we happen to be). And, perhaps even more importantly, a nationalist per-spective also prevents us from seeing not only that, in human terms, a job is a job is a job, wherever it may be created, but that a job created "over there" is a job from which, in the longer term, *and in an open global econ-omy,* Australia (or Germany or Austria or Britain) can benefit as much as Tanzania (or Cambodia or China) does in the short term.

That last remark brings us to the center of things I think. And I want to state what that center is fairly polemically. What is really morally disgusting about nationalism, I want to say, is that it prevents us from thinking seriously in genuinely *human* or humanistic ways. That is, even the most generous-hearted person, whose head is yet stuck in a nationalist perspective, talks and speaks all the time as if the welfare of a fellow national is somehow, intrinsically—just *because* it is the welfare of a fellow national—worth more than the welfare of some other person (any other person) on the planet. Indeed, one may properly say that the unthinking or unstated conviction that this is so is the defining criterion of a nationalist perspective *as* a nationalist perspective. Australians elect John Howard or Kim Beazley to take this perspective on the world. (Individual Australian welfare weighted 1, welfare of others weighted as—at best—some fraction of 1). Britons elect Margaret Thatcher or Tony Blair to apply a similar weighting to the welfare of Britons versus others. Americans elect Ronald Reagan or George W. Bush ... etc.[2]

And the problem with this defining criterion of a nationalist political practice as such a practice *now* is not simply that it is disgusting from a human point of view (for it has always been that), but that in a globalizing world it is both disgusting from a human point of view *and* likely to be increasingly pragmatically ineffective. That is, in a globalizing world, weighting the welfare of non-nationals equally with the welfare of one's fellow nationals is not just a morally better way to behave, it is also the best way to maximize the long-term material welfare of one's own citizens. (Assuming that is what one still desires to do).

These reflections lead us to still wider issues. I have said that nationalism prevents us from "thinking seriously in genuinely human or humanistic ways." But perhaps that is just part of the problem. Perhaps the truth is that we do not, as yet, really know what the words "human" or "humanistic" *mean* in such a context. Perhaps presently these are just words that we cannot fill with any felt existential content. Perhaps also (and relatedly) the words "globe" and "global" are just what the Austrian statesman Metternich said the word "Italy" was in the early nineteenth century— simply a "geographical expression" about which we can *feel* nothing. For

2. I use these First World, indeed Anglo-Saxon, examples because they are the examples that are likely to be closest to home for most of my readers. Needless to say, however, the same generalizations apply to the politicians and leaders of Malaysia, the Philippines, Brazil, Ghana, Iran—to the leaders of *all* nation-states in the world in fact—and whether democratically elected or no.

there is no doubt that still now the words "human," "humanity," "human race," are almost entirely abstractions. Perhaps someone will claim (or perhaps it may be claimed for her) that she "loved humanity." Perhaps she will be awarded (say) the Nobel Peace Prize to indicate that at least some other people believed that she did. But still for all that, it will not be humanity that she loved, or helped, but some particular people, some particular where. There are six billion human beings out there. No one can know them all, or even more than a tiny fraction of them all, so how can one (how can any actual person among that six billion) relate to them all *except* as an abstraction? And abstractions are nearly always affectively empty. They are not called "abstractions" for nothing!

### Nations and Human Civilization

Here, interestingly enough, there is something positive to be said about nationalism, and once again Friedrich List was one of the first to say it. In the same *National System of Political Economy* he says: "As the individual chiefly obtains by means of the nation and in the nation, mental culture, power of production, security and prosperity, so is the civilization of the human race only conceivable and possible by means of the civilization and development of the individual nations."[3] And as he makes clear elsewhere in the same text, and as many subsequent students and studies of nationalism have also claimed, an important part of the civilizing role of nationalism consists in expanding the social scale of human interaction and identification. Thus individuals who once saw themselves as Neapolitan or Piedmontese come to think of themselves as (also) Italian; people who once thought of themselves as Hanoverian or Bavarian come to think of themselves as (also) German; people who once thought of themselves as Gikuyu or Luo come to think of themselves as (also) Kenyan. The notion that the industrialization and modernization of any society brings with it an expansion of the realm of identification from the parochial level of family, village, and clan to the demographically larger and more socially varied level of city, province, and nation, is a standard theme of classical nineteenth-century sociology.[4] Moreover, the closely conjoined notion that such an increase in the scale of individual social interaction and identification is very often accompanied by a *change in language use* (from

3. List, *The National System*, 174.
4. Gellner, *Nations and Nationalism*, and Anderson, *Imagined Communities*, both stress this point.

a mass of—often mutually incomprehensible—local languages or dialects to a single standardized national language encoded in a printed form and used as compulsory vehicle of communication of the citizen with the state and of the state with all its citizens) is an equally common theme in many modern studies of nationalism and nation-building.[5]

For List, and for many other advocates of and apologists for nationalism, these processes represent an increase in the "civility" and "civilization" of human beings in that they also represents a broadening of their social and human sympathies. Individuals who live out their lives on a national rather than on a parochial village or regional scale, learn thereby about an increased variety of human conduct and belief. They also learn simultaneously about the range of variation of norms and social customs which may be found even among the people they are (simultaneously) learning to call "fellow citizens" or "fellow nationals." They learn thereby both a greater tolerance of diversity and a greater capacity to live a positive and personally enriching life amid and through that diversity.

That at least was the claim and hope of nineteenth-century liberal nationalists like List. A range of bloody national and world wars since 1841 have somewhat weakened the more inflated of these civilizing claims for nationalism—especially perhaps among European intellectuals. Nonetheless, there is clearly something to the notion that in expanding the scale of human social interaction, nation-building did (and perhaps still does, in the non-European world) weaken the hold on peoples' minds of at least the most confining sorts of local parochialisms and does involve some "expansion of social consciousness" (as it is often put). And this seems to be the case, even if that expansion may still have its limits, and certainly does not necessarily equate to an expansion of social tolerance, even of all fellow nationals, let alone of foreigners.

Let us therefore, for the sake of argument, accept this civilizing claim for nationalism. Let us, at least for the sake of argument, accept the claim that the movement from a parochial to a national identification is a movement that brings "objectively" human beings closer to be being "subjectively" human beings—closer to the widest possible subjective identity that such beings can possess. The question then arises whether that identity can be expanded still further, from the national to the regional or even continental level. The creation—or attempted creation—of a European

---

5. Karl Deutsch, *Nationalism and Social Communication: An Inquiry into the Foundations of Nationality* (New York: John Wiley and Sons, 1953), is perhaps the classical text here.

Union in Western Europe, and with it the attempt to turn notions like "Europe" and "European" from empty geographical expressions into some sort of subjectively felt identity, poses this question in a pressing political form in one part of the world today. So can it be done? Is it possible, this expansion of subjective identification of human beings beyond the national level?

When considering this question we have available for consultation a great deal of postmodern social and political theorizing about "identity" and "the Other." But personally I do not find it very helpful. Most of this literature insists, properly enough, that any notion of identity presupposes and requires an "Other" to operate at all. Thus a conception of masculinity requires a conception of femininity against which to define itself; a conception of Occidental or Western a conception of Oriental; a conception of youth that of adulthood; a conception of Italian that of non-Italian, a conception of Britishness that of non-Britishness.[6] But all that this tells us (if it tells us anything) is that all possible human identities are parasitical upon notions of difference, and that therefore a desire for all human beings to have one—and *only* one—identity is a self-contradictory desire. It is the desire for an impossibility. But I do not desire human beings to have *only* one identity, so this conclusion is of no interest to me. That is, although it seems to me axiomatic that human beings *en masse* will always have multiple identities, it does not follow from this that *national* identities, as we now have them, need to be a permanent element in that multiplicity. Indeed there were centuries of recorded human history in which human identities were clearly multiple (men/women, children/adults, Moslems, Christians, Taoists, Buddhists, Hindus, nobility and commoners, warriors, artisans, priests, serfs, slaves, etc.) but this multiplicity (which was in fact far more complex and fine-grained than the above list suggests) did not include national identities in the modern sense. Why could not human beings therefore have a future in which an even finer-grained multiplicity of identity reigned (men, women, transsexual, heterosexual, homosexual, bisexual, Moslem, Christian, Taoist, Buddhist, Hindu, agnostic, atheist, African, European, Native American, Native Australasian, Pacific islander, environmentalist, hedonist, member of the Sect of Western Hemisphere Super Puritanical Atheist Transsexuals) without that even greater multiplicity including national identities as we now understand them?

6. For a text making typically heavy weather of laboring this obvious point, see Ihab Hassan, "The Culture of Postmodernism," *Theory, Culture and Society* 2 (1985): 119–31.

But the main reason why social theory of the postmodernist or any other variety is of little utility in answering the question I am interested in, is that social theory speaks only of what *is,* and contents itself with describing and explaining that which *is.* But here I am concerned with what is *not.* That is, asking whether or not X is possible is not like asking whether or not it is green or sticky. It is not, that is to say, a question simply about the world. Rather, it is a question about the world *and* about the actions of the asker (and of other people) in the world. That is, a valid answer to the question, is X possible? is that it is possible if enough people want it enough and act to bring it about. But the answer to the question of whether or not X is green is not—*never* is—(and despite some facile forms of extreme philosophical subjectivism) that it is green if enough people say it is green and act as if it were green. Rather the answer is, quite properly, it is green if it is green. However, the proposition, it is possible if it is possible, does not answer the question of whether or not X is possible. Rather, it begs it.[7]

So in short, the question, can human political identities be extended beyond the national level? can productively be rephrased—rephrased *actively* as it were, as a question about human action, and the motives for and consequences of that action. For example, it can be put in the form, what can be *done* to extend human political identities beyond the national level, or, at least to begin such a process? But questions about possibility are always questions about the world (conceived as an object) *as well as* about subjective action. Thus, even if we are interested in changing the world through our actions, it is still perfectly valid to ask such objectifying questions as what factors in the world are likely to facilitate an extension of identities beyond the national level? and what factors in the world are likely to resist or block such an extension? In fact, there is probably some merit in dealing with these objective questions first, so that a context can be set for the "subjective" or "action" questions.

## *Globalization and the Transcendence of Nationalism*

In the case of the factors facilitating a human transcendence of nationalism, an obvious answer is "the economic changes occurring in the world which I have analyzed at length in this book, and which are usually

7. I got this and many other important insights from Wittgenstein. For some Wittgensteinian insights into the concept of possibility in particular, see my *Marxism and Science,* 156–58 and 164–71.

referred to as 'globalization'"; and since I have already analyzed those changes, and some of their implications at length, I do not need to repeat any of that here.

In the case of the factors likely to resist or block such a transcendence, probably the most significant of these factors at present are the fears and uncertainties of those who have benefited most from the nationalistic pre-globalized economic system of capitalism as it existed up to the 1960s, and as it continues to exist—to an extent—up to now. As should by now be clear, I have in mind here primarily the ordinary worker-citizens of the advanced capitalist societies of the world, rather than the capitalist firms and other organizations that have employed them. For it is the former rather than the latter, I believe, that have most immediately—in the short term—to lose from certain changes associated with globalization.

However, while I believe it is the fears and insecurities of the worker-citizens of the advanced capitalist world—and most especially those fears and insecurities converted into electoral pressure on their national governments—which represent the most important political obstacle to globalization at the moment, it is not the only such obstacle. Another, almost as significant I think, is the comparative newness of nation-states and of national consciousness in many non-European parts of the world. To put it simply, a large part of the non-European world only got into the political nation-state business in the last fifty or so years, and it generally did so out of a background, and *against* a background (in opposition to a background) of European colonial conquest. In many of those societies too, the nation-building process (the transformation of national identities from merely elite identities to broadly felt mass identities) is still going on, is partially or radically incomplete, and in some parts of the world (most notably sub-Saharan Africa) has effectively stalled, or is actually being reversed. In this kind of context the nationalist elites of such countries are hardly likely to welcome any persuasive message to the effect that nationalism has had its day or that important forms of economic and political decision-making need to move beyond the national level. Indeed, they are quite likely to see any such messages as backdoor attempts to reintroduce or reinforce forms of Western economic, cultural, and (indeed) political imperialism. In the case of Africa in particular, such messages are also likely to be perceived as the worst kind of irony, or as the cruelest of jokes. These elites will see a globalist antinationalism as a cruel joke just because in the African case national disintegration *is* happening in many places, but is not leading to some "higher" reality of global integration. On the contrary, it is typically leading to forms of economic and political retrogression, localization, and chaos that are just a part of Africa's increasingly anomalous *isolation* from the globalizing economy.

So these factors then set some of the most important parameters or constraints in which any effective action to transnationalize political activity and political loyalties must take place, and of which such action, and its activists, must take account. So let us take each of them in turn and consider their "action" implications, their implications for the kind of political action that is possible and feasible.

### Nationalism and the Insecurities of the Rich

In the case of the first constraint—the fears, anxieties, and insecurities of the worker-citizens of the advanced capitalist world—the political danger that this factor raises is clear. It is that the privileged states and economic blocs of the world (Japan, the EU, NAFTA) far from pushing globalization on to what I have called a form of "modified Ricardianism," will begin to try and slow down, or even reverse the process, either by the use of national policy instruments, or (more likely) by the use of bloc policies and instruments. We should not underestimate the capacity of these advanced capitalist states, at least if they act in unison, to do this. The reintroduction of capital controls and regulations (especially on a bloc basis), the manipulation of tax rates and of access mechanisms (formal and informal) to their mass markets, could be used to discourage all forms of global capital movements and to try, above all, to halt or slow down global relocations of production activities. In addition, formal and informal protection of domestic agricultural markets and markets for industrial goods, far from being lowered or gradually reduced, could be reintroduced or further increased.

The question is, however, what would be most likely to produce a retreat into these forms of economic nationalism or blocism by the prosperous capitalist nations? The answer is, I think, not far to seek. It would be the eruption of mass forms of social and political opposition to globalization arising from the economic dislocations and insecurities that it is increasingly seen to be generating. The growth in support for right-wing ultranationalist political groups and parties all over Western Europe in the present period suggests that these dangers are not at all theoretical. On the contrary, they point firmly to the kind of pro-globalizing policies that should *not* be pursued in the prosperous parts of the world. In particular, such constraints suggest, as I have already said, that Ricardo's global free movement of labor is not a policy that can be contemplated for, let alone implemented in, the foreseeable future.

However, these same constraints point up, equally clearly, the kind of pro-globalization policies that *should* be pursued in the immediate future in the rich states and blocs of the world. It is important that the world's advanced capitalist states act—and again it would be far easier and better to do this on a bloc basis—to reduce the levels of anxiety of their populations about the globalization process by putting in place *social policies* that make these anxieties and insecurities easier to cope with. I have in mind here large investments in education, training, and retraining programs that can make their working populations as change-adaptive as it is possible for them to be. But I also have in mind the maintenance of good-quality mass access to health, social security, and other programs. For such programs can reduce the increasingly prevalent sense among the worker-citizens of such countries, that they are increasingly being left alone to cope with the consequences of rapid structural change as best they can. It is hard enough to cope with endemic economic and occupational uncertainty. But to do so in a situation where one must also worry about how one will cope with sickness and old age, or with the costs of one's childrens' education, or with the costs of periods of unemployment and/or retraining, is to risk turning mass uncertainty and worry into growing mass rage.[8]

There is, however, a standard objection to those who advocate expansion of state social policies in advanced capitalist countries as part of the necessary cost of coping with structural economic change without social and political polarization. This objection is that, because of other consequences of globalization (notably the need to maintain globally competitive tax rates on capital and labor), these kinds of programs cannot be afforded any longer. However, it is my view that while this may be true on an individual nation-state basis, it need not be true on a bloc (EU or NAFTA) basis. For it may be possible either for these blocs individually, or (even better) by agreement between them, to agree to uniform minimum tax rates and levels of social expenditure—levels that both labor and capital would have to bear *wherever* they located in Western Europe or North America. In addition they could set uniform levels of social security (in the most general sense) from which labor would benefit uniformly

8. This is the view very persuasively argued for by Will Hutton. See W. Hutton, *The State to Come* (London: Vintage, 1997), especially chap. 3.

*wherever* it was located in Western Europe or North America. In other words then, instead of each advanced capitalist state individually giving up the ghost on social policy and then collectively rushing backward into protectionism as the social and political costs of globalization become unsustainable, they need to act *collectively* on tax regimes and on social policy *now* to make the shorter-term transitional costs of globalization bearable for their people. In so acting now they will avert the need for such protectionist backtracking in the future.

There is a way of putting this polemically. One of the first political converts and apostles of neoliberalism or "economic rationalism,"[9] in the Western world—Margaret Thatcher—famously expressed the view that maintaining a successful and dynamic market or capitalist economy was not compatible with also maintaining what she scornfully referred to as the "nanny state"—the postwar British welfare state with its famous rhetorical commitment to care for the basic social needs of ordinary British citizens "from cradle to grave." I wish to argue the diametrically opposite position to this—that the political cost of creating and maintaining a successful and dynamic global capitalist system is the *maintenance* of something like a "nanny state," or rather a kind of "nanny superstate" (a supranational kind of welfare state) in the currently advanced parts of that system. For without such a state or states—the taxes they can levy and the social protections they can provide[10]—the shorter-term social and political costs of globalization for the richest societies of the world may simply prove unsustainable.

9. This is the term favored in Australia. I have always thought it rather odd, if only because it tends to be used primarily by Australian opponents of neoliberalism but seems to concede to the neoliberals their position that all economic views save their own are irrational. However, perhaps one could make a distinction between "rational" and "rational*ist*" here. That is, other economic views are rational but not rationalist (where "rationalist" means something like "derived from abstract and impractical logic-chopping with formal models"). In that case, the term might be rather appropriate.

10. This does not imply, of course, that the social welfare system setup needs to be centrally *managed* and/or *implemented* by some "supranational" bureaucracy, whether in Brussels or anywhere else. In fact I would favor it being managed and implemented in highly varied, localized, and "subnational" ways to provide for greater flexibility and appropriateness to local socioeconomic conditions. But that is another matter, and quite a separate matter from the more fundamental observation that such forms of state (nonmarket) welfare provision can probably not be adequately *funded* and maintained now—in a globalizing world—except on some kind of agreed transnational basis. "Set and raise taxes supranationally, spend them subnationally" might be a good slogan here.

## Nationalism and the Aspirations of the Poor

The second major objective constraint on political globalization is the newness of Third World nationalism. The attachment of existing non-European national elites to the new political entities they have created strongly suggests that a successful politics here would have to depend upon getting such elites to accept and act upon a redefinition of what a nationalist economic policy requires. In particular, as I have repeatedly emphasized, it means encouraging such elites to abandon any notion of national development that involves using economic protectionism as a means to try and reproduce some ideal-typical advanced capitalist society locally by some sort of politically driven, instant, or hothouse means. Rather, and in place of this, developmental states—states and state elites that are actually serious about economic development—must give attention to how, in a context of reducing or abandoning protectionism, they can best make use of their labor and of their other natural resources and other advantages, to find productive and profitable niches in the global economy.

Such a policy does *not*—I wish to emphasize—involve abandoning industrialization and reverting to exclusive concentration on primary product production. But it *does* involve creating, along with TNCs and other types of foreign investor, manufacturing industries that can be competitive both in open domestic markets and in export markets, from the very beginning. It also involves such state elites moving toward domestic economic openness, only as a *quid pro quo* of the advanced capitalist countries doing the same thing, both in agricultural and industrial markets and by means of both bilateral and multilateral trade agreements.

However, and as I have also said, gradual reduction or abandonment of nationalist economic protectionism is unlikely, in itself, to be enough to allow cheap-labor economies to take full advantage of their competitive edge in an open global capitalist economy. To do this they will need extensive infrastructure development in both urban and rural areas. Above all, they will need massive investments in the education and training of their workforces, so that that their workers are not merely far cheaper to employ (in agriculture *and* labor-intensive manufacturing industry) than Western workers, but just as technically skilled (for this will make them doubly attractive to globally mobile capital). It is my view that, once again, these infrastructural and educational investments may be easier to fund and implement on a supranational basis—through various forms of economic union and/or free trade areas formed between or among Third World states.

Even in an open modified Ricardian global economy then, cheap labor *in itself* is not going to be any kind of development asset, unless it is educated and trained, unless it can operate within an advanced and continually advancing economic infrastructure, and unless it lives in conditions of decent civil peace and order (for it is such civil peace and order that makes investment in such labor a reasonable risk). Such reflections make one intensely gloomy about the short- to medium-term development prospects of sub-Saharan Africa, where so many of the world's currently poorest people live, and where (not coincidentally) virtually none of the above conditions are met. I do not have time or space here to comment more extensively on this matter. But I do wish to reiterate the point that if the world is to proceed politically beyond the nation-state, it can do so only by way of an economic platform (of a certain development of what Marxists call "the productive forces") which nation-states have historically superintended. Where, however, states and state elites have chronically failed in this platform-laying task, then the poor worker-citizens of such states are left with only one form of involvement in the global economy open to them. They are forced to become the cheapest and most unskilled kind of migrant labor, both legal and illegal, which lays them open to the most vicious forms of exploitation and discrimination in the societies to which they migrate. Moreover, unskilled transnational laboring is a form of involvement in the global capitalist economy whose growth prospects are most limited.

As I have repeatedly said, free—or even approximately free—global movement of labor is the one item in the Ricardian model that is still a political nonstarter in our world, now and for the foreseeable future. That being the case, a people, any people, can get themselves into a much better—more economically dynamic—development situation, if they can *get capital to come to them,* rather than having to travel thousands of miles to find capital (and often the most primitive and backward forms of capital at that) to employ them. But to do that—to get capital to come to them—certain minimum economic and political conditions have to be met in the regions of the world where the people who desperately need that capital live. Many of the political elites of sub-Saharan Africa are to be roundly condemned for their manifest failure to create those conditions *in Africa* for the people for whom they are supposedly responsible.

## Human Rights, Human Diversity,
### and the Transcendence of Nationalism

So then, social policy to cushion the costs of transition to globalization in the advanced capitalist world, economic and social policies to make cheap labor a competitive trump card in the underdeveloped or peripheral capitalist world. But is that all? That is, are these the only policies that might help move political identities and loyalties on beyond the national level?

No, there are others, and two at least of these are very important. The first of them involves the political use of an abstraction—the abstraction of "human rights." To put it simply, the creation of some effective global or transnational means of enforcing at least some minimal notion of human rights (not, or not as yet I think, the full UN Charter) would be a highly effective means, over time, of filling a notion of a "common humanity" with some affective content. If people everywhere in the world can feel they have an effective guarantee of the most fundamental of all such rights (the right to life) even, and indeed particularly, against their own national governments or political elites, this will, in itself, be an important force in expanding the horizon of mass consciousness beyond the national level. In this context, I am obviously heartened by recent events in Kosovo and East Timor, and equally obviously disheartened by the contrast of those events with others in Rwanda or Sierra Leone or Chechnya. However, and more fundamentally, a genuinely global enforcement of some minimum set of human rights can only occur if it is not left to the vagaries of shifting U.S. State Department or presidential politics, or to cobbled together "NATO" actions, or to equally cobbled together, and underfunded, "Australasian" actions on the Indonesian archipelago. Rather, a permanent standing global peace-enforcing and peace-keeping force needs to be created, possessed of Leviathan levels of firepower and some transnational basis of funding. It will also require its own command structure answerable to some supranational human rights monitoring body.

No doubt the creation of such a force and such a body will be a formidably difficult task in our world of sovereign nation-states with their (universal and therefore self-contradictory) claims to the "monopoly of the means of violence." But at least a start can be made by acceding to the current U.N. secretary-general's demand for a much better equipped and funded U.N. peacekeeping force with some greater proactive powers.

However, if taking abstract human rights seriously is an important way to start seriously denationalizing the world, taking concrete human *diversity* equally seriously, is as important, if not more important. That is, to have genuinely global communication among human beings, we need forms of such communication that take the realities of cultural, religious, and other forms of diversity seriously and respect them (which is not the same as uncritically endorsing any or all of them). This is vital, because without such respect a discourse of "humanity" is likely to be seen (as it is by so many at present) as a disguised discourse of Western cultural hegemony. I am not very optimistic about this issue in a world in which the most effective means of mass global communication are dominated by Murdoch's News Corp and similar organizations (although, in fact, News Corporation's satellite channels are culturally aware and variegated in some rather crude and pragmatic ways). On the other hand, however, the development of the internet does perhaps provide rather more hope for forms of culturally varied global conversation. It may do so, that is, if the question of the class nature of its distribution (an issue everywhere) can be addressed.

But these issues of technical hardware and software (and who owns and controls them), though difficult, are not perhaps the most difficult issues to be faced here. There is a more fundamental philosophical difficulty. The project of a genuinely respectful and culturally diverse global conversation of peoples requires as a prerequisite a universal commitment to an ethic of tolerance. That is, it requires a commitment to a kind of procedural principle which says that all human cultures and religions, merely because they *are* human, are worthy of equal attention and respect, or at least are so until they show themselves not worthy of such respect by transgressing some norm which all other human beings might agree is not to be transgressed. But the problem is that not all—perhaps not most—of the actually existing cultures and religions of the world endorse this tolerance ethic. On the contrary, it is a very condition of commitment to many of them to believe in their epistemological, philosophical *superiority* to other competing cultures and religions. Such commitments can themselves make open and equal conversation almost impossible from the beginning. I have really no idea how this problem might be solved, except perhaps to say that only in conversation—by the very process of conversation itself—is there even any *hope* that greater mutual understanding and tolerance can be created. So the first task is to get global communication going on at least some roughly equal basis, to keep it going, and to see what happens. In the culturally imperialist world of News Corp *et al.,* even that is going to be a hard enough task.

## Conclusions

Two further points by way of conclusion to this chapter. First, it is not my aim in this text to advocate a world in which all people in the world feel (how shall I put it?) "affectively the same or similar" about all other people in the world. In fact I think that such a world, far from being humanly desirable, would be humanly monstrous. For it could only be a world of human *indifference,* a world where literally nobody really cared about anybody. If I were asked who matters most to me, my answer would be totally conventional. It is my partner, my children, my friends and relatives, who are (globally speaking) a tiny few people in number and located on some very particular and small parts of the earth's surface. These people speak the language (English) I happen to speak most fluently. They share many (not all) of my beliefs and values. I am at ease with them. They are at ease with me. They are central to my sense both of who I am, and indeed of who I am not. And I expect that an answer such as the above is—the usual paradox—at once a deeply personal/particular and entirely universal answer. It is, in short, the kind of answer that *everybody* on this planet would give if asked the same question. Generally speaking too, this sense of affective, identity-giving-and-defining community is, for most people on the planet, tied closely to the reality of *locality,* to a particular place or particular set of (small) places on the earth's surface, where they were born; where they grew up, and so forth.

It is for these reasons that the attempted implementation of all economic policies that treat people—or even purport to treat people—as simply some mobile factor of production (called "labor") available to be shunted around the world in precisely the same way as capital is shunted—always meet, in practice, with strong forms of social and communitarian resistance. For people who go a few thousand (or hundreds or tens) of miles to find work have usually been displaced from what makes them happy, and indeed from what makes and keeps them who they are. So the experience of a person, a human being, moving over the earth's surface in pursuit of a job or of better economic opportunities is existentially incommensurable with the "nano-second" electronic movement of a sum of money from Chicago to Singapore. Socialists in particular have always insisted on this crucial difference and resisted all forms of economics that would ignore it and treat labor and capital as ontologically equivalent "factors of production." They have, I believe, been right to do so. But just because they have been right, they must also acknowledge that the global movement of capital is a far more humane (as well as a technically easier way) of bringing about—one hopes, eventually—an equalization of material living standards among workers than is the global movement of labor. And to be fair to them, what conventional economists mean by the "free movement of labor" is a situation in which anybody who wants to move anywhere *can* do so (without legal or political impediment). They do not mean by this phrase a situation in which everybody, or even most people, *have* to do so out of economic necessity whether they wish to or not.

The world I wish to see then is a world in which most people live, and can live, in social contexts and communities in which they can feel secure and "at home" and in which such communities have approximately equal standards of living worldwide. But I also do not see why such communities cannot be embedded in an open global economy, or be part of new geopolitical entities, some of which might be larger—geographically and demographically—than our current nation-states, and yet others far smaller. (One could perhaps conceive the difference between the two types of entities being functional, so that a particular human community could be a member of one such entity for some "governance" purposes and of another for others.) Above all, I wish to see a world in which human diversity and particularity is *not* expressed in ill-informed or stereotyped images of any human "Other" or groups of "Others." Rather I want a world in which that diversity is known and sympathetically understood by all and in which there is widespread openness to, tolerance of, and delight in the diversity itself.

"But is all this *really* possible?" I hear my readers ask. To this my reply is to remind you once again about the peculiarity of the question about whether anything (or anything in the human world) is "possible." This is not simply, I say again, a question about "the human world" conceived in that "objectified" way. It is just as much a question about *you!*

My second concluding point is as follows. Even if the world I have envisioned were to come about, it would not of course be a world of total equality. It would be a world of rough equality of all *workers*—of men and women workers, of Islamic and Christian workers, of black and white workers, of agricultural and industrial and service workers. But it would still retain one massive source of inequality. I refer to that division between those who would still own and (more particularly) control these massive global means of production, communication, and distribution, and those who would still work for them worldwide. In short, the division between those possessed of capital, and those possessed only or mainly of labor as their principal economic asset, would remain. At that point (say a couple of hundred years down the track) I think it might be a good idea, for virtually everybody on the planet, to abolish *that* division too. That should not be done I hasten to add, by abolishing the market, or by making capitalist property the property of some superstate or states. Rather it should be done by, as far as is possible, making ownership of capital universal and roughly equal and by making the management of all enterprises as democratic as possible. Good lord, some embarrassingly old socialist beliefs are showing! On quickly to my conclusions!

# CHAPTER NINETEEN

# Conclusions:
# Globalization and the Left

As the first draft of this book was being completed, in December 1999, the press and mass media focused, briefly but intently, on events surrounding the latest round of WTO discussions on trade liberalization taking place in Seattle. The negotiations ended in failure. But more significantly perhaps, they became, for the first time, a target for mass street demonstrations against the process of economic globalization in general and the global role of transnational corporations in particular. A Sydney morning newspaper reported the following events on its front page of December 2, 1999.

As tear gas canisters exploded and armed riot police were dealing with rioters a few blocks away, the Bangladesh trade delegate Mr. Abdul-Muyeed Chowdhuy[1] was telling demonstrators a little about his homeland and why he was in Seattle.

A small man, wrapped in a jumper, thick coat and beanie, Mr. Chowdhuy explained why he wanted access to his blockaded World Trade Organization conference centre.

"You are very poorly informed," he told them. "In my country people are starving, they drink water from the river. That is why we

---

1. I assume that this is a mistake and that his name was actually Chowdhury or Choudhury and that the reporter, or someone else, simply mistranscribed it. (Small but important factor in cross-cultural understanding—getting peoples' names right.) In any event I have taken the liberty of referring to him as Chowdury in my own text.

are here, We want market access to the rich countries. Until we have done these things, poor people will stay poor and they will still be drinking from the well and the river and getting sick.". . .

There was silence after Mr. Chowdhuy's words, then one young demonstrator piped up: "It's not democratic, man. It's corporate greed and we're here to shut it down."[2]

It seemed to me that that exchange encapsulated, in an almost painfully intense form, the problems that face the world in the era of globalization. For here we have the fleeting encounter of two undoubtedly well-intentioned human beings, apparently both deeply concerned with the same phenomena, but between whom mutual incomprehension is total. One speaks of disease, sanitation, the most basic poverty. The other speaks of democracy. One speaks of access to markets, the other of greedy corporations. Above all, neither has the remotest conception of the life experiences that have formed the values and priorities of the other and so they are both condemned to a (mercifully brief, in this case) dialogue of the deaf.

Reading this newspaper report led me, however, not just to reflect on the events it recorded but upon myself. For I am a Westerner, an Englishman, a "Pom," now an Australian citizen, who has spent an adult life lived among the academic left of the Anglo-Saxon world. Indeed I have many friends and colleagues in that world, which has been my preferred intellectual habitat since I was a young man in the late 1960s. But I have also spent some years living and working in East Africa, traveled and consulted in other parts of Africa and Latin America, and immersed myself for many years in the academic specialization called development studies. This, inevitably, has brought me into close contact with many Third World people, some of whom have also become friends. It has also brought me into direct physical, sensual contact with the realities of severe human poverty and economic underdevelopment. I have lived in peasant villages, walked and talked in urban shantytowns, seen what malnutrition, poverty-induced disease, lack of basic sanitation, mass unemployment, and underemployment mean.

From the time that it first emerged as an interdisciplinary academic specialization in the 1960s development studies always attracted a significant

2. Tom Allard, "Grunge City v World Greed: Restless in Seattle," *The Sydney Morning Herald,* December 2, 1999, p. 1.

number of students and academics of broadly left-wing views. Indeed the personal and intellectual conduits leading from the more specialized world of development studies to the broader world of left-wing academia were always broad and open ones. In particular, an interest in, and study of, the history and present reality of Western *imperialism* is often what links, or linked, the left-wing academic in development studies or area studies to the left-wing academic in history, economics, political science, sociology, literature, and so forth.

Living then in both these worlds—of the development or Third World-ist left, and of the academic left more generally—I did not, for a long time, perceive any significant or intractable differences between them. Both, after all, concerned themselves with the causes of inequality, injustice, oppression in the world, and with the means by which these might be overcome. Both concurred that the division of the world between a rich, powerful, and imperialist West and a poor, oppressed, and exploited Third World was a major—perhaps the major—problem confronting humanity. Representatives of both could be found at the same demonstrations, signing the same petitions, protesting the same "imperialist" actions, whether those were in Vietnam, Guatamala, Iran, or wherever.

Very gradually, however, it became clear to me that this seamless web which seemed to join my own concerns to those of so many other leftist friends and colleagues was not quite so seamless after all. Gradually I saw that nationalism, or more exactly nationalistically structured perceptions of the world, divided my own perspective far more fundamentally from that of many of my friends than I had ever imagined or suspected.

This realization did not come all at once. On the contrary, it came as a number of discrete revelations and observations stretching over many years, revelations and observations which I only later came to see as parts of a single theme or syndrome. The first of these observations was rather narrowly academic. During the late 1970s and early 1980s I was a regular attendee at the History Workshop conferences held annually at Ruskin College in Oxford. The central topics dealt with in these conferences varied widely—from childhood and sexuality, to sport and recreation, to diverse topics in both working-class and feminist history—but almost invariably, if papers dealt with non-European empirical material they were placed in a separate organizational category called Imperialism. And this was true *even if the papers in question dealt with issues directly germane to the advertised leading theme of a conference.* It seemed somehow that, in the eyes of the conference organizers, African or Asian or Latin American people did not have histories of "childhood" or "urbanization" or "sexuality" or "gender divisions of labor" in the same way that European people did.

It was perhaps around the same time (the late 1970s/early 1980s) that I also began to observe that left intellectuals with little or no personal experience of underdeveloped societies tended to focus their intellectual interest predominantly on topics which *linked* a developing country or some region of the developing world, empirically and/or conceptually, to their country or region of origin. Thus, they were usually strongly interested in the doings of Western TNCs, in international trade and investment issues generally, and in topics having to do with the use (and abuse) of overseas aid. But their interest waned markedly when matters more narrowly internal to developing countries—peasant agriculture and rural sociology, patterns of Third World urbanization, political and military institutions in Africa, Latin America—were raised. In fact, I gradually came to think of the category of "Imperialism" as fulfilling much the same purposes for many Western left intellectuals as the category of "International Relations" does for more orthodox scholars—that of clothing parochial or self-regarding interests in a more expansive garb. Provide a course titled "Australia and the Asian Tigers" and two hundred Australian IR students will instantly enroll. Provide a course titled "Anti-Kuomintang Sentiment and the Rise of Small Business in Taiwan," however, and you'll be lucky to get twenty. Similarly, provide a left-wing course titled "Australian Business Interests and Australian Aid to Melanesia" and you'll find every student with left leanings present and correct. Provide a left-wing course titled "Peasant Class Differentiation in the Highlands of Papua New Guinea," however, and you may well struggle for clients, left-wing or otherwise.

In a left intellectual context in particular this comparative lack of interest among many of my European leftist friends and colleagues in the internal workings of Third World or economically underdeveloped societies had one particularly interesting and ironic consequence (and I suppose this was my second disturbing observation in the sequence). In a word, it tended to lead them—or many of them—to treat such societies *as if they were classless.* That is, whereas if they were concerned with Britain, or Australia, or the United States, questions of class structure and the shifting dynamics of that structure, would be central to their concerns, I noticed that, in practice, if not in theory, they tended to speak about Third World societies in terms ("poor countries," "poor nations," "underdeveloped countries") that, as it were, socially homogenized the poverty of those societies. Of course, being leftists, such people might be committed to the abstract theoretical proposition that *no* human society is classless. But this proposition remained abstract insofar as the people concerned had no empirical knowledge of the class structure of Bangladesh, or Brazil, or Malaysia and so could not fill this abstract conviction with any substantive content. In this situation, what my partner often calls the "Oxfam" or "starving babies" conception of underdevelopment often filled the empirical void by assumptive default.

Moreover, and for much the same underlying reasons, many of my European leftist colleagues were often ignorant of the role played by dominant classes in many parts of the non-European world in maintaining, or even exacerbating, problems of underdevelopment—whether that be through support for parasitic or rapacious landlord classes in the countryside, through endemic (and often state-centered) patterns of corruption and rent-seeking, or through the systematic trading by local elites or sections of such elites on ethnic, religious, or other domestic social divisions. This ignorance in turn supported the easy, uninvolved conviction of many leftist friends and colleagues that all the problems of underdevelopment and poverty in the world are simply problems of "imperialism."

But perhaps neither of these first two observations was as worrying as the third, to which they led. This was the observation that European left intellectuals with no close involvement (or no involvement at all) with the non-European world tend to operate with a conception of imperialism that is what I can only call *nationalistic/racial* in its fundamental structure. That is, not only do they see the world as divided between rich and poor *nations* (with, somehow, everybody in the former involved in "imperialistically" exploiting or oppressing everybody in the latter), they also see all non-European peoples as somehow *essentially,* uniquely, equally, and unproblematically qualified to speak about "imperialism," "underdevelopment," and all associated notions. That is, any self-respecting European leftist would not hesitate to question the ideological credentials or motivations of, say, a British public school headmaster discoursing on the wonders of private education. But the same leftist will treat any Bangladeshi person discoursing on anything in Bangladesh, or any Kenyan discoursing on anything in Kenya (or, probably, Africa), or any Iranian discoursing on anything in Iran, as somehow an unchallengeable, "objective" authority, without, as it were, any social location *in* the society about which s/he is discoursing which even might (might) affect his or her perceptions/judgments/opinions.

Another way of putting this is to say that European intellectuals, even left intellectuals, are apt to treat non-European societies as if they were, somehow, less socially and ideologically complex (and thus problematic of interpretation) than their own. And would it be too insulting here to suggest that this may be because such societies are being thought of as "underdeveloped," and "underdeveloped" is here being used as a synonym for "primitive"? Racism, I want to observe, can be a deep and complex thing, and the more sophisticated the person, the more deep and complex—and the more complexly rationalized—it may be. I observe that one of the forms it can take among liberal or liberal-radical Europeans is an unwillingness to apply intellectual criteria and standards of judgments which they would apply to fellow Europeans (both as individuals and as members of particular European societies) to non-European peoples. In a word, such intellectuals often treat such people in socially de-contextualized and racially essentialized ways, ways in which they do not treat fellow Europeans.

Certainly I think we see something of all this in that fleeting exchange between Mr. Abdul-Muyeed Chowdhury and the young American radicals in Seattle. The reporter tells us that "there was silence after Mr. Chowdhury's words." Why was there silence? Because, I would bet, the young people blocking Mr. Chowdury's way regarded his views on poverty and starvation as authoritative, given his skin color, accent, etc. (given his "Third World" ethnicity in fact).[3] But at the same time they wished to

3. To be fair, I must also add here that some intellectuals, politicians, officials from the Third World, are apt to reinforce this kind of behavior by European leftists by legitimizing themselves through the same kind of racist essentialism. "Only Indians can really understand India." "Only Africans can really understand Africa." It is because I think that a lot of so-called postcolonial literature—or at any rate its most popular or "lumpen" appropriations—tends to encourage this sort of essentialism that I find it so distasteful. This is a complex issue, but suffice to say here that a lot of this literature begins from the postmodernist postulate that one's cultural values will significantly determine what one regards as true (so that, as it were, all truths are culturally equal), but ends up endorsing some cultural truths (usually Third Worldist ones) as more equal than others. That is, it ends up, in effect, abandoning the relativism with which it began. In fact this instability is an inevitable consequence of the initial philosophically relativist postulate, which cannot (I will argue elsewhere) be held to consistently without self-contradiction. A lot of postcolonial writing is also distasteful in trading constantly on a kind of guilt-tripping of Western liberals. But that is another complex matter I cannot go into in a footnote. But briefly, in the worst kind of postcolonial discourse (not, I must emphasize, in the best, such asin the work of Homi Bhaba), the postulation of a single, authentic, "Third Worldist" or "postcolonial" voice always entails the denial or occlusion of some aspect or other of the social location of the Third World intellectual (class, caste, gender, ethnicity, religion)

defend their own actions as still right and legitimate. The silence then reflected their need for time to phrase a defense of their own actions in ways that would not conflict with his "authoritative" statements. Support for democracy and opposition to corporate greed are, eventually, the rhetorical terms one of their number finds to try and do this. And almost certainly this choice of defense reflected his view that they (the protesters), being Westerners, could claim close authoritative knowledge of both democracy and corporate greed to match, and offset, Mr. Chowdhury's ethnically given epistemological priority in regard to poverty!

I think it is quite proper to call this exchange "racist" or "racistly distorted" insofar as there is actually no *a priori* reason to suppose that Mr. Chowdury personally is, or ever has been, poor merely because he comes from Bangladesh. But equally there is no reason *a priori* to suppose that he knows less about democracy or about corporate greed merely for the same reason. Also, there is no *a priori* reason to suppose that the protesters know more about democracy or corporate greed than he does merely because they are Westerners, but no *a priori* reason to suppose that they know less either. Also, while the Western protesters almost certainly have witnessed less severe poverty than Mr. Chowdhury, they may, just for that reason, have much less ideological investment than he in explaining it in some ways rather than others. That is, even if Mr. Chowdhury is a more emotionally involved *observer* of poverty in the world than the protesters, he may also be an unreliable *explainer* of it for just that reason. (Perhaps, perhaps not.) But what one can say, and without any "perhaps," is that the meeting between Mr. Chowdhury and the protesters fails, abysmally, as a meeting between human beings. It is simply far too clouded by mutual ignorance and (especially on the protesters' side) by a deadly combination of empirical ignorance and racistly driven stereotypes (the latter often filling the voids created by the former) to lead to any genuine communication at all.

But to return to the core of matters. All these issues reach a new level of both intensity and importance in an economically globalizing world. Because, as I have argued earlier in this book, the short- to medium-term

---

*within* the society on whose behalf s/he claims to speak. In this way, even the question of how this location may itself affect that speaker/writer's perceptions of Africa, India, the Arab world, cannot be posed. That is, it is not simply cultural distance from a society which can be a distorting factor in studying it (the distance between Occidental scholars and the "Orient" they create, most famously). And to assert otherwise, explicitly or implicitly, can itself degenerate into a kind of counterracism. The faults are not all on the Western side in these matters.

effects of the globalization process are likely to include some trade-off between the increase of employment and real incomes in (some parts of) the non-Western world and some decreases of both in (some parts of) the Western world. Therefore, in making a moral and political *judgment* of globalization, it becomes crucial, as I have also said, how one "weights" a job gained in China or Vietnam or Fiji or India against a job lost in Britain or Germany or Australia or Belgium. To repeat; whereas it seems to me that the only humanly defensible weighting is 1=1 (that is, one job counts the same wherever it is, so that if the same capital movement which leads to the loss of 200 jobs in Australia leads to the creation of 450 jobs in China there has been a net human *gain* in welfare), this is not the implicit weighting that any national or nationalistic economic calculus will apply. On the contrary, if the world is viewed dominantly or exclusively from an Australian point of view (for example), with the imagined geopolitical space of Australia also marking the boundary of economic calculation and social judgment, then one job lost in Australia counts "simply" as one job *lost* (unqualifiedly, as it were).

In other words, the process of globalization asks powerful and searching questions about the values of those who are both affected by it and observing it. In the case of those who count themselves on the left it asks such questions as the following:

1. When you talk about "workers," and about the welfare of "workers," are you explicitly or implicitly understanding that term with a particular nationalist prefix ("Australian" workers, "American" workers, "Belgian" workers) or not?
2. When you talk about "employment" or "unemployment," and about the rise and fall of these magnitudes, are you thinking in a particular national context or not?
3. When you talk about an "economy," of "economic relations" and of the growth and welfare prospects and requirements of such an "economy," are you explicitly or implicitly conceptualizing this entity in national terms?
4. When you talk about "class divisions," about "poverty," about "inequality," and about trends in these socioeconomic phenomena, are you thinking in a particular national context or on a global level?

The answers that you will give to these questions are important and significant in that, in the globalization phase of capitalism, one may see the world as moving in one direction looking at it from a national point of view, and in quite another looking at it from a global point of view.[4] Another way of putting that is to say that these conceptual questions—about how our judgments of capitalist development are affected by viewing it from one perspective ("global") rather than from another or others ("national," "regional")—are raised precisely when, and only when, such development reaches its global or globalization phase. In the pre-globalization phase of capitalist development, one might say, judgments of the welfare effects of that development could simply be an unproblematic sum of particular nationalistic or regional judgments. Now they cannot be, because there are trends in employment, income, and welfare emerging on the global level—on the level of a genuinely global capitalist system—which are precisely *sui generis* to that level, and which may in fact be in contradiction, or in partial contradiction, to trends at any given national or regional level.

There is, however, a standard leftist way of avoiding these conceptual and moral complexities. This is to cling to a willful simplicity—to say that trends at the national and global level *are* homogeneous because globalization causes drops in employment and/or in real wages in advanced capitalist countries while at the same time only creating "exploitative," "low-wage" jobs, often with poor working conditions, in underdeveloped countries. In short, the judgment is made that the trends at both the national and the global level are essentially *uniform* in their human welfare implications, being only or mainly damaging in both cases. Oddly enough this brings us back to Mr. Abdul-Muyeed Chowdhury. For only two days after the appearance of *The Sydney Morning Herald* story in which he figures, reference was explicitly made to events in Seattle, and to Mr. Chowdhury in particular, by an ACTU[5] activist being interviewed on Australian national radio. This trade union official expressed his strong satisfaction at the breakdown of the Seattle negotiations. He also opined that similar satisfaction would be felt by workers in the Third World, as well as by the workers "here in Australia," whom he represented. The only Third World people who would benefit from a world of free trade such as the WTO wanted to see, he suggested, were "local bosses and hack government officials" like Mr. Chowdhury.

4. To take one obvious example, it might not be obvious to anyone reading most of the leftist commentary literature on "deindustrialization" and falls in manufacturing employment that, *in the world as a whole,* employment in manufacturing is actually continuing to grow, not decline.

5. Australian Confederation of Trade Unions.

Now I personally have no idea whether workers in the Third World in general were pleased by the breakdown of the WTO talks in Seattle or not. I certainly found this particular trade union view of matters refreshing as, very untypically, it did at least show some recognition of the existence of class divisions, and of possibly related ideological differences, within a Third World country. But at the same time it forced me, once again, to reflect that my life and professional experiences have led me to prioritize one political desire or aspiration above all—to see the poverty of the poorest people of the world ended or at least ameliorated. And it is because I believe that unfettered market access for the goods (agricultural and manufactured) and services produced by poor people to the more prosperous markets of the world *is* a necessary (not sufficient, but necessary) condition of such mass poverty being ended or ameliorated that I support it. If Mr. Chowdhury believes that too, then I support him and not the Seattle protesters or the ACTU official. If Mr. Chowdhury believes that such access is a sufficient (not merely necessary) condition of even alleviating mass poverty in Bangladesh, then I would oppose him as either naïve or in the grip of a class-structured form of self-interest. But I still would not support the protesters or the ACTU official. More particularly, I suspect (and I share this suspicion with many Third World people of varied class backgrounds) that Western trade union demands for raising workers' wages and conditions in Third World countries to Western levels (a demand explicitly reiterated by the ACTU activist in the radio interview) are as much motivated by a nationalistic desire to protect domestic jobs as they are by concern for the welfare of fellow workers abroad.

### Radical Intellectuals and Zero-Sum Games

That suspicion brings me to a still broader issue. Many years ago, in the course of my doctoral research on peasant agriculture in Tanzania, I read an academic article by the American anthropologist George Foster called "Peasant Society and the Image of Limited Good." This article was rather widely discussed and debated at the time, but it has, I imagine, long been forgotten. On the basis of his fieldwork in rural Mexico, Foster argued that peasant societies were distinguished by the ubiquity within them of a conception of what he called limited good—the belief that any good, material or immaterial, available to human beings is in strictly limited supply. In fact all such goods are believed to be in such limited and strictly finite supply that if a person or group *A* obtains more of any good that they possessed previously, this can only have happened at the expense of person or group *B*... who must have absolutely less of the said good. Foster used this idea to explain many things about the peasant people he had studied. In particular he used it to explain why they could not be gotten to believe in the possibility of economic development that could provide benefits to all without costs to any. According to these Mexican peasants, anybody—any local leader or national or international agency—who promised such a thing had to be lying.

As I say, this article was much disputed and debated at the time. In particular many people disputed whether the ethnographic evidence that Foster presented did convincingly demonstrate the existence of this "image" among his Mexican peasant informants, or whether he had overgeneralized what his informants said and did in various ways. An interesting issue. In retrospect, however, I consider it a rather marginal point. Because I now think, not that it is improbable that peasant people believe in the limited good, but that it is highly unlikely that they would not, for as far as I can see, almost everyone does, including many on the left.

In fact, I think that is why Ricardian and neoclassical trade theory generally meets such a skeptical reception from almost everybody outside a narrow circle of its devotees. Quite simply, it suggests that something is possible which most people find both completely counterintuitive and, above all, far too good to be true. It suggests, that is, that while free movement of goods, labor, and capital globally might have short- to medium-term costs for some people, in the longer term it will provide benefits for all, without exception. That is, and concretely, if capital moves to cheap-labor areas of the globe, this may mean short- to medium-term job losses and (even perhaps) drops in real wages for workers in some other parts of the globe. But, in the longer term, or so it is claimed, the higher real incomes of the newly employed, or more remuneratively employed, poor people, will feed back into enhanced demand for goods and services, demand that will provide far more employment than was previously lost by the initial capital movement. In short, and in conventional economic terms, if free movement of goods, capital, and labor leads to faster growth of the world economy as a whole, then in the longer term everybody benefits from that growth.

Now I do not believe this "too good to be true" story either, or at least not in this, its simplest, form. That is, I believe, as I have said repeatedly in this book, that even if globalization does lead to enhanced growth of the global economy, and an enhanced mass of output and income globally, that need not be converted into enhanced material welfare for ordinary people anywhere unless appropriate redistributive political actions are taken. But, with that crucial proviso, I do nonetheless—and against what appears to be the conventional wisdom of Western radicalism, as manifested in Seattle and elsewhere—believe that global movements of capital and (therefore) of jobs are *not* part of some endless zero-sum game in which, as in the limited-good conception, "our" gains are always and for ever "their" losses or *vice versa*. I *do* believe that in the long run, the global capitalist game is a sum-sum game. I believe, that is to say, that it is a game of "expandable" or "unlimited" good, from which *all* can benefit if—but only if—the right "progressive" political conditions prevail.[6]

Moreover, and also rather unfashionably (on the Left at least) I do *not* believe that environmental or ecological constraints on economic growth are immanently about to bring this "unlimited good" game to an end. Certainly environmentally sustainable ways of generating and maintaining economic growth must be found, and found urgently. But I also believe that mass human poverty is, in itself a major cause of environmental damage on this planet[7] and that reducing that poverty would itself be a massive gain for the world's ecosystem.

Recall, however, Keynes's remark that "in the long run we are all dead." Most people only live lives that cover what economists would call the "short- to medium-term." This means that they find—experientially, existentially—that the limited-good conception *does* hold (in many areas of economic and noneconomic life).[8] In short, it is because the "limited

---

6. In this respect I concur with the arguments advanced in part 1 of Paul Krugman's *Pop Internationalism* (Cambridge: MIT Press, 1997), which is also devoted to a critique of the conception of a "zero-sum" world. But again, I feel that he, like many conventional economists, is apt to slip too easily from impeccably logical arguments about the long term to excessively sanguine treatments of short- to medium-term "frictional" or "adjustment" costs.

7. On this, see, for example, nearly all the contributions to F. C. Steady, ed., *Women and Children First: Environment, Poverty and Sustainable Development* (New York: Schenkman, 1993).

8. You lose a wallet or a purse, and it is not returned. You fail to obtain some prize or award that goes to someone else. You discover (to use a topical local example) that you have failed to obtain a ticket to see a favorite Olympic event, because 60 percent of the tickets for that event have been presold at large premiums to the corporate rich. These and millions of other similar experiences constantly reinforce popular perceptions of the world as a "zero-sum" game, a place of "limited good," in which my loss is always another's gain, and *vice versa*. Above all, the whole experience of living in a class-divided society (and we all live in such societies, they are just class-divided in different ways) seems a constant vindication of the "limited good" view. (Indeed a number of critics of Foster, of whom I

good" or "zero-sum" conception of life is so often experientially confirmed that many people, peasant or otherwise, believe it and believe it firmly. After all, a job today, however poor, is better than jam tomorrow, especially if tomorrow is ten or twenty or thirty years away. That this is so is another reason then for rejecting the most optimistic or naïve Ricardian story about free trade. And as I said earlier it is also a good reason for seeking forms of social policy that can provide security and protection for people from at least the worst effects of what economists are apt to coldly dismiss as "frictional" or "adjustment" difficulties. But this said, even these human cost considerations, being essentially short- to medium-term and partial, are *not* reasons for adopting, as so many on the left implicitly do, a "limited good" or "zero-sum" conception of the workings of the capitalist system *tout court*. For again, this is far too often just an intellectual disguise for a deep nationalism. "The capitalist system is in crisis," actually *means* "the capitalist system in Australia is in crisis" or even "the capitalist system in Victoria is in crisis" or even "the largest employers in these two towns in South Australia have just gone bust."

But I make all these judgments, or partial judgments, because, and only

---

was one, pointed out that the class relations under which his Mexican peasant informants lived probably made the "limited good" conception a perfectly rational generalization from their life experiences and not—as he presented it—some quasi-paranoid delusion.) However, having said all that, it remains the case that the limited good conception provides a seriously and fundamentally flawed basis upon which to understand the distribution of wealth and poverty under capitalism, and this is so whether one is trying to understand capitalism nationally or globally. It is absolutely vital to understand that the Industrial Revolution began an era of human *economic* history to which zero-sum game conceptions—"limited good" conceptions—do *not* apply, simply because of the enormous impetus it gave to the process of economic *growth*—to the growth of the total volume of goods and services available for human consumption. That is, industrial capitalism created, for the first time on this planet, a type of human society (capitalism) in which the material prosperity of the few did not *have* to be bought at the cost of the absolute poverty of the many. Marx grasped this point about capitalism firmly, which was *why* indeed he railed against the most extreme forms of class privilege and class oppression under capitalism. Extreme inequalities under capitalism he felt to be uniquely morally opprobrious because they are *not* a technical necessity, a function of low absolute levels of economic productivity (as they were under all precapitalist forms or modes of production). Rather, they are a product of, in the broadest sense, social and political *choice*—of human *volition*. This proposition is true, is the foundation of any properly sophisticated Left politics for the modern world, and is now true (as it was not in Marx's day) for the population of this planet as a whole. That is, as capitalism globalizes, becomes a genuinely global mode of production, so, following Marx's logic, the existence of extreme poverty and dispossession *anywhere on this planet* becomes absolutely morally noxious (because avoidable).

because, I have as a priority a particular political objective (ending or alleviating the poverty of the poorest people in the world), *and* because I hold a particular view of the causality of that poverty. Were I to prioritize another objective (maximizing employment in manufacturing in Australia, or the United Kingdom, or Italy, or in those two towns in South Australia, for example), or had I a different view of the causality of world poverty, then, presumably, I would make other judgments. But that is the point. Globalization forces us to be honest about our priorities and about our beliefs (including our beliefs about causality). Above all, it forces us to confront our parochialisms and to recognize them, perhaps uncomfortably, *as* parochialisms, even when—perhaps especially when—they have been partially occluded, partially rationalized, in hitherto easy forms of supposed "internationalism."

### *Thinking, Feeling, and the Heroism of Intellect*

The thoughts above bring me to the fundamental issue of this concluding chapter. Socialist politics, the politics of the Left traditionally considered, has always been, rhetorically at least, an internationalist politics, a politics of humanity in the broadest sense. Therefore, if it has in fact been as deeply and pervasively compromised or qualified by a (generally implicit) nationalism—and even, yes, racism—as I have suggested, it is hardly surprising if the vast non-leftist bulk of humanity evinces a nationalistic/racist myopia that is explicit, proud, and virulent rather than (as it is on the left) implicit, closeted, and apologetic. For in either case the fundamental human roots of the phenomenon are the same—the limitations of a social creature, *homo sapiens*, which can only feel close to a finite number of its fellow creatures, in a finite social and geographical space, in (usually) a particular and singular language. Those of us on the left should not be calumnied for these deeply human limitations anymore than anyone else should. "Parochialism is the only genuine human universality," I tell my students,[9] and they always laugh more heartily than I expect, probably out of relief.

9. Consider Saul Steinberg's "A View of the World from 9th Avenue" (1976), perhaps best known as the *New Yorker* magazine cover "A New Yorker's View of the World." It is a visual perspective joke, in which Times Square, the Empire State Building, and the Brooklyn Bridge feature massively in the foreground. Beyond them we see a small stretch of water in mid-perspective (the Atlantic Ocean), then a Big Ben and Eiffel Tower as small figures in a rapidly exceeding background, then Moscow as a barely discernible spot, then a haze labeled "Asia." This cartoon has been reproduced ad nauseam and has since been

So the question then is not whether we can feel differently about our need for what Benedict Anderson called an imagined community, whether we count ourselves as "on the left" or not.[10] For, given our present historical location, we plainly cannot do so. The question rather is whether in the future human beings can create imagined communities that are, in both scale and purpose, different from, and more humanly open than, the nationalist ones they have been a part of for the last two hundred years or so. The question is also whether, in the meantime at least, some more reflective human beings across this planet can begin to *think and act* in a consistently antinationalistic and economically globalist way,[11] even if they cannot (or cannot yet) *feel* in those ways.

At bottom these two questions are the same. How, if at all, it is possible for human beings to think and act beyond the constraints of their historical location, constraints that form their very structure of feeling? That is, the principal obstacle in the way of turning a globalizing world into

---

copied across the world. So, on my travels alone, I have seen "The Londoner's View of the World," "The Parisian's View of the World," even "The Muscovite's View of the World." In short, everybody sees the joke immediately and universalizes it, but they universalize it by parochializing it.

10. Anderson, *Imagined Communities*.

11. I have one small suggestion for such an action. I suggest the creation of a web site to be called "Nationalist Absurdities" whose major objective would be to ridicule—in the manner of *Private Eye's* "Dave/Davida Spart" or "Wimmin" columns—absurd or inflated nationalist claims and rhetoric, wherever they may be found. Plainly false or grossly inflated cultural and/or historical claims would be an especially favored target. There would be only two rules for contributions to the web site. Firstly, all contributors must satire or ridicule their own nationalisms and not those of others. Secondly, *all* nationalisms—Palestinian as well as Israeli, Irish as well as British, Croatian as well as Serbian, Basque as well as Spanish, Cuban and Iranian as well as American—would be "fair game." The first rule reflects my view that nationalist ideologues are always more discomforted by internal attacks than external ones. In fact their worldview leads them to expect the latter, but the former they can only respond to by enraged allegations of "treachery." The second rule reflects my view that, whatever may have been the case in the past, there are now no progressive nationalisms, to be accorded protected status. All nationalisms, at least in their more ideologically extreme forms, are now equally anachronistic and equally ridiculous. The web site could be dedicated to, among others, Thomas Masaryk and Romila Thapar. For justification of this, see Eric Hobsbawm's public lecture "Outside and Inside History" and the short article "Identity History Is Not Enough," both republished in his collection *On History* (London: Abacus, 1997), 1–12 and 351–66. In these two pieces Hobsbawm takes the nationalist bull by the horns in a more direct, powerful and moving way than in any of his longer writings on the subject.

a globalized world is at bottom emotional-rational not simply rationalistic. Human beings currently possess identities and loyalties—identities and loyalties we characterize using words like "national," "nationalistic"— which profoundly shape who they are or feel themselves to be. More importantly, and less frequently noted, such identities and loyalties also profoundly shape what contemporary *homo sapiens* regard as "practical," "possible," even "desirable" states of affairs in the world. Thus, as I have said more than once, to think globally is to weight a job anywhere as humanly equal to a job anywhere else. It is to weight a materially secure and expansive human life lived anywhere on this planet as morally equal to such a life lived anywhere else. But though, as it were, I can write such words, I cannot feel what they mean. And neither (I imagine) can my readers. If one asks why I (we) cannot feel this, the answer is, at bottom I think, that human beings in general do not as yet experience enough non-national patterns of human interaction to make such sentiments existentially and affectively real. In a word, we (all of us, all human beings) spend far too much time interacting with our fellow nationals and far too little time interacting with non-nationals for us to be able to treat these kind of abstract ideas as anything other than just that—abstract intellectual ideas. So here, in short, we have a real intractable existential problem. To make globalization both more real and politically progressive we first have to feel what we cannot feel and act on that feeling. Then we have to get others (our fellow citizens) to feel what they cannot feel and to act on that feeling. But is that not just the description of an impossible task? Is it not simply asking the impossible?

Well yes and no. Yes, in the sense that the above is, I think, an accurate enough description of the political and existential problem of globalization that human beings currently confront. But no, in the sense that if such problems were not soluble, and had indeed not been solved by human beings before, human societies and human beings would never have changed at all. And we know that they have. At one time, for example, probably all human beings would have thought that societies that operated on a principle of religious toleration were impossible precisely because they required people to feel what (in sixteenth- or seventeenth-century Europe) they could not feel. But such societies have come about (at least in some parts of the world), so that impossibility was not an impossibility. How was the impossible made possible? It was done, I believe, by some people (at that time a small minority of people) deciding in effect to commit themselves—both intellectually and in political action—to principles that they were intellectually convinced were right even if they could not (then) feel that they were right.

This reflection brings me to a point which I feel especially worthy of note because of its profound unfashionability in the postmodern world in which we live. I will call it *the heroic potential of intellect.* That is, I believe there is a far too common and popular tendency now, even—indeed especially—among intellectuals to stress the acute limitations of intellect. For the intellectual influenced by postmodernism, and indeed by its modernist precursors such as Freudian psychoanalysis, is much more likely to stress the impotence of intellect in the face of human emotion and passion than its capacity to win victories over the latter—albeit slowly and painfully. Thus, when confronted by the kind of problem with which this book is obsessed—the conflict between the abstract intellectual appeal and potential human merit of more widespread universalism and cosmopolitanism and the affective power of identity-giving parochialisms and nationalisms— the postmodernist is very apt to choose parochialism over universalism and excuse the choice as merely the act of a realist.

And truly it seems an immensely long and tortuous road from where humanity is now to any kind of subjectively globalist future. Can we even conceive it as possible for the kind of people for whom the very category "humanity" is still the most affectively empty of abstractions to live in a world in which more localized and particular identities could coexist with, even share part of their affective power with, this wider identity? How can we even conceive creating sufficiently open and culturally varied patterns of human interaction on this globe by which notions of a "common humanity" might be filled with enough existential content by enough people to give it some affective power in the world? How can we even coherently imagine such a state of affairs, let alone bring it about? How indeed? But, to repeat, are our difficulties here any greater than the difficulties a seventeenth-century Englishman might have had conceiving a world of religious toleration? Ordinary contemporary British citizens consider it "inconceivable" and "impossible" that persons should be forbidden from holding public office "merely" because they are Roman Catholic. Are such citizens at any greater political and psychological distance from their seventeenth-century predecessors (who would have thought it equally "inconceivable" and "impossible" that a Roman Catholic *should* hold such office) than we are from my postulated cosmopolitan people of the future? I doubt it. Or, to take another example, the average reluctantly liberal male citizen of virtually any contemporary Western nation-state can be found saying that "*of course* women should have equal rights with men." Is such a contemporary male at any greater political and psychological distance from his Victorian predecessor (who was often not even angry or affronted by demands for equal rights for women simply because he conceived the very notion as preposterous or ridiculous)[12] than we are from my postulated cosmopolitan people of the future? Again, I doubt it.

So what these examples show us is that, yes, individual people, no matter how intellectually convinced, *are* often too weak to make those convictions existentially real against the power of historically ingrained affective identities and loyalties. There is nothing inaccurate about this popular postmodernist generalization about individuals, as a generalization *about individuals.* But what these historical examples also show us is that this generalization overlooks an equally commonplace and just as importantly true generalization—that people can often accomplish together, as a group or movement, what they cannot accomplish alone. To conclude intellectually that a certain state of affairs is desirable, to come together with others similarly convinced, and to work together intensely, determinedly to bring such a state of affairs about (or even to bring it in some small respects closer to reality) is just a thumbnail description of one of the many patterns of collective human activity to which we give the name *politics. Political* activity is, among other things, the kind of activity through which human beings find strength together to do what they cannot do alone. Through political activity states of affairs that are now "merely theoretical," "merely ideal" can (usually very slowly) become states of affairs that are socially, existentially, emotionally real. Politics is (among many other things) a means by which "present-day" people who can *think* that a potential state of affairs is both possible and good but who cannot *feel* either *how* it is possible or *how* it is good, begin the (enormously complex)

---

12. Anyone—any young male or female reader—who is so inured in the present that feminism has created that they doubt that this is true should read, for example, John Stuart Mill's essay *The Subjection of Women* of 1869. It is written, under the profound influence of a woman, by an educated Victorian middle-class man for an educated Victorian middle-class male readership whose prejudices he knew very well (not least because he had previously shared them!). Its whole argumentative structure is bent simply to getting its readers to at least take feminist ideas *seriously.* This was something that, in 1869, he obviously thought a massively difficult task in itself. Getting the same men to actually *believe* feminist ideas he treats as a decidedly secondary objective. *Enfranchisement of Women* by Harriet Taylor Mill, and *The Subjection of Women* by John Stuart Mill, with an introduction by Kate Soper (London: Virago combined edition, 1983).

historical process of turning this intellectually glimpsed potentiality into reality. In doing this these "present" people simultaneously begin the process of creating "future" people—people who *can* feel how that potential state of affairs is both possible and good because for them it is no longer a potential but an actual state of affairs. And that means of course that these future people live lives within social and cultural contexts which for us present people are barely imaginable, but which for them are just pleasantly but unremarkably mundane and everyday.

### An Antinationalist Left Politics

So that is what we need to do now. We need to be intellectually convinced of the desirability of a non-nationalist world, and then we need to act on that desire in order, slowly and gradually, to bring such a world about. And if we are also people who conceive ourselves as being on the left in any sense (meaning, at a minimum, as people for whom the acid test of the desirability of any state of affairs is its implications for those—whomever they are, wherever they are—in greatest material need), then we require, in a phrase, a well worked out *antinationalist left politics.*

Some of the policy content of such a politics can readily be inferred from this book. Continual and implacable opposition to economic protectionist demands, wherever and by whomever they are articulated, is obviously a crucial part—perhaps the most important part—of such a politics at the present time. But almost equally important is the insistence that genuinely flexible labor markets require, as a human prerequisite, comprehensive state-financed forms of social protection and welfare. Strong support for at least a basic set of human rights anywhere and everywhere in the world—and a rejection of all defenses of the denial or abuse of human rights that are based on the concept of nationalist "internal affairs"—must also be a central plank of such a politics. But so must be an open and tolerant attitude to all forms of human and cultural difference—so long as such toleration does not require us to renege on the politically prior human rights commitment. That is, tolerance of cultural diversity cannot lead antinationalist left activists to accept, on grounds of cultural exceptionalism, the treatment of some human beings by other human beings which we would not accept ourselves. To put that more formally and accurately, it cannot lead us to endorse or accept, on cultural exceptionalist grounds, forms of treatment of *any* human beings by other human beings which we could not endorse or accept for *all* human beings.

However, beyond these policy generalities there are more detailed strategic, tactical, and (above all) organizational questions about how such a politics can be institutionalized and made more transnationally effective. Such questions are obviously very difficult ones for any movement that aims to create transnational political practices from the starting point of a world in which politics is still almost (almost, not entirely) exclusively a nationally structured social practice. In other places, therefore—in future publications—I intend to outline in at least some minimal detail what the more specific objectives, modes, and mechanisms of such an antinationalist left politics might be. This book, however, has been restricted to saying both why I think such a politics is needed, and why (above all) *I* need and desire it. But I hope that I am not alone in that need and desire. In fact, if I read the phenomenon of globalization aright, if the analysis of the phenomenon found in this book has any validity, I *cannot* be alone—it is now a sociological impossibility that I should be alone—in that need and desire.

# Ricardo and Unimaginable Realities:
# A Dialogue

I have found, when teaching about the Ricardian doctrine of comparative advantage, that students often find it hard to grasp and also (and this is most interesting) often initially understand it—or rather misunderstand it—in the nationalist way in which Friedrich List and many other critics have done. However, when its logic finally does strike home, together with the practical implications of that logic, I have found that student response is scarcely less incredulous or doubtful than when misunderstanding reigned. To give an idea of what I mean by this I reproduce below a verbatim account of a tutorial conversation I had with an outstanding student for whom light was dawning, as it were, as the conversation developed.

STUDENT: So what you are saying is that in a world which functioned on Ricardian assumptions, all countries would only specialize in the production and trade of goods and services at the top of their comparative advantage schedule?

GK: Yes.

STUDENT: But in the case of Australia that might boil down to only wine production, or only tourism, or only certain types of mining?

GK: Quite possibly, yes.

STUDENT: But the whole country couldn't live off wine production!

GK: What do you mean?

STUDENT: Well, the production of wine, even if expanded to its ecological maximum, could not employ all—or even most—of the current Australian labor force!

GK: Well of course there is not just wine growing, there is wine fermenting and bottling, production of labels and packaging for the wine, all the activities required in wine exporting, not to mention numerous restaurants serving the wine. And anyway, there is a whole infrastructural basis required for wine making and exporting—roads, electrification, ports—not to mention all the spin-off employment generated by spending by the people working in and around the wine trade. After all they have to have houses to live in, will presumably want to eat out, buy clothes, watch movies and videos, etc.

STUDENT: Yes, but even so. The current Australian labor force is over ten million people. How could they all possibly be employed off wine production, even if we include indirect as well as direct employment? And anyway, what about people in Australia who for one reason or another do not want to work in wine or anything to do with wine? Say they have been trained as lawyers, or computer programmers, or architects, and want to use those skills in ways that are not allowed for by the Australian wine economy. What do they do?

GK: Well, on the question of total employment generated, a lot more than you think depends on just *how much* wine was being produced and exported. Remember we are assuming here that Australia would be a specialist wine producer or—more probably—a specialist producer of some types of wine, for a vast, vast world market demand. That being so, the sheer scale and complexity of that production process would certainly allow for a fair few employment opportunities for computer programmers, lawyers etc. But anyway, you are forgetting the other crucial Ricardian assumption—complete free movement of labor globally. So anybody who felt that their skills were not being adequately employed in Australia could move to other parts of the globe where there would be bigger concentrations—and greater variety—of computer programmer employment or lawyer employment, or whatever.

STUDENT: Yes, but where people choose to live isn't just a question of where they can get a job. If people are born and brought up in a certain place, they get attached to that place and the people in it. They may not want to move off to some completely different part of the world, even to get a better job.

GK: Yes, that is very true. You remember I said in my lectures that, whatever the logical merits of the Ricardian free trade model, there are many deep practical problems of implementing it in a world made up of human beings and human societies as we know them, and the point you have just made brings up one of those difficulties. In fact I think it is probably the most fundamental of all the practical difficulties involved in turning the Ricardian model into an actual functioning world economy. But that does not alter the point that an open world labor market would—logically—counteract the employment problems that might be generated by a highly specialized spatial structure of economic activity.

STUDENT: Yes, but anyway . . .

GK: Anyway, what?

STUDENT: This highly specialized global spatial economy, with every part of the world only engaging in the activities at the top of its comparative advantage schedule, is only going to happen, if *everybody* follows the "comparative advantage" rule, yeh? If everybody—every country—plays what you call the Ricardian game?

GK: Yes.

STUDENT: It'll never happen. People—countries—are never going to put their fate so totally into the hands of other countries in that way. And what about defense? Can you really imagine a world in which all countries allowed the production of—say—tanks or military aircraft, to be concentrated entirely in one or two countries in the world. It's a nonsense!

GK: Yes, that's another considerable practical problem, especially in a world of hostile or potentially hostile, states. But . . .

STUDENT: But what?

GK: Well I suspect that Ricardo rather hoped that a world joined so completely together in economic interdependence would be a world in which no one would want—it would not be in anybody's interest—to make war, so defense industries would be redundant.

STUDENT: Oh come on. That's completely unrealistic!

GK: You're probably right.

# Bibliography

## Books, Articles, and Academic Theses

Ackland, N. A. "The Role of Swaps in the Development of the International Financial System." Ph.D. diss., University of Sydney, 2000.

Aganbegyan, A. *The Challenge: Economics of Perestroika*. London: Hutchinson, 1988.

Allard, T. "Grunge City v World Greed: Restless in Seattle." *The Sydney Morning Herald*, December 2, 1999, p. 1.

Allen, C., ed. *Plain Tales from the Raj: Images of British India in the Twentieth Century*. London: Futura, 1976.

Amin, S. *Unequal Development: Essays on the Social Formations of Peripheral Capitalism*. Hassocks: Harvester, 1976.

Amsden, A. H. *Asia's Next Giant: South Korea and Late Industrialization*. New York: Oxford University Press, 1989.

Anderson, B. *Imagined Communities: Reflections on the Origin and Spread of Nationalism*. London: Verso, 1983.

Anker, R. *Gender and Jobs: Sex Segregation of Occupations in the World*. Geneva: International Labour Office, 1997.

Antony, P. D. *John Ruskin's Labour: A Study of Ruskin's Social Theory*. Cambridge: Cambridge University Press, 1983.

Armstrong, P., A. Glyn, and J. Harrison. *Capitalism Since World War II*. London: Fontana, 1984.

Ashcroft, B., C. Griffith, and H. Tiffin, eds. *The Post-Colonial Studies Reader*. London: Routledge, 1996.

Australian Department of Foreign Affairs and Trade: East Asia Analytical Unit. *The

*Indian Economy at the Midnight Hour.* Canberra: Commonwealth of Australia, 1994.

Australian Industry Commission. *The Textiles, Clothing and Footwear Industries.* Vol. 1, *Report.* Canberra: Commonwealth of Australia, 1997.

Baran, P. *The Political Economy of Growth.* New York: Monthly Review Press, 1959.

Bates, R. *Markets and States in Tropical Africa: The Political Basis of Agricultural Policies.* Berkeley and Los Angeles: University of California Press, 1981.

Beckerman, W. *Through Green-Coloured Glasses: Environmentalism Reconsidered.* Washington, D.C.: Cato Institute, 1996.

Berman, M. *All that Is Solid Melts into Air: The Experience of Modernity.* London: Verso, 1983.

Blum, J. *Lord and Peasant in Russia: From the Ninth to the Nineteenth Century.* Princeton: Princeton University Press, 1961.

Braverman, H. *Labor and Monopoly Capital.* New York: Monthly Review Press, 1974.

Bromley, R., and C. Gerry, eds. *Casual Work and Poverty in Third World Cities.* Chichester: John Wiley and Sons, 1979.

Bruce, M. *The Coming of the British Welfare State.* London: Batsford, 1961.

Bryan, D. *The Chase Across the Globe: International Capital and the Contradictions for Nation States.* Boulder, Colo.: Westview Press, 1995.

Bryan, D., and M. Rafferty. *The Global Economy in Australia: Global Integration and National Economic Policy.* St. Leonards, New South Wales: Allen and Unwin, 1999.

Cardoso, F. H. "Humanizing growth—through equity." In UNDP, *Human Development Report 1996,* 31.

Cardoso, F. H., and E. Faletto. *Dependency and Development in Latin America.* Berkeley and Los Angeles: University of California Press, 1979.

Carynnyk-Sinclair, N. "Rural to Urban Migration in Developing Countries, 1950–1970: A Survey of the Literature." International Labour Organisation Working Paper WEP2-19, Geneva, 1974.

Cawthorne, P. "International Sub-contracting and the Australian and Indian Clothing Industries." Department of Economics, University of Sydney, Seminar Series Paper, November 1997.

———. "The Limited Usefulness of National Economic Identity in the Case of an Australian Networking Firm." Department of Economics, University of Sydney, Working Paper 98-10, September 1997.

Chambers, R. *Rural Development: Putting the Last First.* London: Longman, 1983.

Chenery, H., et al. *Redistribution with Growth.* London: Oxford University Press, 1974.

Cipolla, C. M. *The Economic History of World Population.* Harmondsworth: Penguin, 1975.

Cobbett, W. *Rural Rides.* Harmondsworth: Penguin, 1981.

Coulson, A. *Tanzania: A Political Economy.* Oxford: Clarendon Press, 1982.

Cowen, M., and R. Shenton. *Doctrines of Development.* London: Routledge, 1996.

Currie, L. *Taming the Megalopolis: A Design for Urban Growth.* Oxford: Pergamon, 1976.

Curtin, P. D. *The Atlantic Slave Trade: A Census.* Madison: University of Wisconsin Press, 1969.

Deakin, N. *The Politics of Welfare.* London: Methuen, 1987.

Deutsch, K. W. *Nationalism and Social Communication: An Inquiry into the Foundations of Nationality.* New York: John Wiley and Sons, 1953.

Deutsch, K. W., and W. J. Folz, eds. *Nation-Building.* New York: Atherton, 1963.

Dicken, P. *Global Shift: Transforming the World Economy.* 3d ed. London: Chapman, 1998.

Dore, R. *The Diploma Disease: Education, Qualification and Development.* London: Allen and Unwin, 1976.

———. *Land Reform in Japan.* Oxford: Clarendon Press, 1959.

———. *Taking Japan Seriously: A Confucian Perspective on Leading Economic Issues.* Stanford: Stanford University Press, 1987.

Eagleton, T. "Where Will It All End?" (a review of Eric Hobsbawm's *Age of Extremes*). *The Sunday Times,* November 13, 1994, pp. 7–8.

Fage, J. D. "Slavery and the Slave Trade in the Context of West African History." *Journal of African History* 10, no. 3 (1969): 393–404.

Fanon, F. *Black Skins, White Masks.* New York: Grove Press, 1967.

———. *Wretched of the Earth.* Harmondsworth: Penguin, 1967.

Fieldhouse, D. K. *The Theory of Capitalist Imperialism.* London: Longman, 1967.

Figes, O. *A People's Tragedy: The Russian Revolution, 1891–1924.* London: Pimlico, 1996.

Finlay, M. I. *The Ancient Economy.* London: Chatto and Windus, 1973.

Foster, G. "Peasant Society and the Image of Limited Good." *American Anthropologist* 67, no. 2 (1965): 293–315.

Foster, J. *Class Struggle and the Industrial Revolution.* London: Methuen, 1974.

Frank, A. G. *Capitalism and Underdevelopment in Latin America.* New York: Monthly Review Press, 1967.

———. *Dependent Accumulation and Underdevelopment.* New York: Monthly Review Press, 1979.

———. "Dependence Is Dead, Long Live Dependence and the Class Struggle: A Reply to My Critics." *Latin American Perspectives* 1, no. 1 (Spring 1974): 87–106.

———. "The Thirdworldization of Russia and Eastern Europe." In *The Aftermath of "Real Existing Socialism" in Eastern Europe,* ed. J. Hersh and J. D. Schmidt, 1: 39–61. London: Macmillan, 1996.

Fraser, D. *The Evolution of the British Welfare State: A History of Social Policy Since the Industrial Revolution.* London: Macmillan, 1974.

Freyre, G. *The Masters and the Slaves: A Study in the Development of Brazilian Civilization.* New York: Knopf, 1956.

Galeano, E. *The Open Veins of Latin America: Five Centuries of the Pillage of a Continent.* New York: Monthly Review Press, 1973.

Gellner, E. *Nations and Nationalism.* Oxford: Basil Blackwell, 1983.

Gemery, H. A., and J. S. Hogendorn, eds. *The Uncommon Market: Essays on the Economic History of the Atlantic Slave Trade.* New York: Academic Press, 1979.

Genovese, E. D. *Roll Jordan Roll: The World the Slaves Made.* New York: Random House, 1974.

George, S. *How the Other Half Dies.* Harmondsworth: Penguin, 1976.

Gershenkron, A. *Economic Backwardness in Historical Perspective: A Book of Essays.* Cambridge: Belknap Press of Harvard University Press, 1962.

Glyn, A., and J. Harrison. *The British Economic Disaster.* London: Pluto Press, 1980.

Gorz, A. *Ecology as Politics.* Boston: South End Press, 1980.

Halliday, J., and G. McCormack. *Japanese Imperialism Today: Co-prosperity in Greater East Asia.* Harmondsworth: Penguin, 1973.

Hammond, J., and B. L. Hammond. *The Town Labourer.* London: Longman, 1978.
———. *The Village Labourer.* London: Longman, 1978.

Hardoy, J. E., D. Mitlin, and D. Satterthwaite. *Environmental Problems in Third World Cities.* London: Earthscan, 1992.

Harrison, D. *The Sociology of Modernization and Development.* London: Unwin Hyman, 1988.

Harvey, D. *The Condition of Post-Modernity: An Enquiry into the Origins of Cultural Change.* Oxford: Basil Blackwell, 1989.

Hassan, I. "The Culture of Postmodernism." *Theory, Culture and Society* 2 (1985): 119–31.

Hay, J. R. *The Development of the British Welfare State, 1880–1975.* London: Edward Arnold, 1978.

Heyer, J., et al. *Agricultural Development in Kenya.* Nairobi: Oxford University Press, 1978.

Hirst, P. Q., and G. Thompson. *Globalization in Question: The International Political Economy and the Possibilities of Governance.* Cambridge: Polity, 1996.

Hobsbawm, E. J. *The Age of Capital, 1848–1875.* London: Abacus, 1977.
———. *The Age of Empire, 1875–1914.* London: Abacus, 1994.
———. *Age of Extremes: A History of the World, 1914–1991.* London: Jonathan Cape, 1996.
———. *Industry and Empire.* Harmondsworth: Penguin, 1969.
———. *Nations and Nationalism Since 1780: Programme, Myth, Reality.* Cambridge: Cambridge University Press, 1992.
———. *On History.* London: Abacus, 1997.

Hoogvelt, A. *Globalisation and the Postcolonial World: The New Political Economy of Development.* London: Macmillan, 1997.

Hume, D. *A Treatise on Human Nature.* In *David Hume: The Philosophical Works,* ed. T. H. Green and T. H. Grose. Aalen: Scientia Verlag, 1964.

Hutton, W. *The State to Come.* London: Vintage, 1997.

Hyden, G. *Beyond Ujamaa in Tanzania: Underdevelopment and an Uncaptured Peasantry.* London: Heinemann, 1980.

————. "Capital Accumulation, Resource Distribution, and Governance in Kenya: The Role of the Economy of Affection." In *The Political Economy of Kenya*, ed. M. G. Schatsberg, 117–36. New York: Praeger, 1987.

————. *No Shortcuts to Progress: African Development Management in Perspective*. London: Heinemann, 1983.

Israel, J. *The Language of Dialectics and the Dialectics of Language*. Brighton: Harvester, 1979.

Jacobs, M. *The Green Economy: Economy, Sustainable Development and the Politics of the Future*. Vancouver: University of British Columbia Press, 1993.

Jenkins, R. *Dependent Industrialization in Latin America: The Automotive Industry in Argentina, Chile and Mexico*. New York: Praeger, 1977.

————. *Transnational Corporations and Uneven Development: The Internationalization of Capital and the Third World*. London: Methuen, 1987.

Kautsky, K. *The Agrarian Question*. London: Zwan Publishers, 1988.

Kemp, T. *Industrialization in Nineteenth Century Europe*. London: Longman, 1969.

Kiernan, V. "Development, imperialism and some misconceptions." Centre for Development Studies, University of Wales at Swansea, Occasional Paper No. 13, 1981.

Killick, T. *Development Economics in Action; A Study of Economic Policies in Ghana*. London: Heinemann, 1978.

Kimambo, I. N., and A. J. Temu, eds. *A History of Tanzania*. Nairobi: East African Publishing House, 1969.

Kitching, G. *Class and Economic Change in Kenya: The Making of an African Petite-Bourgeoisie, 1905–1970*. London: Yale University Press, 1980.

————. *Development and Underdevelopment in Historical Perspective: Populism, Nationalism and Industrialisation*. 2d ed. London: Methuen, 1989.

————. *Karl Marx and the Philosophy of Praxis*. London: Routledge, 1988.

————. *Marxism and Science: Analysis of an Obsession*. University Park: Pennsylvania State University Press, 1994.

————. "The Marxist Theory of Imperialism and the Historical Study of Underdevelopment." In *Middle Eastern Research and Information Project (MERIP)*, February 1980, pp. 36–42.

————. "Nationalism: The Instrumental Passion." *Capital and Class*, no. 25 (1985): 98–116.

Krugman, P. *The Accidental Theorist: And Other Dispatches from the Dismal Science*. New York: Norton, 1998.

————. "Is Free Trade Passé?" *Economic Perspectives* 1, no. 2 (1987).

————. *Pop Internationalism*. Cambridge: MIT Press, 1997.

Kuhn, T. *The Structure of Scientific Revolutions*. Chicago: University of Chicago Press, 1962.

Kuznets, S. "Economic Growth and Income Inequality." *American Economics Review* 45 (March 1955): 18–19.

Lall, S. *The Indirect Employment Effect of Multinational Enterprises in Developing Countries.* Geneva: International Labour Office, 1979.

———. *The New Multinationals: The Spread of Third World Enterprises.* Chichester: Wiley, 1983.

Landes, D. *The Unbound Prometheus: Technological Change and Industrial Development in Western Europe from 1750 to the Present.* Cambridge: Cambridge University Press, 1969.

———. *The Wealth and Poverty of Nations.* London: Little, Brown, 1998.

Langdon, S. *Multinational Corporations in the Political Economy of Kenya.* London: Macmillan, 1980.

Leeson, N. *Rogue Trader: Nick Leeson—His Own Amazing Story.* London: Warner, 1997.

Leudde-Neurath, R. "State Intervention and Export-Oriented Development in South Korea." In *Developmental States in East Asia,* ed. G. White, 30–67. New York: St. Martin's Press, 1988.

Lewin, M. *Russian Peasants and Soviet Power: A Study of Collectivization.* London: Allen and Unwin, 1968.

Leys, C. *Politics in Britain: An Introduction.* London: Heinemann, 1983.

Leys, C., and M. Mamdani. *Crises and Reconstruction, African Perspectives: Two Lectures.* Stockholm: Nordiska Afrikainstitutet, 1998.

Lipton, M. *Why Poor People Stay Poor: Urban Bias in World Development.* London: Temple Smith, 1977.

List, F. *The National System of Political Economy.* London: Longmans Green, 1916.

Lowe Morna, C. "Surviving Structural Adjustment." *Africa Report* 35, no. 5 (1989): 45–48.

Maddison, A. *Class Structure and Economic Growth: India and Pakistan Since the Moghuls.* London: Allen and Unwin, 1971.

Maier, C. S. *Recasting Bourgeois Europe: Stabilization in France, Germany and Italy in the Decade After World War I.* Princeton: Princeton University Press, 1975.

Maine, Sir H. *Ancient Law: Its Connection with the Early History of Society and Its Relation to Modern Ideas.* London: John Murray, 1906.

Malthus, T. *An Essay on the Principles of Population.* Harmondsworth: Penguin, 1979.

Mandel, E. *Late Capitalism.* London: New Left Books, 1975.

Manning, P. "Notes Toward a Theory of Ideology in Historical Writing on Modern Africa." *Canadian Journal of African Studies* 8, no. 2 (1974): 235–53.

Marcuse, H. *One-Dimensional Man: Studies in the Ideology of Advanced Industrial Society.* London: Sphere, 1968.

Marks, S., and A. Atmore, eds. *Economy and Society in Pre-Industrial South Africa.* London: Longman, 1980.

Martin, H.-P., and H. Schumann. *The Global Trap: Globalization and the Assault on Prosperity and Democracy.* Leichhardt: Pluto Press Australia, 1997.

Marx, K. *Preface to a Contribution to a Critique of Political Economy.* In K. Marx and

F. Engels, *Selected Works in One Volume,* 180–84. London: Lawrence and Wishart, 1968.

McLuhan, M., and Q. Fiore. *The Medium Is the Massage: An Inventory of Effects.* Harmondsworth: Penguin, 1967.

Middlemas, K. *Politics in Industrial Society: The Experience of the British System Since 1911.* London: Andre Deutsch, 1979.

Mill, J. S. *The Subjection of Women.* London: Virago, 1983.

Mitrany, D. *Marx Against the Peasant: A Study in Social Dogamatism.* London: Weidenfeld and Nicolson, 1951.

Mittelman, J. H., ed. *Globalization: Critical Reflections.* Boulder, Colo.: Lynne Rienner, 1996.

Moore, B. *Injustice: The Social Bases of Obedience and Revolt.* London: Macmillan, 1978.

———. *The Social Origins of Dictatorship and Democracy: Lord and Peasant in the Making of the Modern World.* Harmondsworth: Penguin, 1967.

Moorhouse, G. *India Britannica.* London: Harvill Press, 1983.

Myrdal, G. *Asian Drama: An Inquiry into the Poverty of Nations.* Vol. 1. Harmondsworth: Penguin, 1968.

Nicholas, J. G. *Investing in Hedge Funds.* New York: Blumberg Press, 1998.

Nove, A. *The Economics of Feasible Socialism.* London: Unwin Hyman, 1983.

———. *The Economics of Feasible Socialism Revisited.* London: Unwin Hyman, 1991.

O'Brien, P. K., and K. Chaglar. *Economic Growth in Britain and France, 1780–1914: Two Paths to the Modern World.* London: Allen and Unwin, 1978.

O'Connor, E. "A Historiography of Irish Labor." *Labour History Review* 60, pt. 1 (Spring 1995): 21–34.

O'Hanlon, R., and D. Washbrook. "After Orientalism: Culture, Criticism and Politics in the Third World." *Comparative Studies in Society and History* 34 (1992): 141–67.

Ohmae, K. *The Borderless World: Power and Strategy in the Interlinked Economy.* New York: Free Press, 1990.

Packenham, R. A. *The Dependency Movement: Scholarship and Politics in Development Studies.* Cambridge: Harvard University Press, 1992.

Perkin, H. *The Origins of Modern English Society, 1780–1880.* London: Routledge and Kegan Paul, 1969.

Pitkin, H. F. *Wittgenstein and Justice: On the Significance of Lugwig Wittgenstein for Social and Political Thought.* Berkeley and Los Angeles: University of California Press, 1973.

Platt, D.C.M., and G. di Tella. *Argentina, Australia and Canada: Studies in Comparative Development, 1870–1965.* London: Macmillan, 1985.

Polanyi, K. *The Great Transformation: The Political and Economic Origins of Our Time.* Boston: Beacon Press, 1957.

Porter, M. E. *The Competitive Advantage of Nations.* London: Macmillan, 1990.

Post, K. "Peasantization in West Africa." In *African Social Studies: A Radical Reader,* ed. P.C.W. Gutkind and P. Waterman, 241–50. London: Heinemann, 1977.

Potter, D. C. *India's Political Administrators.* Oxford: Clarendon Press, 1986.

Prakash, G. "Can the Subaltern Ride? A Reply to O'Hanlon and Washbrook." *Comparative Studies in Society and History* 34 (1992): 168–84.

———. "Writing Post-Orientalist Histories of the Third World: Perspectives from Indian Historiography." *Comparative Studies in Society and History* 32 (1990): 383–408.

Radice, H., ed. *International Firms and Modern Imperialism.* Harmondsworth: Penguin, 1975.

Ricardo, D. *Principles of Political Economy and Taxation.* Harmondsworth: Penguin 1971.

Ritchken, R. *Derivative Markets: Theory, Strategy and Applications.* New York: Harper-Collins, 1996.

Rodney, W. "African Slavery and Other Forms of Oppression in the Upper Guinea Coast." *Journal of African History* 7, no. 3 (1966): 431–43.

———. *How Europe Underdeveloped Africa.* London: Bogle-L'Ouverture, 1972.

Rubinstein, W. D. *Capitalism, Culture and Decline in Britain, 1750–1990.* London: Routledge, 1993.

Runciman, W. B. *Relative Deprivation and Social Justice.* London: Routledge and Kegan Paul, 1966.

Rutherford, E. *London: The Novel.* London: Arrow, 1998.

Said, E. W. *Culture and Imperialism.* London: Vintage, 1994.

———. *Orientalism.* London: Routledge and Kegan Paul, 1978.

Samuelson, P. *Economics.* Tokyo: McGraw-Hill Kogkusha, 1976.

Scandizzo, P. L., and D. Diakosawas. *Instability in the Terms of Trade of Primary Commodities, 1900–1982.* Rome: Food and Agricultural Organization, 1987.

Schumacher, E. F. *Small Is Beautiful: Economics as if People Mattered.* New York: Harper and Row, 1973.

Schwartz, Herman M. *States Versus Markets: The Emergence of a Global Economy.* 2d ed. Basingstoke: Macmillan, 2000.

Seabrook, J. *The Myth of the Market.* Bideford: Green Books, 1990.

———. *The Race for Riches.* Basingstoke: Green Print, 1989.

Sen, A. *Development as Freedom.* New York: Knopf, 1999.

Senghaas, D. *The European Experience: A Historical Critique of Development Theory.* Leamington Spa/Dover: Berg Publishers, 1985.

Simkin, C.G.F. *The Instability of a Dependent Economy: Economic Fluctuations in New Zealand, 1890–1914.* London: Oxford University Press, 1951.

Simon, J. L., and H. Kahn. *The Resourceful Earth: A Response to Global 2000.* Oxford: Basil Blackwell, 1984.

Sklair, L. "Globalisation." In *Sociology: Issues and Debates,* ed. Steve Taylor, 321–45. London: Macmillan, 1999.

———. *Sociology of the Global System.* 2d ed. Baltimore: Johns Hopkins University Press, 1995.

Skrubbeltrang, F. *Agricultural Development and Rural Reform in Denmark.* Rome: Food and Agricultural Organization, 1953.

Smith, A. *The Wealth of Nations, Books I–III.* Harmondsworth: Penguin, 1982.

Smith, A. D. *Theories of Nationalism.* London: Duckworth, 1971.

———, ed. *Ethnicity and Nationalism.* Leiden: E. J. Brill, 1992.

Smith, S. "Class Analysis Versus World System: A Critique of Samir Amin's Typology of Development." In *Neo-Marxist Theories of Development,* ed. P. Limqueco and B. McFarlane, 73–86. London, Croom Helm, 1983.

Spear, P. *A History of India.* Harmondsworth: Penguin, 1966.

St. Croix, G.E.M. de. *The Class Struggle in the Ancient Greek World.* London: Duckworth, 1981.

Steady, F. C., ed. *Women and Children First: Environment, Poverty and Sustainable Development.* New York: Schenkman, 1993.

Stedman Jones, G. *Outcast London: A Study of the Relationship Between Classes in Victorian Society.* Oxford: Clarendon Press, 1971.

Stilwell, F. "From 'Fightback' and 'One Nation' to an Alternative Economic Strategy." In *Beyond the Market: Alternatives to Economic Rationalism,* ed. S. Rhees, G. Rodley, and F. Stilwell, 189–202. Leichhardt: Pluto Press Australia, 1993.

Stokes, E. *The Peasant and the Raj: Studies in Agrarian Society and Peasant Rebellion in India.* Cambridge: Cambridge University Press, 1978.

Storry, R. *A History of Modern Japan.* Harmondsworth: Penguin, 1968.

Stretton, H. *The Political Sciences: General Principles of Selection in Social Science and History.* London: Routledge and Kegan Paul, 1972.

Taylor, A. J., ed. *The Standard of Living in Britain in the Industrial Revolution.* London: Methuen, 1975.

Thomas, C. *Dependency and Transformation.* New York: Monthly Review Press, 1973.

Thompson, E. P. *The Making of the English Working Class.* Harmondsworth: Penguin, 1968.

———. *William Morris: Romantic to Revolutionary.* London: Merlin Press, 1977.

Thompson, N. W. *The Market and Its Critics: Socialist Political Economy in Nineteenth Century Britain.* London: Routledge, 1988.

———. *The People's Science: The Popular Political Economy of Exploitation and Crisis, 1816–34.* Cambridge: Cambridge University Press, 1984.

Thurow, L. C. *The Future of Capitalism: How Today's Economic Forces Shape Tomorrow's World.* St. Leonards, New South Wales: Allen and Unwin, 1997.

Todaro, M. P. *Economics for a Developing World.* London: Longman, 1977.

Tönnies, F. *Community and Society.* East Lansing: Michigan State University Press, 1957.

Tribe, K. *Land, Labour and Economic Discourse.* London: Routledge and Kegan Paul, 1978.

UNRISD (United Nations Research Institute for Social Development). *States of Disarray: The Social Effects of Globalization.* Geneva: UNRISD, 1995.

Wade, R. *Governing the Market: Economic Theory and the Role of Government in East Asian Industrialization.* Princeton: Princeton University Press, 1990.

———. "State Intervention and 'Outward-looking' Development: Neoclassical Theory and Taiwanese Practice." In *Developmental States in East Asia,* ed. G. White, 68–113. New York: St. Martin's Press, 1988.

Walicki, A. *The Controversy over Capitalism: Studies in the Social Philosophy of the Russian Populists.* London: Oxford University Press, 1969.

Wallerstein, I. *The Capitalist World Economy.* Cambridge: Cambridge University Press, 1979.

Warren, B. *Imperialism, Pioneer of Capitalism.* London: Verso, 1980.

Weber, E. *Peasants into Frenchmen: The Modernisation of Rural France, 1870–1914.* London: Chatto and Windus, 1977.

Weber, M. "The Chinese Literati." In *From Max Weber: Essays in Sociology,* ed. H. H. Gerth and C. W. Mills, 416–44. London: Routledge and Kegan Paul, 1970.

———. "The Social Psychology of the World Religions." In *From Max Weber: Essays in Sociology,* ed. H. H. Gerth and C. W. Mills, 267–301. London: Routledge and Kegan Paul, 1970.

Wegren, S. K. "Rural Migration and Agrarian Reform in Russia: A Research Note." *Europe-Asia Studies* 47, no. 5 (1995): 887–88.

Wells, L. T., Jr. *Third World Multinationals: The Rise of Foreign Investment from Developing Countries.* Cambridge: MIT Press, 1983.

White, G., ed. *Developmental States in East Asia.* New York: St. Martin's Press, 1988.

Wiener, M. J. *English Culture and the Decline of the Industrial Spirit, 1850–1980.* Cambridge: Cambridge University Press, 1981.

Williams, R. *Keywords: A Vocabulary of Culture and Society.* London: Fontana, 1976.

Williams, G. A. *Proletarian Order: Antonio Gramsci, Factory Councils and the Origins of Communism in Italy, 1911–21.* London: Pluto Press, 1975.

Wilmott, P. *Derivatives: The Theory and Practice of Financial Engineering.* New York: Wiley, 1998.

Wolf, E. R. *Peasant Wars of the Twentieth Century.* London: Faber and Faber, 1971.

Wolfe, R. *Farm Wars: The Political Economy of Agriculture and the International Trade Regime.* New York: St. Martin's Press, 1998.

Wolfe, M. *Elusive Development.* Geneva: UNRISD, 1981.

Wolff, R. D. *The Economics of Colonialism.* New Haven: Yale University Press, 1974.

Wood, A. *North-South Trade, Employment and Equality: Changing Fortunes in a Skill-Driven World.* Oxford: Clarendon Press, 1994.

Woodruff, P. *The Men Who Ruled India.* Vol. 2, *The Guardians.* London: Jonathan Cape, 1954.

## Statistical Sources and Compilations

Australian Bureau of Statistics. *Australian Economic Indicators.* Canberra: Common-wealth of Australia, 1991 and 1999.

International Telecommunications Union (ITU). *Yearbook of Statistics 1998.* Geneva: ITU, 1999.

Mitchell, B. R. *British Historical Statistics.* Cambridge: Cambridge University Press, 1988.

OECD Statistics Directorate. *Historical Statistics, 1960–95.* Paris: OECD, 1997.

———. *Main Economic Indicators, 1955–71.* Paris: OECD, 1972.

———. *National Accounts, 1960–1996.* Vol. 1, *Main Aggregates.* OECD: Paris, 1998.

UNCTAD (United Nations Commission on Trade, Aid and Development). *World Investment Report 1994: Transnational Corporations, Employment and the Workplace.* New York: United Nations, 1994.

UNDP (United Nations Development Programme). *Human Development Report 1995.* New York: Oxford University Press, 1995.

———. *Human Development Report 1996.* New York: Oxford University Press, 1996.

———. *Human Development Report 1997.* New York: Oxford University Press, 1997.

———. *Human Development Report 1999.* New York: Oxford University Press, 1999.

World Bank. *World Development Indicators.* Washington, D.C.: World Bank, 2000.

———. *World Development Report 1990.* New York: Oxford University Press, 1990.

———. *World Development Report 2000.* New York: Oxford University Press, 2000.

## Web Site Sources and References

The "Derivatives Bookshop," at www.global-investor.com.

"Ecommerce Bypasses Developing World." NUA InternetSurvey, at www.nua.ie/surveys.

"European Africa Center for Success and Self-Reliance." At www.africasuccess.com.

"Former GM Executive Puts Dream Factory in Brazil." At www.nytimes.com.

"Hedge Fund Research." At www.hfr.com.

"Independence Home Page." The Tibetan independence movement, at www.taklamakaa. org.

Internet Software Consortium, Internet Domain Survey, at www.isc.org/dsview.cgi?domainsurvey/report.html.

Krugman, Paul. "A Raspberry for Free Trade" and "Ricardo's Difficult Idea." "The Unofficial Paul Krugman Web Page," at members.home.net/copernicus/ricardo.html.

NUA Internet Surveys, at www.nua.ie/surveys.

Parliament of Australia web site, at www.aph.gov.au.

"Preamble Center on Globalization." At www.preamble.org/mai.

Tony Blair web site, at www.dicppi.org/speeches.

Worldwide television schedules, at www.tvshow.com/tv/sheds.

# Index